RECREATION AND LEISURE
IN MODERN SOCIETY

RECREATION AND LEISURE
IN MODERN SOCIETY

Sixth Edition

Richard Kraus
Temple University, Professor Emeritus

JONES AND BARTLETT PUBLISHERS
Sudbury, Massachusetts
BOSTON   TORONTO   LONDON   SINGAPORE

World Headquarters
Jones and Bartlett Publishers
40 Tall Pine Drive
Sudbury, MA 01776
info@jbpub.com
www.jbpub.com

Jones and Bartlett Publishers Canada
2406 Nikanna Road
Mississauga, ON L5C 2W6
CANADA

Jones and Bartlett Publishers International
Barb House, Barb Mews
London W6 7PA
UK

Library of Congress Cataloging-in-Publication Data

Kraus, Richard G.
    Recreation and leisure in modern society / Richard Kraus.—6th ed.
        p. cm.
    Includes bibliographical references and index.
    ISBN 0-7637-1678-2
    1. Recreation—North America. 2. Recreation—North America—History. 3.
Leisure—Social aspects—North America. 4. Play—North America—Psychological aspects.
5. Recreation—Vocational guidance—North America. I. Title.

GV51 .K7 2001
790'.097—dc21   00-067856

Production Credits:
Acquisitions Editor: Suzanne Jeans
Associate Editor: Amy Austin
Production Editor: Rebecca S. Marks
Editorial/Production Assistant: Amanda J. Green
Composition: Shepherd, Inc.
Cover Design: Stephanie Torta
Cover Images: Copyright © 2001 PhotoDisc
Printing and Binding: Courier Companies
Cover Printing: Henry Sawyer Co.

Printed in the United States of America
05 04 03 02 01   10 9 8 7 6 5 4 3 2

To John Hutchinson, Ruth and Jimmy Norris, and Vivian O. Wills

CONTENTS

9   Specialized Leisure-Service Areas   248

10   Two Major Leisure-Service Components: Sports and Tourism   285

PREFACE

Recreation and Leisure in Modern Society is the sixth edition of a text that has been used by hundreds of college and university departments of recreation, parks, and leisure studies throughout the United States and Canada. As before, it is designed for use in courses dealing with the history and philosophy of recreation and leisure on the world scene and, more specifically, with the role of organized leisure services today in North American communities.

The book has been heavily revised to reflect societal changes that have occurred in recent years and the challenges that face leisure-service managers in the twenty-first century. While it has been cut back in terms of the number of chapters and pages, it continues to provide in-depth analysis of the basic concepts of recreation and leisure, the motivations and values of participants, and trends in the overall field of organized community services.

Throughout the text, several important themes are emphasized, including the following:

Dramatic shifts in population makeup, including the balance of different age groups, restructured family patterns, and great ethnic and racial diversification in many communities

The impact of sophisticated information technologies on the national economy and business world and on the varied uses of leisure

Linked to these trends, the burgeoning prosperity of the early 2000s has been accompanied by a "winner-take-all" psychology that has left the United States, in particular, with a growing gap between the rich and the poor. In the recreation field itself, there has been a strong drive toward an entrepreneurial, marketing-based approach to the delivery of leisure services, which has undercut the traditional human-service orientation of this field.

As a consequence, such trends as the commodification and privatization of organized recreation programs threaten to create a society in which many disadvantaged individuals have sharply limited leisure opportunities. On the positive side, innovative partnership approaches among agencies and the application of benefits-based management approaches offer a hopeful vision of the future.

Throughout this book, instead of the past approach to characterizing organized leisure services as the almost exclusive domain of public recreation and park agencies, 10 different types of organizations—ranging from nonprofit community organizations or armed forces recreation to sports management and travel and tourism sponsors—are discussed in detail.

ACKNOWLEDGMENTS

Numerous public, private, nonprofit, commercial, and other organizations have contributed material to the text in the form of annual reports, program brochures, and planning studies. Beyond research in such scholarly or professional journals as *Parks and Recreation, Recreation Canada,* the *Journal of Leisure Research, Leisure Studies,* or the *Journal of Park and Recreation Administration,* many contemporary events and social trends were gathered from major newspapers, newsmagazines, and wire services.

In addition to these sources, the author wishes to acknowledge the important contribution made by a number of leading recreation and leisure-studies educators whose writings—both in textbooks and in scholarly articles—influenced his thinking. While it is not possible to name all of these individuals, they include the following: Lawrence Allen, Maria Allison, John Crompton, Dan Dustin, Geoffrey Godbey, Tom Goodall, Karla Henderson, Debra Jordan, John Kelly, Leo McAvoy, James Murphy, Ruth Russell, Wayne Stormann, and Charles Sylvester.

In addition, the author wishes to express his appreciation to Acquisitions Editor, Suzanne Jeans; Editorial/Production Assistant, Amanda Green; Production Editor, Rebecca Marks; Cover Designer, Stephanie Torta; Production Services Coordinator, Doug Nalean-Carlson; Paging Specialist, Sandy Wille; and Copyeditor, Jeanne Patterson for their invaluable assistance.

Richard Kraus, Professor Emeritus
School of Tourism and Hospitality Management
Temple University, Philadelphia, Pennsylvania

CHAPTER 1

RECREATION AND LEISURE:
The Current Scene

◆ ◆ ◆

Parks, recreation, and the leisure services in the twenty-first century continue to experience enormous changes as a result of development in lifestyles, technology, economics, governmental philosophy, and almost every aspect of human endeavor.

These changes present both challenges and opportunities to those citizens and professionals concerned with improving the quality of life for all people through creative, meaningful, leisure opportunities. Professionals in this dynamic field are constantly trying to find new ways to meet the needs, desires, and the potential of our society.[1]

◆ ◆ ◆

INTRODUCTION

Many individuals regard recreation simply as a source of casual fun or pleasure and think of leisure solely as the free time that provides the opportunity to relax and shed work-related responsibilities. However, as this book will show, recreation, parks, and leisure services have become an important part of government operations and a vital program element of many huge nonprofit, commercial, private-membership, therapeutic, and other types of agencies. Today, recreation constitutes a major force in our national and local economies and is responsible for millions of jobs in such varied fields as travel and tourism, popular entertainment and the arts, health and fitness programs, hobbies, and participatory and spectator sports.

Beyond its value as a form of sociability, play also provides major personal benefits in terms of meeting physical, emotional, and other important health-related needs of participants. In a broad sense, the leisure life of a nation reflects its fundamental values and character. The very games and sports, entertainment media, and group affiliations that people enjoy in their leisure help to shape the character and well-being of families, communities, and society at large.

For these reasons, it is the purpose of this text to present a comprehensive picture of the role of recreation and leisure in modern society, including (1) the field's conceptual base; (2) the varied leisure pursuits people engage in; (3) their social and psychological implications; (4) both positive and negative outcomes of play; (5) the network of community organizations that provide recreational programs and related social services; and (6) the development of recreation as a rich, diversified field of professional practice.

VARIED VIEWS OF RECREATION AND LEISURE

For some, recreation means the network of public agencies that provide such facilities as parks, playgrounds, swimming pools, sports fields, and community centers in thousands of cities, towns, counties, or park districts today. They may view these facilities as an outlet for the young or a means of achieving family togetherness or pursuing interesting hobbies, sports, or social activities.

For others, recreation may be found in a senior center or golden age club, a sheltered workshop for mentally retarded individuals, or a treatment center for physical rehabilitation.

Environmentalists may be chiefly concerned about the impact of outdoor forms of play on our natural surroundings—the forests, mountains, rivers, and lakes that are the national heritage of Americans and Canadians.

Without question, recreation and leisure *are* all of these things. They represent a potentially rewarding and important form of human experience and constitute a major aspect of economic development and government responsibility today. It is important to recognize that this is not a new development. Recreation and leisure are concepts that have fascinated humankind since the golden age of ancient Athens. Varied forms of play have been condemned and suppressed in some societies and highly valued and encouraged in others.

Today, for the first time, there is almost universal acceptance of the value of recreation and leisure. As a consequence, government at every level in the United States and Canada has accepted responsibility for providing or assisting leisure opportunities through extensive recreation and park systems. For example, Searle and Brayley have reported that leisure expenditures by the federal government in Canada almost tripled during the 1980s and that annual recreation expenditures by Canadian families rose by 40 percent during a recent five-year period.[2]

Diversity in Participation

Often we tend to think of recreation primarily as participation in sports and games or in social activities and to ignore other forms of play. However, recreation actually includes an extremely broad range of leisure pursuits, including travel and tourism, cultural entertainment or participation in the arts, hobbies, membership in social clubs or interest groups, nature-related activities such as camping or hunting and fishing, attendance at parties or other special events, or fitness activities.

Recreation may be enjoyed along with thousands of other participants or spectators or may be an intensely solitary experience. It may be highly strenuous and physically demanding or may be primarily a cerebral activity. It may represent a lifetime of interest and involvement or may consist of a single, isolated experience.

Motivations for Recreational Participation

In addition to the varied forms that recreation may take, it also meets a wide range of individual needs and interests. While later chapters in this text will describe play motivations and outcomes in fuller detail, they can be summarized as follows.

Many participants take part in recreation as a form of relaxation and release from work pressures or other tensions. Often they may be passive spectators of entertainment provided by television, movies, or other forms of electronic amusement. However, other significant play motivations are based on the need to express creativity, vent hidden talents, or pursue excellence in varied forms of personal expression.

For some participants, active, competitive recreation may offer a channel for releasing hostility and aggression or for struggling against others or the environment in adventurous, high-risk pursuits. Others enjoy recreation that is highly social and provides the opportunity for making new friends or cooperating with others in group settings.

Many individuals take part in leisure activities that involve community service or that permit them to provide leadership in fraternal or religious organizations. Still others take part in activities that promote health and physical fitness as a primary goal. A steadily growing number of participants enjoy participation in the expanding world of computer-based entertainment and communication—including CD-ROMs, interactive video games, and the Internet. Others are deeply involved in forms of so-called elite culture, such as music, drama, dance, literature, and the fine arts. Exploring new environments through travel and tourism or seeking self-discovery or personality enrichment through continuing education or religious activity represent other important leisure drives.

SOCIAL FACTORS PROMOTING THE RECREATION AND PARK MOVEMENT

The social factors that helped bring about the growth of recreation and leisure programs and services in the United States and Canada stemmed from a variety of causes. Some of these involved changes in the economic structure of society or in dramatically shifting gender values and family relationships. Others were rooted in the kinds of social expectations that emerged as we moved from an essentially rural, agrarian society— where government played a limited role—to a complex industrial, urban culture where government assumed increasingly broad functions.

Twelve of these important social trends are described briefly in the following section of this chapter and in fuller detail in later sections.

1. *Increase in Discretionary Time*   A key development underlying the growth of the recreation movement and our national preoccupation with leisure has been the growth of free or discretionary time in the twentieth century.

In modern, post-industrial society, nonwork time has grown markedly for many individuals. Thanks to advanced mechanical equipment and automated processes in factories, agriculture, and the service fields, productive capacity increased dramatically during the second half of the nineteenth century and the first half of the twentieth. In effect, the workweek has been cut in half since the early days of the Industrial Revolution.

In addition, more holidays and longer vacations are now taken for granted by most American and Canadian employees. With improved Social Security benefits and pension plans, as well as medical advances leading to a longer life, many employees today are assured 15 or more years of full-time leisure after retiring from work.

Finally, labor-saving devices in and around the home, such as automatic heating units, snowblowers and lawnmowers, microwave ovens, and frozen foods, have simplified life's demands considerably.

Surprisingly, in the mid- and late 1980s, a number of surveys showed that this trend had been reversed and that there actually had been an increase in workweek hours for many individuals. However, other research has challenged these findings. As Chapter 4 shows, the increase in work hours appears to have been selective, with certain groups in the population (such as affluent professionals or business managers) working longer hours, but with other individuals continuing to have relatively short workweeks. When other factors are taken into account, such as the increase in holidays, vacations, and early retirement and the needs of special population groups like the disabled or underemployed, it is apparent that leisure continues to present a vast opportunity to great numbers of Americans and Canadians today.

2. National Affluence   A second critical factor stemmed from the dramatic growth of the gross national product (GNP) and personal income in the United States and Canada.

Throughout the twentieth century, household income continued to rise steadily in both nations, with the total amount spent on varied forms of recreation increasing from decade to decade. In the late 1990s, annual expenditures on recreation in the United States rose to over $400 billion (see Table 1.1). When one recognizes that the Commerce Department's figures do not include hundreds of billions of dollars spent on travel and tourism, gambling, liquor, and less easily measured forms of amusement or the operational expenses of thousands of public, nonprofit and private leisure-service agencies, it is apparent that total leisure spending is substantially higher than the amounts shown in the table. Some authorities have estimated that annual recreation expenditures in the United States now are a trillion dollars.[3]

For a period of time, chiefly in the 1980s and early 1990s, the national economies of both the United States and Canada experienced a pronounced slump—with growing unemployment rates and enforced cutbacks in government spending that many referred to as an "era of austerity." However, a dramatic economic recovery in the late 1990s and early twenty-first century returned government agencies on all levels to

TABLE 1.1

ANNUAL PERSONAL SPENDING ON RECREATION: 1985–1996

Type of Product or Service	1985	1990	1996
Total Recreation Expenditures (Billions of Dollars)	116.3	281.6	431.1
Percent of Total Personal Consumption	6.6	7.3	8.3
Books and maps	6.5	16.5	23.2
Magazines, newspapers, and sheet music	12.0	21.5	26.5
Nondurable toys and sport supplies	14.6	31.6	45.4
Wheel goods, sports, and photographic equipment	15.6	29.8	42.0
Video and audio products, computer equipment, and musical instruments	19.9	53.8	89.7
Radio and television repair	2.5	4.2	5.1
Flowers, seeds, and potted plants	4.7	11.1	14.9
Admissions to specified spectator amusements	6.7	15.1	22.1
Motion picture theaters	2.6	5.2	6.3
Legitimate theater and opera and entertainments of nonprofit institutions	1.8	5.6	9.3
Spectator sports	2.3	4.4	6.4
Clubs and fraternal organizations except insurance	3.1	8.9	13.0
Commercial participant amusements	9.1	23.0	46.2
Parimutuel net receipts	2.3	3.4	3.5
Other [includes lottery receipts, pets, cable TV, film processing, sports camps, video rentals, etc.]	19.4	62.7	99.6

Sources: *Statistical Abstract of the United States* (U.S. Department of Commerce, 1999). See this source for a fuller explanation of product and service categories.

impressive budget surpluses and expanded service capability and led to consumer confidence and increased spending on recreation. One commentator writes:

> Go ahead, it's safe to say it: *We've never had it so good.* We've got an $8 trillion economy that's cranking out three million new jobs a year, an economy so strong that a lot of us are gorging ourselves on its fruits.
>   . . . [W]e can be honest with ourselves and recognize that on the eve of a new millennium we are living in an age of unparalleled economic prosperity and material comfort, in the most affluent civilization that this long-suffering planet has ever known.[4]

Growing Gap between Rich and Poor   At the same time that millions of newly rich families are enjoying what one economist has described as "luxury fever," there is strong evidence that the middle and lower socioeconomic classes have been left behind. A 2000 report by the Center on Budget and Policy Priorities and the Economic Policy Institute found that

> . . . the incomes of the poor and middle class have declined or stagnated while the incomes of the highest-income families continued to grow. Since the late 1980s, in

two-thirds of the states, the income gap between the richest and poorest families grew. . . . [T]he average income of the poorest fifth of families nationwide actually fell by almost $900 after adjusting for inflation.[5]

As a result, economists have concluded that the United States is the most economically stratified of nations. While a growing class of millionaires is able to enjoy a host of expensive forms of recreation, those in the nation's urban ghettos and rural slums lack even minimal resources for needed recreation—a contrast that has been described as "recreation apartheid."

3. Commodification of Leisure   This contrast is heightened by what has been termed the "commodification" of leisure. Increasingly, varied forms of play today are developed in complex, expensive forms by profit-seeking businesses. More and more, giant conglomerates like Time Warner, Disney, and Viacom have taken over control of huge corporations that run music, television, and movie businesses; and own sports stadiums and professional teams, cruise ships and theme parks, and other leisure operations.

Many elaborate new facilities offering varied forms of recreation are being developed as part of this trend toward commodification. In cities throughout the United States and Canada, huge public fitness centers that include pools, aerobics and dance rooms, and facilities for family play and a host of other activities are being built—often with charges for membership that cost several hundred dollars a year. Many other recreation centers or programs operated by public recreation and park agencies today require the payment of substantial fees that exclude the poor.

4. Population Trends   Another factor that has been responsible for increasing participation in recreation and leisure in the United States and Canada has been the steady growth of the populations in both countries.

Population in the United States, estimated to be about 250 million persons in 1990, reached over 281 million by the turn of the twenty-first century—with striking growth in the number of young and elderly age groups. In Canada, the population stood at 27 million in 1990 and grew to 30.5 million by the end of the decade. Clearly, the growing numbers of potential participants encouraged the development of new recreation facilities and programs to meet their leisure needs on every age level.

Another marked influence on leisure programs has been the dramatic diversification, in racial and ethnic terms, that has taken place, particularly in the United States. As a result of growing waves of immigration from Asian, Latin American, and other third world regions, often with markedly higher birthrates, the nation's identity as a primarily white society based heavily on northern European and English traditions is rapidly shifting.

As later chapters will show, the emphasis in popular culture, sports, and other leisure-related areas reflects these population changes, with African-Americans, Hispanics, and, to a lesser degree, Asian-Americans playing a far more visible role.

Both in public recreation and park agencies and in major youth-serving organizations like the Boy Scouts, Girl Scouts, Boys and Girls Clubs, and YMCA and YWCA, recreation programming and staffing practices today reflect a strong multicultural emphasis. In Canada, both public and nonprofit recreation and park organizations have made programming to reflect the traditions and customs of minority populations—with Indian and Inuit (Eskimo) groups in particular a high priority.

5. *Where People Live: Urbanization and Suburbanization*   A key factor in the early development of the recreation movement was the growth of North America's industrial cities. As millions of immigrants came from impoverished European nations or migrated from rural regions to cities in search of better job opportunities, they tended to huddle together in crowded slum tenements. Without the natural opportunities for outdoor recreation that the countryside provided, it became obvious that leisure posed an increasingly serious problem for a heavily urbanized society.

Thanks to this dramatic growth of the cities, the recreation movement got under way in the United States and Canada. It took the form of playgrounds for children, sports fields for youths and adults, networks of parks throughout our cities, and the establishment of settlement houses, community centers, and other social-service and religious organizations to meet public leisure needs. In addition, throughout both countries, civic-minded individuals joined together to establish symphony orchestras, opera companies, art and natural history museums, and libraries.

Following World War II, there was a widespread move by millions of middle-class families away from the central cities to the suburban areas that surrounded them. The satellite communities they formed quickly established recreation and park systems—often with extensive facilities and programs. Recreation was part of the "good life" that the suburbs offered to many American and Canadian families who moved to them, and they paid taxes to support these services willingly.

More recently, recreation and park development has been seen as a key factor in promoting the revival of many larger cities, as wealthy citizens have moved into newly rehabilitated or developed residential areas (the process has become known as gentrification). Rundown waterfront or factory areas have been transformed into attractive sites for shopping, sightseeing, cultural activities, and entertainment. Recreation has been stressed as critical to making cities more livable, attracting tourists, and retaining middle-class and wealthy residents. In numerous other communities, public recreation and park departments have constructed new water-play parks, tennis complexes, creative arts centers, marinas, and other recreational facilities.

At the same time, there has been a pronounced shift of millions of residents from the older cities of Northern and Midwestern states to such sunbelt states as Florida, Arizona, or Southern California. Millions of older men and women have retired to communities in these states, and many others have moved to them to find jobs in their flourishing economies.

Within each of these population shifts, recreation and leisure play an important role. Many individuals and families place high value on the recreational and cultural opportunities that are available in communities that they are considering moving to, and large corporations regard this factor as an important element with respect to staff recruitment and retention.

Increasingly, outdoor recreation park and recreation resources are being recognized as critical to a community's image and morale. A Winter 2000 report on urban parks by the Lila Wallace–Reader's Digest Fund concludes:

> Across the country in communities of all sizes, parks and open space are getting new attention. Large city parks, converted corner lots, playgrounds, schoolyards, greenways, and bike trails are changing the face of the urban landscape as public officials and residents alike realize that the quality and availability of a neighborhood's parks are a reflection of the community itself.[6]

6. *Influence of Technology*   Over the past several decades, sophisticated technology has played a key role in providing new forms of play for the American and Canadian populations. Outdoor recreation, for example, makes use of increasingly complex and expensive devices in such activities as skydiving, hang gliding, scuba diving, boating, hunting, fishing, roller-blading, skiing, and snowboarding. Computer dating provides a new form of social contact for single adults, and video games offer interactive competition or exposure to new varieties of play settings and "virtual realities."

As an example of the impact of technology on outdoor recreation pursuits, one author describes gadgets that have been created specifically for hunting, or that have been adapted from the military:

> There were Russian Night Vision Goggles to see in the dark, Bionic Ear Scouts to hear things at a greater distance, and target lasers to mark the destination of bullets with precise red dots. There were battery-powered feeders to lure animals into your territory and automatic cameras to keep track of prey while you were in another neck of the woods.[7]

The Internet has become an integral part of travel and tourism, with airlines, cruise ships, resorts, and major parks maintaining web pages that provide information and facilitate reservations and vacation choices.

Within every aspect of professional recreation, park, and leisure-service management, computer software has become indispensable in program planning and scheduling, public relations, fiscal and personnel management, and maintaining agency information systems.

Home-based recreation has become increasingly dependent on varied forms of electronic entertainment, with television, interactive video games, CD-ROMs, cassette players, and similar devices. Some have speculated that reliance on such gadgetry has become an obsession for many individuals, with retreat into a virtual-reality, "cyberworld" environment taking the place of face-to-face social contact with other humans.

One social critic, Robert Putnam, a Harvard University political scientist, has concluded that there has been a sharp decline over the years in Americans' social and civic involvement—with reliance on home-based technological forms of entertainment and communication an important factor (see page 113).

7. *Recreation's Contribution to Health and Fitness*   A key trend during the 1970s and 1980s was the growth of public interest in exercise and physical fitness programs. Realizing that modern life is frequently inactive, sedentary, beset by tensions, and subject to a host of unhealthy habits including overeating, smoking, and drinking, we have developed a wave of popular concern about improving one's health, vitality, and appearance through diet and exercise.

In 1961, it was estimated that fewer than one out of four persons 18 and older exercised on a regular basis. In 1983, *USA Today* reported that more than 100 million Americans took part in swimming, 75 million bicycled, and 35 million jogged. A year later, a Gallup poll found that 59 percent of adults reported that they exercised daily.

Participation in such activities as aerobics, swimming, running and jogging, racquet sports, and similar vigorous pursuits has more than physiological effects. It also has psychological value; those who exercise regularly look and feel better. Experts have concluded that fitness is not a passing phase; the public's desire to be healthy and physically attractive is supported by a wave of continuing publicity, social values, personal vanity, and solid business sense.

Research showed that the most successful fitness programs were likely to be those that provided an ingredient of recreational interest and satisfaction. In a study of dropouts in an employee fitness program in Canada, Wankel found that while all enrollees had physical fitness as a strong initial motivation, those who continued to be involved had other objectives for joining the program. These objectives of a non-health-related nature (e.g., competition, curiosity, develop recreational skills, go out with friends) were consistently rated as more important by the participants than by the dropouts.[8]

However, through the 1990s, there were reports that the rate of adult participation in regular fitness activities was declining. While evidence showed that regular vigorous activity helped to prevent cardiovascular disease, cancer, and a number of other serious illnesses, the percentage of adults taking part in active exercise regimens was sharply lower than at the height of the fitness boom. Similarly, there was strong evidence that children and youth in the United States were increasingly obese and in poor physical condition.

Certain recreational sports such as youth soccer, volleyball, and ice hockey have grown in popularity. According to the National Federation of High School Athletic Associations, fast-pitch softball is the fastest growing high-school sport in the United States. Television coverage of beach volleyball and inclusion of that sport in the Olympics has resulted in thousands of junior and adult volleyball clubs and leagues—including many leagues sponsored by municipal recreation and park departments. With

Thousands of enthusiasts enjoy a marathon race on New York's Verrazano Bridge, ice-skating on Ottawa's Rideau Canal, and contract bridge tournament in Washington hotel.

Places for Play

Extensive sports fields and beach-like swimming pool, both in England. Serpentine roller coaster, named after the Loch Ness Monster, at Busch Gardens, The Old Country, in Williamsburg, Virginia.

the expansion of professional ice hockey, it was reported in 1995 that there were over 24,000 teams registered in U.S.A. Hockey, the Little League of ice hockey, with long waiting lists for ice rink practice time throughout the country.

However, more recent reports indicate that there has been a marked downward trend in participation in other traditional individual and team games. At the same time, a growing number of state school systems have reduced or eliminated physical education requirements, which means that organized recreation programs represent an even more important means of promoting physical fitness for children and youth.

8. *Environmental Concerns* As later chapters on the historical development of recreation and leisure will show, the establishment of public recreation programs in the United States and Canada was closely linked to the growing number of national, state, provincial, and local park systems. In Canada, for example, Searle and Brayley write:

> Recognition of the need to protect our natural resources and to provide opportunities for Canadians to experience their leisure in natural environments and places of historical significance led to the creation of Banff National Park in 1885 by the Canadian Government. Subsequently, this led to the creation of the national parks system, the largest in the world. It has also led to the systematic protection of historic sites. Similar initiatives by provincial park services make an important contribution to the social fabric of the nation and increasingly to the health of its environment.[9]

Outdoor recreation activities such as camping, biking, backpacking, boating, hunting, fishing, skiing, and mountain climbing depend heavily on parks, forest water areas operated chiefly by public recreation and park agencies. However, the concern of many Americans with the health of the nation's outdoor resources stems from more than the need for outdoor recreation spaces. LaPage and Ranney point out that one of the most powerful sources of America's essential cultural fiber and spirit is the land itself. They write:

> The roots of this new nation and its people became the forests and rivers, the deserts and mountains, and the challenges and inspirations they presented, not the ruins of ancient civilizations most other cultures look to for ancestral continuity. Thus, America developed a different attitude and identity.[10]

For such reasons, the environmental movement has received strong support from many recreation advocates and organizations. At the same time, it is recognized that such activities as fishing and hunting are just part of a bigger scene that requires clean—and safe—air and water and wise use of the land.

Growing national concern about the need to protect the environment was buttressed by the 1962 Report of the Outdoor Recreation Resources Review Commission. During the following two decades, there was a wave of federal and state legislative action and funding support in the United States that was designed to acquire open space; to protect imperiled forests, wetlands, and scenic areas; to help endangered species flourish; and to reclaim the nation's wild rivers and trails. This movement was threatened during the early 1980s, when a new national administration in the United States sought to reduce park and open space funding, eliminate conservation programs and environmental regulations, and subject the outdoors to renewed economic exploitation. Again, in the mid-1990s, the effort to open up protected wilderness areas to increased oil drilling, cattle grazing, lumbering, and other commercial uses gained strong political support.

Organizations such as the nonpartisan League of Conservation Voters, National Audubon Society, National Wildlife Federation, Wilderness Society, Sierra Club, and Nature Conservancy have been in the forefront of the continuing battle to protect the nation's natural resources. Numerous outdoor recreation organizations have joined with such groups, in both the United States and Canada, and the struggle will clearly continue as an important political issue in the years ahead.

As the world celebrated Earth Day 2000, thirty years after the first Earth Day in 1970, it was clear that North American air was cleaner and its water purer than for many past decades. There was more protected open space in national parks, wildlife refuges, and wilderness areas. Yet, Whitman writes:

> . . . [S]urveys indicate that only 14 percent to 36 percent of Americans believe that the environment has improved a "great deal" since 1970. And, according to a 1999 Roper poll, 56 percent worry that the next 10 years will be "the last decade when humans will have a chance to save the earth from an environmental catastrophe."[11]

9. *Therapeutic Recreation Service*   An important aspect of the growth of the recreation movement since World War II has been the increased awareness of the leisure needs of persons with physical, mental, or social disabilities.

In both the United States and Canada, there has been a marked expansion of legislation and social welfare programs designed to improve the lives of disabled and dependent aging individuals and to open up new opportunities for them within the mainstream of community life.

In the recreation movement, this trend was most strikingly illustrated by the growth of concern about children and youth with mental retardation, which began in the early 1960s under the administration of President John F. Kennedy. The Kennedy Foundation joined forces with the federal and state governments and professional organizations in physical education and recreation to provide sports opportunities for retarded individuals. This coalition initiated research, supported demonstration projects, helped prepare professional personnel, and gave rise to such major recreation ventures as the Special Olympics program.

In the United States, the Americans with Disabilities Act of 1990 symbolized and gave force to the drive to provide fuller and more equitable life opportunities to persons with disabilities and to assist them in the areas of education, career development, and social involvement. Through the efforts of such professional societies as the National Therapeutic Recreation Society and the American Therapeutic Recreation Association, the practice of recreation specialists in clinical treatment settings has become increasingly sophisticated and recognized as an important element in the care of ill and disabled persons.

Despite such progress, therapeutic recreation service has experienced a number of setbacks over the past two decades. The deinstitutionalization of mental health care in both the United States and Canada has meant that many mental hospitals and special schools for persons with mental retardation have been closed or reduced in scope. Too often, patients or clients who would formerly have been exposed to professionally designed therapeutic recreation programs now live in community settings with limited support services.

Finally, the emergence of managed-care systems with third-party payment by insurance companies that dominate the provision of medical care and rehabilitation has meant that often socially oriented services like therapeutic recreation receive little support. Too often, hospitals have been forced to cut back their programs sharply or have been overwhelmed by excessive patient loads and limited budgetary support.

The problem is particularly acute in a number of Canadian provinces, where dozens of hospitals have been forced to close down, and where patients with critical illnesses or emergency needs for medical assistance are forced to wait long periods for attention.[12]

Under such circumstances, therapeutic recreation as an adjunctive form of treatment inevitably receives a lower level of priority. As a result, therapeutic recreation specialists today are working in a much greater variety of settings and serving entirely new kinds of patient or client populations. In the late 1990s, Riley and Skalko summarized the trend:

> Not only will therapeutic recreation specialists [in the years ahead] provide services in hospital, rehabilitation, and community recreation settings . . . but [they] will increasingly capture service-delivery roles in home health, homeless care, domestic abuse, substance abuse, at-risk youth services, transplant units, adult day services, partial hospitalization, retirement services, and care for the frail elderly.[13]

Such predictions are based on the growing acceptance of recreation itself as a health-related field, but also raise questions with respect to the training, certification, and professional identity of therapeutic recreation specialists, issues discussed in later chapters of this text.

10. *New Leisure Roles for Girls and Women*   Another striking phenomenon of the post–World War II decades was the strong drive by girls and women in the United States and Canada toward playing a more equal role in varied aspects of community life. This trend was also linked with other gender-related concerns, such as the leisure needs and involvements of men and boys and public attitudes and policies with respect to homosexuality.

The feminist movement that gathered force at this time represented a major challenge to sexist beliefs and social customs that had existed for many centuries, during which women were essentially treated as second-class citizens in marital and family life, education, careers, politics, and leisure opportunity.

Distorted and stereotyped views of women's traits and capabilities had meant that from early childhood on, they were often restricted in their play opportunities. They were barred from a variety of athletic, outdoor recreation, social, and cultural involvements— with few exceptions.

As the recreation and park movement expanded, men tended to dominate— particularly in administrative and policy-making roles—while women were relegated to direct leadership or programming roles at salaries far below those of their male counterparts. With the emergence of a vigorous feminist movement and antidiscrimination laws in the 1960s and 1970s, many of these inequities were corrected.

lthough public interest in women's sports continues to be considerably lower than its support for boys' and men's sports, there is growing interest in women's tennis, golf, gymnastics, track and field, and similar events on every level of competition. Participation totals in team sports such as field hockey, soccer, softball, and volleyball have continued to climb steadily. For many, increased participation in vigorous athletics and outdoor pastimes is symbolic of the need to overcome the past view of women as fragile, over-emotional, or lacking in courage and drive. Outstanding women athletes in particular have helped to create a new image of feminine strength, determination, and self-confidence, which is closely linked to women's achieving a higher degree of acceptance in formerly male-restricted fields such as the military, aviation, police and fire departments, law, and medicine.

More and more, young women today are engaging in violent and aggressive contact sports, such as ice hockey, football, and rugby, and even professional boxing. In some cases, they have adopted formerly male behaviors and values linked to sport, such as the abuse of steroid drugs.

Along with such changes, many women have succeeded in overcoming the barriers to participation in formerly male-restricted clubs and semi-secret societies that have historically controlled access to the power structure and success in American and Canadian life. Accompanying these developments, a number of leading scholars have explored the special meaning of leisure in the lives of women and have spearheaded their advancement in the recreation, park, and leisure-service profession.

11. *Decline of Family and Community Values*   Linked to several of the social trends just described, there has been a marked breakdown in the quality of American and Canadian daily life with respect to traditional family values and community relationships.

his deterioration has taken several forms: (1) the fragmentation of family life, with a steady increase in the number of children born out of wedlock, divorces and separations, and single-parent households; (2) the expanding problem of widespread alcohol and drug abuse, particularly among the young; (3) the increase in random and senseless violence, often on an individual basis but also linked to gang-generated conflict in cities large and small; (4) the presence of homeless people in increasing numbers, both on the streets and in parks and under highways and viaducts, in many communities; (5) the ready acceptance of gambling as a solution to the economic problems of states and cities, along with the growing tolerance of veiled forms of prostitution and other commercially linked forms of sexual entertainment; and, finally, (6) an overall sense that the patterns of civility and human decency that should prevail in everyday life have been widely abandoned.

What do these trends have to do with recreation and leisure? First and most obviously, many of the more popular but morally questionable pursuits just described represent a search for pleasure, novelty, and excitement. Secondly, they tend to displace more traditional and constructive forms of play. Thus, they represent a major challenge to recreation managers, leaders, and program planners in public and nonprofit community leisure-service agencies, who must compete with them for the attention of participants and must struggle against their demoralizing effects on community life.

Now, a major segment of the nation's leisure sponsors—the creators and distributors of popular motion pictures and television shows, video games, books, magazines, and even toys—are being blamed for having created a climate that tolerates immorality, crime, sexual and physical abuse of children, and random violence.

Beginning in the 1992 presidential campaign in the United States, attacks were leveled on the producers of television shows for undermining the nation's traditional codes of sexual behavior and parental responsibility. In the years that followed, major political figures have blamed the "cultural elite"—particularly executives and creative leaders in the communications and entertainment media—for deliberately promoting sensational themes or publicizing events, personalities, shocking crimes, and distorted relationships, which has resulted in a decline of family values and civic morality.

With several devastating examples of teenage boys carrying out slaughters of students and teachers in American schools during the late 1990s, such problems aroused a new wave of concern. In response, a growing number of public and nonprofit leisure-service organizations have initiated innovative, comprehensive programs designed to serve "at-risk" youth—in many cases with strikingly positive results.[14]

Beyond such programs, however, the broader role of leisure-service agencies, along with religious organizations, the schools, and parents' groups, will need to mount more intensive and focused efforts to promote family stability in American life and to overcome the effects of poverty, intergroup conflicts, and the negative impact of destructive forms of play.

12. *Growth of Organized Leisure-Service Field* A dramatic expansion in the number and influence of several major types of organized recreation, park, and leisure-service sponsors has also occurred over the past several decades. At the time of World War II, such organizations tended to fall under two primary headings: public recreation and park departments and voluntary, nonprofit youth-serving organizations. As Chapter 9 will show, in the years that followed, a number of other forms of leisure-service sponsors gained steadily in membership and public support. Today, recreation and leisure-service providers may be classified under eight major categories. These are:

1. *Government agencies*—federal, state, and provincial agencies, and local departments of recreation and parks—that provide leisure services as a primary function, as well as hundreds of other agencies (such as those concerned with social service, education, special populations, and the armed forces) that offer or assist recreation programs as a secondary responsibility.

2. *Voluntary organizations*, which are nongovernmental, nonprofit agencies, both sectarian and nonsectarian, serving the public at large or selected elements of it with multiservice programs that often include a substantial element of recreational opportunity. Such organizations include national youth programs like the Boy Scouts and Girl Scouts and the YMCA, YWCA, and YM-YWHA.

3.   *Private membership organizations*, such as golf, tennis, yacht, athletic, and country clubs, along with a wide range of service clubs and fraternal bodies, that provide recreational and social activities for their own members and in some cases assist community recreation needs as well. Under this heading are the recreation sponsors connected to residence, as in the case of swimming pools, sports or fitness complexes, or clubs attached to leisure villages, apartment or condominium units, or retirement communities.

4.   *Commercial recreation enterprises*, including a great variety of privately owned, for-profit businesses, such as ski centers, bowling alleys, nightclubs, movie houses or theaters, health spas or fitness centers, dancing schools, amusement or theme parks, and other enterprises that provide leisure services.

5.   *Employee recreation programs* (formerly called industrial recreation), which serve those who work for given companies or other employers by providing recreation, often as part of a total personnel benefits package, linked to other services concerned with employee health and fitness.

6.   *Armed forces recreation*, which, while it is obviously a form of government-sponsored activity, is unique in its setting and purpose. Each of the major branches of the armed forces tends to operate an extensive network of recreation facilities and programs.

7.   *Campus recreation*, which includes intramural athletics or sports clubs, social activities, trip-and-travel programs, performing arts groups, entertainment, lounges, film series, and numerous other forms of recreation on college and university campuses.

8.   *Therapeutic recreation services*, including any type of program designed to meet the needs of persons with physical or mental disabilities, individuals with poor health, dependent aging persons, socially deviant persons in correctional facilities or other treatment settings, and similar special groups.

In addition to these eight types of sponsors, two other distinct areas of recreational involvement have given rise to a whole host of leisure-service providers. Within the diversified fields of *sports participation and spectatorship*, and *travel, tourism, and hospitality management*, public, private, commercial and other sponsors today constitute huge industries, making a total of ten special areas of leisure-service operations.

Need for Professional Leadership

Within each of these fields of specialization, there is a growing need for qualified professional leadership. Too often, people assume that the task of organizing and conducting recreation programs is a relatively simple one and that "anyone" can do it without specialized training. They do so because they realize that many youths and adults in our society do provide recreational leadership *without* such training. Volunteer leaders or coaches in the Scouting movement, Little League, hospitals, and similar organizations often help run excellent programs.

However, the professional's assignment within the organized recreation field tends to be far more complex and difficult than that of the typical volunteer leader or coach. It must involve carefully thought-out goals and objectives and often requires sophisticated planning techniques.

To pick a dramatic example, in such large-scale commercial recreation enterprises as the far-flung Disney theme park operations, including Disneyland in California; Disney World, Epcot Center, and other attractions in Florida; and other parks in Japan and

France, the immense investment that is at stake requires shrewd marketing, management, and creative design approaches. Literally hundreds of millions of dollars are involved in such ventures.

Even when the scope of the program is on a lesser scale, professional management involves such varied tasks as planning and building recreation facilities that may range from golf courses to swimming complexes, supervising leadership and maintenance personnel, carrying out effective public relations campaigns, and assessing public needs and demands. Often it will require working closely with boards or commissions, advisory groups, or civic officials; it may also involve effective liaison with other levels of government.

In the case of therapeutic programs that serve persons with disabilities, the recreation specialist may need an intensive knowledge of illness and its effects, medical terminology, anatomy, kinesiology, and psychopathology. Those working with the aging must have a solid understanding of geriatrics and gerontology and should be aware of the varied roles played by other community agencies that work with older populations.

On all levels, recreation professionals should be familiar with a wide range of activities and their potential values and outcomes. They should possess the skills needed for direct leadership and supervision, group dynamics, and patient or client assessment, and have the ability to carry out basic evaluation or research and write literate and meaningful reports. Underlying each of these areas of competence, there is a need for recreation professionals to be fully aware of the meaning of recreation and leisure in human society and of the history and traditions of this field.

Emerging Professional Identity

As employment in recreation, park, and leisure-service agencies and programs grew over the past several decades, it gained public recognition as a flourishing career field. Millions of men and women became employed in various specialized sectors of leisure service, with hundreds of thousands holding professional-level jobs as recreation leaders, supervisors, planners, managers, and resource specialists.

Emerging professionalism had a number of important aspects: (1) the identification for the first time of *recreation* as a specialized field of service, making significant contributions to society and requiring unique competencies and skills; (2) heightened visibility for the field itself and the development of channels for influencing public policy in matters related to recreation and leisure; and (3) a higher level of status for those working in the field, accompanied by the widespread acceptance of recreation as a legitimate field of social responsibility. Particularly through the efforts of national, state, and provincial societies, higher standards for practice were developed and the first steps of certification and accreditation were set in motion.

Influence of Professional Specialization

As the overall leisure-service field expanded, each of its specialized disciplines also gained strength and a sense of unique identity. Specialists also began to form their own professional societies in such areas as armed forces recreation, therapeutic recreation, campus recreation, and employee services. In some cases, they established their own certification processes and set up linkages to other professional disciplines functioning in areas related to their specializations.

It must therefore be understood that recreation leadership and management does not represent a single, unified field of professional practice today. Its practitioners have varying areas of responsibility and have developed specialized missions and operational strategies suited to their unique service areas.

However, representatives of each of the ten types of program sponsors within the overall leisure-service field have a common concern with the provision of constructive recreation programs that meet societal needs and contribute to individual physical and mental health and positive community relationships. Increasingly, they are joining together in partnerships that share human, fiscal, and other agency resources to achieve such goals. It is essential that all leisure-service practitioners seeking to be regarded as professionals recognize that they must have more than nuts-and-bolts competence in conducting program activities.

In addition to such competence, recreation professionals must meet high standards of specialized training, be affiliated with appropriate professional societies, and have a rich understanding of the full range of public leisure needs and of the social challenges that face this field.

CHALLENGES FACING THE LEISURE-SERVICE FIELD

This chapter has outlined a number of the critical social trends that were responsible for the growth of recreation's popularity in modern society—and that also pose a number of serious challenges to its practitioners and planners. Leisure-service professionals must therefore be able to deal creatively with the following kinds of questions.

How can the organized recreation movement contribute to public understanding of leisure's role in daily life and to upgrading the level of the public's choices of leisure pursuits?

What role can public, voluntary, therapeutic, and other community-based agencies play in helping to reduce crime, violence, substance abuse, and other serious societal problems?

How can recreation contribute to promoting positive intercultural understanding and relationships and to enriching the lives of persons with disabilities?

How can the organized recreation movement play a meaningful role in a society that has increasingly become dominated by commercial interests—particularly conglomerates in the mass media of communication and entertainment—that place dollar profits at a higher priority than important human values?

In an era marked by striking economic prosperity, how can recreation and leisure-service professionals develop programs designed to serve the less fortunate in society?

Particularly for practitioners in park agencies that sponsor outdoor recreation services or manage extensive natural resources, what policies will serve important ecological needs in the years ahead?

PURPOSES OF THIS TEXT

This text is intended to provide comprehensive information that will be helpful to its readers in developing sound personal philosophies and gaining a broad awareness of the leisure-service field and in answering questions not with learned-by-rote solutions, but rather through intelligent analysis, critical thinking, and problem solving.

Leisure-service professionals should have in-depth understanding of the full range of recreational needs and motivations and agency programs and outcomes. This understanding should be based on a solid foundation with respect to the behavioral and social principles underlying recreation and leisure in contemporary society.

To have a sound philosophy of the goals and values of recreation and leisure in modern life, it is essential to understand recreation's history—and to be aware of its social, economic, and psychological characteristics in today's society. Should recreation be regarded chiefly as an amenity or should it be supported as a form of social therapy? What are the recreation needs of such populations as girls and women, the aging, the disadvantaged, racial minorities, persons with disabilities, or others who have not been served fully in the past?

What environmental priorities should recreation and park professionals fight to support, and how can outdoor forms of play be designed to avoid destructive ecological outcomes? How can leisure-service practitioners strike a balance between entrepreneurial management approaches, which emphasize fiscal self-sufficiency, and human-service programming that responds to the issues raised in this chapter?

Recently, columnist Neal Peirce wrote:

> A quarter century from now, what will urban America be like? Ravaged wastelands? Or supportive, progressive communities with parks and kids at play?[15]

Peirce goes on to point out that low-income communities are critically underserved—in sharp contrast to the park and recreation facilities provided in comfortable middle-class suburbs. He cites examples of a number of cities throughout the United States where crime has declined when recreation programs were expanded, and quotes Newark, New Jersey's Mayor Sharpe James: "We are going to recreate or we are going to incinerate. The choice is ours."

Throughout this text, such issues are discussed in detail. Through a vivid depiction of the field's conceptual base, history, and current status; through an examination of existing agencies and programs; and through a comprehensive summary of research studies and recent reports, the reader should gain a full, in-depth understanding of the role of recreation and leisure in modern society.

Although this text promotes no single philosophical position, its purpose is to clarify the values promoted by recreation and leisure in modern society. Ultimately, these values will be responsible for the field's ability to flourish as a significant form of governmental or voluntary-agency service or as a commercial enterprise.

SUMMARY

This chapter provides an introduction to the study of recreation, park, and leisure services, seen as vital ingredients in the lives of Americans and Canadians and as growing areas of career opportunity and professional responsibility.

It outlines several of the unique characteristics of leisure involvement, such as the diverse forms of recreational involvement and play motivations shared by persons of all ages and backgrounds. It then presents several important factors or social trends that have promoted the growth of the recreation and park movement during the twentieth century. These trends range from the increase of discretionary time and growing affluence to expanded interest in the creative arts and concern about the natural environment. Emphasis is placed on the development of the organized recreation system over the past several decades, with a discussion of different types of leisure-service agencies that are responsible for facility development and activity program management.

The chapter ends by briefly describing the emergence of the recreation, park, and leisure-service profession and emphasizing the need for specialized educational preparation for those holding responsible positions in this field. It also suggests a number of critical social challenges that will face leisure-service practitioners in the years ahead; these will be discussed more fully in the chapters that follow.

QUESTIONS FOR CLASS DISCUSSION OR ESSAY EXAMINATIONS

1. Identify and discuss at least three important social factors (example: increased affluence) that have contributed to the growth of recreation and leisure concerns over the past several decades.
2. What are the special meanings and values of recreation and leisure for different population groups in modern society, based on socioeconomic, age, gender or ability/disability factors?
3. This chapter briefly summarizes the emergence of professional leadership in recreation and parks management roles. Why should leisure-service professionals be expected to have an understanding of the history, psychology, and sociology of recreation and leisure?
4. What do you regard as some of the most critical challenges facing recreation and leisure-service agencies and practitioners in the years that lie ahead? Justify your response.

ENDNOTES

1 Tony Mobley and Dan Newport, *Parks and Recreation in the 21st Century* (National Recreation and Park Association and National Symposium Committee Report, 1996): 9.

2 Mark Searle and Russell Brayley, *Leisure Services in Canada: An Introduction* (State College, Pa.: Venture Publishing, 1993): 3.

3 Daniel Stynes, "Leisure—The New Center of the Economy," in Geoffrey Godbey, ed., *Issue Papers* (Pennsylvania State University and Academy of Leisure Sciences, 1993): 11–17.

4 Dick Polman, "Prosperity," *Philadelphia Inquirer* (20 September 1998): 5.

5 "How Wide Is the Nation's Income Gap?" *Philadelphia Inquirer* (30 January 2000): D-7.

6 *Focus: Urban Parks 2000.* (Periodic Report, Lila Wallace–Readers Digest Fund): 1.

7 John Steinbreder, "Technohunters," *New York Times Magazine* (30 November 1997): 114.

8 Leonard Wankel, "Personal and Situational Factors Affecting Exercise Involvement: The Importance of Enjoyment," *Research Quarterly for Exercise and Sport* (Vol. 56, No. 3, 1985): 281.

9 Searle and Brayley, *op. cit.:* 2–3.

10 W. F. LaPage and S. R. Ranney, "America's Wilderness: The Heart and Soul of Culture," *Parks and Recreation* (July 1988): 24.

11 David Whitman, "It's a Breath of Fresh Air," *U.S. News and World Report* (17 April 2000): 16.

12 James Brooke, "Full Hospitals Make Canadians Wait and Look South," *New York Times* (16 January 2000): 15.

13 Bob Riley and Thomas Skalko, "The Evolution of Therapeutic Recreation," *Parks and Recreation* (May 1998): 69.

14 Peter Witt and John Crompton, "A Paradigm of the Times," *Parks and Recreation* (December 1999): 66–75.

15 Neal Peirce, "We Are Going to Recreate or Incinerate," *Philadelphia Inquirer* (15 September 1994): 31.

CHAPTER 2

BAJIC CONCEPTJ:
Philosophical Analysis of Play, Recreation, and Leisure

◆ ◆ ◆

What would life be without play? Play is fun, freedom, a way to socialize, our reward after hard work. When we play at something, we enjoy it for its own sake. It's a refuge from ordinary life where one is exempt from the usual obligations, customs, and rules. Play is our brain's favorite way of learning. . . . We evolved through play. Our culture thrives on play.[1]

◆ ◆ ◆

INTRODUCTION

Any consideration of the broad field of recreation and leisure should begin with a clarification of terms and concepts. The words *play*, *leisure*, and *recreation* are frequently used interchangeably, as if they meant the same thing. However, while related, they have distinctly different meanings and it is important for both students and practitioners in this field to understand their varied implications and the differences among them.

The rationale for stressing such conceptual understanding is clear-cut. Just as a doctor must know chemistry, anatomy, kinesiology, and other underlying sciences in order to practice medicine effectively, so the recreation and park professional must understand the meaning of leisure and its motivations and satisfactions if he or she is to provide effective recreation programs and services.

Similarly, the leisure scholar should not withdraw from the real world of leisure programming and participation by focusing only on abstract or theoretical models of free-time behavior. Instead, the scholar should become familiar with the profession of recreation service and should contribute to its effective performance. Such conceptual understandings are critical to the development of a sound philosophy of recreation service and to interpreting leisure-service goals and outcomes to the public at large.

THE MEANING OF PLAY

The word *play* is derived from the Anglo-Saxon *plega*, meaning a game or sport, skirmish, fight, or battle. This is related to the Latin *plaga*, meaning a blow, stroke, or thrust. It is illustrated in the idea of striking or stroking an instrument or playing a game by striking a ball. Other languages have words derived from a common root (such as the German *spielen* and the Dutch *spelen*) whose meanings include the playing of games, sports, and musical instruments. *Webster's New International Dictionary* offers several definitions of the noun *play*. Primary meanings include:

> a brisk handling, using, or plying; as, the play of a sword; any exercise or series of actions intended for diversion; a particular amusement; a game; a sport.[2]

Other dictionary meanings of play include stage exhibitions or dramatic presentations; any form of amusement or frolic; the act of carrying on a game; a way of acting or proceeding, often with the implication of deception or trickiness; or action or movement, as in the play of life. Play is traditionally thought of as a child's activity, in contrast to recreation, which is usually described as an adult activity. Today, however, it is recognized that people of all ages take part in play.

Historical Perspectives

In ancient Greece, play was assigned a valuable role in the lives of children, based on the writings of Plato and Aristotle. The Athenians placed great value on developing qualities of honor, loyalty, and beauty and other elements of productive citizenship in children. For them, play was an integral element of education and was considered a means of positive character development and teaching the values of Greek society.

Later, as the Catholic Church gained dominance among the developing nations of western Europe, play came to be regarded as a social threat. The body was thought to detract from more spiritual or work-oriented values, and every effort was made to curb the pleasurable forms of play that had been popular in the Greek and Roman eras.

Gradually, however, educators and philosophers like Froebel, Rousseau, and Schiller came to the defense of play as an important aspect of childhood education. For example, Froebel wrote of play as the highest expression of human development in childhood:

> Play is the purest, most spiritual activity of man at this stage. . . . A child that plays thoroughly with self-active determination, perseveringly until physical fatigue forbids, will surely be a thorough, determined man, capable of self-sacrifice for the promotion of the welfare of himself and others.[3]

EARLY THEORIES OF PLAY

In the nineteenth and early twentieth centuries, a number of influential scholars evolved comprehensive theories of play—explaining how it had developed and its role in human society and personal development.

Surplus-Energy Theory

The English philosopher Herbert Spencer, in his mid-nineteenth-century work *Principles of Psychology*, advanced the view that play was primarily motivated by the need to burn up excess energy. He was influenced by the earlier writings of Friedrich von Schiller, who had suggested that when animals or birds were fully fed and had no other survival needs, they vented their exuberant energy in a variety of aimless and pleasurable forms of play. Spencer saw play among children as an imitation of adult activities; the sport of boys, such as chasing, wrestling, and taking one another prisoner, involved "predatory instincts."

Recreation Theory

An early explanation of play that was regarded as the converse of the Schiller-Spencer view was developed by Moritz Lazarus, a German philosopher, who argued that rather than serving to *burn up* excess energy, the purpose of play was to *conserve* or *restore* it. In other words, when one is exhausted through toil, play recharges one's energy for renewed work. Lazarus distinguished between physical and mental energy, pointing out that when the brain is "tired" (provided that it is not overtired), a change of activity, particularly in the form of physical exercise, will restore one's nervous energy. To illustrate, the desk worker who plays tennis after a long day's work simultaneously discharges surplus physical energy and restores mental energy.

Instinct-Practice Theory

A more elaborate explanation of play was put forward by Karl Groos, a professor of philosophy at Basel, who wrote two major texts—one in 1896 on the play of animals and another in 1899 on the play of humans.

Groos argued that play helped animals survive by enabling them to practice and perfect the skills they would need in adult life. He concluded that the more adaptable and intelligent a species was, the more it needed a period of protected infancy and childhood for essential learning to take place. Thus among humans there was a lengthy early period during which children engaged in varied activities to perfect skills before they really needed them.

Modern ethologists who have systematically studied the behavior of animals and birds in interaction with each other and with their environment have identified varied forms of play that appear to illustrate the instinct-practice theory. For example, much play among young animals, particularly primates, involves aggressive teasing and mock battles. Such play represents a ritualized form of combat, in which the combatants practice their fighting skills and learn to interact with each other in establishing a "pecking order."

Anthropologists who have observed preindustrial tribal societies point out that "playing house" is often a form of rehearsal for adult roles. In some African rural villages, it may involve both technical and social skills, as boys and girls build and thatch small houses and make various tools and utensils. Often the play forms are gender-related: boys typically make axes, spears, shields, slings, bows, and arrows or build miniature cattle kraals, while girls make pottery for cooking real or imaginary food or perhaps weave mats or baskets of plaited grass.

Catharsis Theory

The catharsis theory is based on the view that play—particularly competitive, active play—serves as a safety valve for the expression of bottled-up emotions. Among the ancient Greeks, Aristotle saw drama as a means of purging oneself of hostile or aggressive emotions; by vicarious sharing in the staged experience, onlookers purified themselves of harmful feelings. A number of early twentieth-century writers expanded this theory. Harvey Carr, an American psychologist, wrote:

> Catharsis . . . implies the idea of purging or draining of that energy which has *anti-social possibilities.* . . . The value of football, boxing, and other physical contests in relieving the pugnacious tendencies of boys is readily apparent as examples. Without the numberless well-organized set forms of play possessed by society which give a harmless outlet to the mischievous and unapplied energy of the young, the task of the teacher and parent would be appalling.[4]

Coupled with the surplus-energy theory, the catharsis theory suggested a vital necessity for active play to help children and youth burn up excess energy and provide a socially acceptable channel for aggressive or hostile emotions and drives.

TWENTIETH-CENTURY CONCEPTS OF PLAY

During the first three decades of the twentieth century, a number of psychologists and educators examined play, particularly as a developmental and learning experience for children.

Self-Expression Theory

Two leading physical educators, Elmer Mitchell and Bernard Mason, saw play primarily as a result of the need for self-expression. Humans were regarded as active, dynamic beings with the need to find outlets for their energies, use their abilities, and express their personalities. The specific types of activity that an individual engaged in were, according to Mitchell and Mason, influenced by such factors as physiological and anatomical structure, physical fitness level, environment, and family and social background.[5]

In addition to these elements, the "self-expression" theory also suggested that certain universal wishes of humankind were influential in shaping play attitudes and habits. These included: (1) the wish for new experience; (2) the wish for participation in a group enterprise; (3) the wish for security; (4) the wish for response and recognition from others; and (5) the wish for the aesthetic.

Play as a Social Necessity

Joseph Lee, who is widely regarded as the father of the play movement in America and who promoted the establishment of numerous playgrounds and recreation centers, was instrumental in the public acceptance of play as an important force in child development and community life.

Lee believed that play contributed to the wholesome development of personal character because it involved lessons of discipline, sacrifice, and morality. He saw it as more than mere pleasurable pastime, but rather as a serious element in the lives of children and—along with his contemporary pioneer, Luther Halsey Gulick—he considered it a vital element in community life. This view extended itself to a literal application of play as a means of preparing children for the adult work world. Wayne Stormann points out that play was considered a useful form of manual training because it coordinated bodily functions, promoted health, and prepared children for the "indoor confinement," first of schools and then of factory life.[6]

Typologies of Play Activity

In the twentieth century, more and more social and behavioral scientists began to examine play empirically. One such investigator, the French sociologist Roger Caillois, examined the play experience itself by classifying the games and play activities that were characteristic of various cultures and identifying their apparent functions and values. Caillois established four major types of play and game activity: agon, alea, mimicry, and ilinx.

Agon refers to activities that are competitive and in which the equality of the participants' chances of winning is artificially created. Winners are determined through such qualities as speed, endurance, strength, memory, skills, and ingenuity. Agonistic games may be played by individuals or teams; they presuppose sustained attention, training and discipline, perseverance, limits, and rules. Clearly, most modern games and sports, including many card and table games involving skill, are examples of agon.

Alea includes those games or contests over whose outcome the contestant has no control; winning is the result of fate rather than the skill of the player. Games of dice, roulette, and baccarat, as well as lotteries, are examples of alea.

Mimicry is based on the acceptance of illusions or imaginary universes. It includes a class of games in which players make believe, or make others believe, that they are other than themselves. For children, Caillois writes:

> The aim is to imitate adults. . . . This explains the success of the toy weapons and miniatures which copy the tools, engines, arms and machines used by adults. The little girl plays her mother's role as cook, laundress and ironer. The boy makes believe he is a soldier, musketeer, policeman, pirate, cowboy, Martian, etc.[7]

Ilinx consists of play activities based on the pursuit of vertigo or dizziness. Historically, ilinx was found in primitive religious dances or other rituals that induced the trancelike state necessary for worship. Today it may be seen in children's games that lead to dizziness by whirling rapidly, and in the use of swings and seesaws. Among adults, ilinx may be achieved through certain dances involving rapid turns or through such amusement park rides as rollercoasters.

Contrasting Styles of Play   Caillois also suggested two extremes of play behavior. The first of these, which he calls *paidia,* involves exuberance, freedom, and uncontrolled and spontaneous gaiety. The second, *ludus,* is characterized by rules and conventions and represents calculated and contrived activity. Each of the four forms of play may be conducted at either extreme of *paidia* or *ludus* or at some point on a continuum between the two.

Anthropological Analysis of Play

Other social scientists have focused on the functions of play within different human societies. In tribal cultures, they have found it to be a form of behavior that is connected to many aspects of daily life and linked to major events and ceremonies.

Play behavior is commonly found at rites of birth, coming of age, marriage, and death and burial—indeed, all of our important social events tend to be incorporated into social observances that include a rich element of play, such as games and sports, dance, music, costumed parades, and dramatic reenactments of religious or historical events.

The Play Element in Culture

Probably the most far-reaching and influential theory of play as a cultural phenomenon was advanced by the Dutch social historian, Johan Huizinga, in his provocative work *Homo Ludens* (Man the Player).

Huizinga presents the thesis that play pervades all of life. He sees it as having certain characteristics: it is a voluntary activity, marked by freedom and never imposed by physical necessity or moral duty. It stands outside the realm of satisfying physiological needs and appetites. It is separate from ordinary life both in its location and its duration, being "played out" within special time periods and in such special places as the arena, the card table, the stage, and the tennis court. Play is controlled, says Huizinga, by special sets of rules, and it demands absolute order. It is also marked by uncertainty and tension. Finally, it is not concerned with good or evil, although it has its own ethical value in that its rules must be obeyed.

In Huizinga's view, play reveals itself chiefly in two kinds of activity—contests *for* something and representations *of* something. He regards it as an important civilizing influence in human society and cites as an example the society of ancient Greece, which was permeated with play forms. He traces historically the origins of many social institutions as ritualized forms of play activity. For example, the element of play was initially dominant in the evolution of judicial processes. Law consisted of a pure contest between competing individuals or groups. It was not a matter of being right or wrong; instead, trials were conducted through the use of oracles, contests of chance that determined one's fate, trials of strength or resistance to torture, and verbal contests. Huizinga suggests that the same principle applies to many other cultural institutions:

> In myth and ritual the great instinctive forces of civilized life have their origin: law and order, commerce and profit, craft and art, poetry, wisdom, and science. All are rooted in the primeval soil of play.[8]

While Huizinga's view may seem extreme, it may be illustrated by examining two aspects of contemporary life: war and the business world.

War as Play   Although we tend to regard play as nonserious, it may obviously be carried on for stakes as important as life or death. High-risk sports such as hang gliding or extremely violent spectator sports are the most obvious examples of this. Indeed, Huizinga points out that war itself developed historically as a kind of game. The elements of competing national armies (teams), stratagems and deception, elaborate codes for prisoners, hostages and noncombatants, permissible weapons, and honorable behavior all support the idea of war as a game on a giant scale. Until recently, armies went off to fight in a spirit of national celebration.

One future British field marshal wrote to his aunt during the Crimean War, "Man shooting is the finest sport of all." Others describe war as life's greatest experience: "Indescribably exciting, filled with the thunder of cannon, the clash of steel, clatter of horse's hooves, and blare of the trumpet."

Play in the Business World   Huizinga's thesis may also be illustrated in the world of business, as in takeover battles waged through the 1990s by giant corporations. Today, much business practice—including the development of new technology, advertising strategies, personnel "raids," and even the pervasive practice of company spying—suggests that business is often approached as an exciting game.

The modern industrial leader (as revealed in a study of 250 top executives in leading American companies) likes to take calculated risks and is fascinated by new techniques. This person views a career in terms of options and possibilities as if it were a huge game. Such a person's character may reveal a number of contradictions: at once cooperative and competitive, detached and playful, but also compulsively driven to succeed; a team player or a hopeful superstar; a team leader or a rebel against bureaucratic regulations; a "jungle fighter" or a loyal company member.

Beyond this, the "investment game" is an obvious form of gambling for many participants. One analyst points out that growing numbers of investors today have developed a passion for talking and trading stocks, checking their holdings and possible buys incessantly on the Internet, and turning investment itself into a sport or legal wager—with the stock market itself being viewed increasingly as a "pastime." For many, it becomes an addiction.

PSYCHOLOGICAL ANALYSIS OF PLAY

Over the past several decades, numerous authorities in the fields of psychology and psychoanalysis have examined play and its role in personality development, learning theory, mental health, and related areas.

Play in Personality Development

A respected child psychologist, Lawrence K. Frank, points out that play is important to the psychological and emotional development of children. He writes:

> Play, as we are beginning to understand, is the way the child learns what no one can teach him. It is the way he explores and orients himself to the actual world of space and time, of things, animals, structures, and people. Through play he learns to live in our symbolic world of meaning and values, of progressive striving for deferred goals, at the same time exploring and experimenting and learning in his own individual way. Through play the child practices and rehearses endlessly the complicated and subtle patterns of human living and communication which he must master if he is to become a participating adult in our social life.[9]

Psychoanalytical Perspectives on Play

Sigmund Freud, the father of modern psychoanalysis, had a number of distinctive views regarding the meaning and purpose of play. Freud saw play as a medium through which children are able to gain control and competence and to resolve conflicts that occur in their lives. He felt that children are frequently overwhelmed by their life circumstances, which may be confusing, complex, and unpleasant. Through play, they are able to reexperience threatening events, and so to control and master them. In this sense, play and dreams serve a therapeutic function for children.

In general, Freud felt that play represented the child's way of dealing with reality—in effect, by playing with it, making it more acceptable, and exerting mastery over it. He wrote:

> Might we not say that every child at play behaves like a creative writer, in that he creates a world of his own, or, rather, rearranges the things of his world in a new way which pleases him? It would be wrong to think he does not take his play seriously; on the contrary he takes his play very seriously and he expends large amounts of emotion on it. *The opposite of play is not what is serious but what is real.*[10]

A number of Freud's other theories, such as the "pleasure principle" and the "death wish," have also been seen as having strong implications for the analysis of play. The Freudian view of play influenced many psychotherapists and educators in their approach to childhood education and treatment programs. Bruno Bettelheim, Erik Erikson, and Anna Freud, Freud's daughter, all experimented with the use of play in treating disturbed children.

Play as Creative Exploration

Other contemporary theories of play emphasize its role in creative exploration and problem solving. Studies of arousal, excitement, and curiosity have led to two related theories of play: the *stimulus-arousal* and *competence-effectance* theories.

Stimulus-Arousal

This approach is based on the observation that both humans and animals constantly seek stimuli of various kinds, both to gain knowledge and to satisfy a need for excitement, risk, surprise, and pleasure. Often this is connected with the idea of fun, expressed as light amusement, joking, and laughter.

However, the expectation that play is always light, enjoyable, pleasant, or humorous can be misleading. Often, play activities can be frustrating, boring, unpleasant, or even physically painful—particularly when they lead to addiction (as in the case of drug, alcohol, or gambling abuse) and subsequent ill health or economic losses.

Arousal-seeking play may often be centered about experiences that are not overtly pleasant or safe, such as high-risk, outdoor adventure pastimes. A professor of psychology at Johns Hopkins University, Marvin Zuckerman discovered that many individuals rate high on a "sensation-seeking" scale. Such men and women abhor monotony and boredom, are eager to try risky sports and outdoor pursuits, and have varied and exciting sexual partners and involvements. Even in their jobs, such sensation seekers welcome challenge and excitement; they tend to experiment with drugs and are frequent involved in hedonistic activities.

The essential point of this theory is that play often serves not to *reduce* drives and tensions but instead to *create* and *satisfy* them, and thereby the player achieves a sense of arousal and emotional release.

Competence-Effectance

A closely related theory holds that much play is motivated by the need of the player to test the environment, solve problems, and gain a sense of mastery and accomplishment. Typically, it involves experimentation or information-seeking behavior in which the player—whether human or animal—observes the environment, tests or manipulates it, and observes the outcome.

Beyond this, the player seeks to develop *competence*, defined as the ability to interact effectively with the environment. Often this is achieved through repetition of the same action even when it has been mastered. The term *effectance* refers to the player's need to be able to master the environment and, even when uncertainty about it has been resolved, to produce desired effects in it.

Cziksentmihalyi's "Flow" Principle   Related to this is Mihaly Cziksentmihalyi's view of play as a process in which ideally the player's skills are pitched at the challenge level of the tasks. If the task is too simple, it may become boring and lacking in appeal. If it is too difficult, it may produce anxiety and frustration, and the player may discontinue activity or change the approach to it so it becomes more satisfying.

Beyond this idea, Cziksentmihalyi suggests that there is a unique element in true play, which he identifies as a sense of flow. This is the sensation players feel when they are totally involved with the activity. It involves a feeling of harmony and full immersion in play; at a peak level, players might tend to lose their sense of time and their surroundings and even to experience an altered state of being. Such flow, he argues, could be found in some work situations, but it is much more commonly experienced in play such as games or sports.[11]

Play Defined

It is difficult to arrive at a single definition of play because it takes so many forms and appears in so many contexts. However, a general definition would describe it as a form of human or animal activity or behavioral style that is self-motivated and carried on for intrinsic, rather than external, purposes. It is generally pleasurable and is often marked by elements of competition, humor, creative exploration and problem solving, and mimicry or role playing. It appears most frequently in leisure activities, but may be part of work. It is typically marked by freedom and lack of structure, but may involve rules and prescribed actions, as in sports and games.

THE MEANING OF LEISURE: SIX VIEWS

Over the past several decades, the statement has frequently been made that one of the most crucial challenges of the present day is the need to come to grips with the "new leisure." What exactly is leisure?

For the Athenians particularly, leisure was the highest value of life, and work the lowest. Since the upper classes were not required to work, they were free to engage in intellectual, cultural, and artistic activity. Leisure represented an ideal state of freedom and the opportunity for spiritual and intellectual enlightenment. Within modern philosophies of leisure that have descended from this classical Athenian view, leisure is still seen as occurring only in time that is not devoted to work. However, it is considered far more than just a temporary release from work used to restore one for more work.

Etymologically, the English word *leisure* seems to be derived from the Latin *licere*, meaning "to be permitted" or "to be free." From *licere* came the French *loisir*, meaning "free time," and such English words as *license* (originally meaning immunity from public obligation) and *liberty*. These words are all related; they suggest free choice and the absence of compulsion.

The early Greek word *scole* or *skole* meant "leisure." It led to the Latin *scola* and the English *school* or *scholar*—thus implying a close connection between leisure and education. The word *scole* also referred to places where scholarly discussions were held. One such place was a grove next to the temple of Apollo Lykos, which became known as the *lyceum*. From this came the French *lycée*, meaning "school"—again implying a bond between leisure and education.

The Classical View of Leisure

Aristotle regarded leisure as "a state of being in which activity is performed for its own sake." It was sharply contrasted with work or purposeful action, involving instead such pursuits as art, political debate, philosophical discussion, and learning in general. The Athenians saw work as ignoble; to them it was boring and monotonous. A common Greek word for work is *ascholia*, meaning the absence of leisure—whereas we do the opposite, defining leisure as the absence of work.

How meaningful is this classical view of leisure today? It has two flaws. First, it is linked to the idea of an aristocratic class structure based on the availability of slave labor. When Aristotle wrote in his *Treatise on Politics* that "it is of course generally understood that in a well-ordered state, the citizens should have leisure and not have to provide for their daily needs," he meant that leisure was given to a comparatively few patricians and made possible through the strenuous labor of the many.

In modern society, leisure cannot be a privilege reserved for the few; instead, it must be widely available to all. It must exist side by side with work that is respected in our society, and it should have a meaningful relationship to work.

The implication is that leisure should be calm, quiet, contemplative, and unhurried, as implied by the word *leisurely*. Obviously, this concept would not apply to those uses of leisure today that are dynamic, active, and demanding or that may have a degree of extrinsic purpose about them.

Leisure as a Symbol of Social Class

The view of leisure as closely related to social class stemmed from the work of Thorstein Veblen, a leading American sociologist of the late nineteenth century. Veblen showed how, throughout history, ruling classes emerged that identified themselves sharply through the possession and use of leisure. In his major work, *The Theory of the Leisure Class,* he pointed out that in Europe—during the feudal and Renaissance periods and finally during the industrial age—the possession and visible use of leisure became the hallmark of the upper class.

Veblen attacked the "idle rich"; he saw leisure as a complete way of life for the privileged class, regarding them as exploiters who lived on the toil of others. He coined the phrase "conspicuous consumption" to describe their way of life throughout history because of this greater working class leisure, and because many members of extremely wealthy families continue to work actively in business, politics, or other demanding professions.

To some degree, however, Veblen's analysis is still relevant. The wealthy or privileged class in modern society—although its members may not have an immense amount of free time—continues to engage in a wide variety of expensive and prestigious leisure activities. They tend to travel widely, entertain, patronize the arts, and engage in exclusive and high-status pastimes. Although rarely called the "leisure class" today, this group continues to define itself through its use of leisure.

Leisure as Unobligated Time

The most common approach to leisure is to regard it as unobligated or discretionary time. In a number of sociological references, this concept of leisure is clearly stated. The *Dictionary of Sociology* offers the following definition:

> Leisure is the free time after the practical necessities of life have been attended to. . . . Conceptions of leisure vary from the arithmetic one of time devoted to work, sleep, and other necessities, subtracted from 24 hours—which gives the surplus time— to the general notion of leisure as the time which one uses as he pleases.[12]

This view of leisure sees it essentially as time that is free from work or from such work-related responsibilities as travel, study, or social involvements based on work. It also excludes time devoted to essential life-maintenance activities, such as sleep, eating, or personal care. Its most important characteristic is that it lacks a sense of obligation or compulsion. This approach to defining leisure is most popular among economists or sociologists who are particularly concerned with trends in the economic and industrial life of the nation.

While this appears to be convenient and largely a matter of arithmetic (subtracting work and other obligated tasks from the 24 hours that are available each day and coming out with a block of time that can be called leisure), it has some built-in complexities. For example, is it possible to say that *any* time is totally free of obligation or compulsion or that any form of leisure activity is totally without some extrinsic purpose?

For example, some uses of free time that are not clearly work or paid for as work may contribute to success at work. A person may read books or articles related to work, attend evening classes that contribute to work competence, invite guests to a party because of work associations, or join a country club because of its value in establishing business contacts or promoting sales. Within community life, those nonwork occupations that have a degree of obligation about them—such as serving on a school board or as an unpaid member of a town council—may also be viewed as part of a person's civic responsibility.

The strict view of leisure as time that lacks *any* obligation or compulsion is suspect. If one chooses to raise dogs as a hobby or to play an instrument in an orchestra, one begins to assume a system of routines, schedules, and commitments to others.

Stebbins discusses the concept of obligation as an aspect of leisure experience, pointing out that so-called "semi-leisure" may degenerate into "anti-leisure," defined by Godbey as

> . . . activity which is undertaken compulsively, as a means to an end, for a perception of necessity, with a high degree of externally imposed constraints, with considerable anxiety, and with a minimum of personal autonomy. . . .[13]

Leisure as Activity

A fourth common understanding of leisure is that it is activity in which people engage during their free time. For example, the International Study Group on Leisure and Social Science defines it thus:

> Leisure consists of a number of occupations in which the individual may indulge of his own free will—either to rest, to amuse himself, to add to his knowledge and improve his skills disinterestedly and to increase his voluntary participation in the life of the community after discharging his professional, family, and social duties.[14]

An American sociologist, Bennett Berger, echoes this concept by pointing out that the sociology of leisure during the 1950s and 1960s consisted of "little more than a reporting of survey data on what selected samples of individuals do with the time in which they are not working, and the correlation of these data with conventional demographic variables."

Obviously, this concept of leisure is closely linked to the idea of recreation, since it involves the way in which free time is used. Early writers on recreation stressed the importance of activity; for example, Jay B. Nash urged that the recreative act be thought of as an active, "doing" experience. Recuperation through play, he wrote, is not wholly relegated to inertia—doing nothing—but is gained through action.

For many individuals, Nash's view of leisure would be too confining. They would view relatively passive activities, such as reading a book, going to a museum, watching a film, or even dozing in a hammock or daydreaming, to be appropriate leisure pursuits—along with forms of active play.

Leisure as a State of Being Marked by Freedom

This fifth concept of leisure places the emphasis on the perceived freedom of the activity and on the role of leisure involvement in helping the individual achieve personal fulfillment and self-enrichment. Neulinger writes:

> To leisure means to be engaged in an activity performed for its own sake, to do something which gives one pleasure and satisfaction, which involves one to the very core of one's being. To leisure means to be oneself, to express one's talents, one's capacities, one's potentials.[15]

This concept of leisure implies a lifestyle that is *holistic,* in the sense that one's view of life is not sharply fragmented into a number of spheres such as family activities, religion, work, and free time. Instead, all such involvements are seen as part of a whole in which the individual explores his or her capabilities, develops enriching experiences with others, and seeks "self-actualization" in the sense of being creative, involved, expressive, and fully alive.

The idea of leisure as a state of being places great emphasis on the need for perceived freedom. Recognizing the fact that some constraints always exist, Godbey defines leisure in the following way:

> Leisure is living in relative freedom from the external compulsive forces of one's culture and physical environment so as to be able to act from internal compulsion in ways which are personally pleasing and intuitively worthwhile.[16]

Such contemporary leisure theorists stress the need for the true leisure experience to yield a sense of total freedom and absence from compulsion of any kind. Realistically, however, there are many situations in which individuals are pressured to participate or in which the activity's structure diminishes his or her sense of freedom and intrinsic motivation.

Beyond this, many individuals become so caught up in the leisure activities they pursue that their daily lives are dominated by them. Mark Jury tells the story of a Philadelphian enrolled in a Moto-Cross seminar at Pocono International Raceway. He was in a hurry to carry out his prescribed exercise because his wife would soon finish showing their cats in a competition at a nearby resort, and the two of them would then be driving back to Philadelphia to watch their daughter compete in a baton-twirling contest. The man explained that he would return to the Poconos the next day for the American Motorcycle Association qualifying race—but would have to hurry back to Philadelphia again for a monthly bridge game.

"What do you do in your spare time?" joked one of the cyclists.

"I work," replied the man.[17]

Too often, such individuals tend to be dominated by a consumer mentality, in which they engage in a host of games, hobbies, social pursuits, or other activities as part of a crowded, hectic lifestyle. Psychiatrist Erich Fromm suggested in *The Sane Society* that people today suffer from a lack of autonomy and self-direction in leisure and recreation, as in other areas of their lives. As consumers, they are manipulated and sold products that they do not really need or understand. Marketing techniques in the twentieth century have created a receptive orientation—in which the aim is to "drink in," to have something new all the time, to be a passive, alienated recipient of leisure goods that are thrust upon one. Fromm writes of the consumer:

> He does not participate actively, he wants to "take in" all there is to be had and to have as much as possible of pleasure, culture and what not. Actually, he is not free to enjoy "his" leisure; his leisure-time consumption is determined by industry, as are the commodities he buys; his taste is manipulated, he wants to see and to hear what he is conditioned to want to see and to hear; entertainment is an industry like any other, the customer is made to buy fun as he is made to buy dresses and shoes. The value of the fun is determined by its success on the market, not by anything which could be measured in human terms.[18]

Leisure as Spiritual Expression

A sixth way of conceptualizing leisure today sees it in terms of its contribution to spiritual expression or religious values. For example, during the early decades of the twentieth century, play and recreation were often referred to as uplifting or holy kinds of human experiences. In a systematic study of the professional literature of this period, Charles Sylvester found numerous references to God, Christ, divine ends, or other terms that suggested a clear linkage between leisure and religion.[19]

Writing from a Judeo-Christian perspective, Paul Heintzman and Glen Van Andel point out that both work and leisure have traditionally been viewed as parts of a God-ordained whole in which work and play complement each other, with the Sabbath serving as a time for both worship and leisure. Leisure, they argue, is seen as a theological virtue through the Christian doctrines of creation, rest, worship and celebration, freedom, and grace. They continue:

> From the new age paradigm, the leisure experience is characterized by a mystical or spiritual feeling of being connected with oneself, with all else, and a sense of oneness with the universe. [It may also] facilitate spiritual experiences as "extreme states of consciousness" which may be similar to "peak" experiences of self-actualization or "flow" experiences.[20]

John Hultsman points out that our tendency is to think about leisure within the context of Western philosophical thought and social values. However, he writes, in the modern industrial world, marked as it is by such influences as urbanization, bureaucratization, and commodification, it becomes difficult to experience true leisure. We have become slaves to our technology and to the frenetic, busy, and pressured way of life that it imposes. However, in such non-Western philosophies or religious systems of belief as Confucianism, Hinduism, Zen Buddhism, and Taoism, leisure may be viewed within an entirely different framework. In such settings, life itself tends to be more serene and harmonious, simple rather than complex, and natural rather than contrived.

The various facets of existence—play, education, work, and social and family relations—are not compartmentalized, but rather are part of a seamless whole in a truly integrated lifestyle. Beyond this, Zuefle argues that concerns about the natural environment inevitably require coming to terms with the connection between religion, spirituality, and nature.[21]

Leisure Seen in Relationship to Work

While it is generally accepted that, by definition, leisure does not exist *during* work, it nonetheless may have a connection with work. Two theories that present alternative views of this relationship are the "compensatory" and "spillover" theories.

Compensatory Theory of Leisure   According to this theory, leisure stems from and is influenced by work, in the sense that leisure is used to compensate for the strains or demands of work. For example, if work is extremely boring and repetitive, or involves a great deal of stress or physical exertion, leisure may be used to provide a contrast in the individual's daily life. Burch writes:

> The compensatory hypothesis suggests that whenever the individual is given the opportunity to avoid his regular routine, he will seek a directly opposite activity.[22]

To illustrate: the clerical worker, bound to a desk and kept indoors during the working day, might choose to take part in hunting, fishing, or hiking during leisure hours—in direct contrast to the work environment.

Spillover Theory of Leisure   This theory suggests that leisure becomes an extension of work. This is the reverse of the compensatory theory. The individual may enjoy work so much—either in terms of its basic focus or the creative or social satisfactions it provides—that its themes are repeated in his or her leisure pursuits.

For example, the truck driver who enjoys long hours of highway driving may also have a hobby of riding motorcycles or restoring and exhibiting antique cars. The commercial artist in an advertising agency may do watercolor painting during vacations.

Distinguishing between work and nonwork may also be complex. The same activity may be carried on by an individual with the only distinction between work and nonwork being whether the person is receiving pay for participation, along with the differences of motivation that may result from this. This is critical to the idea of defining one's time as free or obligated. Kelly, for example, has suggested a typology of leisure in relation to work. Within his framework, four types of leisure appear: (1) *unconditional leisure*—activity independent of work influence and freely chosen as an end in itself; (2) *coordinated leisure*—activity similar to work in form or content (such as a work activity carried on at home as a hobby), but not required by the job; (3) *complementary leisure*—activity independent of work in its form and content but in which the need to take part is influenced by one's work, as in the case of a business manager involved in the work of community organizations because he or she is expected to be; and (4) *recuperative* or *preparatory* leisure nonwork activity related to work by its form or purpose.[23]

Leisure Defined

Recognizing that each of the six concepts of leisure just presented stems from a different perspective, a general definition that embraces several of the key points follows:

Leisure is that portion of an individual's time that is not directly devoted to work or work-connected responsibilities or to other obligated forms of maintenance or self-care. Leisure implies freedom and choice and is customarily used in a variety of ways, but chiefly to meet one's personal needs for reflection, self-enrichment, relaxation, or pleasure. While it usually involves some form of participation in a voluntarily chosen activity, it may also be regarded as a holistic state of being or even a spiritual experience.

THE MEANING OF RECREATION

In a sense, recreation represents a fusion between play and leisure and is therefore presented as the third of the important concepts that provide the framework for this overall field of study.

The term itself stems from the Latin word *recreatio*, meaning that which refreshes or restores. Historically, recreation was often regarded as a period of light and restful activity, voluntarily chosen, that permits one to regain energy after heavy work and to return to work renewed. This view is essentially the same as the recreation theory of play described earlier. Even in the modern era, this point of view is often expressed.

This point of view lacks acceptability today for two reasons. First, as most work in modern society becomes less demanding, many people are becoming more fully engaged, both physically and mentally, in their recreation than in their work. Thus, the notion that recreation should be light and relaxing is far too limiting. Second, the definition of recreation as primarily intended to restore one for work does not cover the case of persons who have *no* work, but who certainly need recreation to make their lives meaningful.

In contrast to work, which is often thought of as tedious, unpleasant, and obligatory, recreation has traditionally been thought of as light, pleasant, and revitalizing. However, this contrast too should be rethought. A modern, holistic view of work and recreation would be that *both* have the potential for being pleasant, rewarding, and creative and that *both* may represent serious forms of personal involvement and deep commitment.

CONTEMPORARY DEFINITIONS

Most modern definitions of recreation fit into one of three categories: (1) recreation has been seen as an activity carried on under certain conditions or with certain motivations; (2) recreation has been viewed as a process or state of being—something that happens within the person while engaging in certain kinds of activity, with a given set of expectations; and (3) recreation has been perceived as a social institution, a body of knowledge, or a professional field.

Typically, definitions of recreation found in the professional literature have included the following elements:

1. Recreation is widely regarded as *activity* (including physical, mental, social, or emotional involvement) as contrasted with sheer *idleness* or complete *rest.*
2. Recreation may include an extremely wide range of activities, such as sports, games, crafts, performing arts, fine arts, music, dramatics, travel, hobbies, and social activities. They may be engaged in by individuals or by groups and may involve single or episodic participation or sustained and frequent involvement throughout one's lifetime.
3. The choice of activity or involvement is voluntary, free of compulsion or obligation.
4. Recreation is prompted by internal motivation and the desire to achieve personal satisfaction, rather than by extrinsic goals or rewards.
5. Recreation is dependent on a state of mind or attitude; it is not so much *what* one does as the reason for doing it, and the way the individual *feels* about the activity, that makes it recreation.
6. Although the primary motivation for taking part in recreation is usually pleasure seeking, it may also be meeting intellectual, physical, or social needs. In some cases, rather than provide "fun" of a light or trivial nature, recreation may involve a serious degree of commitment and self-discipline and may yield frustration or even pain.

Within this framework, many kinds of leisure experiences may be viewed as recreation. They may range from the most physically challenging pursuits to those with much milder demands. Watching television, listening to a symphony orchestra, reading a book, or playing chess are all forms of recreation.

Voluntary Participation

While it is generally accepted that recreation participation should be voluntary and carried out without any degree of pressure or compulsion, often this is not the case. We tend to be influenced by others, as in the case of the youngster whose parents urge him to join a Little League team, or the gymnast or figure skater who is encouraged in the thought that he or she might become a professional performer.

Although ideally recreation is thought of as being free of compulsion or obligation, once one has entered into an activity—such as joining a company bowling league or playing with a chamber music group—one accepts a set of obligations to the other members of the team or group. Thus, recreation cannot be entirely free and spontaneous and, in fact, assumes some of the characteristics of work in the sense of having schedules, commitments, and responsibilities.

Motives for Participation

Definitions of recreation generally have stressed that it should be conducted for personal enjoyment or pleasure—ideally of an immediate nature. However, many worthwhile activities take time to master before they yield the fullest degree of satisfaction. Some complex activities may cause frustration and even mental anguish—as in the

Adventurous Outdoor Recreation

Pocono Whitewater, Ltd., in Jim Thorpe, Pennsylvania, offers rafting excitement and paintball skirmishing. Mormon youth on canoeing trip leap from cliff into lake.

Gentler Pastimes

Pet-loving families let their dogs frolic off-leash in Sarasota County, Florida's Paw Park. Westchester County, New York, and Vero Beach, Florida, among many other communities, sponsor outstanding arts programs. In Montgomery County, Maryland, older women enjoy gardening hobby.

case of the golf addict who is desperately unhappy because of poor putting or driving. In such cases it is not so much that the participant receives immediate pleasure as that he or she is absorbed and challenged by the activity; pleasure will probably grow as the individual's skill improves.

What of the view that recreation must be carried on for its own sake and without extrinsic goals or purposes? It is essential to recognize that human beings *are* usually goal-oriented, purposeful creatures. James Murphy and his coauthors have identified different recreational behaviors that suggest the kinds of motives people may have when they engage in activity. They include:

Socializing behaviors—activities such as dancing, dating, going to parties, or visiting friends, in which people relate to one another in informal and unstereotyped ways.

Associative behaviors—activities in which people group together because of common interests such as car clubs, stamps-, coin-, or gem-collecting groups or similar hobbies.

Competitive behaviors—activities including all of the popular sports and games, but also competition in the performing arts or in outdoor activities in which individuals compete against the environment or even against their own limitations.

Risk-taking behaviors—an increasingly popular form of participation in which the stakes are often physical injury or possible death.

Exploratory behaviors—in a sense, all recreation involves some degree of exploration; in this context, it refers to such activities as travel and sightseeing, hiking, scuba diving, spelunking, and other pursuits that open up new environments to the participant.[24]

To these they add: *vicarious experience,* such as watching movies or sports events; *sensory stimulation,* which might include drug use, sexual involvement, or listening to rock music; or *physical involvement* for its own sake, as opposed to competitive games. Creative arts, intellectual pursuits, or community volunteerism might also be considered important categories of recreational experience.

Recreation as an Emotional State

Recognizing that different people may have many different motives for taking part in recreation, Gray and Greben suggest that it should not be thought of simply as a form of activity. Instead, they argue that recreation should be perceived as the *outcome* of participation—a "peak experience in self-satisfaction" that comes from successful participation in any sort of enterprise. They write:

> Recreation is an emotional condition within an individual human being that flows from a feeling of well-being and self-satisfaction. It is characterized by feelings of mastery, achievement, exhilaration, acceptance, success, personal worth, and pleasure. It reinforces a positive self-image. Recreation is a response to aesthetic experience, achievement of personal goals, or positive feedback from others. It is independent of activity, leisure, or social acceptance.[25]

Depth of Involvement   The degree to which many individuals become deeply committed emotionally to their recreational interests may be illustrated within the realms of sports and popular entertainment. So fervently do many Americans and Canadians root for popular sports teams and stars that sports have increasingly been referred to as a form of religion (see page 289).

The glorification of leading athletes as folk idols and the national preoccupation with such major events as the Stanley Cup, the World Series, or the Super Bowl both demonstrate the degree to which sports—as a popular form of recreation—capture the emotional commitment of millions of Americans and Canadians today.

*S*imilarly, the popular fascination with leading entertainment figures makes the same point. We have made legends and deities out of a few great performers. The brilliant rock-and-roll entertainer, Elvis Presley, died at the age of 42 as an overweight, drug-dependent, and burned-out saloon singer. Nonetheless, million of fans maintain shrines to him, collect his albums and memorabilia, and make pilgrimages to Graceland, his Tennessee home. The anniversary of his death is marked by a solemn Death Week each August, with candlelit processionals and prayers. Elvis is believed to be able to heal the ill, emotionally troubled, or physically disabled; for many, he has become a religion in his own right.

Social Acceptability

Another question arises with respect to defining recreation. Should activity that is often widely disapproved, such as drug use, be regarded as a form of recreation? One school of thought maintains that *any* form of voluntarily chosen, pleasurable, leisure-time activity should be regarded as recreation. This view seems to be supported by those behavioral scientists and writers in recent years who have begun to refer to "recreational sex" or "recreational drug use."

Other writers take the opposite view—that recreation must be wholesome for the individual and for society and must serve to recreate the participant physically, psychologically, spiritually, or mentally. Some even argue that recreation should be clearly distinguished from mere amusement, time-filling, or negative forms of play. Rojek characterizes this approach to defining recreation and leisure as an element in "moral regulation" theory, in which different noneconomic societal institutions are used to control and "civilize" the behavior of the working classes.[26]

Whether or not one accepts this position, it is important to recognize that all publicly financed programs must have significant goals and objectives in order to deserve and obtain support. It therefore becomes necessary to make an important distinction. Recreation, as such, may not imply social acceptability or a set of socially oriented goals or values. When, however, it is provided as a form of community-based service, supported by taxes or voluntary contributions, it must be attuned to prevailing social values and must be aimed at achieving desirable and constructive results.

The task of determining exactly what is socially acceptable or morally desirable is a complex one, particularly in a heterogeneous society with many different religious groups and with laws that may vary greatly from state to state or even county to county.

Our attitudes toward varied leisure pursuits have been ambiguous from a moral perspective. Certain forms of gambling have traditionally been morally or legally disapproved. Compulsive gambling is seen as an illness, and the law prohibits private gambling games, the "numbers" game, and similar pastimes. Yet, we legalize gambling, and many of our states depend heavily for income on licensed casinos or state lotteries. Similarly, many churches sponsor bingo games, a form of gambling. Is one form of gambling recreation because it is countenanced, and another not?

Apart from the obvious point that it is difficult to make such distinctions, it should be stressed that recreation is carried on within a social context. It must respond to social needs and expectations, and it is influenced by prevailing social attitudes and values. Indeed, although we tend to think of recreation as a form of *personal* involvement or experience, it must also be defined as a *social* institution.

Recreation as a Social Institution

Increasingly, recreation has become identified as a significant institution in the modern community, involving a form of collective behavior carried on within specific social structures. It has numerous traditions, values, channels of communication, formal relationships, and other institutional aspects.

Once chiefly the responsibility of the family, the church, or other local social bodies, recreation has now become the responsibility of a number of major agencies in our society. These may include public, voluntary, or commercial organizations that operate parks, beaches, zoos, aquariums, stadiums, or sports facilities. Recreational activities may also be provided by organizations such as hospitals, schools, correctional institutions, and branches of the armed forces. Clearly, recreation has emerged as a significant social institution, complete with its own national and international organizations and an extensive network of programs of professional preparation in colleges and universities. Increasingly, recreation is widely referred to as a *business* or *industry*, involving a cluster of major profit-seeking categories of leisure-related enterprises.

Beyond this development, over the past century there has been general acceptance of the view that community recreation, in which citizens take responsibility for planning and supporting organized leisure services to meet social needs, contributes significantly to democratic citizenship. Hemingway, for example, contrasts two contrasting patterns—"participatory" and "representative" democracy—and discusses the role of leisure in contributing to "social capital."[27]

Stormann carries the point further by examining the role of recreation in contributing to community development. He describes the work of neighborhood groups in developing vest-pocket parks and community gardens in Loisaida, a primarily Puerto Rican section of New York City's Lower East Side. Men and women involved in transforming littered vacant lots into productive and pleasant environments gained a larger vision of what their community might become and learned to work with other social activists on health care, education, housing, and job development. Stormann writes:

> Leisure is invested with communalism and divested of privatism. The empty and dangerous, garbage-infested, unused space became the impetus for an overpowering leisure time. Unused space became meaningful "urban space" [and led to positive] democratic human relations.[28]

Leisure Opportunity and "Social Justice"   From a broader perspective, Allison makes the case that organized recreation—seen as a social institution intended to provide the "good life" for all citizens—often fails to meet the need of historically disenfranchised or marginalized groups, such as "women, people of color, individuals with disabilities, gays and lesbians, the poor, and the elderly." For example, she writes:

> Individuals with disabilities and the elderly suffer a host of injustices around issues of organizational exclusion, discrimination, and stigmatization [with] structural and institutional barriers that continue to diminish the rights and opportunities of these individuals in . . . recreation/travel environments (e.g., employment opportunities, program accessibility).[29]

Recreation Defined

Acknowledging these contrasting views of the meaning of recreation, the following definition of the term is offered. Recreation consists of human activities or experiences that occur in leisure time. Usually, they are voluntarily chosen for intrinsic purposes and are pleasurable, although they may involve a degree of compulsion, extrinsic purpose, and discomfort, or even pain or danger. Recreation may also be regarded as the emotional state resulting from participation or as a social institution, a professional career field, or a business. When provided as part of organized community or voluntary-agency programs, recreation should be socially constructive and morally acceptable in terms of prevailing community standards and values.

RELATIONSHIPS AMONG PLAY, LEISURE, AND RECREATION

Obviously, the three terms discussed in this chapter are closely interrelated. Leisure, for example, provides an opportunity to carry on both play and recreation. Much of our free time in modern society is taken up by recreation, although leisure may also include such activities as continuing education, religious practice, or community service, which are not usually thought of as forms of recreation.

In turn, it should be understood that although play and recreation tend to overlap, they are not identical. *Play* is not so much an activity as a form of behavior—marked stylistically by teasing, competition, exploration, or make-believe. Play can occur during work or leisure, whereas recreation takes place only during leisure.

Recreation obviously includes many forms of play, but it also may involve distinctly nonplaylike activities such as traveling, reading, going to museums, and other cultural or intellectual activities. As a social institution, recreation has broader applications than play or leisure in two ways: (1) recreation is often provided by institutions that do *not* have leisure as a primary concern, such as the armed forces or business concerns; and (2) recreation agencies often provide *other* social or environmental services and may in fact become an important linkage between municipal governments and the people they serve.

Leisure is a subject of scholarly study for many economists and sociologists; it also has come increasingly under the scrutiny of psychologists and social psychologists. However, to the public at large, leisure tends to be a somewhat abstract or remote concept. Although many academic departments and some community agencies use the term *leisure* in their titles, it lacks a sense of urgency or strong appeal as a public issue or focus of government action.

Of the three terms, *recreation* is at once the most understandable and significant for most persons. It is easily recognizable as an area of personal activity and social responsibility, and its values are readily apparent for all age groups and special populations as well. For these reasons, it will be given primary emphasis in the chapters that follow, particularly in terms of program sponsorship and professional identity.

Role of Recreation and Leisure in Professional Education Curricula

Both recreation and leisure are the focus of higher education curricula for individuals planning to enter the overall leisure-service field. Mannell and Kleiber point out that they demand different teaching emphases. Leisure studies scholars, they write, draw on the knowledge and approaches of both the social and management sciences, with their findings reported in varied national and international journals and conferences dealing with leisure studies. They continue:

> Most college and university recreation and leisure studies programs encourage their students to integrate and understand the interplay between "people," "resource" and "policy" issues.
>
> In other words, leisure studies curricula require students to study individual and group leisure behavior as a function of social and cultural factors, the planning and management of natural and built resources for free time use, and policy/management issues associated with the provision of public and private leisure services.[30]

The themes that have just been introduced will be explored more fully throughout this text, as the historical development of recreation and play and the evolution of the present-day leisure-service system are described. Throughout, issues related to the social implications of recreation and leisure and to the role of recreation and park professionals will be fully discussed, along with the challenges that will face practitioners in this field in the twenty-first century.

SUMMARY

Play, recreation, and leisure represent important basic concepts that are essential aspects of the overall field of organized leisure services. They have been explored by philosophers, psychologists, historians, educators, and sociologists from ancient Greek civilizations to the present.

Play may best be understood as a form of activity or behavior that is generally non-purposeful in terms of having serious intended outcomes, but that is an important element in the healthy growth of children and in other societal functions. The chapter presents various theories of play, ranging from the classical views of Herbert Spencer and Karl Groos to more contemporary concepts that link play to Freudian theory or to exploratory drives of human personality.

Six concepts of leisure are presented that depict it as the possession of the upper classes or aristocrats through history as free time or activity, as a state of being, and as a form of spiritual expression. Recreation is also explored from different perspectives, with a key issue being whether it must be morally constructive or socially approved to be considered recreation. The role of recreation as an important contemporary social institution and force in economic life is also discussed.

QUESTIONS FOR CLASS DISCUSSION OR ESSAY EXAMINATIONS

1. This chapter presents several perspectives on play, including a review of traditional definitions of play, its role as a social ritual in community life, and its contribution to personality development. Which of these do you find most interesting and useful? Why?

2. Recreation has been simply defined as socially desirable activity carried on voluntarily in free time for purposes of fun or pleasure. Critically analyze this definition. For example, must activity always be considered socially desirable in order to be regarded as recreation? Is recreation always pleasurable? Is it always carried on voluntarily? What elements would you add to this definition to make it more meaningful?

3. The chapter presents two contrasting views of leisure—one as the slow-paced, relaxed, or contemplative use of free time and the other as active participation in a wide range of often challenging or demanding activities. Which of these do you believe is the more accurate picture of leisure today?

4. Discuss the contrasting meanings of play, leisure, and recreation, and show how they overlap and differ from each other in their separate meanings. Which of the three do you feel is the more useful term as far as public understanding of this field is concerned?

ENDNOTES

1   Diane Ackerman, "Why We Need to Play," *Parade Magazine* (25 April 1999): 12.

2   *Webster's New International Dictionary* (Springfield, Mass.: G. and C. Merriam Co., 1954).

3   Friedrich Froebel, cited in George Torkildsen, *Leisure and Recreation Management* (London: E. and F. N. Spon, 1992): 48–49.

4   Harvey Carr, cited in H. C. Lehman and P. A. Witty, *The Psychology of Play Activities* (New York: A. S. Barnes, 1927): 19.

5   The original source of this theory was W. P. Bowen and Elmer D. Mitchell, *The Theory of Organized Play* (New York: A. S. Barnes, 1923).

6   See Wayne Stormann, "The Recreation Profession, Capital and Democracy," *Leisure Sciences* (Vol. 15, No. 1, 1993): 51.

7   Roger Caillois, *Man, Play, and Games* (London: Thames and Hudson, 1961): 21.

8   Johan Huizinga, *Homo Ludens: A Study of the Play Element in Culture* (Boston: Beacon Press, 1944, 1960): 5.

9   Lawrence K. Frank, quoted in R. Hartley and R. Goldenson, *The Complete Book of Children's Play* (New York: Thomas Y. Crowell, 1963): 43.

10 Sigmund Freud, quoted in M. J. Ellis, *Why People Play* (Englewood Cliffs, N.J., 1973): 60.

11 See Mihalyi Cziksentmihalyi, *Beyond Boredom and Anxiety* (San Francisco: Jossey Bass, 1975).

12 See M. H. Neumeyer and E. Neumeyer, *Leisure and Recreation* (New York: Ronald Press, 1958): 19.

13 Robert Stebbins, "Obligation as an Aspect of Leisure Experience," *Journal of Leisure Research* (Vol. 32, No. 1, 2000): 153.

14 See I. Cosgrove and R. Jackson, *The Geography of Recreation and Leisure* (London: Hutchinson University Library, 1972): 13.

15 John Neulinger, *The Psychology of Leisure* (Springfield, Ill.: Charles C. Thomas, 1974): xi.

16 Geoffrey Godbey, *Leisure in Your Life: An Exploration* (Philadelphia: W. B. Saunders, 1981): 10.

17 Mark Jury, *Playtime! Americans at Leisure* (New York: Harcourt Brace Jovanovich, 1977): 76.

18 Erich Fromm, *The Sane Society* (New York: Fawcett, 1955): 124.

19 Charles Sylvester, "The Ethics of Play, Leisure and Recreation in the Twentieth Century, 1900–1965," *Leisure Sciences* (vol. 9, 1987): 173–188.

20 Paul Heintzman and Glen Van Andel, "Leisure and Spirituality," *Parks and Recreation* (March 1995): 22, 24.

21 David Zuefle, "The Spirituality of Recreation," *Parks and Recreation* (September 1999): 40–41.

22 W. R. Burch, Jr., "The Social Circles of Leisure: Competing Explanations," *Journal of Leisure Research*, (Vol. I, 1969): 125–127.

23 John R. Kelly, "Work and Leisure: A Simplified Paradigm," Journal of *Leisure Research* (Vol. 4, 1972): 50–62.

24 James Murphy et al. *Leisure Service Delivery Systems: A Modern Perspective* (Philadelphia: Lea and Febiger, 1973): 73–76.

25 David Gray and Seymour Greben, "Future Perspectives," *Parks and Recreation* (July 1974): 49.

26 Chris Rojek, *Capitalism and Leisure Theory* (London: Tavistock, 1985): 42.

27 J. L. Hemingway, "Leisure, Social Capital, and Democratic Citizenship," *Journal of Leisure Research* (Vol. 31, No. 2, 1999): 150–165.

28 Wayne Stormann, "Recreation's Role in Community Development: Community Re-creation," *Journal of Applied Recreation Research* (Vol. 21, No. 2, 1996): 161.

29 Maria Allison, "Leisure, Diversity, and Social Justice," *Journal of Leisure Research* (Vol. 32, No. 1, 2000): 4.

30 Roger Mannell and Douglas Kleiber, *A Social Psychology of Leisure* (State College, Pa.: Venture Publishing, 1997): 11.

CHAPTER 3

EARLY HISTORY OF RECREATION AND LEISURE

◆ ◆ ◆

In the year A.D. *80, the Colosseum opened with what must stand as quite the longest and most disgusting mass binge in history. . . . Various sorts of large-scale slaughter, both of animals and men, were appreciatively watched by the Emperor Titus and a packed audience for 100 days. . . . Titus was quite happy footing the enormous bill just as he and his father, the imperial Vespasian, had already footed the bill for building this vast arena. Such payments were the privilege of power.*[1]

In the long run, industrialization brought the reduction of work-time. The hours per year committed to work have declined in the industrial West in a range from 3,000–3,600 to 1,800–2,000 from 1840 to the present. . . . This redistribution of time has been accompanied by a drastic "repackaging" of leisure hours making possible new forms of leisure time, including the typically modern notions of free evenings, the weekend, paid summer vacations, as well as a lengthy childhood and retirement.[2]

◆ ◆ ◆

INTRODUCTION

To provide a meaningful background for the study of recreation and leisure in modern society, it is helpful to have a clear understanding of its role in the past. To some, history may seem dull, boring, or meaningless, especially if taught with an emphasis on simply memorizing dates and names of rulers or battles. Such an approach, dealing with the bare skeleton of events, lacks vitality and human interest.

Instead, history should be presented as a rich panorama of humanity's past existence. It should provide a tapestry of people, places, events, and social forces—showing the role of religion, education, and government and the customs and values of different cultures, their arts, sports, and pastimes. By becoming familiar with earlier historical epochs, we are better able to understand and deal effectively with the present. As the philosopher George Santayana said, "Those who cannot remember the past are condemned to repeat it."

THE PLAY OF EARLY SOCIETIES

One would expect a chronological study to begin by examining the play of prehistoric peoples during the Paleolithic and Neolithic epochs. However, relatively little is known about the nature of leisure and play in these early periods.

We have tended to focus on what have been called existing "primitive" societies as a means of speculating on what life may have been like for prehistoric human groups. The term *primitive* has often been applied to present-day or recently observed tribal societies in North or Central America, the Pacific Islands, Africa, or other regions of the world that have not developed in terms of written language or technological systems. It should not be implied that these groups were or are inferior to other societies. Indeed, they often have highly complex social structures, religious practices, art forms, or ways of surviving in natural environments. However, because the word primitive may have negative connotations, it is preferable to refer to such societies as "tribal, pretechnological" cultures.

Tribal people do not make the same sharp distinction between work and leisure that we in more technologically advanced societies do. While we set aside different periods of time for work and relaxation, a tribal, pretechnological society has no such precise separations. Instead, work is customarily done when it is available or necessary, and it is often infused with rites and customs that lend it variety and pleasure.

In such tribal societies, work tends to be varied and creative, rather than being a narrow, specialized task demanding a sharply defined skill, as in modern industry. Work is often accompanied by ritual that is regarded as essential to the success of the planting or harvesting or to the building or hunting expedition. The ritual may involve prayer, sacrifice, dance, or feasting, which thus becomes part of the world of work.

Origins of Games and Sports

In tribal societies, play may have many sources. Popular games are often vestiges of warfare—now practiced as a form of sport. Occasionally play activities depict historical events, transportation practices, or the use of household or farming implements. When an activity is no longer useful in its original form (such as archery for hunting or warfare), it may become a form of sport. Often, the origin is religious ritual, in which games are played to symbolize a continuing struggle between good and evil or life and death.

The game of *tlachtli,* which was widely practiced in Central America centuries ago, is an example of such a contest. Tlachtli courts were about 200 feet long and 30 feet wide and were situated near temples. A stone ring was fixed about halfway up the wall at either end. The players struck a rubber ball with their knees or hips, the purpose being to drive it through one of the hoops. Blank writes:

> The rubber ball used in the ancient game symbolized the sun, and by making it carom across the court, players hoped to perpetuate the daily arc of the heavenly sphere. . . . Mesoamerican ball was no schoolyard shoot-around: Win or lose, the athletes played for keeps. . . . [I]n pre-Columbian games, members of the losing team were commonly offered up for ritual sacrifice, their hearts cut out with blades of razor-sharp obsidian. That's one way to shorten the post-game interviews.[3]

A vivid example of the linkage of sport and warfare in tribal societies is found in the Willigiman—Wallalua and Wittaia tribes of New Guinea. Every week or so, these two neighboring mountain peoples, who have the same language, dress, and customs, arrange a formal battle at one of their traditional fighting grounds. As described by anthropologists who observed the tribes during the 1960s, these frays seem more like a dangerous field sport than true war:

> Each battle lasts but a single day, always stops before nightfall (because of the danger of ghosts) or if it begins to rain (no one wants to get his hair or ornaments wet). The men are very accurate with their weapons—they have all played war games since they were small boys—but they are equally adept at dodging, and hence are rarely hit by anything.[4]

In addition to arranged contests, however, the two New Guinea tribes (who, despite their cultural similarities, regard each other with hatred) also practice sneak raids, during which they mercilessly slaughter men, women, and children. Victories are celebrated by *etais*, or victory dances, and are part of an unending cycle of fighting, death, mourning, and revenge.

This fascination with warfare dominates the play of young boys in these tribes; when they are four or five years old, they join older boys in a variety of games that help to prepare them for the formal warfare organized by their elders. The play of girls is different:

> . . . not as free as the boys, they spend less time at play; at a very early age their energy is channeled into the purposeful pursuits of female life. Long before boys begin to behave like men, girls are little women—planting, cultivating, cooking, and doing a great variety of other more complicated tasks. . . . Still, while they are children they are not without some childish pleasures. Occasionally they even compete with their male contemporaries and are more than able to hold their own, playing at war with little cane spears and short grass darts.[5]

Other Play Functions   On the North American continent, play has had similar functions among Indian tribes, helping to equip the young for adult life. Indian boys practiced warriors' skills and were taught to survive unarmed and unclothed in the wilderness. Girls were taught the household crafts expected of mature women. Through dancing, singing, and storytelling, both sexes learned of the history and religion of their cultures. Among such southwestern American Indian tribes as the Navajo, Zuni, or Hopi, shamans or medicine men practiced healing rites that made use of chanting, storytelling, dancing, sacred "kachina" dolls, and elaborate, multicolored sand paintings.

Among North American Indians, games were sometimes so seriously regarded that captains of losing teams were sacrificed; sports were a modified form of warfare, as in the lacrosse games of the Choctaw and Cherokee Indians. These contests often involved as many as a thousand young braves and continued for hours over considerable distances, resulting in numerous injuries and deaths. It is believed that they were a means not only of testing warriors in battlelike situations but of keeping their fighting spirits high. Indeed, lacrosse was known as the "little brother of war."

Roots of Sport in Tribal Cultures

New Guinea tribesmen battle daily, and warriors dance to celebrate victory. Boys play warlike games to learn skills needed as adults.

RECREATION AND LEISURE IN PRE-CHRISTIAN CIVILIZATIONS

As prehistoric societies advanced, they developed specialization of functions. Humans learned to domesticate plants and animals, which permitted them to shift from a nomadic existence based on hunting and food-gathering to a largely stationary way of life based on grazing animals and planting crops.

Ultimately, ruling classes developed, along with soldiers, craftsmen, peasants, and slaves. As villages and cities came into being and large estates were tilled (often with complex water storage and irrigation systems) and harvested by lower-class workers, upper-class societies gained power, wealth, and leisure. Thus, in the landed aristocracy of the first civilizations that developed in the Middle East during the five millennia before the Christian era, we find for the first time in history a leisure class.

Ancient Egypt

The Egyptian culture was a rich and diversified one; it achieved an advanced knowledge of astronomy, architecture, engineering, agriculture, and construction. The Egyptians had a varied class structure, with a powerful nobility, priesthood, and military class and lesser classes of workers, artisans, peasants, and slaves. This civilization, which lasted from about 5000 B.C. well into the Roman era, was richly recorded in paintings, statuary, and hieroglyphic records.

The ancient Egyptians led a colorful and pleasant life; it is said of them that their energies were directed to the arts of living and the arts of dying. They engaged in many sports as part of education and recreation, including wrestling, gymnastic exercises, lifting and swinging weights, and ball games. Bullfighting was a popular spectacle and, at least at its inception, was religiously motivated. Music, drama, and dance were forms of religious worship as well as social entertainment. The Egyptians had complex orchestras that included various stringed and percussive instruments. Groups of female performers were attached to temples, and the royal houses had troupes of entertainers who performed on sacred or social occasions.

Ancient Assyria and Babylonia

The land known as the "fertile crescent" between two great rivers, the Tigris and the Euphrates, was ruled by two powerful empires, Assyria in the north and Babylon in the south. These kingdoms were in power for approximately 26 centuries, from about 2900 B.C. until the invasion by Alexander the Great in 330 B.C. Like the ancient Egyptians, the Assyrians and Babylonians had many popular recreation activities, such as boxing, wrestling, archery, and a variety of table games.

In addition to watching dancing, listening to music, and giving banquets, Assyrians were also devoted to hunting; the nobles of Assyria went lion hunting in chariots and on foot, using spears. The chase was a daily occupation, recorded for history in numerous reliefs, sculptures, and inscriptions. As early as the ninth century B.C., early parks were established as sites for royal hunting parties. They also provided settings for feasts, assemblies, and royal gatherings. On the estates of other monarchs during the ninth and tenth centuries B.C. were vineyards, fishponds, and the famed hanging gardens of Babylon.

Ancient Israel

Among the ancient Israelites, music and dancing were performed for ritual purposes as well as for social activities and celebrations. The early Hebrews distinguished dances of a sacred or holy character from those that resembled pagan ceremonies. While there are no wall reliefs or paintings to tell of dance as performed by the ancient Hebrews, there are abundant references to this practice in the Old Testament. Dance was highly respected and was particularly used on occasions of celebration and triumph.

Like other pre-Christian societies, the ancient Hebrews also engaged in hunting, fishing, wrestling, and the use of such weapons as the sword and javelin for both recreational and defensive purposes. As for leisure itself, their major contribution was to set aside the seventh day—the Sabbath—as a time for people to rest from work and to worship their creator.

Ancient Greece

In the city-states of ancient Greece, particularly in Athens during the so-called Golden Age of Pericles from about 500 to 400 B.C., humankind reached a new peak of philosophical and cultural development. The Athenians took great interest in the arts, in learning, and in athletics. These pursuits were generally restricted to the wellborn, aristocratic noblemen, who had full rights of citizenship including voting and participation in affairs of state. Craftsmen, farmers, and tradespeople were also citizens, but had limited rights and less prestige. Labor was performed by slaves and foreigners, who outnumbered citizens by as much as two or three to one.

The amenities of life were generally restricted to the most wealthy and powerful citizens, who represented the Athenian ideal of the balanced man—a combined soldier, athlete, artist, statesman, and philosopher. This ideal was furthered through education and the various religious festivals, which occupied about 70 days of the year. The arts of music, poetry, theater, gymnastics, and athletic competition were combined in these sacred competitions.

Sports appear to have been part of daily life and to have occurred mainly when there were mass gatherings of people, such as the assembly of an army for war or the wedding or funeral of some great chieftain. There were also bardic or musical events, offering contests on the harp and flute, poetry, and theatrical presentations. Physical prowess was celebrated in sculpture and poetry, and strength and beauty were seen as gifts of the gods.

From earliest childhood, Athenian citizens engaged in varied athletic and cultural activities. Young children enjoyed toys, dolls, carts, skip ropes, kites, and seesaws. When boys reached the age of seven, they were enrolled in schools in which gymnastics and music were primary elements. They were intensively instructed in running and leaping, wrestling, throwing the javelin and discus, dancing (taught as a form of military drill), boxing, swimming, and ball games.

Greek Philosophy of Recreation and Leisure   The Athenian philosophers believed strongly in the unity of mind and body and in the strong relationship of all forms of human qualities and skills. They felt that play activity was essential to the healthy physical and social growth of children.

Plato believed that education should be compulsory and that it should provide natural modes of amusement for children:

> Education should begin with the right direction of children's sports. The plays of childhood have a great deal to do with the maintenance or nonmaintenance of laws.[6]

Changes in the Greek Approach to Leisure   The ancient Greeks developed the art of town planning and customarily made extensive provisions for parks and gardens, open-air theaters and gymnasiums, baths, exercise grounds, and stadiums. During the time of Plato, the gymnasium and the park were closely connected in beautiful natural settings, often including indoor halls, gardens, and buildings for musical performances. Early Athens had many public baths and some public parks, which later gave way to privately owned estates.

A gradual transition occurred in the Greek approach to leisure and play. At first, all citizens were expected to participate in sports and games, and the Olympic games were restricted to free-born Greeks only. Gradually, however, the religious and cultural functions of the Olympic games and other festivals were weakened by athletic specialization and commercialism. In time, sports and other forms of activity such as drama, singing, and dance were performed only by highly skilled specialists (drawn from the lower classes, or even slaves) who trained or perfected their skills throughout the year to appear before huge crowds of admiring spectators.

Ancient Rome

Like the Greek city-states, the Roman republic during its early development was a vigorous and manly state. The Roman citizen, although he belonged to a privileged class, was constantly ready to defend his society and fight in its wars. He willingly participated in sports and gymnastics, which kept his body strong and his spirit courageous. Numerous games held in connection with the worship of various Roman gods later developed into annual festivals. Such games were carefully supervised by the priesthood and were supported by public funds, frequently at great cost. The most important of the Roman games were those that celebrated military triumphs, which were usually held in honor of the god Jupiter, the head of the Roman pantheon.

Like the early Greeks, young Roman children had toy carts, houses, dolls, hobbyhorses, stilts, and tops and engaged in many sports and games. Young boys were taught various sports and exercises such as running and jumping, sword and spear play, wrestling, swimming, and horseback riding. The Romans, however, had a different concept of leisure than the Greeks. Although the Latin words for "leisure" and "business" are *otium* and *negotium*, suggesting the same view of leisure as a positive value (with work defined negatively as a lack of leisure), the Romans supported play for utilitarian rather than aesthetic or spiritual reasons. The Romans were much less interested than the Athenians in varied forms of cultural activity. Although they had many performing companies, usually composed of Greek and southern Italian slaves, the Romans themselves did not actively participate in the theater.

Even more than the Greeks, the Romans were systematic planners and builders. Their towns generally included provisions for baths, open-air theaters, amphitheaters, forums for public assemblies, stadiums, and sometimes parks and gardens. They developed buildings for gymnastic sports, modeled after the Greek *palaestra* and including wrestling rooms, conversation areas for philosophers, and colonnades where games might be held in winter despite bad weather. Wealthier Romans often had private villas, many with large gardens and hunting preserves.

As the empire grew more powerful, the simple agricultural democracy of the early years, in which all male Romans were citizens and free men, shifted to an urban life with sharply divided classes. There were four social levels: the *senators*, who were the richest, holding most of the land and power; the *curiae*, who owned more than 25 acres of land and were officeholders or tax collectors; the *plebs*, or free common people, who owned small properties or were tradesmen or artisans; and the *coloni*, who were lower-class tenants of the land.

The society became marked by the wealth and profiteering of businessmen and speculators, with the cooperation of the rulers and governing officials. In time, a huge urban population of plebs lived in semi-idleness, since most of the work was done by coloni and slaves brought to Rome. Gradually it became necessary for the Roman emperors and senate to amuse and entertain the plebs; they did so with doles of grain and with public games—thus the slogan "bread and circuses."

As early as the reign of the Emperor Claudius in the first century A.D., there were 159 public holidays during the year, 93 of which were devoted to games at public expense, including many new festivals in honor of national heroes and foreign victories. By A.D. 354, there were 200 public holidays each year, including 175 days of games. Even on working days, the labor began at daybreak and ended shortly after noon during much of the year.

As leisure increased and the necessity for military service and other forms of physical effort declined for the Roman citizen, he began to do fewer things for himself. The normal practice was for him to be entertained or to follow a daily routine of exercise, bathing, and eating.

Roman citizens were no longer as active in sports as they had once been. They now sought to be amused and to entertain their guests with paid acrobats, musicians, dancers, and other artists. Athletes now performed as members of a specialized profession with unions, coaches, and training schools and with conditions of service accepted and approved by the emperor himself.

Corruption of Entertainment.   Gradually, the focus on the traditional sports of running, throwing, and jumping gave way to an emphasis on human combat—first boxing and wrestling and then displays of cruelty in which gladiators fought to the death for the entertainment of mass audiences. By the time of Emperor Tiberius (A.D. 14–37), competitive sport in the Roman Empire had become completely commercialized. To maintain political popularity and placate the bored masses, the emperors and the senate provided great parades, circuses, and feasts. The Roman games featured contests that were fought to the death between gladiators using various weapons, on foot, on horseback, or in chariots. Even sea battles were fought in artificially constructed lakes in the Roman arenas. Imported wild beasts, such as tigers and elephants, were pitted against each other or against human antagonists. Christians, in particular, were slaughtered in such games. Tacitus wrote that many

> were dressed in the skins of wild beasts, and exposed to be torn to pieces by dogs in the public games, were crucified, or condemned to be burnt; and at nightfall serve in place of lamps to light the darkness, Nero's own gardens being used for the purpose.[7]

Both animals and humans were maimed and butchered in cruel and horrible ways. Spectacles were often lewd and obscene, leading to a mass debauchery, corruption, and perversion that led to a profound weakening of the Roman state.

EARLY CHRISTIAN ERA: DARK AND MIDDLE AGES

Under attack by successive waves of northern European tribes, the Roman Empire finally collapsed. For a period of several centuries, Europe was overrun with warring tribes and shifting alliances. The organized power of Rome, which had built roads, extended commerce, and provided civil order, was at an end. Gradually the Catholic Church emerged to provide a form of universal citizenship within Europe.

Having suffered under the brutal persecutions of the Romans, the early Christians condemned all that their pagan oppressors had stood for—especially their hedonistic way of life. Indeed, the early church fathers believed in a fanatical asceticism, which in the Byzantine, or Eastern, Empire was marked by the Anchorite movement—with its idea of salvation through masochistic self-deprivation.

Many aspects of Roman life were forbidden during the Dark and Middle Ages. The stadiums, amphitheaters, and baths that had characterized Roman life were destroyed. The Council of Elvira ruled that the rite of baptism could not be extended to those connected with the stage, and in A.D. 398 the Council of Carthage excommunicated those who attended the theater on holy days. The great spectacles and organized shows of imperial Rome were at an end. The Roman emphasis on leisure was replaced by a Christian emphasis on work. The influential Benedictine order in particular insisted on the dignity of labor. Their rule read, "Idleness is the great enemy of the soul. Therefore, monks should always be occupied either in manual labor or in sacred readings."

It would be a mistake, however, to assume that the Catholic Church eliminated all forms of play. Many early Catholic religious practices were based on the rituals of earlier faiths. Priests built churches on existing shrines or temple sites, set Christian holy days according to the dates of pagan festivals, and used such elements of pagan worship as bells, candles, incense, singing, and dancing.

Pastimes in the Middle Ages

Despite disapproval from the church, many forms of play continued during the Middle Ages; Medieval society was marked by rigid class stratification; below the nobility and clergy were the peasants, who were divided into such ranks as freemen, villeins, serfs, and slaves.

Life in the Middle Ages, even for the feudal nobility, was crude and harsh. Manors and castles were little more than stone fortresses—crowded, dark, and damp. Knights were responsible for fighting in the service of their rulers; between wars, their favorite pastimes were hunting and hawking.

Leisure Pursuits
in Ancient Lands

Heros of Greek mythology, Ajax and Achilles, play an early form of checkers. Gladiators fight to the death in third century B.C. Roman mosaic. During the Middle Ages, knights joust outside castle walls, and townspeople enjoy street theater in Breughel painting.

Hunting skill was considered a virtue of medieval rulers and noblemen. The sport was thought to be helpful in keeping hunters from the sin of idleness (a vigorous and tiring sport, it was also believed to prevent sensual temptation). Hunting also served as a useful preparation for war. In a later era, the Italian Machiavelli pointed out that since the main concern of the prince must be war, he must never cease thinking of it. In times of peace, thoughts of war should be directed to the sport of hunting.

Other pastimes during the Middle Ages were various types of games and gambling, music and dance, sports, and jousting. The games played in castles and medieval manors included early forms of chess, checkers, backgammon, and dice. Gambling was popular, although forbidden by both ecclesiastical and royal authority.

The control of sexual behavior was also a preoccupation of the Catholic Church during the Dark and Middle Ages. Its concept of natural, acceptable sex was narrow. It was to take place in marriage only, for procreative purposes. Too much desire was a sin, as was sex in daylight hours. Conjugal relations were also forbidden during menstruation and pregnancy, as well as on Sundays and certain holidays. Kleiner writes:

> Guidelines were laid out in penitentials, handbooks for priest-confessors. In order to define what was "natural," the monks who wrote these books also had to convey what was unnatural. The result is some of the kinkiest literature of *any* time period. [One German penitential written in 1094 described] a smorgasbord of 194 sexual transgressions—from bestiality to sex with a nun—in colorful detail.[8]

As the chaos of the Dark Ages yielded to greater order and regularity, life became more stable. Travel in reasonable safety became possible, and by the eleventh century commerce was widespread. The custom of jousting emerged within the medieval courts, stemming from the tradition that only the nobility fought on horseback; common men fought on foot. Thus the term chivalry (from the French *cheval*, meaning horse) came into being. By the dawn of the twelfth century, the code of chivalry was developed, having originated in the profession of arms among feudal courtiers. (The tournament was a contest between teams, and the joust was a trial of skill between two individual knights.) An elaborate code of laws and regulations was drawn up for the combat, and no one below the rank of esquire was permitted to engage in tournaments or jousting.

Games of the Common People   Meanwhile, what of the life of the peasantry during the Middle Ages? Edward Hulme suggests that life was not all work for the lower classes. There were village feasts and sports, practical joking, throwing weights, cockfighting, bullbaiting, and other lively games. "Ball games and wrestling, in which men of one village were pitted against men of another, sometimes resulted in bloodshed."[9]

There was sometimes dancing on the green, and, on holidays, there were miracle and morality plays (forms of popular religious drama and pageantry). However, peasants usually went to bed at dark, reading was a rare accomplishment, and there was much drinking and crude brawling. For peasants, hunting was more a means of obtaining food than a sport. Although the nobility usually rode through the hedges and trampled the fields of the peasantry, peasants were not allowed to defend their crops against such forays or even against wild animals. If peasants were caught poaching, they were often maimed or hanged as punishment.

Typically, certain games were classified as rich men's sports and others as poor men's sports; sometimes a distinction was also made between urban and rural sports. As life in the Middle Ages became somewhat easier, a number of pastimes emerged. Many modern sports were developed at this time in rudimentary form.

The people of the Middle Ages had an insatiable love of sightseeing and would travel great distances to see entertainments. There was no religious event, parish fair, municipal feast, or military parade that did not bring great crowds of people. When the kings of France assembled their principal retainers once or twice a year, they distributed food and liquor among the common people and provided military displays, court ceremonies, and entertainment by jugglers, tumblers, and minstrels.

An illustration of the extent to which popular recreation expanded during the Middle Ages is found in the famous painting of children's games by the Flemish artist, Pieter Breughel. This painting depicts more than 90 forms of children's play, including marbles, stilts, sledding, bowling, skating, blindman's bluff, piggyback, leapfrog, follow-the-leader, archery, tug-of-war, doll play, and dozens of others, many of which have lasted to the present day.

THE RENAISSANCE

Historians generally view the first half of the Middle Ages in Europe (roughly from A.D. 400 to 1000) as the Dark Ages, and the next 400 to 500 years as *le haut Moyen Age* or high Middle Age. The Renaissance is said to have begun in Italy about A.D. 1350, in France about 1450, and in England about 1500. It marked a transition between the medieval world and the modern age. The term "renaissance" means rebirth and describes the revived interest in the scholarship, philosophy, and arts of ancient Greece and Rome that developed at this time. More broadly, it also represented a new freedom of thought and expression, a more rational and scientific view of life, and the expansion of commerce and travel in European life.

As the major European nations stabilized during this period under solidly established monarchies, power shifted from the church to the kings and their noblemen. In Italy and France, particularly, the nobility became patrons of great painters, sculptors, musicians, dancers, and dramatists. These artists were no longer dominated by the ideals and values of the Catholic Church, but were free to serve secular goals. A great wave of music and literature swept through the courts of Europe, aided by the development of printing. Dance and theater became more complex and elaborate, and increasingly lavish entertainments and spectacles were presented in the courts of Italy and France.

Play as Education

Varied forms of play became part of the education of the youth of the nobility at this time. The French essayist, Michel de Montaigne, in discussing the education of children, wrote:

> Our very exercises and recreations, running, wrestling, music, dancing, hunting, riding, and fencing will prove to be a good part of our study. . . . It is not a soul, it is not a body, that we are training up; it is a man, and we ought not to divide him into two parts.[10]

The Athenian philosophy that had supported play as an important form of education was given fuller emphasis during the Renaissance by such educators and writers as Francois Rabelais, John Locke, and Jean Jacques Rousseau.

In early sixteenth-century France, Rabelais advanced a number of revolutionary theories on education, emphasizing the need for physical exercises and games as well as singing, dancing, modeling and painting, nature study, and manual training. His account of the education of Gargantua describes play as an exercise for mind and body.

Locke, an Englishman who lived from 1632 to 1704, was also concerned with play as a medium of learning. He recommended that children make their own playthings and felt that games could contribute significantly to character development if they were properly supervised and directed. "All the plays and diversions of children," he wrote, "should be directed toward good and useful habits." Locke distinguished between the play of children and recreation for older youth and adults. "Recreation," he said, "is not being idle . . . but easing the wearied part by change of business."

INFLUENCE OF THE PROTESTANT REFORMATION

The Reformation was a religious movement of the 1500s that resulted in the establishment of a number of Protestant sects whose leaders broke away from Roman Catholicism. It was part of a broader stream that included economic, social, and political currents. In part it represented the influence of the growing middle classes, who allied with the nobility in the emerging nations of Europe to challenge the power of the church.

The new Protestant sects tended to be more solemn and austere than the Catholic Church. Calvin established an autocratic system of government in Geneva in 1541 that was directed by a group of Presbyters, morally upright men who controlled the social and cultural life of the community to the smallest detail. They ruthlessly suppressed heretics and burned dissenters at the stake. Miller and Robinson describe the unbending Puritanism in Geneva:

> "Purity of conduct" was insisted upon, which meant the forbidding of gambling, card playing, dancing, wearing of finery, singing of gay songs, feasting, drinking and the like. There were to be no more festivals, no more theaters, no more ribaldry, no more light and disrespectful poetry or display. Works of art and musical instruments were removed from the churches.[11]

Throughout Europe, there was an aura of grim dedication to work and a determination to enforce old codes against play and idleness.

Puritanism in England

The English Puritans waged a constant battle to limit or condemn sports and other forms of entertainment during the period from the sixteenth to the eighteenth century. Maintaining strict observation of the Sabbath was a particular issue.

Anglican clergy during the Elizabethan period bitterly attacked stage plays, church festival gatherings, dancing, gambling, bowling, and other "devilish pastimes" like hawking and hunting, holding fairs and markets, and reading "lascivious and wanton books."

James I, however, recognized that the prohibition of harmless amusements like dancing, archery, and the decorating of maypoles caused public anger. In 1618 he issued a *Declaration on Lawful Sports*, in which he asked, "When shall the common people have leave to exercise, if not upon the Sundayes and holy daies, seeing they must apply their labour and win their living in all working daies?" James stressed the military value of sport and the danger of an increase in drinking and other vices as substitute activities if sport were denied to people.

DEVELOPMENT OF PARKS AND RECREATION AREAS

During the Middle Ages, the need to enclose cities within protective walls necessitated building within a compact area that left little space for public gardens or sports areas. As the walled city became more difficult to defend after the invention of gunpowder and cannon, residents began to move out of the central city. Satellite communities developed around the city, but usually with little definite planning.

As the Renaissance period began, European town planning became characterized by wide avenues, long approaches, handsome buildings, and similar monumental features. The nobility decorated their estates with elaborate gardens, some of which were open to public use, as in Italy at the end of the thirteenth century. There were walks and public squares, often decorated with statuary. In some cases, religious brotherhoods built clubhouses, gardens, and shooting stands for archery practice that were used by townspeople for recreation and amusement.

Three major types of large parks came into existence during the late Renaissance. The first were royal hunting preserves or parks, some of which have become famous public parks today, such as the four-thousand-acre Prater in Vienna and the Tiergarten in Berlin. Second were the ornate and formal garden parks designed according to the so-called French style of landscape architecture. Third were the English garden parks, which strove to produce naturalistic landscape effects. This became the prevailing style in most European cities. In England, there were beginning efforts at city planning during the eighteenth century. Business and residential streets were paved and street names posted. Since it was believed that overcrowding led to disease (in the seventeenth century, London had suffered from recurrent attacks of the plague), an effort was made to convert open squares into gardens and to create more small parks. Deaths from contagious disease declined during each successive decade of the eighteenth century, and this improvement was believed to have been due to increased cleanliness and ventilation within the city.

Use of Private Estates

From 1500 to the latter part of the eighteenth century, the European nobility developed increasingly lavish private grounds. These often included topiary work (trees and shrubbery clipped in fantastic shapes), aviaries, fishponds, summer houses, water displays, outdoor theaters, hunting grounds and menageries, and facilities for outdoor games. During this period, such famed gardens as the Tuileries and the Luxembourg in Paris as well as Versailles were established by the French royalty; similar gardens and private estates were found all over Europe. Following the early Italian example, it became the custom to open these private parks and gardens to the public—at first occasionally and then as a regular practice.

Popular Diversions in England

Great outdoor gardens were established to provide entertainment and relaxation. Vauxhall, a pleasure resort founded during the reign of Charles II, was a densely wooded area with walks and bowers, lighting displays, water mills, fireworks, artificial caves and grottoes, entertainment, eating places, and tea gardens. The park was supported by the growing class of merchants and tradesmen, and its admission charge and distance from London helped to "exclude the rabble."

Following the Restoration period in England, Hyde Park and St. James Park became fashionable centers for promenading by the upper classes during the early afternoon. Varied amusements were provided in the parks—wrestling matches, races, military displays, fireworks, and illuminations on special occasions. Aristocrats, merchants, and tradesmen all rode, drove carriages, and strolled in the parks. Horse racing, lotteries, and other forms of gambling became the vogue.

Among the lower classes, tastes in entertainment varied according to whether one lived in the country or city. Countrymen continued to engage vigorously in such sports as football, cricket, wrestling, or "cudgel playing," and to enjoy traditional country or Morris dancing and the singing of old folk songs.

Concerns about Leisure: Class Differences

Gradually, concerns about the growing number of holidays and the effect of leisure activities on the working classes began to be voiced. In France, for example, in the eighteenth century, wealthy individuals had the opportunity for amusement all week long—paying social visits, dining, and passing evenings at gaming, at the theater, ballet, or opera, or at clubs. In contrast, the working classes had only Sundays and fête days, or holidays, for their amusements, La Croix points out, however, that these represented a third of the whole year; in addition to those holidays decreed by the state, many other special celebrations had been either authorized or tolerated by the Catholic Church. Many economists and men of affairs argued that the ecclesiastic authorities should be called upon to reduce the number. Voltaire wrote in 1756:

> Twenty fête days too many in the country condemn to inactivity and expose to dissipation twenty times a year ten millions of workingmen, each of whom would earn five pence a day, and this gives a total of 180 million livres . . . lost to the state in the course of a twelve-month. This painful fact is beyond all doubt.[12]

In the larger cities in France, many places of commercial amusement sprang up. Cafes provided meeting places to chat, read newspapers, and play dominoes, chess, checkers, or billiards.

RECREATION IN AMERICA: THE COLONIAL PERIOD

We now cross the Atlantic to examine the development of recreation and leisure in the early American colonies. First, it needs to be recognized that when English and other settlers came to the New World, they did not entirely divorce themselves from the customs and values of the countries they had left. Commerce was ongoing; governors and military personnel traveled back and forth; and newspapers, magazines, and books were exchanged regularly. Thus, there was a constant interchange of ideas and social trends; one historian has summed it up by saying that an Atlantic civilization existed that embraced both sides of the great ocean. Michael Kraus writes:

> What came from the New World . . . was embedded . . . in the pattern of European life. The revolutions of the sixteenth and seventeenth centuries—political, scientific, religious, and commercial—make for a remarkable fertility of speculation and social reorientation. . . . The era of democratization was thus well begun, and this, truly, was in large measure the creation of the Atlantic civilization.[13]

Despite this linkage, the North American settlements represented a unique and harsh environment for most Europeans who arrived during the period of early colonization. The first need of seventeenth century colonists was for survival. They had to plant crops, clear forests, build shelters, and in some cases defend themselves against attack by hostile Indian tribes. More than half of the colonists who arrived on the Mayflower did not survive the first harsh winter near Plymouth. In such a setting, work was all-important; there was little time, money, or energy to support amusements or public entertainment. Without a nobility possessing the wealth, leisure, and inclination to patronize the arts, there was little opportunity for music, theater, or dance to flourish. But the most important hindrance to the development of recreation was the religious attitude.

Restrictions in New England

The Puritan settlers of New England came to the New World to establish a society based on a strict Calvinist interpretation of the Bible. Although the work ethic had not originated with the Puritans, they adopted it enthusiastically. Idleness was detested as the "devil's workshop," and a number of colonies passed laws binding "any rougs, vagabonds, sturdy beggards, masterless men or other notorious offenders" over to compulsory work or imprisonment.

Puritan magistrates attempted to maintain curbs on amusements long after the practical reasons for such prohibitions had disappeared. Early court records show many cases of young people being fined, confined to the stocks, or publicly whipped for such "violations" as drunkenness, idleness, gambling, dancing, or participating in other forms of "lascivious" behavior. Yet, despite these restrictions, many forms of play continued. Football was played by boys in Boston's streets and lanes, and although playing cards (the "devil's picture-books") were hated by the Puritans, they were freely imported from England and openly on sale.

Other ordinances banned gambling, drama, and nonreligious music, with dancing—particularly between men and women—also condemned. There was vigorous enforcement of the Sabbath laws; Sunday work, travel, or recreation, even "unnecessary and unseasonable walking in the streets and fields," was prohibited. Merrymaking on religious holidays such as Christmas or Easter was banned.

Leisure in the Southern Colonies

A number of the southern colonies had similar restrictions during the early years of settlement. The laws of Virginia, for example, forbade Sunday amusements and made imprisonment the penalty for failure to attend church services. Sabbath-day dancing, fiddling, hunting, fishing, and cardplaying were strictly banned. Gradually, however, these stern restrictions declined in the southern colonies. There the upper classes had both wealth and leisure from their large estates and plantations, on which the labor was performed by indentured servants and slaves. Many of them had ties with the landed gentry in England and shared their tastes for aristocratic amusements. As southern settlers of this social class became established, plantation life became marked by lavish entertainment and hospitality.

Such "unlawful games" as bear-baiting, bull-baiting, bowling, cards, cockfighting, quoits, dice, football, ninepins, and tennis were usually forbidden to workingmen, servants, apprentices, and students. Yet it is clear that they enjoyed these forbidden activities frequently.

Decline of Religious Controls

Despite the stern sermons of New England ministers and the severe penalties for infractions of the established moral code, it was clear that play became gradually tolerated in the colonies. In terms of gambling, the lottery was introduced during the early 1700s and quickly gained the sanction and participation of the most esteemed citizens. Towns and states used lotteries to increase their revenue and to build canals, turnpikes, and bridges. This "acceptable" form of gambling helped to endow leading colleges and academies, and even Congregational, Baptist, and Episcopal churches had lotteries "for promoting public worship and the advancement of religion."

In the realm of sexual behavior, the practice of bundling was widely accepted. A fairly open invitation to premarital sexual activity, bundling permitted engaged couples to sleep together through the night, separated by a low wooden board. Despite the supposedly rigorous religious principles in New England, there is much evidence that

> among New Englanders of all social classes in the early part of the eighteenth century . . . fornication if followed by marriage, no matter how long delayed, was considered a venial sin, if sin at all.[14]

Even in the area of drinking, the climate began to change despite the very strong opposition of the Puritan magistrates in New England. Under Puritan law, drunkards were subject to fine and imprisonment in the stocks, and sellers were forbidden to provide them with any liquor thereafter. A frequent drunkard, according to Earle, was punished by having a large *D* made of "Redd Cloth" hung around his neck or sewn on his clothing, and he lost the right to vote. Yet, by the early part of the eighteenth century, taverns were widely established throughout New England, providing places where gentlemen might "enjoy their bowl and bottle with satisfaction" and engage in billiards, cards, skittles, and other games.

Gradually, restrictions against play were relaxed in New England and elsewhere. Recreation became more acceptable when amusements could be attached to work, and thus country fairs and market days became occasions for merrymaking. Social gatherings with music, games, and dancing were held in conjunction with such work projects as house raisings, sheepshearing, logrolling, or cornhusking bees. Many social pastimes were linked to other civic occasions such as elections or training days for local militia. On training days in Boston, over a thousand men would gather on the Boston Common to drill and practice marksmanship, after which they celebrated at nearly taverns.

By the mid-1700s, the stern necessity of hard work for survival had lessened, and religious antagonism toward amusements had also declined. However, the Sunday laws continued in many settlements, and there was still a strong undercurrent of disapproval of play. Certain religious groups refused to relax their firm opposition to all forms of play.

Parks and Conservation in the Colonial Era

Compared with the nations of Europe, the early American colonies showed little concern for developing parks. With land so plentiful around the isolated settlements along the eastern seaboard, there seemed to be little need for such planning. Even in the earliest colonies, however, particularly in New England, a number of towns and villages established "commons" or "greens," used chiefly for pasturing cattle and sheep but also for military drills, market days, and fairs. Similar open areas were established in towns settled by the Spanish in the South and Southwest, in the form of plazas and large squares in the center of towns or adjacent to principal churches.

Beautiful village greens established during the colonial period still exist throughout Massachusetts, Connecticut, Vermont, and New Hampshire. In the design of new cities, the colonists began to give attention to the need for preserving or establishing parks and open spaces. Among the first cities in which such plans were made were Philadelphia, Savannah, and Washington, D.C.

Early Conservation Efforts

Almost from the earliest days of settlement, there was concern for the conservation of forests and open land. As early as 1626 in the Plymouth Colony, the cutting of trees without official consent was prohibited by law. The Massachusetts Bay Colony passed the Great Ponds Act in 1641, which set aside 2,000 bodies of water, each over 10 acres in size, for such public uses as "fishing and fowling." The courts supported this conservation of land for recreational use. Pennsylvania law in 1681 required that for every five acres of forest land that were cleared, one was to be left untouched. Other laws prohibiting setting woods on fire or cutting certain types of trees were enacted long before the Revolution.

As early as the late seventeenth century, Massachusetts and Connecticut defined hunting seasons and established rules for hunting certain types of game. Although originally a means of obtaining food, hunting rapidly became a sport in the colonies.

What appeared to be an inexhaustible supply of wildlife began to disappear with the advance of settlements and the destruction of the forests. Wildfowl in particular were ruthlessly hunted, especially in New England, and so unlicensed had the destruction of the heath hen become in New York that in 1708 the province determined to protect its game by providing for a closed season. Thus, before the Revolution, the colonists had shown a concern for the establishment of parks and urban open spaces and for the conservation of forests and wildlife.

NINETEENTH-CENTURY CHANGES: IMPACT OF INDUSTRIAL REVOLUTION

During the nineteenth century, great changes took place in both Europe and the United States. It was a time of growing democratization, advancement of scientific knowledge and technology, and huge waves of immigration from Europe to the New World. More than any other factor, the Industrial Revolution changed the way people lived, and it also had a major effect on popular patterns of recreation and leisure. By the early decades of the twentieth century, leisure was more freely available to all, and a widespread recreation movement had begun in the United States and Canada.

The Industrial Revolution extended from the late eighteenth through the twentieth century. Science and capital combined to increase production, as businessmen invested in the industrial expansion made possible by newly invented machines. Industry moved from homes and small workshops to new mills and factories with mechanical power. The invention of such devices as the spinning jenny, the water frame, the weaving machine, and the steam engine—during the 1760s—drastically altered production methods and increased output.

Urbanization

Throughout the Western world, there was a steady shift of the population from rural areas to urban centers. Because factory wages were usually higher than those in domestic industry or agriculture, great numbers of people moved to the cities to work. Millions of European peasant families immigrated because of crop failures, expulsion from their land, religious or social discrimination, or political unrest. The American population increased rapidly. When Andrew Jackson became president in 1829, about 12.5 million people lived in the United States. By 1850 the total had reached 23 million, and a decade later America's population was 31 million. In the large cities, the proportion of foreign born was quite high: 45 percent of New York City's population in 1850 was foreign born, mostly Irish and German.

About 85 percent of the population in 1850 was still rural, living in areas of less than 2,500 population. However, as more and more people moved into factory towns and large cities along the eastern seaboard or around the Great Lakes, the United States became an urban civilization.

Rural townspeople and foreign immigrants moved into the congested tenement areas of growing cities, living in quarters that were inadequate for decent family life. Often a family lived crowded in a single room under unsanitary and unsafe conditions. The new urban slums were marked by congestion and disease; their residents were oppressed by low wages and recurrent unemployment and by monotonous and prolonged labor, including the use of young children in mills, mines, and factories and at piecework tasks at home.

The Availability of Leisure

The trend in manual occupations in Europe from the late Middle Ages to 1800 was toward longer working hours. With industrialization, the average working day in both France and England climbed from 12 hours in about 1700 to a 14- to 18-hour day in 1800. By 1850, the average workweek in French cities was about 70 hours. In addition, the number of holidays provided during the year was sharply reduced.

The peak of working hours appears to have been reached during the first half of the nineteenth century. Gradually, pressure by trade unions and industrial legislation improved the situation. In England, for example, factory acts during the first 40 years of the nineteenth century removed the youngest children from factories and limited the working hours of others. The hours of labor were limited by law to 10 per day in 1847; a 9-hour day was won by contract for most workers between 1869 and 1873. By 1919, the 8-hour day had been formally adopted in nearly all European countries.

Acceptance of the Protestant Work Ethic

The Puritan ideal, which glorified work and condemned leisure and play, became even stronger as a consequence of the Industrial Revolution. In the United States, dedication to work became a hallmark of American life. As industrialization became more widespread, there was a renewed emphasis on the importance of "honest toil" and a strong antagonism expressed against play. Religious leaders supported the 10- or 14- hour workday as part of the "wholesome discipline of factory life."

Work was considered the source of social and moral values, and therefore the proper concern of the church, which renewed its attack upon most forms of play. The church condemned many commercial amusements as "the door to all the sins of iniquity." As late as 1844, Henry Ward Beecher, a leading minister, savagely attacked the stage, the concert hall, and the circus, charging that anyone who pandered to the public taste for commercial entertainment was a moral assassin.

GROWTH OF POPULAR PARTICIPATION IN RECREATION

Despite such efforts, which were fueled by a religious revival before the Civil War, the first half of the nineteenth century saw a gradual expansion of popular amusements in the United States.

The theater, which had been banned during the American Revolution, gradually gained popularity in cities along the eastern seaboard and in the south. Large theaters were built to accommodate audiences of as many as 4,000 people. Performances were usually by touring players who joined local stock companies throughout the country in presenting serious drama as well as lighthearted entertainment, which later became burlesque and vaudeville. By the 1830s, about 30 traveling shows were regularly touring the country with menageries and bands of acrobats and jugglers. Ultimately the latter added riding and tumbling acts and developed into circuses.

Drinking also remained a popular pastime. At this time, the majority of American men were taverngoers. Printed street directories of American cities listed tavernkeepers in staggering numbers. J. Larkin writes that as the nation's most popular centers of male sociability:

> . . . taverns were often the scene of excited gaming and vicious fights and always of hard drinking, heavy smoking, and an enormous amount of alcohol-stimulated talk. . . . Taverns accommodated women as travelers, but their barroom clienteles were almost exclusively male. Apart from the dockside dives frequented by prostitutes, or the liquor-selling groceries of poor city neighborhoods, women rarely drank in public.[15]

Hypocrisy in Public Life

Particularly with respect to sexual behavior, a double standard was widely accepted in American communities. Despite the moral code that condemned sexual dalliance through much of the nineteenth century, prostitution was generally tolerated. Typically, one leading madam in Washington, D.C., was regarded as an upstanding taxpayer and was never troubled by the law. Serving prominent government officials and lobbyists, she

> . . . maintained a classic "parlor house," a sanctuary where "men of wealth and distinction" were wined, dined, and sexually served by women "noted for their youth, beauty, and social refinement."[16]

Growing Interest in Sport

A number of sports gained their first strong impetus during the early nineteenth century. Americans had enjoyed watching amateur wrestling matches, foot races, shooting events, and horse races during colonial days and along the frontier. In the early 1800s, professional promotion of sports events began as well.

Professionalism in Sports   Crowds as large as 50,000 drawn from all ranks of society attended highly publicized boating regattas, and five- and ten-mile races of professional runners during the 1820s. The first sports promoters were owners of resorts or of commercial transportation facilities such as stagecoach lines, ferries, and, later, trolleys and railroads.

These new sports impresarios initially made their profits from transportation fares and accommodations for spectators; later, they erected grandstands and charged admission.

Horse racing flourished; both running and trotting races attracted crowds as large as 100,000 spectators. Prize fighting also gained popularity as a professional contest. It began as a brutal, bare-knuckled sport that was often prohibited by legal authorities; but by the time of the Civil War, gloves were used and rules established, and boxing exhibitions were becoming accepted. Baseball was enjoyed as a casual diversion in the towns of New England through the early decades of the nineteenth century (in the form of "rounders" or "town-ball"), and amateur teams, often organized by occupation (merchants and clerks, or shipwrights and mechanics), were playing on the commons of large eastern cities by the mid-1850s.

*S*ocial class differences played a strong influence on sports involvement and attendance. George Will points out that professional baseball initially appealed to the brawling urban working classes:

> The sport was so tangled up with gambling and drinking that its first task was to attract a better class of fans. This it did by raising ticket prices, banning beer, not playing on Sundays, and giving free tickets to the clergy. Most important, baseball replaced wooden ball parks with permanent structures of concrete and steel [with impressive lobbies and other architectural features].[17]

Racial and Ethnic Influences on Leisure

Throughout the period before the Civil War, slaves living on southern plantations had relatively few opportunities for leisure or recreation. Particularly for black field hands, work hours were long and oppressive; however, Sundays were free of work and could be spent fishing, hunting, socializing, or pursuing other leisure activities, as well as religious worship. In describing the slave community in the antebellum South, John Blassingame points out that house slaves were sometimes permitted to organize balls and parties. On most plantations, work was suspended for a short time after crops were raised in the fall or during the Christmas season. Some plantation owners arranged feasts for their slaves and even permitted them to visit neighboring plantations at such times.

Blassingame comments that however oppressive plantation life was, slaves managed to create a number of unique cultural forms that lightened their burden and helped to maintain morale in an area of life free from the control of their masters:

> Among the elements of slave culture were: an emotional religion [that combined Christian elements with earlier African rites], folk songs and tales, dances, and superstitions. His thoughts, values, ideals and behavior were all greatly influenced by these processes. . . . [T]he more they were immune from the control of whites, the more the slave gained in personal autonomy and positive self-concepts.[18]

Similarly, the large numbers of European immigrants who came to the United States during the nineteenth century tended initially to practice their own folk customs, games, sports, and traditions in separate ethnic groupings—until, with succeeding generations, they gradually blended into the overall American pattern of leisure pursuits.

CHANGING ATTITUDES TOWARD PLAY

During the last half of the nineteenth century, the Industrial Revolution was flourishing with factories, expansion of urban areas, and railroads criss-crossing the country. Free public education had become a reality in most regions of the country, and health care and life expectancy were improving. As the industrial labor force began to organize into craft unions, working conditions improved, levels of pay increased, and the hours of work were cut back. Children, who had worked long, hard hours in factories, mines, and big-city sweatshops, were freed of this burden through child labor legislation.

Gradually, the climate grew more receptive toward play and leisure. Although the work ethic was still widely accepted and there was almost no public provision for recreation, leisure was about to expand sharply. The strong disapproval of play that had characterized the colonial period began to disappear.

By the 1880s and 1890s, church leaders recognized that religion could no longer arbitrarily condemn all play and offered "sanctified amusement and recreation" as alternatives to undesirable play. Many churches made provisions for libraries, gymnasiums, and assembly rooms.

The growth of popular amusements, such as music, vaudeville, theater, and dance that had characterized the first half of the century, became even more pronounced. Popular hobbies such as photography caught on and were frequently linked to new outdoor recreation pursuits. Sports was probably the largest single area of expanded leisure participation, with increasing interest being shown in tennis, archery, bowling, skating, bicycling, and team games like baseball, basketball, and football.

Athletic and outdoor pastimes steadily became more socially acceptable. Skating became a vogue in the 1850s, and rowing and sailing also grew popular, especially for the upper social classes.

The Muscular Christianity movement—so named because of the support given to it by leading church figures and because sports and physical activity were thought to build morality and good character—had its greatest influence in schools and colleges, which began to initiate programs of physical education and athletic competition. In addition, the newly founded Young Men's Christian Association based its program on active physical recreation.

College Sports

In America, colleges initiated their first competitive sports programs. In colonial New England, youthful students had engaged in many pastimes, with some tolerated by college authorities and others prohibited. The first college clubs had been founded as early as 1717, and social clubs were in full swing by the 1780s and 1790s. By the early nineteenth century, most American colleges had more or less officially recognized clubs and their social activities. The founding of social fraternities in the 1840s and the building of college gymnasiums in the 1860s added to the social life and physical recreation of students.

Intercollegiate sports competition in rowing, baseball, track, and football was organized. The first known intercollegiate football game was between Princeton and Rutgers in 1869; interest spread rapidly, and by the late 1880s college football games were attracting as many as 40,000 spectators.

Amateur Sports

Track and field events were widely promoted by amateur athletic clubs, some of which, like the New York Athletic Club, had many influential members who formed the Amateur Athletic Union and developed rules to govern amateur sports competition. Gymnastic instruction and games were sponsored by the German *turnvereins*, the Czech *sokols*, and the YMCA, which had established some 260 large gymnasiums around the country by the 1880s and was a leader in sports activities.

Other Activities

Other popular pastimes included croquet, archery, lawn tennis, and roller-skating, which became so popular that skating rinks were built to accommodate thousands of skaters and spectators. Women began to participate in recreational pastimes, enjoying gymnastics, dance, and other athletics in school and college physical education programs. Bicycling was introduced in the 1870s, and within a few years hundreds of thousands of people had become enthusiasts. During the last decades of the nineteenth century, there was a growing vogue for outdoor activities. Americans began to enjoy hiking and mountain climbing, fishing and hunting, camping in national forests and state parks, and nature photography.

During the late 1800s, a number of economic factors also combined to promote sports interest. With rising wages and a shorter workweek, many workers began to take part in organized sports on newly developed sports fields in city parks. Cheap train service carried players and fans to games, and newspapers publicized major sporting events to build circulation.

GROWTH OF COMMERCIAL AMUSEMENTS

Particularly in larger cities, new forms of commercial amusement sprang up or expanded during the nineteenth century. The theater, in its various forms, was more popular than ever. Dime museums, dance halls, shooting galleries, bowling alleys, billiard parlors, beer gardens, and saloons provided a new world of entertainment for pay. In addition to these, many cities had "red light districts" where houses of prostitution flourished. Drinking, gambling, and commercial vice gradually became serious social problems, particularly when protected by a tacit alliance between criminal figures and big-city political machines.

Amusement parks grew on the outskirts of cities and towns, often established by new rapid transit companies offering reduced-fare rides to the parks in gaily decorated trolley cars. Amusement parks featured such varied attractions as parachute jumps, open-air theaters, band concerts, professional bicycle races, freak shows, games of chance, and shooting galleries. Roller coasters, fun houses, and midget-car tracks also became popular.

Reduction in Work Hours

Throughout this period, there was steady pressure to reduce the workweek, both through industry-labor negotiation and legislation. Benjamin Hunnicutt points out that the effort to obtain shorter work hours was a critical issue in reform politics in the United States throughout the nineteenth century and up until the period of the Great Depression:

> It was an issue for the idealistic antebellum (pre–Civil War) reformers. It had a prominent place in the Populists' Omaha platform and the Bull Moose platform, and appeared in both the Democratic and Republican platforms as late as 1932.[19]

The eight-hour day had been a union objective for many years in the United States, paralleling efforts to reduce the workweek in other countries. In 1868, Congress established the eight-hour day by law for mechanics and laborers employed by or under contracts with the federal government. Following the 1868 law, labor unions made a concerted effort to obtain the eight-hour day in other areas, and in 1890 began to achieve success.

Overall, the average workweek declined from 69.7 hours per week for all industries (including agriculture) in 1860 to 61.7 hours in 1890, and to 54.9 hours in 1910. As a consequence, during the last half of the nineteenth century, concerns about increases in free time began to appear—including fears about the dangers of certain forms of play and the broader question of what the potential role of leisure might be in the coming century.

Concerns about Leisure

Intellectual and political leaders raised searching questions. The English author Lord Lytton commented, "The social civilization of a people is always and infallibly indicated by the intellectual character of its amusements." In 1876, Horace Greeley, a leading American journalist, observed that although there were teachers for every art, science, and "elegy," there were no "professors of play." He asked, "Who will teach us incessant workers how to achieve leisure and enjoy it?" And, in 1880, President James Garfield declared in a speech at Lake Chautauqua, "We may divide the whole struggle of the human race into two chapters: first, the fight to get leisure; and then the second fight of civilization—what shall we do with our leisure when we get it."

This new concern was an inevitable consequence of the Industrial Revolution. Americans now lived in greater numbers in large cities, where the traditional social activities of the past and the opportunity for casual play were no longer available.

THE BEGINNING RECREATION MOVEMENT

The term *recreation movement* is used here to describe forms of leisure activity that are provided in an organized way by social agencies, either governmental or voluntary, with the intent of achieving desirable social outcomes.

The Adult Education Movement

During the early nineteenth century, there was considerable civic concern for improving intellectual cultivation and providing continuing education for adults. Again, this was found in other nations as well; in France, workers' societies were determined to gain shorter workdays and more leisure time for adult study and cultural activities, and they pressed vigorously for the development of popular lectures, adult education courses, and municipal libraries.

In the United States, there was a growing conviction that leisure, properly used, could contribute to the idealistic liberal values that were part of the American intellectual heritage. As early as the founding of the republic, such leaders as Thomas Jefferson and John Adams had envisioned the growth of a rich democratic culture. Adams is said to have written of his children's and America's future:

> I must study Politicks and War that my sons may have liberty to study Mathematicks and Philosophy. My sons ought to study Mathematicks and Philosophy, Geography, Natural History, Naval Architecture, Navigation, Commerce and Agriculture, in order to give their Children a right to study Painting, Poetry, Musick, Architecture, Statuary, Tapestry and Porcelaine.[20]

One of the means of achieving this dream took the form of the Lyceum movement, a national organization with more than 900 local chapters. Its program consisted chiefly of lectures, readings, and other educational events reflecting the view that all citizens should be educated in order to participate knowledgeably in affairs of government.

The Lyceum movement was widely promoted by such organizations as Chautauqua, which sponsored both a lecture circuit and a leading summer camp program in upstate New York for adults and families, with varied cultural activities, sports, lectures, and other educational features. While the professed purpose of Chautauqua was education, it actually provided substantial entertainment and amusement to its audiences as well. By the twentieth century, circuit Chautauquas were formed, in a fusion of the Lyceum movement and independent Chautauquas, to provide educational programs, culture, and entertainment.

A closely related development was the expansion of reading as a recreational experience, which was furthered by the widespread growth of free public libraries. This development was linked to the adoption of compulsory universal education and to the increasing need for better-educated workers in the nation's industrial system. As an example of the growing interest in cultural activity, the arts and crafts movement found its largest following in the United States in the beginning of the twentieth century. Between 1896 and 1915, thousands of organized groups were established throughout the country to bring artists and patrons together, sponsor exhibits and publications, and promote the teaching of art in the schools.

The Development of National, State, and Municipal Parks

Concern for preservation of the natural heritage of the United States in an era of increasing industrialization and despoilment of natural resources began in the nineteenth century. The first conservation action was in 1864, when Congress set aside an

Early North American Pastimes

Hunting was popular recreation in the mid-nineteenth century, and huge crowds attend walking races and other sports. As early stadiums and arenas are built, an international bowling tournament is held at Madison Square Garden in 1909. Before parks and public sports fields are available, children play "baseball" in slum alleyway.

extensive area of wilderness primarily for public recreational use, consisting of the Yosemite Valley and the Mariposa Grove of Big Trees in California. This later became a national park. The first designated national park was Yellowstone, founded in 1872. In 1892 the Sierra Club was founded by John Muir, a leading Scottish-born conservationist who, along with Theodore Roosevelt, encouraged national interest in the outdoors and ultimately the establishment of the National Park Service.

All such developments did not lend themselves immediately to an emphasis on recreation. The primary purpose of the national parks at the outset was to preserve the nation's natural heritage and wildlife. This contrasted sharply with the Canadian approach to wilderness, which saw it as primitive and untamed. Parks, as in Great Britain and Europe, were seen as landscaped gardens, and intensive development for recreation and tourism guided early Canadian policy. Indeed, Banff National Park was initially a health spa, and early provincial parks were designed to be health resorts.[21]

State Parks   As federal park development gained momentum in the United States, state governments also became concerned with the preservation of their forest areas and wildlife. As early as 1867, Michigan and Wisconsin established fact-finding committees to explore the problem of forest conservation; their example was followed shortly by Maine and other eastern states. Within two decades, several states had established forestry commissions. Between 1864 and 1900, the first state parks were established, as were a number of state forest preserves and historic parks.

Municipal Parks   Until this time, North America had lagged far behind Europe in the development of municipal parks, partly because America had no aristocracy with large cultivated estates, hunting grounds, and elaborate gardens that they could turn over to the public. The first major park to be developed in an American city was Central Park in New York; its design and the philosophy on which it was based strongly influenced other large cities during the latter half of the nineteenth century.

There had long been a need for open space in New York City. During the first 30 years of the nineteenth century, plans were made for several open squares to total about 450 acres, but these were not carried out completely. By the early 1850s, the entire amount of public open space in Manhattan totaled only 117 acres. Pressure mounted among the citizens of the city for a major park that would provide relief from stone and concrete. The poet William Cullen Bryant wrote:

> Commerce is devouring inch by inch the coast of the island, and if we would rescue any part of it for health and recreation it must be done now. All large cities have their extensive public grounds and gardens, Madrid and Mexico [City] their Alamedas, London its Regent's Park, Paris its Champs Elysées, and Vienna its Prater.[22]

There was concern about the reckless and haphazard course of urban growth in the nineteenth century, which had been guided almost exclusively by narrow commercial interests. Reformers were disturbed not only by the obvious "social failures"—the growing number of criminals, prostitutes, alcoholics, and insane—but also by the effects of the relentless commercial environment on the culture of cities. Large public parks came to be seen as "necessary institutions of democratic recreation and indispensable antidotes to urban anomie."

When the public will could no longer be denied, legislation was passed in 1856 to establish a park in New York City. Construction of the 843-acre site began in 1857. Central Park, designed by landscape architects Frederick Law Olmsted and Calvert Vaux, was completely man-made: "Every foot of the park's surface, every tree and bush, as well as every arch, roadway and walk has been fixed where it is with a purpose." The dominant need was to provide, within the densely populated heart of an immense metropolis, "refreshment of the mind and nerves" for city dwellers through the provision of greenery and scenic vistas. The park was to be heavily wooded and to have the appearance of rural scenery, with roadways screened from the eyes of park users wherever possible. Recreational pursuits permitted in the park included walking, pleasure driving, ice skating in the winter, and boating—but not organized or structured sports. It also was designed to provide needed social controls to prevent misuse of the park environment or destructive behavior by the "lower" classes.

County Park Systems   In later years, planning began for what was to become the nation's first county park system in Essex County, New Jersey. Bordering the crowded industrial city of Newark, it was outlined in a comprehensive proposal in 1894 that promised that the entire cost of the park project would be realized through tax revenues from increased property values. Set in motion in the following year, the Essex County park system proved to be a great success and set a model to be followed by hundreds of other county and special district park agencies throughout the United States and Canada in the early 1900s.

Establishment of Voluntary Organizations

During the nineteenth century, a number of voluntary (privately sponsored, nonprofit) organizations were founded that played an important role in providing recreation services, chiefly for children and youth. One such body was the Young Men's Christian Association, founded in Boston in 1851 and followed by the Young Women's Christian Association 15 years later. At first, the Y's provided fellowship between youth and adults for religious purposes. They gradually enlarged their programs, however, to include gymnastics, sports, and other recreational and social activities.

Another type of voluntary agency that offered significant leisure programs was the settlement house—neighborhood centers established in the slum sections in the East and Midwest. Among the first were University Settlement, founded in New York City in 1886, and Hull House, founded in Chicago in 1889. Their staffs sought to help poor people, particularly immigrants, adjust to modern urban life by providing services concerned with education, family life, and community improvement.

The Playground Movement

To understand the need for playgrounds in cities and towns, it is necessary to know the living conditions of poor people during the latter decades of the nineteenth century. The wave of urbanization that had begun earlier had now reached its peak. The urban population more than doubled—from 14 to 30 million—between 1880 and 1900 alone. By the century's end, there were 28 cities with over 100,000 residents because of the recent waves of migration. A leading example was New York, where nearly five out of every six of the city's 1.5 million residents lived in tenements in 1891. Social reformers of the period described these buildings as crowded, with dark hallways, filthy cellars, and inadequate cooking and bathroom facilities. In neighborhoods populated by poor immigrants, there was a tremendous amount of crime, gambling, gang violence, and prostitution.

Boston Sand Garden—A Beginning   Within poor working class neighborhoods, there were few safe places where children might play. The first such facility—and the one that is generally regarded as a landmark in the development of the recreation movement in the United States—was the Boston Sand Garden. The city of Boston had been the arena for many important developments in the park and recreation movement in the United States. The Boston Common, established in 1634, has generally been regarded as the first municipal park; a 48-acre area of green rolling hills and shady trees, it is located in the heart of the city. Boston was also the site of the first public gardens with the establishment of an outstanding Botanic Garden in 1838.

The famous Boston Sand Garden was the first playground in the country designed specifically for children. A group of public-spirited citizens had a pile of sand placed behind the Parmenter Street Chapel in a working class district. Young children in the neighborhood came to play in the sand with wooden shovels. Supervision was voluntary at first, but by 1887 when ten such centers were opened, women were employed to supervise the children. Two years later, the city of Boston began to contribute funds to support the sand gardens. So it was that citizens, on a voluntary basis, began to provide play opportunities for young children.

New York's First Playgrounds   In the nation's largest city, Walter Vrooman, founder of the New York Society for Parks and Playgrounds, directed the public's attention to the fact that in 1890 there were 350,000 children without a single public playground of their own. Although the city now had almost 6,000 acres of parkland, none of it was set aside specifically for children. Civic leaders pointed out that children of working parents lacked supervision and were permitted to grow up subject to various temptations. Vrooman wrote that such children

> are driven from their crowded homes in the morning . . . are chased from the streets by the police when they attempt to play, and beaten with the broom handle of the janitor's wife when found in the hallway, or on the stairs. No wonder they learn to chew and smoke tobacco before they can read, and take a fiendish delight in breaking windows, in petty thievery, and in gambling their pennies.[23]

Gradually, the pressure mounted. Two small model playgrounds were established in poor areas of the city in 1889 and 1891 by the newly formed New York Society for Parks and Playgrounds, with support from private donors. Gradually, the city assumed financial and legal responsibility as many additional playgrounds were built in the years that followed, often attached to schools.

The period between 1880 and 1900 was of critical importance to the development of urban recreation and park programs. More than 80 cities initiated park systems; a lesser number established "sand gardens," and, shortly after, playgrounds, Illinois passed a law permitting the establishment of local park districts in which two or more municipalities might join together to operate park systems.

EFFECTS OF RACIAL AND ETHNIC DISCRIMINATION

Throughout this period, public and nonprofit youth-serving organizations often discriminated against members of racial or ethnic minorities. As late as the 1930s and 1940s, prejudice against those perceived as lower-class "undesirables" or those from less-favored European nations was evidenced in many organizations. Such practices reflected widespread attitudes of snobbery, as well as the nativist political agitation of the nineteenth century that opposed the flow of immigration from Europe, preached hatred against Catholics and Jews, and barred citizens of color from mainstream American life.

Prejudice Against Minorities

Generally, the most severe discrimination was leveled against African-Americans who, though no longer slaves, were kept in a position of economic servitude through the practice of sharecropping and were without civil, political, or judicial rights in the southern and border states. However, there was an extreme degree of prejudice against Mexican-Americans and other Hispanics of mixed racial origins. For example, Anglo settlers in Texas regarded Mexicans as savage "heathens" who had historically practiced human sacrifice, and saw them as a decadent and inferior people. Most prejudice was expressed in racial terms.

A popular journal, the *Southern Review*, expressed the dominant feeling of many white Americans at this time with respect to "mongrelism"—the term often applied to mixing among different racial groups. In time, intermarriage between whites and blacks or American Indians was defined as "miscegenation" and forbidden by law through much of the country.

There was also widespread prejudice expressed against Asian-Americans, mostly Chinese nationals who began to arrive in California in the mid-1800s and who worked on the transcontinental railroad. As the number of Asians grew, so did xenophobia. Americans viewed them as heathens who could not readily be assimilated within the nation's essentially Anglo-Saxon framework, and condemned them as unsanitary, immoral, and criminal. Based on such prejudice, Chinese were often the victims of mob violence, particularly at times of national depression, and were barred from entry into the United States by the Oriental Exclusion Acts of 1882 and 1902.

Similar views were frequently expressed against Americans of African origin, who were increasingly barred from social contact, economic opportunity, or recreational involvement with whites by a wave of state legislation and local ordinances in the late nineteenth and early twentieth centuries.

RECREATION AND PARKS: EARLY TWENTIETH CENTURY

For the majority of Americans, however, the beginning of the twentieth century was an exciting period marked by growing economic and recreational opportunity. By 1900, 14 cities had made provisions for supervised play facilities. Among the leading cities were Boston, Providence, Philadelphia, Pittsburgh, Baltimore, Chicago, Milwaukee, Cleveland, Denver, and Minneapolis. In Canada, there was a similar thrust, although it relied more heavily on voluntary community associations.

At the same time, municipal parks became well established throughout the United States. In addition to the urban parks mentioned earlier, the first metropolitan park system was established by Boston in 1892. In the West, San Francisco and Sacramento, California, as well as Salt Lake City, Utah, were among the first to incorporate large open spaces in town planning before 1900. The New England Association of Park Superintendents, the predecessor of the American Institute of Park Executives, was established in 1898 to bring together park superintendents and promote their professional concerns.

Growth of Public Recreation and Park Agencies

Gradually, the concept that city governments should provide recreation facilities, programs, and services became widely accepted. By 1906, 41 cities were sponsoring public recreation programs, and by 1920, 465. More and more states passed laws authorizing local governments to operate recreation programs, and between 1925 and 1935 the number of municipal recreation buildings quadrupled.

Municipalities were also discovering new ways to add parks. Many acquired areas outside their city limits, while others required that new real estate subdivision plans include the dedication of space for recreation. Some cities acquired major park properties through gifts. The pattern that began to develop was one of placing a network of small, intensively used playgrounds throughout the cities, particularly in neighborhoods of working-class families, and placing larger parks in outlying areas.

Federal Park Expansion

As president, Theodore Roosevelt, a dedicated outdoorsman, encouraged the acquisition of numerous new areas for the federal park system, including many new forest preserves, historic and scientific sites, and wildlife refuges. Thanks in part to his assistance and support, the Reclamation Act of 1902, which authorized reservoir-building irrigation systems in the West, was passed, along with the Antiquities Act of 1906, which designated the first national monuments. Establishment of the U.S. Forest Service in 1905 and of the National Park Service 11 years later helped place many of the scattered forests, parks, and other sites under more clearly defined policies for acquisition, development, and use.

EMERGENCE OF THE RECREATION MOVEMENT: THREE PIONEERS

As the recreation field developed during the first three decades of the twentieth century, several men and women emerged as influential advocates of play and recreation. Three of the most effective were Joseph Lee, Luther Halsey Gulick, and Jane Addams.

Joseph Lee

Regarded as the "father" of the playground movement, Joseph Lee was a lawyer and philanthropist who came from a wealthy New England family. Born in 1862, he took part in a survey of play opportunities conducted by the Family Welfare Society of Boston in 1882. Shocked to see boys arrested for playing in the streets, he organized a playground for them in an open lot, which he helped supervise. In 1898, Lee helped create a model playground on Columbus Avenue in Boston that included a play area for small children, a boys' section, a sports field, and individual gardens.

Lee's influence soon expanded; he was in great demand as a speaker and writer on playgrounds and served as vice president for public recreation of the American Civic Association. President of the Playground Association of America for 27 years, he was also the president and leading lecturer of the National Recreation School, a one-year program for carefully selected college graduates.

Lee's view of play was idealistic and purposeful. In *Play in Education*, he outlined a set of major play instincts that he believed all children shared and that governed the specific nature of play activities. He believed that play forms had to be taught and that this process required capable leadership. Lee did not make a sharp distinction between work and play, but saw them as closely related expressions of the impulses to achieve, to explore, to excel, and to master.

Luther Halsey Gulick

Another leading figure in the early recreation movement was Luther Halsey Gulick. A physician by training, he developed a special interest in physical education and recreation. He also had a strong religious orientation, as did many of the early play leaders. Beginning in 1887, Dr. Gulick headed the first summer school of "special training for gymnasium instructors" at the School for Christian Workers (now Springfield College) in Massachusetts. He was active in the YMCAs in Canada and the United States, was the first president of the Camp Fire Girls, and was instrumental in the establishment of the Playground Association of America in 1906. Gulick lectured extensively on the significance of play and recreation and taught a course in the psychology of play as early as 1899. He also vigorously promoted expanded recreation programs for girls and women.

Gulick distinguished play from recreation. Gulick defined play as "doing that which we want to do, without reference primarily to any ulterior end, but simply for the joy of the process." But, he went on to say, play is not less serious than work:

> The boy who is playing football with intensity needs recreation as much as does the inventor who is working intensely at his invention. Play can be more exhausting than work, because one can play much harder than one can work. No one would dream of pushing a boy in school as hard as he pushes himself in a football game. If there is any difference of intensity between play and work, the difference is in favor of play. Play is the result of desire; for that reason it is often carried on with more vigor than work.[24]

Jane Addams

Jane Addams was a social work pioneer who established Hull House in Chicago. Her interest in the needs of children and youth, and in the lives of immigrant families and the poor in America's great cities, led her to develop outstanding programs of educational, social, and recreational activities. Beyond this, she was a leading feminist pioneer and so active a reformer that she was known as "the most dangerous woman in America."

Mary Duncan points out that Jane Addams, along with a number of other recreation and park leaders in the late nineteenth and early twentieth centuries, was part of a wider radical reform movement in America's cities. Joining with muckraking editors, writers, ministers, and other social activists, they

> continually fought city hall, organized labor strikes, marched in the street, gave public speeches, and wrote award-winning articles deploring the living conditions of the poor. The issues and problems they faced were well defined: slavery, the aftermath of the Civil War, thousands of new immigrants, slums, child labor, disease, the suffrage movement, World War I, and a rapidly industrializing nation.[25]

Contrasting Roles of Recreation Pioneers

Although Lee, Gulick, and Addams were described as muckraking radicals, it is clear that they also were individuals who worked through the major societal institutions of government and voluntary agencies. Addams, for example, helped to found the Playground Association of America, encouraged the Chicago School Board's involvement in playground and recreational sports programs, and supported the early development of the Chicago Park District. Indeed, these early recreation pioneers often walked a tightrope between their desire on the one hand to promote individuality, to give youth the opportunity for creative development, and to overcome old barriers of prejudice and class distinction and the need on the other hand to maintain order and control and to indoctrinate youth with traditional social goals.

While these three fought to help the downtrodden and illiterate immigrant families living in crowded urban slums, they were also using recreation to maintain the status quo and enforce traditional values. Play was seen as a means of "Americanizing" foreigners and perpetuating and protecting the traditional small-town, moralistic, white Anglo-Saxon heritage that had dominated national culture over the past century. Recreation would be used as a way of repressing the "overwhelming temptation of illicit and soul-destroying pleasures."

EMERGING NEW LIFESTYLES

However, such views of recreation, play, and leisure were not shared by the entire population. The early twentieth century was a time when the traditional Victorian mentality that had been taught and enforced by the home, school, and church was being challenged. For the first time, many young women took jobs in business and industry in cities throughout the country. With relative freedom from disapproving, stern parental authority, and with money to spend, they frequented commercial dance halls, boat rides, drinking saloons, social clubs, and other sources of popular entertainment. Kathy Peiss describes the new freedom for working class youth in general:

> [t]hey fled the tenements for the streets, dance halls, and theaters, generally bypassing their fathers' saloons and lodges. Adolescents formed social clubs, organized entertainments, and patronized new commercial amusements, shaping, in effect, a working-class youth culture expressed through leisure activity.[26]

Part of what appealed to young people were the playgrounds, parks, public beaches, and picnic grounds. However, often these were considered too tame and unexciting, and more and more young people became attracted to commercial forms of entertainment involving liquor, dancing, and sex that were viewed by the establishment as immoral and dangerous. Increasingly, organized recreation programs were promoted by churches, law enforcement agencies, and civic associations in an attempt to resist the new, hedonistic forms of play. They sought to promote traditional, idealistic activities, such as youth sports, music, games, crafts, and dramatic activities, as a way to repress the urge for more "sinful" behavior.

PUBLIC CONCERNS ABOUT THE USE OF LEISURE

To some degree, the support for public recreation was based on the fear that without public programs and facilities adult leisure would be used unwisely. Many industrial leaders and civic officials believed that the growth of leisure for the working classes represented a dangerous trend; when unemployment increased they expressed concern about what idle men would do with their time. Similarly, when the eight-hour workday laws first came under discussion, temperance societies prepared for increased drunkenness, and social reformers held international conferences on the worker's spare time and ways to use it constructively.

The major concern, however, was for children and youth in the large cities and their need for healthful and safe places to play. Indeed, much "juvenile delinquency" arose from children being arrested for playing on city streets.

Authorities during this period reported reduced rates of juvenile delinquency in slum areas where playgrounds had been established. A probation officer of the juvenile court in Milwaukee described "a very noticeable dropping off of boys coming before the court" and a disappearance of "dangerous gangs," concluding that playgrounds and social centers were "saviors" for American youth. Typically, the judge of the juvenile department of the Orange County Court in Anaheim, California, noted that after

the opening of supervised playgrounds in the public park in the summer of 1924, juvenile delinquency decreased. During the first six months of 1925, it was 70 percent less than for the same period in 1924.[27]

Concern about Commercial Amusements

At this time, there was also fear that unregulated and unsupervised places of commercial amusement posed a serious threat to children and youth. Commercially sponsored forms of entertainment and recreation had grown rapidly during the early twentieth century, with many new pool and billiard parlors, dance halls, vaudeville shows and burlesque, and other amusement attractions.

In major cities such as Milwaukee, Detroit, Kansas City, and San Francisco, extensive recreation surveys scrutinized the nature of commercial amusements, the extent and kind of their patronage, and their character. There was much concern about movies and stage performances, with frequent charges that they were immoral and led to the sexual corruption of youth.

A high percentage of privately operated dance halls had attached saloons that were freely patronized by young girls. Dancing seemed to be only a secondary consideration. Pickups occurred regularly, often of young girls who had come to cities from the nation's farms and small towns with a presumed degree of innocence; so-called "white slavers," who trapped or recruited girls and women into prostitution, appeared to ply their trade with little interference. Dance halls were often attached to disreputable rooming houses, and girls in their early and middle teens were easily recruited into prostitution.

The same studies that examined commercial amusements also surveyed the socially approved forms of recreation. They found that in many cities the schools were closed in the evening and throughout the summer, that libraries closed at night and on weekends, that churches closed for the summer, and that publicly provided forms of recreation were at a minimum. Jane Addams concluded that the city had "turned over the provision for public recreation to the most evil-minded and the most unscrupulous members of the community."

Gradually, pressure mounted for more effective control of places of public amusement. In city after city, permits were required for operating dance halls, pool parlors, and bowling alleys, and for the sale of liquor.

There was also a fear that Americans were moving away from the traditional active ways of using their leisure to pursuits in which they were passive spectators. Some critics commented that instead of believing in the wholesome love of play, Americans now had a love of being "played upon." It had become wholly outdated to make one's own fun.

Emerging Mass Culture

Such complaints and fears were the inevitable reactions of civic leaders to what they perceived to be a threat to traditional morality and values. The reality is that America in the early decades of the twentieth century was undergoing massive changes in response to changing economic and social conditions. These included the emergence of new middle-class and working-class people who had the time and money to spend on leisure, as well as a steady infusion of varied ethnic peoples who contributed new ideas and values to American society.

Part of the change involved a growing rejection of authoritarian family structures and church-dominated social values, as well as a readiness to accept new kinds of roles for young people and women. All of these influences resulted in a new mass culture that emerged during the new century. John Kasson writes:

> At the turn of the century this culture was still in the process of formation and not fully incorporated into the life of society as a whole. Its purest expression at this time lay in the realm of commercial amusements, which were creating symbols of the new cultural order.[28]

Kasson goes on to point out that nineteenth-century America was governed by a coherent set of values—highly Victorian in nature and directed by a self-conscious elite group of ministers, educators, and reformers drawn chiefly from the Protestant middle class of the urban Northeast. These apostles of culture preached the values of character, moral integrity, self-control, sobriety, and industriousness. They believed that leisure should be spent in ways that were edifying and that had moral and social utility. They founded museums, art galleries, libraries, and symphony orchestras, and they lent moral sanction to the recreation and park movement. However, they were unable to exert a significant influence on the growing masses of urban working classes and new immigrant groups.

As a single example of the new craze for excitement and freedom in leisure, a host of amusement parks were developed close to various cities around the country. Typically, they put together a mélange of popular attractions, including bathing facilities, band pavilions, dance halls, vaudeville theaters, sideshows, circus attractions, freak displays, food and drink counters, and daredevil rides of every description.

MAJOR FORCES PROMOTING ORGANIZED RECREATION SERVICES

At the same time that mass culture was providing new kinds of pastimes that challenged traditional community values and standards, the forces that sought to guide the American public in what they regarded as constructive uses of leisure were becoming active.

Growth of Voluntary Organizations

In the opening decades of the twentieth century, a number of important youth-serving, nonprofit organizations were formed, either on a local basis or through nationally organized movements or federations. The National Association of Boys' Clubs was founded in 1906, the Boy Scouts and the Camp Fire Girls in 1910, and the Girl Scouts in 1912. Major civic clubs and community service groups such as the Rotary Club, Kiwanis, and the Lions Club were also founded between 1910 and 1917.

By the end of the 1920s, these organizations had become widely established in American life and were serving substantial numbers of young people. One of every seven boys in the appropriate age group in the United States was a Scout. The YMCA and YWCA had more than 1.5 million members in 1926.

Playground Association of America

In the early 1900s, leading recreation directors called for a conference to promote public awareness of and effective practices in the field of leisure services. Under the leadership of Luther Halsey Gulick, representatives of park, recreation, and school boards throughout the United States met in Washington, D.C., in April 1906. Unanimously agreeing upon the need for a national organization, the conference members drew up a constitution and selected Gulick as the first president of the Playground Association of America. The organization had President Theodore Roosevelt's strong support.

A basic purpose of the Playground Association was to develop informational and promotional services to assist people of all ages in using leisure time constructively. Field workers traveled from city to city, meeting with public officials and citizens' groups and helping in the development of playgrounds and recreation programs. In order to promote professional training, the association developed *The Normal Course in*

Play, a curriculum plan of courses on play leadership on several levels. In keeping with its broadening emphasis, the organization changed its name in 1911 to the Playground and Recreation Association of America, and in 1926 to the National Recreation Association. It sought to provide the public with a broader concept of recreation and leisure, and to promote recreation as an area of government responsibility.

Recreation Programs in World War I

The nation's rapid mobilization during World War I revealed that communities adjacent to army and navy stations and training camps needed more adequate programs of recreation. The Council of National Defense and the War Department Commission on Training Camp Activities asked the Playground and Recreation Association to assist in the creation of a national organization to provide wartime community recreation programs. The association established the War Camp Community Service, which utilized the recreation resources of several hundred communities near military camps to provide wholesome recreation activities for both military personnel and civilians.

At its peak, WCCS employed a national staff of approximately 3,000 paid workers who organized programs in 755 cities with the help of more than 500,000 volunteers. At other military bases in the United States and Europe, organizations like the Young Men's Christian Association sponsored canteens and other morale-boosting services.

ROLE OF THE SCHOOLS

As indicated earlier, a number of urban school boards had initiated after-school and vacation play programs as early as the 1890s. This trend continued in the twentieth century. Playground programs were begun in Rochester, New York, in 1907; in Milwaukee, Wisconsin, in 1911; and in Los Angeles, California, in 1914. These pioneering efforts were strongly supported by the National Education Association, which recommended that public school buildings be used for community recreation and social activities.

With such support, public opinion encouraged the expansion of organized playground and public recreation programs in American communities. Between 1910 and 1930, thousands of school systems established extensive programs of extracurricular activities, particularly in sports, publications, hobbies, and social- and academic-related fields. And, in 1919, the first college curriculum in recreation was established at Virginia Commonwealth University.

In addition to playgrounds, other facilities of the schools that could be useful for recreational purposes were assembly rooms and gymnasiums, swimming pools, music and arts rooms, and outdoor areas for sports and gardening. Education for the "worthy use of leisure" was vigorously supported as an important goal for secondary schools throughout the United States.

Outdoor Recreation Developments

The role of the federal and state governments in promoting outdoor recreation was enlarged by the establishment of the National Park Service in 1916 and an accelerated pattern of acquisition and development of outdoor areas by the U.S. Forest Service. In 1921, Stephen Mather, Director of the National Park Service, called for a National Conference on State Parks. This meeting made it clear that the Park Service was primarily to acquire and administer areas of national significance; it led to the recommendation that state governments take more responsibility for acquiring sites of lesser interest or value.

Park administrators began to give active recreation a higher priority in park design and operation. The founding of the American Association of Zoological Parks and Aquariums in 1924 was an indication that specialized recreational uses of parks were becoming widespread in American communities.

The End of Shorter Hours

At the same time that the recreation movement continued to gain impetus, a reverse trend took place as the movement to shorten the workweek and provide workers with more free time gradually slackened. Benjamin Hunnicutt points out that the most dramatic increase in free time occurred in the period between 1901 and 1921, when the average workweek dropped from 58.4 hours to 48.4 hours, a decline never before or since equaled.[29]

Since the mid-nineteenth century, shorter hours and higher wages had been a campaign issue for progressive politicians. Union pressure, legislation, and court decisions achieved the eight-hour day in jobs under federal contracts, sections of the railroad industry, and certain hazardous occupations. The policy was supported by the findings of scientific management experts like Frederick Taylor, who argued that workers' efficiency declined significantly after eight hours. It also responded to a trend in other industrialized nations, such as France, Germany, Italy, and Belgium, to approve legal restriction of working time, based on the 8-hour day or 48-hour workweek.

New problems began to arise in the American economy though as overproduction and "economic maturity" left the nation with an excess of goods and services. Many leading businessmen and economists began to promote a "New Gospel of Consumption" during the 1920s. They argued that the way to stimulate the economy was not to provide more leisure, but to increase productivity and public spending on a broad range of consumer goods.

IMPACT OF THE GREAT DEPRESSION

Following the flourishing 1920s, the Great Depression of the 1930s mired the United States—as it did much of the industrial world—in a period of almost total despair. The Depression resulted in mass unemployment and involuntary idleness for American workers. By the end of 1932, an estimated 15 million people, nearly one-third of the labor force, were unemployed. Banks crashed, home and farm mortgages were foreclosed, and breadlines appeared everywhere. The nation was at its lowest ebb.

As part of a broad plan to combat the effects of the Depression, the federal government soon instituted a number of emergency work programs related to recreation. Richard Knapp points out that the Federal Emergency Relief Administration, established early in 1933, financed construction of recreation facilities such as parks and swimming pools and hired recreation leaders from the relief rolls. A second agency, the Civil Works Administration, was given the task of finding jobs for 4 million people in 30 days! Among other tasks, this agency built or improved 3,500 playgrounds and athletic fields in a few months.

Both the National Youth Administration and the Civilian Conservation Corps carried out numerous work projects involving the construction of recreational facilities. During the five years from 1932 to 1937, the federal government spent an estimated $1.5 billion developing camps, buildings, picnic grounds, trails, swimming pools, and other facilities. The Civilian Conservation Corps helped to establish state park systems in a number of states that had no organized park programs before 1933. According to Knapp, projects under the Works Progress Administration spanned the nation and built or improved 12,700 playgrounds, 8,500 gymnasiums or recreation buildings, 750 swimming pools, 1,000 ice skating rinks, and 64 ski jumps.[30]

These programs initiated under President Franklin D. Roosevelt's New Deal had a beneficial effect on the development of the recreation and park movement throughout the United States: they made it clear that leisure was an important responsibility of government.

Sharpened Awareness of Leisure Needs

The Depression helped to stimulate national concern about problems of leisure and recreational opportunity. For example, a number of studies in the 1930s revealed a serious lack of recreation programs for young people, especially blacks, girls, and rural youth.

In the early 1930s, the National Education Association carried out a major study of leisure education in the nation's school systems and issued a report, *The New Leisure Challenges the Schools,* which urged the educational establishment to take more responsibility for this function and for enlarging the school's role in community recreation. Shortly thereafter, the National Recreation Association examined the public recreation and park programs in a number of major European nations and published a detailed report that included implications for American policy makers.

The American Association for the Study of Group Work studied the overall problem and in 1939 published an important report, *Leisure: A National Issue.* Written by Eduard Lindeman, a leading social work administrator who had played a key role in government during the Depression, the report stated that the "leisure of the American people constitutes a central and crucial problem of social policy."[31]

Lindeman urged that, in the American democracy, recreation should meet the true needs of the people. Pointing out that American workers were gaining a vast national reservoir of leisure estimated at 390 billion hours per year, he suggested that the new leisure should be characterized by free choice and a minimum of restraint. He urged, however, that if leisure were not to become "idleness, waste, or opportunity for sheer mischief," a national plan for leisure had to be developed, including the widespread preparation of professionally trained recreation leaders.

A NATION AT WAR

World War II, in which the United States became fully involved on December 7, 1941, compelled the immediate mobilization of every aspect of national life: manpower, education, industry, and a variety of social services and programs.

The Special Services Division of the U.S. Army provided recreation facilities and programs on military bases throughout the world, making use of approximately 12,000 officers, even more enlisted personnel, and many volunteers. About 1,500 officers were involved in the Welfare and Recreation Section of the Bureau of Naval Personnel, and expanded programs were offered by the Recreation Service of the Marine Corps. These departments were assisted by the United Service Organizations (USO), which was formed in 1941 and consisted of the joint military effort of six agencies: the Jewish Welfare Board, the Salvation Army, Catholic Community Services, the YMCA, the YWCA, and the National Travelers Aid. The USO functioned in the continental United States and outside of camps and in clubs, hostels, and lounges throughout the western hemisphere. The American National Red Cross established approximately 750 clubs in wartime theaters of operations throughout the world and about 250 mobile entertainment units, staffed by more than 4,000 leaders. Its military hospitals overseas and in the United States involved more than 1,500 recreation workers as well.

Many municipal directors extended their facilities and services to local war plants and changed their schedules to provide programs around the clock. Because of the rapid increase in industrial recreation programs, the National Industrial Recreation Association (later known as the National Employee Services and Recreation Association) was formed in 1941 to assist in such efforts. Also, the Federal Security Agency's Office of Community War Services established a new Recreation Division to assist programs on the community level. This division helped set up 300 new community programs throughout the country, including numerous child-care and recreation centers, many of which continued after the war as tax-supported community recreation programs. The Women's Bureau of the U.S. Department of Labor developed guidelines for recreation and housing for women war workers, based on their needs in moving from their home environments into suddenly expanded or greatly congested areas.

By the end of World War II, great numbers of servicemen and servicewomen had participated in varied recreation programs and services and thus had gained a new appreciation for this field. Many people had been trained in recreation leadership (more than 40,000 people were in the Special Services Division of the U.S. Army alone) and were ready to return to civilian life as professionals in this field.

SUMMARY

This chapter shows the long history of recreation, play, and leisure by discussing their roles during the ancient civilizations of Assyria, Babylonia, and Egypt; then in the Greek and Roman eras; and during the Middle Ages, the Renaissance, and the pre-Revolutionary period in the North American colonies, extending to the mid-twentieth century.

Religion and social class were major factors that influenced recreational involvement in terms of either prohibiting certain forms of activity or assigning them to one class or another. Leisure, seen as an aristocratic devotion to knowledge, the arts, athletics, philosophy, and contemplation in ancient Athens, took a different form in Rome where it became a political instrument devoted to perpetuating the rule of the Roman emperors by entertaining and placating the common people.

During the Dark and Middle Ages, the Catholic Church placed a strong value on work and worship and sought to prohibit forms of play that had descended from pagan sources. However, such activities as sports and games, music, dance, the theater, and gambling persisted, even under the stern condemnation of the new Protestant sects that gained influence during the period of the Reformation. At this time, class distinctions in terms of appropriate forms of play became clearly evident in England, France, and other European nations. However, the value of play as a form of childhood education was championed in the writings of numerous educators and philosophers of that era.

In the pre-Revolutionary American colonies, New England Puritans were very strict in their condemnation of most recreational pursuits. After an initial conservative period, however, play and varied social pursuits flourished in the plantations of the southern colonies, which had been settled by members of the English gentry who used slaves and indentured servants to make their own leisure possible.

The chapter traces the influence of the Industrial Revolution, which brought millions of immigrants from Europe to America where they lived in crowded tenements in large cities or in factory towns. It also led to increased attempts to impose the stern strictures of the Protestant work ethic on the nation's population.

By the middle of the nineteenth century, however, religious opposition to varied terms of play and entertainment began to decline. Sports became more popular and accepted and, after reaching a high point at mid-century, work hours began to decline. Four major roots of what was ultimately to become the recreation and park movement appeared: (1) the establishment of city parks, beginning with New York's Central Park, and the later growth of county, state, and national parks; (2) the growing interest in adult education and cultural development; (3) the appearance of playgrounds for children, sponsored first as charitable efforts and shortly after by city governments and the public schools; and (4) the development of a number of nonprofit, youth-serving organizations that spread throughout the country.

Popular culture gained momentum during the "Jazz Age" of the 1920s, with college and professional sports, motion pictures and radio, new forms of dance and music, and a host of other crazes capturing the public's interest. While the Great Depression of the 1930s had a tragic impact on many families, the efforts of the federal government to build recreation facilities and leisure services to provide jobs and a morale boost for the public at large meant that the Depression was a powerful positive force for the recreation movement in general.

By the early 1940s, organized recreation service was firmly established in American life, and both government officials and social critics began to raise searching questions about its future role in postwar society.

QUESTIONS FOR CLASS DISCUSSION OR ESSAY EXAMINATIONS

1. Contrast the attitudes toward sports and other uses of leisure that were found in ancient Greece with those found in the Roman Empire. How did their philosophies differ, and how did the Roman philosophy lead to a weakening of that powerful nation? Could you draw a parallel between the approach to leisure and entertainment in ancient Rome and that in the present-day United States?

2. Trace the development of religious attitudes and policies regarding leisure and play from the Dark and Middle Ages, through the Renaissance and Reformation periods, to the colonial era in seventeenth and eighteenth century North America. What differences were there in the approach to recreation between the northern and southern colonies at this time?

3. In the second half of the nineteenth century, the roots of what was to become the modern recreation and park movement appeared. What were these roots (i.e., the adult education or Lyceum movement), and how did they relate to the broad social needs of Americans?

4. Three important pioneers of the early recreation movement in the United States were Lee, Gulick, and Addams. Summarize some of the key points of their philosophies and their contributions to the playground and recreation developments in the pre–World War I era. Describe the conflict between the traditional Victorian values and code of morality and the emerging popular culture, especially during the 1920s.

5. Trace the expanding role of government in terms of sponsoring recreation and park programs during the first half of the twentieth century, with emphasis on federal policies in wartime and during the Depression of the 1930s. What were some of the growing concerns about leisure during this period?

ENDNOTES

1 John Pearson, *Arena: The Story of the Colosseum* (New York: McGraw-Hill, 1973): 7.

2 Gary Cross, *A Social History of Leisure Since 1600* (State College, Pa.: Venture Publishing): 73.

3 Jonah Blank, "Playing for Keeps," *U.S. News and World Report* (28 June 1999): 64.

4 "The Ancient World of a War-Torn Tribe," *Life* (28 December 1972): 73.

5 R. Gardner and K. Heider, *Gardens of War: Life and Death in the New Guinea Stone Age* (New York: Random House, 1968): 63.

6 Plato, *The Laws,* translated by R. G. Bury (Cambridge: Harvard University Press, 1926, 1961): 23.

7 Lincoln Kirstein, *Dance: A Short History of Classical Theatrical Dancing* (New York: G. P. Putnam, 1935): 57.

8 Carolyn Kleiner, "Sexuality," *U.S. News and World Report* (23 August 1999): 76.

9 E. M. Hulme, *The Middle Ages* (New York: Holt, 1938): 604.

10 Fred Leonard, *A Guide to the History of Physical Education* (Philadelphia: Lea and Febiger, 1928): 55.

11 N. Miller and D. Robinson, *The Leisure Age* (Belmont, Calif.: Wadsworth, 1963): 66.

12 Paul La Croix, *France in the Middle Ages* (New York: Frederick Ungar, 1963): 346.

13 Michael Kraus, *The Atlantic Civilization: 18th Century Origins* (Ithaca, N.Y.: Cornell University Press, 1949): 3.

14 James Truslow Adams, *Provincial Society, 1690–1763* (New York: Macmillan, 1973): 159.

15 J. Larkin, "The Secret Life of a Developing Country (Ours)," *American Heritage* (September–October 1988): 60.

16 Francis Clines, "Archeology Find: Capital's Best Little Brothel," *New York Times* (18 April 1999): 22.

17 George Will, Review of G. Edward White, "Creating the National Pastime," *New York Times Book Review* (7 April 1996): 11.

18 John Blassingame, *The Slave Community: Plantation Life in the Antebellum South* (New York: Oxford University Press, 1972): 42.

19 Benjamin Hunnicutt, "The End of Shorter Hours," *Labor Review* (Vol. 3, 1984): 373–374.

20 John Adams to Abigail Adams, May 1780, *Adams Family Correspondence III* (Cambridge, Mass.: Harvard University Press, 1973): 342.

21 Paul Heintzman, "Wilderness and the Canadian Mind: Impact Upon Recreation Development in Canadian Parks," (*NRPA Research Symposium, 1997*): 75.

22 See H. H. Reed and S. Duckworth, *Central Park: A History and a Guide* (New York: Clarkson N. Potter, 1967): 3.

23 Walter Vrooman, "Playgrounds for Children," *The Arena* (July 1894): 286.

24 Luther H. Gulick, *A Philosophy of Play* (New York: Scribner, 1920): 125.

25 Mary Duncan, "Back to Our Radical Roots," in Thomas Goodale and Peter Witt, eds., *Recreation and Leisure: Issues in an Era of Change* (State College, Pa.: Venture Publishing, 1980): 287–295.

26 Kathy Peiss, *Cheap Amusements: Working Women and Leisure in Turn-of-the-Century New York* (Philadelphia: Temple University Press, 1986): 57.

27 James Rogers, "The Child and Play," *Report on White House Conference on Child Health and Protection* (1932): 27.

28 John Kasson, *Amusing the Millions: Coney Island at the Turn of the Century* (New York: Hill and Wang, 1978): 3–4.

29 Benjamin Hunnicutt, "Historical Attitudes Toward the Increase of Free Time in the Twentieth Century: Time for Leisure, for Work, for Unemployment," *Loisir et Societe* (Vol. 3, 1980): 196.

30 Richard Knapp, "Play for America: The New Deal and the NRA," *Parks and Recreation* (July 1973): 23.

31 Eduard Lindeman, *Leisure: A National Issue* (New York: American Association for the Study of Group Work, 1939): 32.

CHAPTER 4

RECREATION AND LEISURE IN THE MODERN ERA

◆ ◆ ◆

During the 1950s and 1960s, organized recreation had a marked impact on community life. The growing movement was advanced by an increasing concern for physical fitness; programs for the ill, aged, and disabled; an upsurge in outdoor recreation and park development; involvement in the arts; professional education; unification of the parks and recreation professional organization; and the impact of civil unrest and youth dissent. . . . During this time, recreation and leisure services . . . came to be seen as an opportunity system to improve the quality of life, reduce social pathology, build constructive values in citizens, and generally make communities better places to live.[1]

◆ ◆ ◆

INTRODUCTION

From the end of World War II to the turn of the twenty-first century, recreation, park, and leisure services evolved from a relatively minor area of government responsibility and nonprofit agency or business function to an enormous, complex enterprise.

This chapter chronicles the expansion and diversification of the recreation movement, seen against the broader background of social and economic change in the United States and Canada. In addition to describing these elements, the chapter presents a number of trends in leisure involvement and professional services that were influenced by environmental, demographic, social, and economic trends in the postwar era.

These included: (1) growing concern about the natural environment and government's role in protecting it; (2) stronger emphasis on recreation's role in combating poverty and racial tensions; (3) programs designed to serve girls and women more fully, along with disabled persons and the elderly; (4) the emergence of a number of specialized disciplines and professional groups serving the military, business, private-membership groups, and other interests; and (5) a period of economic austerity during the 1980s and early 1990s, followed by a dramatic upsurge in the nation's economy during the last years of the century.

POST–WORLD WAR II EXPECTATIONS

Immediately after World War II, expectations for the growth of leisure in the United States were high. In the 1950s and 1960s, it was predicted that leisure—usually defined as nonwork or discretionary time—would expand dramatically and have an increasing influence on the lives of Americans in the years ahead.

Think tanks like the Rand Corporation or the Hudson Institute and special planning bodies like the National Commission on Technology envisioned futurist scenarios with such alternatives as lowering the retirement age to 38, reducing the workweek to 22 hours a week, or extending paid vacations to as many as 25 weeks a year. Other authorities predicted that the three-day or four-day workweek, which some companies had been experimenting with, would soon be widespread.

It was also assumed that leisure would become an increasingly important source of personal values and life satisfaction for many Americans. There was widespread agreement that the work ethic was declining sharply, with work in the industrial era having become more and more specialized, routine, and unfulfilling. Leisure was seen as having immense potential, and writers and educators like David Gray and Seymour Greben suggested that it offered new possibilities for confronting such social problems as human misery and suffering, health and fitness concerns, environmental and energy problems, and worker dissatisfaction.

In the early and mid-1990s, widespread company downsizing and other business trends led to the firing of millions of employees and an atmosphere of economic pessimism. With the strong business recovery of the late 1990s, unemployment declined sharply, prosperity was widespread, and government budgets began to show surpluses on every level.

EXPANSION OF RECREATION AND LEISURE

Through it all, recreation and leisure witnessed an immense growth in participation. There was a steady increase in sports, the arts, hobbies, outdoor recreation, and fitness programs, along with a parallel expansion of home-based entertainment through the use of stereo, television, videocassette recorders, and other electronic equipment.

Influence of National Affluence

An important factor in the growth of recreational participation was the national affluence of the postwar years. The gross national product rose from $211 billion in 1945 to over a trillion dollars annually in 1971. In the late 1950s, it was reported that Americans were spending $30 billion a year on leisure—a sum that seemed huge then but was just one-tenth of what it was to become in the 1980s. Elsewhere, this author states:

> Involvement in varied forms of recreation exploded during this period. Visits to national forests increased by 474 percent between 1947 and 1963, and to national parks by 302 percent during the same period. Overseas pleasure travel increased by 440 percent, and attendance at sports and cultural events also grew rapidly. Sales of golf equipment increased by 188 percent, of tennis equipment by 148 percent, and use of bowling lanes by 258 percent. Hunting and fishing, horse-racing attendance, and

copies of paperback books sold all gained dramatically and—most strikingly—the number of families with television sets grew by 3,500 percent over this 16-year period.[2]

Government recreation and park agencies dramatically expanded their budgets, personnel, facilities, and programs until the mid-1970s. Then, many federal, state, and local agencies were forced by funding cuts to cut back or freeze budgets. At the same time, the recreation and park profession continued to grow in numbers and public visibility. Pre-professional curricula were established in many colleges and universities during the 1960s and 1970s, and several national organizations, including the National Recreation Association, the American Recreation Society, and the American Institute of Park Executives, merged to form the National Recreation and Park Association—a stronger and more unified voice for the park and recreation field overall.

Effect of Demographic Changes: Suburbanization and Urban Crises

In the years immediately after World War II, which had disrupted the lives of millions of servicemen and women, great numbers of young couples married. Within a few years, many of these new families with young children moved from the central cities to new homes in surrounding suburban areas. In these suburban communities, recreation for growing families became an important concern. Most suburbs were quick to establish new recreation and park departments, hire personnel, and develop programs and facilities to serve all age groups—often in concert with local school districts.

At the same time, the population within the inner cities changed dramatically. With the rapid mechanization of agriculture in the South and the abandonment of the sharecropper system, millions of southern blacks moved to the cities and industrialized areas of the Northeast, the Midwest, and the West in search of jobs and better opportunities. Growing numbers of Hispanic immigrants surged into the cities from the Caribbean islands and Central America. Generally, these new residents were accustomed to rural living and had limited job skills; they posed serious problems of health, housing, welfare, and social control for the cities.

TRENDS IN PROGRAM SPONSORSHIP

As a result of such population shifts and changes in lifestyle, a number of trends in recreation program functions and in the role to be played by government emerged. These included: (1) programs aimed at improving physical fitness; (2) emphasis on environmental concerns; (3) activities and services designed to meet special age-group needs; (4) recreation for persons with disabilities; (5) increasing programming in the arts; (6) services for the economically and socially disadvantaged; and (7) programs concerned with the needs of racial and ethnic minorities.

Physical Fitness Emphasis

Beginning in the 1950s, there was a strong emphasis on the need to develop and maintain the physical fitness of youth. In both world wars, a disappointingly high percentage of male draftees and enlistees had been rejected by the armed forces for physical reasons. Then, after World War II, comparative studies such as the Kraus-Weber tests

International Trend

In countries around the world, recreational participation grew rapidly. In Japan, this three-tiered golf driving range and artificial ski slope were typical of huge new facilities, including immense indoor pools and artificial-snow ski areas. Trout streams continued to be overwhelmed by enthusiasts.

showed that American youth were less fit than the youth of several other nations. This led schools to strengthen their programs of physical fitness, and many public recreational departments expanded their leisure activities to include fitness classes, conditioning, jogging, and sports for all ages.

A similar trend was found in Canada, where the government passed a National Physical Fitness Act in 1943, pioneering legislation that was motivated by the need to improve the level of fitness for recruits for the Canadian armed forces. In the decades that followed, this act was interpreted broadly:

> It enabled the federal government to train instructors, develop school curricula in physical education, provide direct fitness programs, and enter into agreements with the provinces for the financial support of provincial fitness initiatives. During the decade following the introduction of the act, numerous initiatives were undertaken and, more importantly, a public expectation was created concerning government involvement in leisure service provision.[3]

Environmental Concerns

A key concern of the recreation field has been the environment. In the postwar period, it became evident that there was a critical need to preserve and rehabilitate the nation's land, water, and wildlife resources. We had permitted the great rivers and lakes to be polluted by waste, forests to be ruthlessly razed by lumbering interests, and wildlife to be ravaged by over-hunting or lack of adequate breeding areas or by chemical poisons and invasion of their environments. Greater and greater demands had been placed on our natural resource bank, with open space shrinking at an unprecedented rate.

In the late 1950s, President Dwight Eisenhower and the Congress formed the Outdoor Recreation Resources Review Commission to investigate this problem. The result was a landmark, heavily documented report in 1962 that helped to promote a wave of environmental efforts by federal, state, and municipal governments. The Federal Water Pollution Control Administration divided the nation into 20 major river basins and promoted regional sewage treatment programs in those areas. The Water Quality Act of 1965, the Clean Water Restoration Act of 1966, the Solid Waste Disposal Act of 1965, the Highway Beautification Act of 1965, and the Mining Reclamation Act of 1968 all committed the United States to a sustained program of conservation and protection of its natural resources. Another major piece of legislation was the Wilderness Act of 1964, which gave Congress the authority to declare certain unspoiled lands permanently off-limits to human occupation and development.

Many states and cities embarked on new programs of land acquisition and beautification and developed environmental plans designed to reduce air and water pollution. Nonprofit organizations like the American Land Trust, The Nature Conservancy, and the Trust for Public Lands took over properties encompassing hundreds of thousands of acres—many of them donated by large corporations—for preservation or transfer to public agencies for recreational use. Such programs were accompanied by efforts within federal agencies like the National Park Service, the Forest Service, the Fish and Wildlife Service, and the Bureau of Land Management to meet public needs for outdoor recreation.

The environmental progress of the 1960s and 1970s was, however, soon to be halted. In the early 1980s, federal expenditures for parks and environmental programs were sharply reduced, the rate of land acquisition was cut back, and government policies regulating the use of wild lands for mining, timber cutting, grazing, oil drilling, and similar commercial activities were dramatically relaxed. Outdoor recreation and park enthusiasts and conservation organizations engaged in a continuing battle with Secretary of the Interior James Watt, and to a lesser degree with his successors, to protect the nation's parks and forests from encroachment and neglect.

While national outdoor recreation planning ended in 1981, a number of major studies continued to assess the nation's natural resources and environmental concerns through the two decades that followed.[4]

Meeting Age-Group Needs

In addition to the demographic trends cited earlier, three other important changes in the nation's population that gathered force in the postwar decades were: (1) the dramatic rise in the birth rate, with millions of children and youth flooding the schools and community recreation centers; (2) the lengthening of the population's life span, resulting in a growing proportion of elderly persons in society; and (3) the increasing incidence of marital breakup and divorce and of children born out of wedlock, leading to a huge number of single-parent households.

In response to these trends, thousands of governmental and nonprofit organizations expanded their programs for children and youth, and numerous youth sports leagues like Little League, Biddy Basketball, and American Legion Football recruited millions of participants. At the other end of the age range, public and nonprofit organizations developed golden age clubs or senior centers, often with funding from the federal government through the Administration on Aging.

The high divorce rate and growing number of single-parent households confirmed the need for recreation programs to provide day-care services for children of working parents and to meet other leisure-related needs. Religious organizations in particular are stressing family-oriented programming today in an effort to strengthen marital bonds and improve parent-child relationships.

Special Recreation for Persons with Disabilities

An area of increased emphasis in the postwar era was the provision of special services for persons with physical and mental disabilities. As in the environmental field, this trend was strengthened by federal legislation (see page 249). Various government agencies concerned with rehabilitation were expanded to meet the needs of individuals with disabilities, especially the large numbers of returning veterans who sought to be integrated into community life.

The federal government sharply increased its aid to special education. In recreation, assistance was given to programs serving children, youth, and adults with developmental disability. Beginning in the mid-1960s, there was an increased emphasis on

Special Recreation Activities

Physically disabled persons engage in a variety of sport and outdoor recreation activities today—in a therapeutic exercise pool at RCH, Inc., in San Francisco; a seaside excursion sponsored by the North East Passage program in New England; and a national wheelchair tennis tournament. Disabled in a car accident, ballet dancer Marc Brew continues to perform in New York.

developing social and recreational programs for aging persons in both institutional and community settings. Overall, the specialized field of what came to be known as therapeutic recreation service expanded steadily in this period.

With the establishment of the National Therapeutic Recreation Society in the mid-1960s and the American Therapeutic Recreation Association in the 1980s, professionalization in therapeutic recreation service developed rapidly. The establishment of curriculum guidelines for courses in professional preparation, the setting of program standards, and the development of registration and certification plans all served to make this field a significant specialized area within the broad leisure-service field.

Increased Interest in the Arts

Following World War II, the United States embarked on an expansion of cultural centers, museums, and art centers. In part this represented a natural follow-up to the stimulus that had been given to art, theater, music, and dance by emergency federal programs during the Great Depression. Another element, however, was that Americans had now come to respect and enjoy the arts—as spectators and participants.

Through the 1970s and early 1980s, community arts activities continued to flourish, with the assistance of federal funding through the National Endowment for the Arts, which helped to support state arts units, choreographers and composers, and individual performers and companies. In the mid- and late 1980s, some decline in attendance at music, drama, and dance events was noted, possibly due to declining federal support and to the increasing public interest in home-based video entertainment. To meet this challenge, many cultural organizations in the fine and performing arts, as well as many museums, libraries, and similar institutions, have developed new methods of fund-raising by diversifying their offerings and marketing them to a broader community audience. As an example, art, natural history, and science museums today offer lectures, tours, classes, films, innovative displays, special fund-raising dinners, and other events designed to attract a wide spectrum of patrons.

Despite such efforts, attacks on public funding for the arts continued into the 1990s, and many music, drama, and dance organizations were forced to cut back sharply in their programs.

Recreation's Antipoverty Role

An important development of the 1960s was the expanded role given to recreation as an important element in President Lyndon Johnson's "war on poverty." Initially, the nation's concern about the economically and socially disadvantaged had been aroused by a widely read book on poverty in America by Michael Harrington—published in 1962 at a time of great prosperity for most citizens.

During the 1930s and 1940s, a number of federal housing programs had provided funding to support small parks, playgrounds, or centers in public housing projects. Now, a new wave of legislation, such as the Economic Opportunity Act of 1964, the Housing and Urban Development Act of 1964, and the Model Cities program approved in 1967, provided assistance for locally directed recreation programs to be conducted by disadvantaged citizens themselves in depressed urban neighborhoods. Other federal programs, such as the Job Corps, VISTA (Volunteers in Service to America), and the Neighborhood Youth Corps, also included recreation-related components.

Linkage of Antipoverty and Race-Related Programming

In the mid-1960s, destructive riots erupted in a number of major American cities, with a shattering loss of life and housing. Occurring chiefly in ghetto neighborhoods where blacks and Hispanics lived, these riots stemmed from a number of causes. Later research disclosed that among the causes were increasing frustration over continuing job and educational discrimination, unheeded protests against the justice system and poor community services, *and* inadequate recreation and park programs and facilities for minority groups.

In a number of cases, riots began as a protest by African-Americans against police who were turning off hydrants that afforded children and youth a measure of summer relief on steaming city streets—where no swimming pool was accessible. In other cases, they stemmed from the overall lack of parks, playgrounds, or other recreation facilities in inner-city neighborhoods, as compared to wealthier sections. Yet it was also recognized that to a great degree the situations were aggravated by the frustration, anger, and boredom felt by boys and men who were unemployed and had little to do but mill about in the streets or taverns.

In an effort to "cool" the hot summers and prevent further rioting, many of the antipoverty programs of the mid- and late 1960s placed their emphasis on serving minority groups in urban slums. Hundreds of millions of dollars were granted each year to local governments and to organizations of "indigenous" residents to provide enriched recreation services aimed particularly at youth. These included sports and social activities, cultural pursuits, job-training and tutorial programs, and trips and similar recreation activities.

On a national scale, Job Corps, VISTA, Neighborhood Youth Corps, and an aggregate of special projects known as Community Action Programs continued into the 1970s but were gradually terminated in the years that followed.

COUNTERCULTURE: YOUTH IN REBELLION

Paralleling the period of the urban riots, what came to be known as the *counterculture* made its appearance in America. The term *counterculture*, as John Kelly points out, is generally applied to a movement that develops in opposition to an established and dominant culture—often in political, religious, or lifestyle terms—that manifests itself in language, symbols, and behavior.

The counterculture movement in the United States during the 1960s was part of a larger youth movement that challenged the political, economic, and educational establishments in a number of other nations around the world. Here, it symbolized the rebellion of young people against parental authority and the curricular and social controls of schools and colleges. Much of it stemmed from mass protests against the Vietnam War as students initiated strikes and takeovers of administrative offices in a number of universities.

Rock music and lyrics that challenged traditional values became popular, and many young people joined "hippie" communes or fled to neighborhoods like Haight-Ashbury in San Francisco or the East Village in New York City, where they experimented with drugs and a variety of alternative lifestyles.

Rejection of the Work Ethic

A significant aspect of the counterculture movement was its rejection of work as the be-all and end-all of one's life—and of the widely accepted goal of "making it" in the business or professional world.

As Chapter 3 has shown, a deep-rooted belief in the value of hard work, which was linked to an essentially conservative, industrious, and moralistic view of life, had long been a fundamental tenet of American society.

However, since World War II, there had been a retreat from the stern precepts of the Protestant work ethic. As establishment values and monetary success were undermined in the thinking of young people during the counterculture period, leisure satisfactions assumed new importance. Writers urged new, holistic approaches to the use of free time that would integrate varied aspects of human personality and lead to the self-actualization spoken of by Maslow and other psychologists.

By 1981, a poll by the Louis Harris survey organization found that:

78 percent of all working Americans feel that "people take less pride in their work than they did 10 years ago."

73 percent believe that "the motivation to work hard is not as strong today as it was a decade ago."

69 percent feel that our workmanship is worse than it was.

63 percent simply believe that "most people do not work as hard today as they did 10 years ago."[5]

Changing Lifestyles in Post-World War II Era

Youth lifestyles changed radically from this formal college prom in the 1950s to a swinging singles poolside party in the 1960s.

DRIVES FOR EQUALITY BY DISADVANTAGED GROUPS

Another important aspect of the counterculture movement was that it provided a climate within which various populations in American society that had historically been disadvantaged were encouraged to press vigorously for fuller social and economic rights.

Racial and Ethnic Minorities

For racial and ethnic minorities there was a strong thrust during the 1960s and 1970s toward demanding fuller recreational service in terms of facilities and organized programs. In response, many public recreation and park departments not only upgraded these traditional elements, but also began to provide mobile recreation units that would enter impacted neighborhoods with cultural, social, and other special services. Building on projects that had been initiated during the "war on poverty" and the period of urban riots, many departments initiated classes, workshops, festivals, and holiday celebrations designed to promote ethnic pride and intercultural appreciation.

Through legislation, Supreme Court decisions, other judicial orders, and voluntary compliance, public, nonprofit, and commercial facilities were gradually desegregated through the 1970s and 1980s. Major youth and adult social membership organizations like the Boy Scouts and Girl Scouts and the YMCA and YWCA, which had tended to maintain segregated units for racial minorities or to not serve them at all, opened up their memberships and in some cases identified racial justice as a high-priority mission for the years ahead.

In terms of the broader culture, many members of racial and ethnic minorities began to achieve great success in such leisure-related areas as college and professional sports and popular entertainment, such as music, television, and motion pictures.

Progress for Women

In the 1960s and 1970s, feminist groups mobilized themselves to attack two major areas of gender-based discrimination in recreation and leisure: (1) employment practices and (2) program involvement. A number of studies showed that women tended to secure fewer high-level administrative positions and were paid lower salaries than men in recreation and park departments throughout the United States.

However, in response to equal opportunity laws and other pressures, governmental recreation and park departments and other agencies began to hire women in greater numbers than in the past. Several states hired their first women park rangers, naturalists, and park superintendents; and in a number of cities women were appointed as directors of the recreation and park departments. A fundamental principle in community recreation has been that all persons should be given an equal opportunity, regardless of sex, religion, race, or other personal factors. However, in the postwar decades, it became evident that this principle had not been applied toward participation of girls and women in public recreation programs in either the United States or Canada. To document the preferential treatment given to males as participants in public and nonprofit agency recreation programs, Michael Heit and Don Malpass studied program differentiation by gender in the Sport and Fitness Division of the Ontario, Canada, Ministry of Culture and Recreation. Their findings clearly documented the unequal provision of programs for females.[6]

In the United States, similar investigations, when combined with pressure from women's groups, legislation like Title IX of the Education Amendments Act of 1972, and lawsuits directed at colleges, school boards, and various community recreation agencies, led to significant changes in public recreation programming. As a result, girls and women today have a far greater range of sport and physical recreation opportunities than they did in the past.

A significant development at this time involved the merger of formerly sex-separated organizations into groups serving both sexes, such as the Boys and Girls Clubs of America.

Gays and Lesbians

A third group of persons who traditionally have been disadvantaged in American society consists of homosexuals. During the counterculture era, they began to mobilize themselves as an economic and political force. In the 1960s and 1970s, many gay and lesbian groups began to organize and promote their recreational and social activities openly on college campuses and in community life. In a number of cities, they had to fight through the courts for the right to take part in community celebrations, parades, and other civic events. In the 1980s and 1990s, with heavily attended Gay Games—athletic events featuring thousands of homosexual participants—and with gay and lesbian themes becoming commonplace in the movies, at the theater, and on television, this population began to achieve a much higher degree of acceptance within the sphere of leisure activity.

In other cases, when they have sought to enter homosexual groups as such in big-city St. Patrick's Day Parades, or when they held a huge gay festival at Florida's Walt Disney World, a number of conservative Christian organizations protested vigorously. In retaliation, when rural Cobb County, Georgia, passed a resolution condemning the gay lifestyle as incompatible with its values, gay groups and their allies pressured the International Olympic Committee to withdraw some of its featured events from the county after they had already been scheduled to take place there as part of the 1996 Olympics.

The Elderly in Community Life

Although the counterculture was primarily a youth movement in the United States and abroad, it also prompted many middle-aged and older persons to examine their value systems and their status in community-life.

The elderly at this time represented a fourth group of disadvantaged persons in the sense that they were generally regarded and treated as powerless individuals, who were both physically and economically vulnerable. However, under the leadership of such growing organizations as the American Association of Retired Persons and the much smaller Gray Panthers, elderly persons began to mobilize and exert political clout in order to obtain improved benefits. With support from various federal programs, including the Administration on Aging, senior citizens' groups and golden age clubs around the United States began to offer diversified programs of health care, social services, nutrition, housing and transportation assistance, and recreation.

Programming for Persons with Disabilities

Although significant progress had been made following World War II, both treatment-centered and community-based programming for persons with disabilities received a major impetus during the counterculture period. Like other disadvantaged groups that had essentially been powerless, persons with disabilities began to act as their own advocates, demanding their rights and opportunities.

Disabled persons began to mobilize politically, to promote positive legislation and increased community services for those with physical, mental, or social disabilities. At the same time that therapeutic recreation specialists have begun to include a broader range of disabilities within their scope of service, numerous organizations have gone one step farther and promoted such innovative programming as theater arts for physically disabled individuals, skiing for those with visual disabilities, and a full range of sports and track-and-field events for the mobility-impaired.

ERA OF AUSTERITY AND FISCAL CUTBACKS

Despite this general picture of positive progress, the recreation, parks, and leisure-service field faced a serious threat in the 1970s and 1980s as mounting costs of government led to tax protests and funding cutbacks in states and cities across the United States.

As early as the mid-1970s, a number of older industrial cities in the nations's "rust belt" began to suffer from increased energy costs, welfare and crime problems, and expenses linked to rising infrastructure maintenance problems. Along with some suburban school districts confronted by skyrocketing enrollments and limited tax bases, such communities experienced budget deficits and the need to freeze expenditures.

In 1976, a tax limitation law was passed in New Jersey, and in 1978 California's much more radical Proposition 13 sharply reduced local property tax rates and assessment increases. A "tax revolt" soon spread rapidly across the United States. By the end of 1979, statutory provisions had been approved in 36 states that either reduced property, income, or sales taxes or put other types of spending limits in place. Austerity budgets had to be adopted in many communities, counties, and other governmental units. Typically, Proposition 13 resulted in major funding cutbacks for parks, libraries, recreation, social services, and street sweeping and maintenance, while police and fire departments tended to be protected against cuts.

Expanding Use of Revenue Sources

Many local recreation and park agencies adopted the policy of instituting or raising fees and charges for participation in programs, for use of the facilities, for rental of equipment, and for other types of involvement in a wide range of leisure activities and services. In the past, it had generally been the practice to provide all basic play opportunities, particularly for children and youth, without charge and to impose fees only for classes with special expenses or for admission to facilities such as skating rinks, swimming pools, golf courses, or tennis courts—often with arrangements made for annual permits at modest cost.

The revenues gained from such sources usually amounted to no more than 5 or 10 percent of a department's operating budget. However, Crompton and McGregor found that between 1964–1965 and 1990–1991 there was, in real dollar terms, a 259 percent increase in the self-generated revenues of local public recreation and park agencies.[7] In a study of 372 local public leisure-service agencies in Illinois, the average self-generated income of responding departments was found to be 32.7 percent of total department operating expenses by the late 1980s. What this meant was that more and more public departments either were imposing new charges on programs like day camps, sports league registration, classes, or outings, or were raising the level of existing fees—often to the point where substantial numbers of families could not afford to pay them.

Acceptance of Marketing Orientation   Directly linked to this trend was the widespread acceptance of an entrepreneurial, marketing-oriented approach to recreation and park programming and administration. It was argued by both educators and practitioners that it was necessary to be aggressive in seeking out new program opportunities and creative in responding to fiscal challenges—rather than relying on past, and often outmoded, formulas or policies.

References were being made to recreation as an "industry" in both the popular and the professional literature. Typically, in 1986, the *American Association for Leisure and Recreation Reporter* described the recreation field as a mosaic of thousands of businesses woven directly or subtly into the American economy.

In other professional publications, it was argued that managers of recreation and park programs, directors of nonprofit youth organizations, and operators of commercial play facilities were all essentially in the same "business"—that of meeting the public's leisure needs and interests. *Trends*, published by the National Recreation and Park Association and the National Park Service, agreed:

> Managed recreation is a profession that provides services to consumers of all demographic stripes and shades. Under this designation, a public park superintendent is in the same business as a resort owner . . . a theme park operator and the fitness directors of a YMCA.[8]

It was often argued that in order to compete effectively public recreation agencies had to adopt the philosophy and businesslike methods of successful companies. This meant that at every stage of agency operations—from assessing potential target populations and planning programs to pricing, publicizing, and distributing services—sophisticated methods of analysis and businesslike approaches to attracting and satisfying "customers" were to be used.

Privatization of Recreation and Park Operations

As a second type of response to the era of austerity that began in the 1980s, many recreation, park, and leisure-service agencies resorted to privatization—subcontracting or developing concession arrangements with private organizations—to carry out functions that they could not themselves fulfill as economically or efficiently.

This has become a major thrust in American life as the role of government has been challenged. Many cities now rely on private businesses to construct or maintain facilities, provide food and health services, or manage a variety of other formerly public functions. In a number of cases, prisons and correctional institutions are managed by for-profit companies under contract with public authorities, and several cities have experimented with assigning private organizations the responsibility for running all or part of their school systems.

As for recreation and parks, numerous public departments have contracted with private businesses to operate golf courses, tennis complexes, marinas, and other facilities under contractual agreements that govern the standards they must meet and the rates they may impose. Particularly in the construction of massive new facilities such as sports stadiums and arenas, similar arrangements have been made with commercial developers or businesses for private funding of all or part of construction expenses, with long-term leases being granted to owners of major sports teams.

Impact of Funding Cuts

In 1978, the National Urban Recreation Study reported that hiring freezes and staff cutbacks had taken place in a majority of urban park and recreation departments during the preceding five years. Two years later, a study of U.S. cities having over 150,000 in population found that a majority of the responding recreation and park departments had experienced major cutbacks, which necessitated manpower freezes and staff discharges, program eliminations, rejection of bond issues, and reduced facility maintenance.[9]

Some reports suggest that many municipal and county recreation and park agencies have weathered the financial crisis that followed the tax revolt and have reached a point of relative stability. A study of small-town public recreation departments in several western and midwestern states by Ellen Weissinger and William Murphy found that, while these departments had experienced somewhat similar cutbacks to those reported in larger cities, they have generally avoided drastic reductions in staff and programs.[10]

However, the reality is that in many larger cities, which have the greatest number of poor families—and are marked by high welfare statistics, school dropouts, drug and alcohol abuse, youth gangs, and random violence—recreation and park programs today offer only the most minimal opportunities. The facilities that are provided are often vandalized and covered with graffiti, staff members are threatened, and overall agency operations are extremely limited.

Beyond this, Jack Foley and Veda Ward point out that in the most severely disadvantaged communities, such as South Los Angeles, nonprofit sports groups like Little League, Pony League, AAU swimming, and gymnastic and track clubs (which use public facilities but rely on volunteer leaders and membership fees) do not exist. There is also no commercial recreation in the form of movie theaters, malls, skating rinks, or bowling alleys. They continue:

> Boys and Girls Clubs, YMCAs and YWCAs, Scouts, and so forth, which rely on business and community support, are under-represented and financed in poor communities. A market equity policy (one gets all the recreation one can buy) [has] created a separate, unequal, and regressive City of Los Angeles recreation system. Many city parks [in wealthier neighborhoods] raise from $50,000 to $250,000 annually from user fees and donations for state-of-the-art services, while recreation centers in South Los Angeles exist on small city subsidies and what money they can squeeze out of the parents of poor children.[11]

EXPANSION OF OTHER RECREATION PROGRAMS

In sharp contrast with this negative picture, other forms of recreation services have flourished over the past three decades. Today, the largest single component of leisure services is the diversified field of commercial recreation businesses. Travel and tourism; fitness spas; professional sports and sports equipment; the manufacture and sale of hobbies, toys, and games; and varied forms of popular entertainment represent only part of this major sector of leisure involvement.

Similarly, most of the other areas of specialized recreation programming, such as therapeutic recreation, employee services, campus recreation, and private-membership and residential leisure services, have expanded steadily. In each case, these fields have sharpened their own identities and public images by developing professional societies or business associations, sponsoring national and regional conferences, publishing newsletters and magazines, and in some cases establishing continuing education and certification programs.

This striking expansion of the organized leisure-service field is illustrated in Table 4.1, which provides an overview of 20 different kinds of public, private, and commercial agencies based on a survey conducted in the mid-1980s. As later chapters of this text will show, these leisure-service organizations may be classified within 10 major groups that serve the public in the United States and Canada.

TABLE 4.1

TYPES OF FACILITIES AND/OR AGENCIES (CLASSIFIED BY SIZE OR POPULATIONS SERVED)

Type of Facility	Mean Size†
Private golf courses/country clubs	183 acres
Resort hotels/motels	102 units
Racquetball/tennis clubs	745 members
YMCAs/YWCAs	4,119 members
Multi-purpose athletic clubs	4,294 members
Campgrounds/trailer parks	145 sites
Sport/recreation camps	369 daily capacity
Theme/amusement parks	Insufficient sample
Corporate rec/fitness centers	5,239 number of employees
Retirement/life core centers	405 units
Rehabilitation hospitals	416 beds
Zoos	8,105 daily capacity
Military installations	26,973 populations served
Stadiums/arenas/tracks	Insufficient sample
Secondary schools/school districts	7,174 enrollment
Colleges/universities	14,627 enrollment
Correctional institutions	546 units
State recreation facilities	800,546 population served
County recreation departments	295,981 population served
Municipal recreation departments	81,451 population served

†Mean is the arithmetic average
Source: *Recreation, Sports and Leisure* (August 1985): 13.

TRENDS IN THE 1990s

The concluding section of this chapter describes several important demographic, social, economic, and technological trends of the 1990s that influenced the provision of recreation and leisure services in the years immediately before the turn of the century.

Continuing Diversification

As this chapter has shown, the overall recreation and park movement shifted from a primary focus on programs sponsored by local, public, tax-supported agencies to a much broader emphasis on several different kinds of commercially sponsored, private, or special-interest types of organizations. Apart from the issue of preparing future professionals in the varied leisure-service specialties, this trend suggests the overall need to broaden the public awareness of this field.

Economic Stratification: Income Gaps and "Luxury Fever"

Historically, the United States was viewed as a land of opportunity, in which every individual might climb the socioeconomic ladder and in which the middle class represented the backbone of society.

During the 1990s, these assumptions were sharply reversed. Several new studies on the growing concentration of American wealth and income challenged the nation's cherished self-image. Bradsher writes:

> They show that rather than being an egalitarian society, the United States has become the most economically stratified of industrial nations. . . . Indeed the drive [under the so-called Contract with America] to reduce federal welfare programs and cut taxes is expected to widen disparities between rich and poor.[12]

In part, this development stemmed from the emergence of a winner-take-all mentality in American business and public life, as more and more Americans compete for ever fewer and bigger prizes, encouraging "economic waste, income inequality, and an impoverished cultural life."[13] As part of this trend, which began in the 1980s and gained momentum in the 1990s, the annual compensation of CEOs at large firms rose from $1.8 million to $10.6 million—an increase of almost 500 percent from 1990 to 1998. In the latter year, top executives pocketed, on-average, 419 times the earnings of a typical production worker, a ratio far higher than that in any other industrialized nation. In many cases, they were being rewarded for having downsized hundreds of thousands of employees at the major corporations they headed to achieve higher profits and stock returns for investors.

While the number of wealthy families was growing steadily, in the mid-1990s it was reported that the nation's poverty rate had risen to its highest level in 10 years, with the number of children living in poverty higher than at any time since 1964. Meanwhile, the middle class was declining, both in terms of numbers, income, and morale. Labor Secretary Robert Reich concluded:

> Today's middle class is split into three groups. An underclass largely trapped in center cities, increasingly isolated from the core economy; an overclass of those who are posi-

tioned to profitably ride the waves of change; and in between, the largest group, an anxious class, most of whom hold jobs but who are justifiably . . . uneasy about their own standing and fearful for their children's futures.[14]

Implications for Leisure   What did this growing separation of American society into rich and poor mean for recreation and leisure? First, a growing number of individuals had become immensely wealthy. In 1999, it was reported that 4.1 million of the nation's 102 million households had a net worth of $1 million or more.

In what seemed to be a vivid replay of Thorstein Veblen's view of "conspicuous consumption" (see page 33), these individuals were caught up in what Cornell economist Robert Frank described as *luxury fever*—a rage to spend wildly on vehicles, clothing, toys and hobbies, and a host of other possessions.[15]

Multimillion-dollar megamansions were being built throughout the country, often on relatively small lots. Many of the newly rich were paying huge sums to build elaborate swimming pools or buy luxury yachts or giant motor homes for vacation travel. One billionaire's ex-wife demanded $4,400 a day to raise their daughter after divorce, and parents began paying sports coaches $70 an hour—sometimes more—to coach their youngsters in Little League baseball skills.

Some wealthy school districts developed elaborate plans for new schools. An elite private school in Westchester County, New York, set out to build a $25 million structure on 100 acres, resembling a small college:

> . . . offering the 400 students 2 ice rinks and 4 basketball courts in a giant field house, 12 athletic fields and 6 tennis courts outdoors, and a 500-seat auditorium. The property itself is a little Eden, with thickly wooded hills and vales.[16]

Meanwhile, children in less affluent neighborhoods or school districts often attend schools that lack even the most minimal resources for play, as well as spaces and equipment for classes. Throughout the nation at century's end, the growing gap between rich and poor evidenced itself in such jarring contrasts in terms of recreation, parks, and leisure opportunities.

Growing Conservatism in Social Policy

Accompanying the nation's division into rich and poor social classes, there was a pronounced shift in the late 1980s and early 1990s toward more conservative social and economic policies. This trend took many forms, including a sharp withdrawal of assistance for welfare and for inner-city programs serving the economically disadvantaged.

Conservative forces initiated a wave of legislation striking down affirmative action policies that had assisted African-American, Hispanic, and other minorities in gaining access to education or career settings. Harsher curbs on immigration from third-world regions were enacted, and bilingual education programs were discarded in many districts—a policy seen by many as racially motivated.

Particularly in the mid-1990s, there were renewed efforts to open up the nation's parks and forests to economic exploitation and to reduce support for environmental education programs.

There were continuing assaults on federal support for the National Endowment for the Arts and other cultural programs. *Time Magazine*'s arts critic Robert Hughes described the all-out assault on federal funding as unenlightened, uneconomic, and undemocratic:

> . . . [t]he present [leadership in Congress means to sever] all links between American government and American culture. It wants the federal government to give no support at all to music, theater, ballet, opera, film, intelligent television, literature, history, archaeology, museum work, architectural conservation, and the visual arts. It intends to abolish federal funding for the National Endowment for the Arts, the National Endowment for the Humanities, and the Corporation for Public Broadcasting. And it wants to do it tomorrow.[17]

Through the 1990s, although the nation's crime rate continued to decline steadily, the numbers of those imprisoned in state, federal, and local jails rose steadily. With a vindictive attitude toward those convicted even of minor drug offenses, prison policies increasingly abandoned efforts to rehabilitate prisoners—and instead adopted increasingly severe and punitive practices.

California's higher education system, which had offered a four-year degree at little or no cost to every qualified citizen, faced major funding cuts that compelled sharp rises in tuition charges. Miller writes:

> . . . [B]asic tuition charges have more than doubled since 1991 [while] spending on prisons has increased almost eight times as fast as spending on higher education. . . . Meanwhile, hundreds of public libraries have closed, cut their hours, or been unable to buy books, leaving one of the nation's richest states last in per capita library services. . . . Three out of every four schools need major plumbing, electrical, or roof repairs, says the U.S. General Accounting Office, making them the worst such facilities of any state.[18]

Through the middle years of the decade, newspaper headlines illustrated the impact of conservative political thrusts in American life in such areas as mandates for child welfare, nursing home beds for the elderly, health care, environmental protection enforcement, legal help for the urban poor, and youth programs. The widespread decline in support for needed public services and the harsh resistance to government policies benefiting minorities and the poor inevitably posed a severe challenge to many public and nonprofit leisure-service organizations during the early and mid-1990s.

Commodification and Privatization of Leisure Services

The final years of the twentieth century saw a pronounced blurring of functions among different types of organizations in American society: governmental, nonprofit, private, and commercial. Instead of having clearly marked areas of responsibility and program operations in the leisure-service field, these separate kinds of organizations began to overlap each other through partnership or cosponsorship arrangements, by expanding their missions and undertaking new, innovative ventures, and by adopting new fiscal policies. This overall trend had two related components: *commodification* and *privatization*.

Commodification   Simply defined, commodification describes the process of taking any product or service and commercializing it by designing and marketing it to yield the greatest degree of financial return or profit.

Political scientist Sebastian De Grazia described the fuller meaning of this trend:

> Commodification of leisure is understood as a necessary element in the subordination of the entire social system to the reproduction of capitalism and its institutional structure. The consequence to the worker is surrendering to forms of leisure which turn away from self-defining, creative experience and, instead, consume vast quantities of market-produced goods and services.[19]

On the national scene, as part of the effort to gain fuller financial support in an increasingly consumer-oriented society, art museums, libraries, and theater, orchestra, and ballet companies have all become centers of popular entertainment, offering chartered trips abroad, film series and lecture programs, social events, and jazz concerts.

On a broader scale, huge conglomerates were formed during the 1990s, such as the Viacom and CBS mergers or the linkage of Time Warner and America Online, which dominate the nation's leisure through the operation of media empires (television, newspapers, magazines, and music companies) or theme parks, sports teams and stadiums, cruise lines, and similar ventures.

Fee-Based Public Recreation   Even when recreation programs are provided by public local or nonprofit agencies, price tags are placed today on almost every kind of sponsored recreational opportunity. Typically, the annual or seasonal program brochures of public recreation and park agencies list varied classes, aquatic or sports facilities, camps, tournaments, or special events—invariably with attached fees and charges that may run into several hundreds of dollars.

Privatization   As described earlier in this chapter, privatization refers to the growing practice of having private corporations take on responsibility for providing services, maintaining facilities, or performing other functions formerly carried out by government agencies.

During the 1990s, privatization grew increasingly widespread in such areas as the so-called prison industry, in which growing numbers of commercial businesses gained contracts for managing prisons or correctional centers or such civic functions as trash removal, building maintenance, or the operation of utility or water-supply systems. In terms of public recreation and park privatization, the most striking event at this time was the 1998 contract for a private group, the Central Park Conservancy, to operate New York's famous and historic Central Park, with joint public and private funding.

Privatization has a second important meaning with respect to recreation and leisure, when it refers to the withdrawal of major segments of the population from participation in shared communal events and programs—a marked trend of the 1990s. In 1995, Harvard political scientist Robert Putnam published an article, "Bowling Alone," in a small scholarly journal that raised a national firestorm of concern.

Putnam's thesis, backed by a wealth of documentation, was that Americans had increasingly withdrawn from varied forms of civic engagement—churchgoing, membership in Parent-Teacher Associations, unions, and a host of other social networks that contribute to what he calls "social capital" and a sense of connectedness. Bowling, which Putnam cites as a metaphor, suffered a precipitous decline in league activity, although it continues to be a popular sport.[20]

Clearly, the need to revive community involvement and the interconnectedness among different social groups and generations represents a major continuing challenge for the overall leisure-service field, a topic discussed more fully in Chapter 12.

New Environmental Initiatives

As this chapter has shown, the nation's support for environmental protection and the recovery of polluted lakes and streams, as well as the continuing acquisition and preservation of wilderness areas, faced a sharp challenge during the 1980s and early 1990s.

Several decades of neglect and overcrowding had left the nation's park system and forest in a precarious state. In 1997, *Time Magazine* cited Yellowstone as a leading example:

> There is little doubt that the preservationists are losing ground. The ills that beset the nation's first and still most magnificent park affect the park system as a whole: underfunding and overcrowding, pollution, encroaching commercial development, invasion of exotic species, and the decline of natural, historical, and cultural treasures.[21]

With national concern mounting, park authorities and Congress moved ahead in the years that followed. In a number of the major parks, they instituted new fees to gather additional revenue and restricted automobile traffic into interior sections. Increasingly, corporate sponsors to assist in parks maintenance were recruited, and major environmental organizations like the National Park Trust provided support for the acquisition of new parks and wildlands.

In 1998, the federal government announced a moratorium on the construction of new logging roads in the national forests and discontinued the use of numerous older roads to permit huge areas to return to a natural state. Later, in 2000, they initiated plans to remove a number of major dams that had threatened the survival of fish populations in New England, although similar efforts were strongly resisted in the Northwest.

Although public concerns focused chiefly on the ecological recovery of parks and wilderness areas, they also were directed to problems of clean air and water that affected major metropolitan areas. At the same time, as Chapter 7 will show, major efforts were made in such older cities as Baltimore and Boston to revive waterfront and disused industrial areas. In such settings, cities developed such new harbor facilities as aquariums, museums, sports stadiums, marinas, theme parks, and other cultural and entertainment attractions—both to improve their image and attract tourists and to serve their own residents with appealing leisure programs.

Reported Decline of Leisure

As Chapter 3 points out, a leading cause of the growth of the recreation movement throughout this century was the increase in free time—stemming from the shortened workweek, expanded vacations and holidays, longer periods of retirement, and greater use of labor-saving devices. The expectation in the 1950s was that this trend would be accelerated by the increased use of automation, and that this would lead to much more leisure time for those in the workforce.

However, the decline in the workweek came to a halt at mid-century, and the average hours of work remained relatively stable in the period that followed. In the 1980s, reports began to indicate that a change was taking place in terms of work hours.

A *Wall Street Journal/NBC News* survey report in 1986 found that a substantial number of Americans claimed to have more work and less leisure than in the past. In 1987 the Louis Harris polling organization found that the number of hours the average American worked each week had risen from 40.6 in 1973 to 48.4 in 1983. At the same time, leisure hours had declined from 26.2 to 17.7 hours a week, with the trend being most evident among the nation's most affluent sectors.

In the early 1990s, *The Overworked American: The Unexpected Decline of Leisure*, a book by Harvard economics professor Juliet Schor, summed up these and other studies to conclude that Americans had lost as much as 160 hours of leisure a year—a full month—due to heightened work demands.[22]

In Canada, a study authorized by the Federal Minister of Human Resources Development concluded that the number of employees in longer hour jobs had been rising steadily since the 1970s, with 10 percent of all adult male workers and 6 percent of all female workers now working more than 50 hours per week—and with two-income families hit doubly hard.

In January 2000, *U.S. News and World Report* concluded that Americans were working 208 more hours a year than two decades ago and now work more hours than any country in the advanced industrial world—the equivalent of eight more weeks a year than the average Western European.[23]

Disputed Findings   However, these reports were seriously disputed before long. Other research studies suggested that work schedules had *not* increased for most Americans over the past three decades. Making use of systematic time diaries kept by a cross-section of working adults over the 1960s, 1970s, and 1980s, sociologist John Robinson of the University of Maryland concluded that leisure hours had actually risen by about 10 percent during this period.

His research also disclosed specific changes in the way that leisure hours were allocated to various activities. For example, he found that fitness participation had declined by 10 percent between 1985 and 1990. Among 22 physical recreation or fitness activities, only walking, bicycling, and basketball had gained in popularity during this period. Gardening and yard work; calisthenics and general exercise; jogging and running; and dancing, aerobics, and swimming as exercise had all declined.

Robinson also suggested that certain groups of Americans actually do have less free time or feel greater work pressures. These include working women and single parents who must combine work with family responsibilities, parents who have unconventional work schedules, and individuals who have lost well-paying jobs and must now work at two or three different jobs to meet their responsibilities.

In 1995, Hamlin reported the findings of a three-year study conducted by the NPD Group, a marketing research firm in Park Ridge, Illinois, which analyzed daily activity reports of 3,000 adults chosen to reflect the national population.[24] This study found that Americans were working slightly less and playing more over the period recorded, on average.

Additional data on work hours reported in the 1990s was drawn from surveys conducted by the Bureau of Labor Statistics, of 400,000 nonfarm businesses and additional thousands of randomly selected households:

> The survey of businesses suggests the average workweek [of production and nonsupervisory employees] in the companies studied "trended down" from 38.8 in the mid-1960s to 36.1 in the mid-1970s, 34.9 in the mid-1980s, and 34.6 in 1998.[25]

A key element affecting work and leisure patterns consists of the socioeconomic level and job categories of those studied. Business executives, professionals, and "knowledge workers" tend to work long hours and are increasingly under heavy stress and time pressures due, as indicated, to the invasion of the home by computers, E-mail, the Internet, cell phones, and pagers.

For such individuals, Mark Hunter writes, the traditional distinction between work and leisure is blurred today—particularly for families in which both parents must work to maintain an upscale lifestyle.[26] Similarly, James Lardner writes that in a "work-happy America that is enjoying unparalleled prosperity" at the end of the twentieth century many modern managers and professionals have become highly competitive, success-driven "workaholics."[27]

Two other evidences of the increased emphasis given to work and career success during the 1990s were: (1) the rapid increase in the number of school districts throughout the United States shuffling the traditional calendar and imposing mandatory summer school attendance for millions of pupils,[28] and (2) the reality that millions of working adults now are forced to work nontraditional schedules within an exploding 24-hour economy.

Stores open around the clock, the need to accommodate the time schedules of other nations in a globalized economy, and the expansion of night-shift jobs have created a new "all-night" world:

> The 24-hour day may take a toll on family life, especially among people expected to work the nonstandard hours demanded by the new economy. . . . Fewer than one-third of all employed Americans 18 or older have a standard workweek, defined as 35 to 40 hours, Monday through Friday, on a fixed daytime schedule.[29]

Desire for More Free Time and Simpler Lifestyle

Among those groups that *are* experiencing increased work time and work pressures, there appears to be a trend toward achieving a simpler, less pressured, and more rewarding lifestyle. In many cases, this involves deliberately resisting job demands that require more work or that represent a threat to family life. Some individuals are even accepting part-time positions at lesser salaries. In a *Time*/CNN poll of representative adults, 61 percent agreed that earning a living today "requires so much effort that it is difficult to find time to enjoy life."

In a dramatic example of workers balancing work pressures against quality-of-life needs, several thousand workers at the General Motors plant in Janesville, Wisconsin, agreed in November 1994 to reject company demands that they work a 50-hour week to compensate for a sharply reduced workforce. Although they welcomed the overtime pay involved, these union employees felt that the increased hours and heightened pace of work would create stress and lead to accidents—and that they would rather have more free time than more money.

The implications of this trend for the recreation field are clear. For those who seek to develop simpler and more relaxed lives, recreation, park, and leisure-service agencies must provide a rich array of challenging and satisfying experiences for their free-time enrichment. And for those who genuinely suffer from work overload and a shortage of leisure time, David Scott urges the recreation profession to use strategies that will help them to use their scarce free hours more productively. He writes:

> Leisure-service agencies must strive to insure convenience in program offerings [by scheduling] programs or services at times that are convenient for the clients [or by scheduling] some form of child care . . . or dual programming for children and adults.[30]

Technological Impacts on Leisure

Beyond the effects of technological innovation described in Chapter 3, a number of other scientifically based advances had a major impact on American leisure in the final decades of the twentieth century.

Many of these had to do with forms of travel. Apart from uses of computers in terms of tourism planning and reservations, electronic guidance systems are able to direct an automobile trip through every turn until a destination is reached. Electronic navigation simulators created by companies like Maptech, Inc., provide piloting assistance for boating enthusiasts. For the family that is on vacation, movies and video games replace license-plate Bingo, as cars become entertainment centers, with the latest audio and video technology that is being displayed at consumer electronic shows.

Home environments have become increasingly "smart," with "Nanny cams" that watch over sleeping babies or "intelligent" wallpaper that turns the wall of a room into a television screen, virtual aquarium, or other visual feature. Home theater systems control lighting, stereo and CD systems, window shades, satellite service, and laser discs, while other lines accommodate the family's telephones, fax machines, and modems—all at a distance.

Television, video games, and children's toys represent impressive examples of technology's impact on family leisure. Today, almost 80 percent of homes have cable or satellite television, and many studies report that about 40 percent of Americans' free time is spent watching the home screen. Seplow and Storm write:

> For half a century now, television has been gobbling up time the way a good running back gobbles up yardage. Regardless of income, education, or any major demographic indicator, Americans have made television the unrivaled consumer of their free time. [Apart from recent findings that television watching is beginning to decline among young people] nothing has remotely weakened its grip. Americans spend more time watching television than working out, reading, using the computer, working in the garden, and going to church—*combined.*[31]

Numerous critics have bemoaned the cultural level of most television programs, from inane situation comedies or fake wrestling bouts to news broadcasts that endlessly report crime and the continuing emphasis on sex and violence in many rock and rap music shows. As a single example, many psychologists and sociologists regard popular talk programs as "freak shows" that trivialize social issues and exploit troubled people who are often presented as pathetic losers.

Horrifying new games featuring zombies and vampires offer scary action, creepy characters, and taut suspense and—while sometimes designated for mature audiences, ages 17 and up—are often available to children.

Perhaps the most attacks on entertainment media have involved the violence- or horror-focused video games that have evolved from such harmless products as *Pong* or *Pac-Man*. Today, games that are generally described as "first-person shooter games" provide impressively rendered, full-color combat zones, in which the player carries out the kind of murderous rampage that real teenagers—addicts of such games—actually conducted at Columbine High School in Littleton, Colorado, and several other schools across the nation.[32]

Similar concerns have been expressed about the Internet, which—apart from its uses in business, government, or other major systems—has also become a means of social exchange through computer bulletin boards and chat rooms. The dangers involved in Internet use such as exposure of children to sexual predators, breakdown of privacy barriers, victimization through "con" games, or the risk of becoming obsessed with it—to the point of becoming seriously withdrawn from other social involvements—are discussed in Chapter 12.

Concern about Family Values

A final important problem that arose in American society over the past few decades involved the severe erosion in the civility and quality of everyday life. Social critics and political campaigners have stressed the need to strengthen family values, but the problem goes far beyond this. The increased reliance on drugs, gambling, and indiscriminate or commercialized sex; the shocking examples of random violence; the accelerating rate of imprisonment; and the presence of growing numbers of homeless persons on city streets are all indications of the breakdown of community life.

Some writers have concluded that the nation has undergone a spiritual crisis in recent years. A Princeton University sociologist of religion sees this as a major challenge for the nation's churches:

> Americans . . . say they are repelled by materialism, yet admit to being caught up in it. They say they feel under constant pressure, working too much and neglecting family life, yet they are ready to work even longer hours for more money. They say they are troubled by widespread poverty, yet esteem wealth.[33]

A vivid illustration of what many regard as the nation's selfishness and moral drift was found on the cover of the *New York Times Magazine* in November 1998—presented as a satirical statement of popular values:

> *Election Day, 1998.* We, the relatively unbothered and well-off, hold these truths to be self-evident: That Big Government, Big Deficits, and Big Tobacco are bad, but that big bathrooms and 4-by-4's are not; that American overseas involvement should be restricted to trade agreements, mutual funds, and the visiting of certain beachfront resorts; that markets can take care of themselves as long as they take care of us; that an individual's sex life is nobody's business, although highly entertaining; and that the only rights that really matter are those which indulge the Self.[34]

In addition to the kinds of privatization discussed earlier in this chapter, there is another kind of withdrawal today from experiences shared with others—a retreat of millions of Americans to secure existences behind the walls of private communities, or to the entertainment provided by television, CD-ROMs, and video games in one's own home rather than that provided in community social settings. What appears to be lacking is a shared sense of responsibility and communal values that would bring people together to build bridges between groups that are separated by gender, race, generation, or other differences.

What does this have to do with recreation and leisure? It is the leisure activities that are the key elements in current popular culture—namely, movies, television, music, and video games—that are being blamed for many of the pathologies of community life today. However, recreation practitioners cannot simply condemn and seek to censor or control such forms of entertainment, but must provide alternatives in the form of active, positive, and challenging recreational opportunities and must effectively educate for the creative and constructive use of leisure by all age groups.

It is an ugly paradox that while middle-class or wealthy Americans are able to afford a huge range of positive and appealing forms of play, the poorest citizens with the greatest need for healthful and enriching leisure experiences are provided with only minimal recreation facilities and programs.

A critical challenge for all recreation, park, and leisure-service practitioners in the years ahead will be to gather evidence of the social value and outcomes of organized recreation programs and to incorporate these in benefits-based management approaches in the years ahead.

Increased determination to move in such socially oriented directions was shown in the mid- and late 1990s, when growing numbers of public recreation and park agencies addressed themselves to important community problems—with special emphasis on programming for "at-risk" youth. Numerous examples of such programs are cited in Chapter 6 and Chapter 7.

National Prosperity: A Happy "Problem"

A final important development in the mid- and late 1990s was the dramatic economic recovery that saw the net worth of American families rise rapidly, with sharply declining unemployment and the appearance of impressive budget surpluses on all levels of government.

In city after city and state after state, mayors and governors bubbled with optimism at the turn of the century. In June 2000, at the annual meeting of the United States Conference of Mayors, it was agreed that urban America's biggest challenge was *prosperity*:

> The mayors complained about too many high-skill jobs and not enough people to fill them; too many well-off people moving back to the city and not enough houses for all of them . . . and too much demand for parks and serenity and not enough open space to offer the new city dwellers appalled by sprawl.[35]

The impact of this flourishing economic trend on the organized recreation, park, and leisure-service field is outlined in Chapter 7 through Chapter 9 of this text. First, however, we examine the personal and societal values and outcomes of recreation in contemporary culture.

SUMMARY

The years following World War II represented a period of immense change in the lives of Americans. From 1945 to the early 1970s, it was a time of prosperity and optimism for most families. As great numbers of young people—generally white and working- or middle-class—moved into suburban areas, recreation and park programs flourished and leisure was seen as part of the good life.

Recognizing that a substantial part of the population continued to live in urban slums, with limited economic and social opportunities, the federal government launched a "War on Poverty," in which recreation played a significant role. Under pressure from the civil rights movement, many recreation and park agencies began to give a higher level of priority to serving minorities. With the inner-city riots of the mid- and late 1960s, this effort was expanded throughout the country. At the same time, the counterculture movement, which saw young people rebelling against traditional authority and establishment values, transformed the society with its resistance to the work ethic and its acceptance of drugs.

The late 1960s and 1970s were also a time when minority groups—including women, the elderly, persons with disabilities, or those with alternative sexual lifestyles—began to demand greater social, economic, political, and leisure opportunities. For them, recreation represented a means of gaining independence and achieving their fullest potential.

Beginning in the 1970s and intensifying during the decade that followed, recessions, inflation, rising costs of welfare and crime, and declining tax bases created an era of austerity that affected many government agencies. With sharp cutbacks in their budgets, many recreation and park agencies imposed severe staffing and maintenance cuts and relied more fully on fees and privatization to maintain their programs. The entrepreneurial marketing strategy that prevailed widely at this time meant that many public departments were forced to give less emphasis to socially oriented programming.

At the same time, a wave of political conservatism in areas related to race relations, the criminal justice system, services for the poor, and environmental programs gained support. Studies in the 1980s and 1990s indicated that many Americans were working longer hours, due both to changes in family patterns and technological influences on business—although other reports indicated that many employees have shorter workweeks.

At the end of the 1990s, with economic prosperity and more positive social and environmental concerns gaining acceptance, the place of recreation and leisure in contemporary life appeared to be more secure than ever.

QUESTIONS FOR CLASS DISCUSSION OR ESSAY EXAMINATIONS

1. During the 1950s and 1960s, Americans became sharply aware of environmental problems and the federal government took action to curb pollution and protect open spaces. What were some of the key events in this process, and how did it affect the recreation and park movement? Describe the changes that occurred with respect to federal environmental policy in the 1980s and 1990s.

2. Poverty, racial unrest, and the youth counterculture movement were important trends or concerns during the 1960s and 1970s. What actions did government take with respect to these problem areas, and how did they affect public values and behavior with respect to recreation? Some critics suggest that the breakdown in family values and social stability of the last two decades had its roots in this earlier period. Could you make a case for this argument?

3. Immediately after World War II, social forecasters predicted that free time would increase greatly by the turn of the twenty-first century and that society would adopt humanistic leisure interests and lifestyles, largely replacing the work ethic. From the perspective of the mid- and late 1990s, what has actually happened?

ENDNOTES

1 J. Murphy, E. W. Niepoth, L. Jamieson, and J. Williams, *Leisure Systems: Critical Concepts and Applications* (Champaign, Ill.: Sagamore Publishers, 1991): 94.

2 See Richard Kraus, *Leisure in a Changing America: Multicultural Perspectives* (New York: Macmillan College Publishing, 1994): 61.

3 Mark Searle and Russell Brayley, *Leisure Services in Canada: An Introduction* (State College, Pa.: Venture Publishing, 1993): 20.

4 Carter Betz, "National Outdoor Recreation Assessments," *Parks and Recreation* (January 1999): 22.

5 See Daniel Yankelovich, "The Work Ethic Is Under-Employed," *Psychology Today* (May 1982): 6.

6 Michael Heit and Don Malpass, *Do Women Have Equal Pay?* (Ontario, Canada: Ministry of Culture and Recreation, 1995).

7 John Crompton and Brian McGregor, "Trends in the Financing and Staffing of Local Government Park and Recreation Services," *Journal of Park and Recreation Administration* (Vol. 21, No. 1, 1994): 22.

8 J. Zenger, "Leadership: Management's Better Half," *Trends* (Vol. 4, No. 3, 1987).

9 Richard Kraus, *New Directions in Urban Parks and Recreation: A Trends Analysis Report* (Temple University and Heritage Conservation and Recreation Service, 1980): 6.

10 Ellen Weissinger and William Murphy, "A Survey of Fiscal Conditions in Small-Town Public Recreation Departments from 1987 to 1991," *Journal of Park and Recreation Administration* (Vol. 11, No. 3, 1993): 61–71.

11 Jack Foley and Veda Ward, "Recreation, the Riots and a Healthy L.A.," *Parks and Recreation* (March 1993): 68.

12 Keith Bradsher, "Gap in Wealth in U.S. Called Widest in West," *New York Times* (17 April 1995): 1.

13 See Robert Frank and Philip Cook, *"The Winner Take All Society,"* (New York: The Free Press, 1995).

14 Robert Reich, cited in "A New Profile of Middle Class," *Employee Services Management* (May/June 1995): 4.

15 Robert Frank, *Luxury Fever: Why Money Fails to Satisfy in an Era of Excess* (New York: The Free Press, 1999).

16 Lisa Foderaro, "Plan for Elite School in Westchester Divides Haves and Have-Mores," *New York Times* (1 August 1999): 27.

17 Robert Hughes, "Pulling the Fuse on Culture," *Time* (7 August 1995): 61.

18 Matthew Miller, "Explaining California's 'Mississippification,' " *U.S. News and World Report* (18 May 1998): 32.

19 Sebastian de Grazia, cited in J. S. Shivers and L. J. DeLisle, *The Story of Leisure: Context, Concepts, and Current Controversy* (Champaign, Ill.: Human Kinetics, 1996): 173.

20 Robert Putnam, *Bowling Alone: The Collapse and Revival of American Community* (New York: Simon and Schuster, 2000).

21 Michael Satchell, "Parks in Peril," *U.S. News and World Report* (21 June 1997): 24.

22 Juliet Schor, *The Overworked American: The Unexpected Decline of Leisure* (New York: Basic Books, 1991).

23 A later report indicated that growing numbers of Americans—44 percent—now regard themselves as "workaholics." See editorial "No Time to Slow Down," *U.S. News and World Report* (26 June 2000): 14.

24 Suzanne Hamlin, "Does It Go?" *New York Times* (6 September 1995): C-1.

25 Janny Scott, "Working Hard, More or Less," *New York Times* (10 July 1999): B-7.

26 Mark Hunter, "Work, Work, Work! It's Taking Over Our Lives . . . ," *Modern Maturity* (May/June 1999): 38.

27 James Lardner, "World-Class Workaholics," *U.S. News and World Report* (20 December 1999): 42.

28 Jodi Wilgoren, "Summer Classes Expanding in Push to Improve Skills." *New York Times* (5 July 2000): A-1.

29 Marian Uhlman, "More and More, Ours Is An All-Night World," *Philadelphia Inquirer* (11 June 1999): A-1

30 David Scott, "Time Scarcity and Its Implications for Leisure Behavior and Leisure Delivery," *Journal of Park and Recreation Administration* (Vol. 11, No. 3, 1993): 51–60.

31 Stephen Seplow and Jonathan Storm, "How TV Redefined Our Lives," *Philadelphia Inquirer* (30 November 1997): A-1.

32 Michael Marriott, "New Heights (or Depths) of Blood and Gore," *New York Times* (17 February 2000): G-6.

33 Peter Steinfelds, "Beliefs," *New York Times* (23 August 1997): 9.

34 See Nicholas Lemann, "The New American Consensus: Government of, by, and for the Comfortable," *New York Times* (1 November 1998): 37.

35 Timothy Egan, "Urban Mayors Share The (Not Unwelcome) Burden of Coping with Prosperity," *New York Times* (13 June 2000): A-18.

CHAPTER 5

PERSONAL LEISURE PERSPECTIVES:

Motivations, Values, and Age Group Factors

◆ ◆ ◆

Soccer practice, dance class, play rehearsal, Boy Scouts. Be at Tuesday football practice or be benched in Saturday's game. First graders carry daily planners. Family vacations, not to mention family dinners, take a back seat to basketball. . . . Now some parents in Wayzata, Minnesota, a prosperous, purposeful community, of high-achieving, energetic children and color-coded family calendars, have decided that it is all too much.

    They are concerned that too little time with parents means that children are missing the stabilizing, character-shaping experiences of rituals like suppertime conversations and family outings. And, especially in the wake of school shootings in which the killers' parents often seemed to know little about their children's lives, they are worried that the influence of peers and the media and commercialism may be outweighing the influence of parents.[1]

◆ ◆ ◆

INTRODUCTION

Having reviewed the history of leisure on the world scene and over the past three decades on the North American continent, we now examine it from personal and societal perspectives. This chapter outlines the varied motivations that impel individuals in different age groups to take part in a wide range of recreational and play activities. It presents the values and benefits of leisure, as well as the constraints that limit participation. It examines the influence of demographic factors such as gender, race or ethnicity, socioeconomic class, and similar elements on recreational involvement. While each of these elements is discussed separately in this chapter, in daily life they all are closely interwoven.

MOTIVATIONS FOR RECREATIONAL PARTICIPATION

Through the years, a number of researchers have studied the reasons that people give for taking part in recreation as a generalized experience. For example, in 1980, Rick Crandall summarized a list of 17 motivational factors identified by a cross section of American adults as reasons for taking part in varied forms of leisure activity. They included such motivations as: enjoying nature and escaping civilization; escaping from routine and responsibility; physical exercise and health-related benefits; social contact and companionship; creativity and aesthetic expression; gaining a sense of power and influence; altruism and being of service to others; excitement or thrill-seeking; enrichment of one's personality or self-actualization; and escaping boredom.[2]

Personal Influences on Leisure Motivations

Depending on the life stage of the individual, different kinds of recreational motivations may prevail. For example, systematic studies of the reasons why children engage in competitive sports programs have yielded the following kinds of ranked responses: (1) to have fun; (2) to improve my skills; (3) to stay in shape; (4) to do something I am good at; and (5) for the excitement of competition.

In studies of the recreational motivations of adults, Kelly found that these included such elements as the need for rest and relaxation, excitement, self-expression, enjoying companionship, or to escape pressure from one's spouse.[3]

Gender obviously has a powerful impact on leisure needs and choices. In an extensive study of several thousand adult women in the province of Ontario, Canada, researchers Bolla, Dawson, and Harrington identified the basic meanings of leisure for women and described their subjective experiences reported during leisure involvement. These included such elements as the feeling of competence, security, or playfulness and the expression of serenity, femininity, or assertiveness. Clearly, such factors were closely tied to their motivations for taking part in leisure pursuits.[4]

Motivations Linked to Major Activity Areas

The reasons for taking part in recreational activities also tend to be influenced by the nature of the activities themselves. In some cases, participation may be linked to a set of specific personal benefits. For example, Clough, Shepherd, and Maughan examined a sample of recreational long-distance runners and found that these marathoners had motivations linked to such underlying needs as health, challenge, and personal well-being. They listed the following kinds of benefits to be gained from running: (1) it keeps me fit; (2) it keeps me healthy; (3) it provides me with a physical challenge; (4) it gives me a sense of achievement; (5) it helps me relax; (6) it gives me more energy in my other activities; and (7) it increases my self-discipline.[5]

Still other research has identified the major purposes of an individual taking part in wilderness recreation such as extended hiking and camping, backpacking, rock climbing, or similar pursuits to include such elements as responding to the splendor of nature; resting and relaxation; enjoying adventure, challenge, and contact with others; escaping the pressures of modern, urban life; or living in simple and natural ways.

Simon Priest examined the function of privacy as part of camping in the Canadian wilderness and identified such personal needs and values as:

Personal autonomy—the need to avoid being manipulated or dominated by others; to safeguard one's individuality

Emotional release—providing for respite from the psychological tensions and stresses of everyday life

Intimacy—being part of a small social unit, achieving a close personal relationship with others involved in the wilderness experience[6]

Often, leisure motivations are shaped by the interplay of both participants and activities at different levels of skill, experience, or difficulty. For example, Williams, Schreyer, and Knopf examined river floating as experienced by several different types of participants: beginners, novices, and those with both narrow and broad past floating adventures. They found that motivations included such categories as escape, challenge, action, autonomy, self-awareness, learning activity, and interest in nature. However, these motivations varied considerably according to the experience background of those studied. For example, less experienced participants rated escape as a primary motivation, while more advanced floaters rated challenge or learning activity as primary goals.[7]

Social and Affiliation Drives

The need to be part of a social group and to have friends who provide companionship, support, and intimacy is at the heart of much recreational involvement. It helps to explain why people join sororities, fraternities, or other social clubs, senior citizen centers, tour groups, or other settings where new acquaintances and potential friends may be met. It is an underlying element in sports in terms of the friendships and bonds that are formed among team members.

Excitement and Challenge Motivations

A great deal of recreational involvement today is based on the need for excitement and challenge, particularly in such outdoor recreation activities as skiing, mountain climbing, or hang gliding, or in active, highly competitive individual or team sports.

Risk recreation and outdoor adventure pursuits have become increasingly popular program elements, and they serve the needs of individuals who have a strong sensation-seeking drive. For many people, such urges are met through spectatorship—by watching action-oriented movies or television shows—or in the form of video games based on high-speed chase or conflict. For others, ballooning, skydiving, parasailing, amateur stock car racing, or scuba diving satisfy risk-related motivations.

While varied forms of deviant social behavior, such as gang fighting, vandalism, or other types of juvenile crime, are not commonly thought of as leisure pursuits, the reality is that they often are prompted by the same need for thrills, excitement, and challenge that other, more respectable recreation pursuits satisfy.

Hedonistic Motivations

Similarly, many leisure pursuits today are based on the desire for pleasure of a sensual nature. These include a wide range of activities, such as gambling, drug or alcohol use, or direct or indirect sexual involvement, that are essentially hedonistic.

Such motivations are part of the normal range of leisure behavior for many individuals in modern society and, in fact, have existed in many cultures throughout history. While they have been condemned or prohibited in some societies, and while laws still exist in most North American communities to control gambling, drinking, drug use, or commercialized sex, public participation and spending on these activities continue to be high.

PERSONAL VALUES OF RECREATIONAL INVOLVEMENT

We now turn to an examination of the positive values of recreational involvement, as demonstrated by systematic research studies. In describing the major areas of human development, behavioral scientists use such terms as *cognitive* (referring to mental or intellectual development), *affective* (relating to emotional or feeling states), and *psychomotor* (meaning the broad area of motor learning and performance). Because these terms are somewhat narrow in their application, this chapter will instead use the more familiar terms *physical, emotional, social,* and *mental* development, together with a fifth category, *spiritual* experience.

Physical Values and Outcomes

Active recreational pursuits such as sports and games, dance, and even such moderate forms of exercise as walking or gardening have significant positive effects on physical development and health. The value of such activities obviously will vary according to the age and developmental needs of the participants. For children and youth, the major need is to promote healthy structural growth, fitness, endurance, and the acquisition of physical qualities and skills. It is essential that children learn the importance of fitness and develop habits of participation in physical recreation that will serve them in later life. This is particularly important in an era of electronic gadgets, labor-saving devices, and readily available transportation, all of which save time and physical effort but encourage a sedentary way of life.

The physical fitness of American children became a matter of serious national concern when the Kraus-Weber tests after World War II showed the fitness of American boys and girls to be much lower than that of children in other nations. Expanded programs of physical education and community sports for youth helped American schoolchildren to improve their fitness levels at this point.

Despite such efforts, however, it became apparent in the 1980s that American youth were *not* fit. "It's the best kept secret in America today," commented the chairman of the President's Council on Physical Fitness and Sport. "It's a disgrace." Based on national surveys of 19,000 children between the ages of 6 and 17, the council reported that 40 percent of boys and 70 percent of girls were unable to do more than a single pull-up, and fitness experts generally agreed that athletic ability had sagged steadily over the past two decades. As recently as the late 1990s, fresh research reports indicate that this situation has not improved and that American boys and girls suffer from a pronounced sedentary lifestyle—including growing reliance on physically passive forms of play.

Recognizing that the picture is less promising among America's children and youth than among its adults, what are the *specific* benefits of vigorous recreation activity for all age groups? These have been clearly documented in such areas of concern as obesity and cardiovascular health.

Control of Obesity

Scientists agree that physical activity plays a major role in weight control. Obesity among American adults has grown steadily and is now a serious health problem in this country. Per capita energy consumption has decreased as much as 10 percent over the past 50 years because of the use of automobiles and other mechanical devices and the popularity of television and spectator sports.

Numerous medical studies have documented the serious impact of obesity on people of all ages. According to research reported in 1992 by the U.S. Department of Agriculture Nutrition Research Center, overweight teenagers are more likely to suffer from such illnesses as heart disease, colon cancer, arthritis, and gout than are other adolescents through their life span. By the age of 45 they begin to die at a higher-than-usual rate, and when they reach their 70s their risk of death is twice that of those who were normal size as teenagers.[8]

Apart from the psychological, sociological, and other factors that tend to promote obesity, one critical cause has to do with the sedentary lifestyle of many Americans. Regular, vigorous exercise is a key element in maintaining healthy body weight. For example, experts have calculated the exact number of calories burned per hour by various types of activities, such as handball, running, swimming, jogging, tennis, or cycling. Jogging at the rate of 12 minutes per mile will burn up between 480 and 600 calories per hour for a 158-pound adult. Running for one hour at a pace of 7.5 miles per hour will burn up 800 calories. In contrast, watching television uses only 80 calories per hour—just 15 more than sleeping.

Preserving Cardiovascular Health

Of all fitness-related aspects of active recreation, maintaining cardiovascular health has represented the highest priority. Until recently, Americans were known to have more coronary attacks than the people of any other nation, with heart and circulatory system diseases claiming nearly a million lives each year. The continuing rise in the number of such deaths is believed to have been partly caused by the fact that more people are escaping such illnesses as pneumonia or tuberculosis and living to the age when degenerative vascular disease becomes more of a threat. Doctors have also noted, however, an alarming increase of mortality from cardiovascular illness among comparatively young adults, especially males.

In the early 1990s, heart attack was identified as the leading cause of death in the United States, killing about 500,000 people a year. In 1992, a report by the American Heart Association classified physical inactivity as a major risk factor for heart disease, with a sedentary lifestyle being every bit as bad for one's heart as smoking, high cholesterol, or high blood pressure. Supporting this report, the director of epidemiology at the Institute for Aerobics Research in Dallas stated that 20 percent to 30 percent of Americans engage in so little physical activity that they are at especially high risk for developing the clogged arteries that lead to heart attacks.

On the basis of long-term population studies, authorities have generally recommended that a minimum of three half-hour periods of vigorous aerobic exercise with pulse-rate targets keyed to one's age is necessary to have a desired cardiovascular impact. However, recent research involving thousands of men and women indicates that even moderate forms of exercise, including such activities as walking, stairclimbing, gardening, or housework have a beneficial long-term effect on one's health. While high-intensity, pulse-pounding workouts yield the most dramatic benefits, more modest forms of exercise do yield significant benefits.

Beyond these findings, other research has demonstrated that regular exercise reduces the incidence of diabetes, colon cancer among men and breast and uterine cancer among women, stress and hypertension, strokes, osteoporosis, and other serious illnesses.

Need for Recreation Motivation

However, exercise alone, in the form of solitary aerobic activity or body conditioning, is not likely to become a long-term health measure if it lacks sociability or recreational atmosphere. Summerfield and Priest point out that more than half of all adults exercise intermittently and that, of those who start an exercise program, less than half will still be exercising six months later.[9]

Wankel found, in a study of adult fitness programs in a Canadian industrial setting, that the key factors associated with people continuing to engage regularly in group exercise had to do with the need for sociability, competition, and developing recreational skills. Thus, the most effective fitness activities are likely to be those with enjoyable recreational elements.[10]

As a consequence, many colleges and universities, YMCAs and YWCAs, and company recreation programs designed to serve employees have initiated fitness centers and programs in order to promote active play and conditioning activities within a recreational framework. In both the United States and Canada, federal authorities have joined together with professional societies and educational agencies to stimulate public interest and involvement in physical fitness and sports.

Outdoor Recreation's Appeal

The National Outdoor Leadership School sponsors hundreds of classes, trips, and leadership training programs each year around the world in varied outdoor skills, including rock climbing, backpacking, kayaking, and other outdoor pursuits. Many family groups enjoy skiing, shown here at Sugarbush, Vermont, which offers a variety of special children's programs.

In Canada, for example, in the late 1970s and 1980s, Fitness Canada, a program section of the Fitness and Amateur Sport Directorate of the federal government, sponsored extensive research and promotional efforts to encourage Canadians to become more physically active. A private, independent, and nonprofit communications company was established to spearhead this effort through public service advertising and a host of cosponsored special events and campaigns.

Emotional Values and Outcomes

What are the specific ways in which recreation contributes to emotional well-being? Millions of people who function within a presumable normal range of behavior tend to suffer from tension, boredom, stress, frustration, and an inability to use their leisure in satisfying ways. Mental depression afflicts an estimated 35 million people in the United States. The feeling of engagement and control over one's life that may be achieved in leisure is critical to sound mental health. Iso-Ahola and Weissinger point out that many psychologists base their treatment on this principle—seeking to help patients develop freedom and control in their lives, as well as the kind of engagement with others in leisure that contributes to psychological well-being.[11]

Relaxation and Escape

Going beyond these broad categories of leisure benefits, Chubb and Chubb have suggested that one of the most important psychological benefits of recreation is relaxation. Some people obtain this through physical activity, others from reading or other mental pastimes, and still others by dozing, daydreaming, or taking it easy. Relaxation, they write,

> provides a respite from life's worries and pressures, relieves feelings of tension and fatigue, and restores mental efficiency. Most people need it after a day's work, following an emotionally disturbing experience, or part way through a long period of involvement in one task.[12]

Overcoming Loneliness

Another important contribution of recreation to mental health consists of its role in providing social contact, friendship, or intimacy with others. Loneliness is a widespread phenomenon: typically, as many as three-quarters of all college students report being lonely during their first term away from home. Loneliness can have unpleasant and even life-threatening consequences and often is directly linked to alcoholism, physical illness, or suicide.

In a poll taken by *Psychology Today*, loneliness was the most frequently mentioned personal problem, with 38 percent of female and 43 percent of male readers saying they often felt lonely.

Stress Management

A closely related value of recreation is its usefulness in stress reduction. A leading authority on stress, Dr. Hans Selye, defines it as the overall response of the body to any extreme demand made upon it, which might include threats, physical illness, job pressures, and environmental extremes—or even such life changes as marriage, divorce, vacations, or taking a new job. Increasing amounts of stress in modern life have resulted in many individuals suffering from migraine or tension headaches, allergies, ulcers and ulcerative colitis, hypertension, and a number of psychosomatic illnesses, as well as accident proneness.

Once it was thought that the best approach to stress was rest and avoidance of all pressures, but today there is an awareness that some degree of stress is desirable and healthful. Today, researchers point out that physical activity can play a significant role in stress reduction. Typically, people work off anger, frustration, and indignation by taking long walks or engaging in some kind of physical activity such as chopping wood. All of the body's systems—the working muscles, heart, hormones, metabolic reactions, and the responsiveness of the central nervous system—are strengthened through stimulation. Following periods of extended exertion, the body systems slow, bringing on a feeling of deep relaxation. Attaining this relaxed state is essential to lessening the stress reaction.

Indeed, for many individuals, strenuous physical activity does more than reduce tension; it may actually promote a state of elation or euphoria. So-called "runner's high" results from the appearance of chemicals called endorphins which are produced by the brain and pituitary gland following prolonged exercise. Endorphins help the body control pain and produce a strong sense of well-being. High-risk activities such as rock climbing, mountaineering, white-water canoeing, hang gliding, or wilderness backpacking may literally provide a sense of emotional release and an improved outlook, which helps to overcome tension in daily life.

PLAY AS EMOTIONAL RELEASE

Another important benefit of leisure activity is that it can provide strong feelings of pleasure and satisfaction and can serve as an outlet for discharging certain emotional drives that, if repressed, might produce emotional distress or even mental illness.

The role of pleasure is increasingly recognized as a vital factor in emotional well-being. Some researchers have begun to analyze the simple concept of fun—defined as intense pleasure and enjoyment and an important dimension of social interactional leisure. In a review of studies on the "anatomy of joy," Natalie Angier reports that scientists are finding that sensations like optimism, curiosity, and rapture—as opposed to puritan condemnation of pleasure—

> . . . not only make life worth living, but also make life last longer. They think that euphoria unrelated to any ingested substance is good for the body, that laughter is protective against the corrosive impact of stress, and that joyful people outlived their bilious, whining counterparts.[13]

Self-Actualization

Linked to the issue of emotional well-being is *self-actualization,* a term that became popular in the 1970s chiefly through the writings of Abraham Maslow, who stressed the need for individuals to achieve their fullest degree of creative potential. Maslow developed a convincing theory of human motivation in which he identified a number of important human needs, arranging them in a hierarchy. As each of the basic needs is met in turn, a person is able to move ahead to meet more advanced needs and drives. Maslow's theory includes the following ascending levels of need:

Physiological needs: food, rest, exercise, shelter, protection from the elements, and other basic survival needs

Safety needs: self-protection needs on a secondary level—protection against danger, threats, or other forms of deprivation

Social needs: needs for group associations, acceptance by one's fellows, giving and receiving affection and friendship

Ego needs: needs for enhanced status, a sense of achievement, self-esteem, confidence, and recognition by others

Self-actualization needs: needs for being creative, and realizing one's maximum potential in a variety of life spheres

Obviously, play and recreation can be important elements in satisfying at least the last three, highest levels of need in Maslow's hierarchy. In his writing, Maslow stressed the need for individuals to be more spontaneous and creative and to find fulfillment in a variety of expressive activities—both work and play.[14]

Healthy Balance of Work and Play

For most people, emotional well-being is greatly strengthened if they are able to maintain a healthy balance of work and recreation in their lives. Today, we recognize that there can be *too much* commitment to work, resulting in the exclusion of other interests and personal involvements that help to maintain mental health.

Alexander Reid Martin, a psychiatrist who served for 12 years as chairman of the American Psychiatric Association's Committee on Leisure Time and Its Uses, wrote extensively on the problem of leisure in relation to mental health today. Martin pointed out that the Protestant work ethic and the overemphasis on work values in our society made it extremely difficult for many people to use their leisure in self-fulfilling and satisfying ways. In his professional practice, he found many highly successful people who could justify their lives only through work and material accomplishment and who felt intensely guilty about play and leisure. Often they suffered from what Martin called "weekend neurosis," and it was not uncommon for them to have severe psychological upsets while on vacation.[15]

Workaholism   The tendency to place excessive emphasis on work, at the expense of other avenues of expression, has been popularly termed "workaholism." For some people, work is an obsession and they are unable to find other kinds of pleasurable release. For those who find their work a deep source of personal satisfaction and commitment, this may not be an altogether undesirable phenomenon.

Leading authorities on business management and personnel practices now stress the need for business executives to find outside pleasures that open up, diversify, and enrich their lives. The guilt that successful people too often have about play must be assuaged, and they must be helped to realize that, with a more balanced style of life, they are likely to be more productive in the long run—and much happier in the present.

SOCIAL VALUES OF RECREATION

Another important area in which recreation promotes favorable personal development involves healthy socialization. Many adults today find their primary social contacts and interpersonal relationships not in their work lives, but in voluntary group associations during leisure hours.

Clearly, different types of recreation groups and programs impose a set of social norms, roles, and relationships that participants must learn to accept—and that contribute to their own social development. Even in the relatively free environment of outdoor recreation, where people hike, camp, or explore the wilderness in ways of their own choosing, interaction among participants is a key element in the experience.

For children, play groups offer a realistic training ground for developing both cooperative and competitive skills. Through group participation, children learn to interact with others to accept group rules and wishes, and, when necessary, to subordinate their own views or desires to those of the group. They learn to give and take, to assume leadership or follow the leadership of others, and to work effectively as part of a team.

Sport and Social Development

One form of play that has been widely assumed to have a positive effect on participants is sport. Wilderson and Dodder comment that sport is an institution that reflects the cultural ethos of a society and helps socialize its participants into accepting normative value patterns. Sport has been credited with producing or reinforcing such qualities as

> emotional maturity, moral values, self-reliance, self-sacrifice, effective citizenry, respect for authority, democratic ideals, mental health, academic success, competitive spirit, manliness, and, of course, Godliness.[16]

Similarly, Frey and Massengale point out that the values associated with school sports are those widely accepted in American society. They include striving for excellence, achievement, humility, loyalty, self-control, respect for authority, self-discipline, hard work, and deferred gratification. However, these authors contend that the structure of modern school sports at all levels no longer permits the inculcation of these values:

> Goal displacement has taken place. Building character and enhancing education have been replaced as guiding values by the desire for profit, power, prestige, notoriety, visibility, community support, and organizational survival. Modern school sports . . . profess the goals and values of a participatory or amateur model [but] operate under the structure of commercial enterprise.[17]

Even in the conduct of youth sports in community-based leagues, destructive values based on overemphasis on winning tend to poison the atmosphere. In one recent episode, the father of a young Massachusetts hockey player fatally beat another father over a disagreement at a "pick-up" game:

> Parental outbursts at youth sports are getting more frequent and violent, many coaches and parents say. They attribute it to increased participation in sports, greater pressure to compete aggressively, and parents' unrealistic expectations that their children will win lucrative athletic scholarships.
>
> "In 25 years, we've never seen this many reports, and the kinds of assaults are getting much more violent," said Bob Still, president of the National Association of Sports Officials, in Racine, Wisconsin.[18]

Realistically, the benefits of sports participation depend heavily on the circumstances under which games are played. Truly amateur sports competition may foster positive and unselfish values, while commercialized, high-pressure sports in big-time universities may be responsible for fostering a host of hypocritical and manipulative practices. Such traits as the ability to play by the rules, show good sportsmanship, and win or lose gracefully are often given little support in such institutions.

One of the most frequently expressed justifications of sport as a form of social development is that it provides a medium through which children and youth learn to compete, thus supposedly becoming equipped to survive in a tough, "dog-eat-dog" adult world. Yet there is evidence that our national emphasis on competition and glorification of winning as an all-consuming goal has serious undesirable effects on character. Increasingly, the goal of building competitive fervor through sport is being challenged.

Play and Social Mobility

Recreation is also believed to lead to improved social mobility for children and youth by opening up new horizons of awareness—even to lead directly to career opportunities. Again, sport provides a valuable example. The point has frequently been made that high-school sports too often discourage emphasis on scholarship and divert school resources and student energies from the goal of academic excellence. Outstanding high-school graduating seniors may find it almost impossible to get academic scholarships, while star halfbacks who can barely read or write find dozens of coaches beating at their doors with attractive offers for full scholarships and more.

On the other hand, sociological studies of midwestern high-school boys have shown that, on all social class levels, athletes performed on a higher level academically than nonathletes and that proportionally more athletes than nonathletes were motivated to attend college. Almost five times as many nonathletes as athletes dropped out of high school; in general, participation in student activity programs seems to be closely related to the school's holding power and provides constructive outlets for students' social and psychological needs.

In general, the odds against youthful athletes gaining college scholarships or, beyond that, moving into the professional ranks, are daunting. In the mid-1990s, Thomas writes:

> Of the 400,000 high-school seniors who play football or basketball, only about 20,000 will be signed by the 1,000 colleges affiliated with the National Collegiate Athletic Association. Some 5,000 will play for the 400 colleges in the National Association of Independent Athletics and 3,000 for the 500 members of the National Junior College Athletic Association.
>
> What's more, while virtually all two-year and four-year colleges offer varsity athletics, no more than 300 routinely grant full athletic scholarships. . . .[19]

For those talented athletes who do play on varsity college teams, the odds against making it to the professional sports ranks are proportionately far greater. However, for those who complete their college degrees, athletics may clearly represent an important means of achieving social mobility.

Viewed more broadly, recreation provides an early form of exposure and training ground for *all* sorts of career directions for children and youth. Early experience in arts and crafts may lead to an occupational interest in construction, design, commercial art, carpentry, and similar career possibilities. Children with scientific or mathematical hobbies may gradually sharpen their interests through school and college study and ultimately make science, mathematics, or computer work their lifelong occupation. Similarly, many other forms of recreational involvement help young people to become aware of their own skills and talents and of the careers that these might lead to.

INTELLECTUAL VALUES OF RECREATION

Of all the personal benefits of play and recreation, probably the least widely recognized are those involving intellectual or cognitive development. Play is typically thought of as physical activity rather than mental—and has by definition been considered a nonserious form of involvement. How then could it contribute to intellectual growth?

Researchers have slowly come to realize that physical recreation tends to improve personal motivation and make mental and cognitive performance more effective. Numerous studies, for example, have documented the effects of specific types of physical exercise or play on the development of young children.

Other research studies have shown a strong relationship between physical fitness and academic performance. While a number of these studies have focused on formal instructional programs, others have utilized less structured experimental elements. Several studies have shown that playfulness as a personal quality is closely linked to creative and inventive thinking among children.

Play as a Way of Learning

In the past, play was viewed as a frivolous activity, and children were discouraged from playing in order to devote fuller effort to serious learning activities. Today, we recognize that play does contribute to cognitive growth and, indeed, may provide a uniquely effective way of learning. How does this happen?

The leading psychologist in the field of child development over the past several decades was the late Jean Piaget, professor at the University of Geneva and director of the *Institut Rousseau*. Piaget suggested that there are two basic processes to all mental development—*assimilation* and *accommodation*. Assimilation is the process of taking in, as in the case of receiving information in the form of visual or auditory stimuli. Accommodation is the process of adjusting to external circumstances and stimuli. In Piaget's theory, play is specially related to assimilation, the process of mentally digesting new and different situations and experiences. Anything important that has happened is reproduced in play; it is a means of assimilating and consolidating the child's emotional experiences.

In the late 1990s, the findings of a long-term study of the effectiveness of high-quality early childhood day care demonstrated that children who had been exposed to this program far outperformed others who had not, both on academic and cognitive tests, and were more likely to attend college or hold high-skill jobs. Games were an important element in these experimental day-care programs.[20]

Games also have been used to help children learn simple scientific, mathematical, and linguistic concepts. One firm provides game kits and visual aids that use playlike approaches to teach number relationships and mathematical symbols; puzzle boxes and equation games are just two of these approaches. Other games deal with civics, government, history and political science, banking, international trade, geometry, and physics.

On another level, a reporter for *Forbes* magazine points out that business executives frequently enjoy high-level competitive play in games such as contract bridge, chess, or backgammon, and that they value competence in these pastimes in the people they employ. Investment advisors in particular recognize the risk-taking elements involved in such games and the need for strategic flair in taking calculated risks. Whether the game is poker, gin rummy, bridge, backgammon, or chess, the skills involved are all equally important in business.[21]

Evidence that leisure-time activities are linked to academic performance is found in a 1986 report of the U.S. Department of Education. In a study of 30,000 high-school sophomores and 28,000 seniors, the researchers found that "the more activities students were involved in, the higher they ranked" on such measures as grades and test scores. Only 10 percent of the students who participated in four or more activities—such as varsity athletics, cheerleading, debate or drama, band activities, chorus or dance, hobby clubs, or similar groups—had grade point averages of less than 2.0, as opposed to 30 percent of all students.

SPIRITUAL VALUES OF RECREATION AND LEISURE

A final area in which recreation and leisure make a vital contribution to the healthy growth and well-being of human beings is within the spiritual realm. The term *spiritual* is commonly taken to be synonymous with religion, but here it means a capacity for exhibiting humanity's higher nature—a sense of moral values, compassion, and respect for other humans and for the earth itself. It is linked to the development of one's inner feelings, a sense of order and purpose in life, and a commitment to care for others and to behave responsibly in all aspects of one's existence.

How does recreation contribute in this respect? Pieper and others have suggested that in their leisure hours, humans are able to express their fullest and best selves. Leisure can be a time for contemplation, for consideration of ultimate values, for disinterested activity. This means that people can come together simply as people, sharing interests and exploring pleasure, commitment, personal growth, beauty, nature, and other such aspects of life.

In part, the use of outdoor settings for organized recreation experiences is based on the view of the natural world as "God's great temple," which has often been expressed in literature on the outdoors. Such settings often provide places for wilderness retreats, Bible study, or other religiously oriented programs. The Zen Buddhist view that sees God in every aspect of nature, and in the relationships of human beings with the natural world, underlies this concept. For men and women who accept the challenge of being alone in the natural world, even in perilous circumstances, the experience may often be a highly religious one.

RECREATION AS AN INTEGRATIVE EXPERIENCE: HOLISTIC WELLNESS

Thus far this chapter has examined the important personal values of recreation and leisure involvement from five different perspectives: physical, emotional, social, intellectual, and spiritual. It is essential to recognize that these are *not* distinctly separate components of human development, but are instead closely interrelated from a *holistic* perspective.

Wellness Concept of Health

Traditionally, health has been conceptualized as the absence of disease or, more positively, as the quality of personal physical fitness. Increasingly, however, the modern view of wellness holds that a variety of physical, emotional, social, and other factors underlie health in the fullest sense—and that these varied factors help to support and strengthen each other. McDowell writes that true wellness is a holistic state of being that is closely linked to one's leisure life.[22]

He goes on to say that leisure values, the breadth and depth of one's leisure interests, and the degree to which one uses leisure with purpose and joy are all part of holistic wellness. As indicated earlier, numerous research studies have confirmed that active and satisfying leisure experiences throughout one's life span contribute significantly to emotional and physical well-being and to successful aging. Such findings are reinforced by a growing body of evidence confirming the linkage of emotional, physical, and intellectual well-being. The concept of psychosomatic illness, in which an emotional state affects physical health, has long been accepted by medical authorities.

Within this framework, positive leisure experiences may make an important contribution to wellness through their role in stress management, building positive interpersonal relationships, overcoming loneliness and isolation, providing healthy physical outlets, reinforcing a sense of personal worth and competence, and reducing the overdependence on work that is pervasive in modern life.

Emotional Intelligence

A second illustration of the linkage of qualities that were formerly thought of as distinctly separate aspects of human personality is found in the newly coined term *emotional intelligence*. This concept suggests that the traditional view of intelligence as a purely intellectual quality or as a key factor in academic or professional success is far too narrow. Instead, recent studies of effective performers in high-tech work settings indicate that the most successful team members are not those with the highest IQs, the most impressive academic credentials, or the best scores on achievement tests.

Those who excelled at times of crisis or innovation, Goleman writes, were the individuals who exhibited rapport, empathy, cooperation, persuasion, and the ability to build consensus among co-workers.[23]

The potential of youth-serving agencies for incorporating goals related to developing higher levels of emotional intelligence seems clear. Throughout social activities, club programs, sports, outdoor recreation, and leadership development projects, this approach would appear to be a rewarding new direction for organized leisure-service leadership. That many recreation agencies are already achieving such values is illustrated in a research report by McCormick, White, and McGuire, which documented the effectiveness of summer camp programs for children with mental retardation in such areas as: (1) improving consideration for others; (2) developing ability to work in groups; (3) improving social skills; (4) improving communication skills; (5) developing feelings of success through participation in activities; (6) improving sense of personal worth; and (7) improving decision-making and problem-solving skills.[24]

INFLUENCE OF DEMOGRAPHIC FACTORS: AGE GROUPINGS

The influence of one's age on recreational values and patterns of participation has been analyzed in numerous recreation and leisure-service programming textbooks. Typically, key stages of the life span are identified, together with details of the growth process and developmental tasks to be accomplished at each stage.

Apart from differences of individual personalities within each age bracket, there is also the reality that developments in modern technology, economic and social trends, and shifts in family relationships have been responsible for major changes in age-related norms of human behavior. Our patterns of birth and parenthood have been radically altered by innovative technology in medical practice. We now have the potential for mothers to give birth to their own daughters' babies through the surgical implant of fertilized ova. Similarly, men can now father babies for many years after their own deaths.

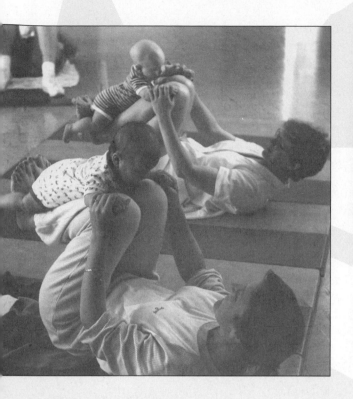

Community recreation serves the full age range, from this "Mommy and Me" mother-and-infant movement class in Long Beach, California, to the tap routine performed by older women at the Community Dance Center at Texas Women's University. Older men and women both exercise vigorously today.

Gail Sheehy lists some of the physical and social changes affecting age groupings over the past few decades:

Nine-year-old girls are developing breasts and pubic hair. Nine-year-old boys are carrying guns to school. Sixteen-year-olds can "divorce" a parent. Thirty-year-old men still live at home with Mom. Forty-year-old women are just getting around to pregnancy. Fifty-year-old men are forced into early retirement.[25]

Today, children are exposed to the realities of life and mature physically at a much earlier point than in the past. At the same time, paradoxically, they have a longer period of adolescence and schooling before entering the adult workforce. Adults now tend to marry later and have fewer children. Older people have a much longer period of retirement, and a significantly greater number of elderly persons live active and adventurous leisure lives today than in the past.

To fully understand the impact of societal trends on public involvement in recreation, park, and leisure-service programs, it is helpful to examine each major age group in turn.

PLAY IN THE LIVES OF CHILDREN

Childhood is the age group that includes children from early infancy through the preteen years. Throughout this period, play satisfies important developmental needs in children—often helping to establish values and behavior patterns that will continue throughout a lifetime. Psychologists have examined the role of play at each stage of life, beginning with infancy and moving through the preschool period, middle and late childhood, and adolescence.

Susanna Millar points out that children typically move through several stages: (1) solitary play, carried on without others nearby; (2) parallel play, in which children play side by side without meaningful interplay; (3) associative play, in which children share a common game or group enterprise but concentrate on their own individual efforts rather than group activity; and (4) cooperative play, beginning at about age three, in which children actually join together in games, informal dramatics, or constructive projects. By the age of six or seven, children tend to be involved in loosely organized play groups, leading to much more tightly structured and organized groups in the so-called gang age between eight and twelve.[26]

The important role of play in child development is illustrated by Lynn Barnett, who summarizes a number of the values and outcomes of constructive forms of leisure activity for children. These include play's demonstrated contribution to cognitive development, including problem solving and creative thinking, based on its flexible or experimental nature, which helps the child's transition from concrete experiences to abstract thought processes.[27]

Typically, we tend to think of childhood as a happy time, picturing it in literature or other forms of entertainment as a period of innocence—marked by a warm nostalgic glow. Television shows of the 1950s, for example, generally idealized the American family in terms of love, support, and security. Within this context, family play was presented as an experience that all could share, one with elements of companionship, humor, and self-discovery. Over the past three decades, however, a number of major changes have taken place that have radically changed the lives of children in terms of their family and neighborhood environments, the community services provided to meet their needs, and the commercial forces that entertain them and shape their personal values and view of the world.

Decline of the Family Structure

A major problem facing the American family involves the steadily growing divorce and separation rate, as well as the spiraling number of out-of-wedlock births and increasing employment of women in both one-parent and two-parent households.

In the mid-1990s, the U.S. Census Bureau confirmed that the percentage of single parents raising children had continued to rise dramatically; 54 percent of all children under age six now lived in families in which the sole parent or both parents worked. As a consequence, the number of "latchkey" children—who are twice as likely to abuse alcohol, tobacco, or marijuana as children with parental supervision—represents an increasing social problem.

If anything, children in affluent homes are likely to be overscheduled, both with family chores and school assignments, and with a host of scheduled classes, clubs, sports, and similar pursuits (see page 123).

In contrast, children in economically disadvantaged households—predominantly in urban ghettos or rural slums—tend to have few resources for constructive play. In the early 1990s, the National Commission on Children reported that there was ample evidence that the poverty rates for children had risen sharply over the past three decades. A Tufts University report showed that the proportion of children living in suburban settings whose family income fell below the poverty line had risen by 76 percent, compared to 56 percent in inner cities and 36 percent in rural areas.

Nevertheless, the problem of inadequate recreational opportunities for the poor remains most severe in America's inner cities. Poor children have fewer toys, games, books, or trips to the zoo or beach; they seldom have access to special classes, vacation day camps—or even well-equipped and staffed playgrounds, recreation centers, or pools in communities where such facilities have been vandalized or dominated by drug dealers or youthful gangs.

At the same time, youngsters in such settings often are subject to pathologies that are made worse by poverty, such as alcoholism, drug abuse, violence, and other negative forces. Lacking the ability to provide for safe, supervised play after school or during vacation periods, many working parents in inner-city slums must choose between the enforced boredom of locking children in their apartments during free hours or days or "street roulette"—the sometimes fatal dangers of outside play.

Lack of Settings for Play

The lack of adequate, safe public settings for play was made evident in a number of studies during the 1990s that showed that many municipal playgrounds were unsafe—either poorly supervised or with dangerous equipment and surfacing. While wealthier families were able to send their children to private play ventures like Gymboree or Discovery Zone, poorer families did not have this choice.

Some critics point out that the attitudes of Americans toward children's play can be seen in the changing face of public playgrounds. In a safety-conscious and litigation-minded society, they write, many cities have removed the jungle gyms, swings, and other climbing structures that provided meaningful challenge to youngsters and have substituted a dull and "dumbed-down," heavily rubber-matted environment lacking in real creative play potential.

At the same time, in a climate that demands unrelenting emphasis on teaching basic academic skills and preparing children in the lowest grades for statewide testing, many schools are cutting back on unstructured schoolyard play and eliminating recess:

> Play has long been a schoolyard staple, a pageant of play replete with drama and intrigue, tears and reconciliation. But today, it's disappearing for America's kids. More than 40 percent of school districts across the country, including those in Atlanta and Chicago, have done away with recess or are considering it.[28]

Influence of Commercial Media: Violence and Sex

A third important influence on the lives of children today stems from the overwhelming barrage of violence and sex-laden stimuli contained in the movies, television shows, video games, and music that saturate their environment.

In the early 1980s, Marie Winn documented what she termed "the loss of childhood" of America's children, based on hundreds of interviews with children in the upper elementary grades. She comments that within an amazingly short span of time, society's most fundamental attitudes toward children have been transformed. Where parents once felt obliged to shelter their children from life's vicissitudes, she writes, today many parents believe that children must be exposed early to adult experiences and life's realities in order to survive in an increasingly uncontrollable world. She continues:

> The Age of Protection has ended. An Age of Preparation has set in. And children have suffered a loss. As they are integrated at a young age in the adult world, in every way their lives have become more difficult, more confusing—in short, more like adult lives.[29]

Outside the confines of a stable family structure with good parental supervision, children are surrounded by a permissive, highly charged sexual atmosphere in terms of readily available pornographic literature and X-rated cable television movies. Younger and younger children are able to acquire alcohol, marijuana, or other drugs. Their sense of humanity is undermined by increasingly realistic video games that feature sex and gore, vampires and demons—or contain such scenes as ripping out an opponent's heart in *Mortal Kombat* or drilling holes in scantily clad teenage girls in *Night Trap*.

Physical Fitness of Youth

The physical fitness of children has steadily deteriorated largely because of their heavy dependence on mass media for entertainment and reliance on physically passive forms of play. A 1993 report by the American Alliance for Health, Physical Education, and Recreation sums up statistics showing that today's students are less fit—and more overweight—than children in previous generations. Similarly, findings of the National Center for Health Statistics showed in 1995 that the proportion of American children who are overweight has more than doubled over the last three decades. Such reports confirm that a critical task facing both the educational and leisure-services systems of the United States in the years ahead is to encourage and provide more opportunities for active play of all kinds for children and youth.

Within this framework, the role of organized recreation agencies and programs would appear to be clear. The role must be to provide healthy and constructive forms of leisure involvement for children that will act as positive forces to counter the destructive aspects of today's culture. From a physical, emotional, and social perspective, it will be essential for recreation programs to involve greater numbers of children and youth, particularly those from broken families or in poverty-ridden settings who suffer from the highest degree of risk in terms of the likelihood of their reaching adulthood safely and enjoying a happy and fulfilling life.

An Optimistic Picture

Despite the negative trends that have just been presented, it is encouraging to know that American children, by and large, are far more optimistic about the world and their place in it, than one might have expected. A national survey in 1999 of 1,740 youngsters, ages 6 to 14, in 25 cities found the following:

> . . . [K]ids are very happy to be kids, and they don't view the world as the nasty place their parents perceive it to be. Nine out of 10 say they feel safe in their schools and neighborhoods. While parents list crime, violence, and guns as the worst aspects of being a child today, such concerns are way down the list for kids. Their gripes are the timeless laments of childhood: "getting bossed around," homework, chores.[30]

However, the study also found that most children were "in no rush to grow up" and were not in a hurry to become teenagers.

RECREATION IN THE LIVES OF ADOLESCENTS

The teenage population, which began to climb in the early 1990s following years of decline, is expected to keep growing until 2019, according to U.S. Census Bureau projections. By then, there will be 30 million Americans between ages 13 and 19, up from 24.6 million in 1990.

Psychologists who have done extensive research into the lives of adolescents document a significant relationship between their recreational habits and their emotional and social development. Beth Kivel writes that in the past researchers have tended to focus on cognitive, emotional, social, and biological aspects of adolescent development and identity formation. She writes:

> Recently, however, researchers from all disciplines—psychology, social psychology, sociology—have broadened their focus to include the central contexts that contribute to a young person's identity—school, family, work, peers, and, more recently, leisure.[31]

Early studies found that the self-image of teenagers was closely related to their involvement in school activities. High-school students with a high degree of self-esteem tended to take part in team sports, musical groups, publications, outdoor recreation, and social activities. Those with a low degree of self-esteem were much less involved.

In studies of high-school subcultures, researchers have identified three distinct groups of adolescents: (1) the "fun" subculture, similar to the collegiate world of football, fraternities, sororities, dates, cars, and drinking; (2) the "academic" subculture of serious students who work hard, get the best grades, and are career-oriented; and (3) the "delinquent" subculture, which rebels against the whole school enterprise and is associated with "negativism, hedonism and violence."

One study, by Kleiber, Larson, and Csikszentmihalyi, examines the ways in which high-school students use their time for "productive" (school and work-oriented), "maintenance" (related to personal care and daily living needs) and "leisure" (socializing, sports, television, and similar activities) involvement. They focused on leisure activities that combined the fun element with the need for exertion and effort, which they referred to as transitional activities. Commenting that many adolescents tend to be bored and disinterested in purposeful and productive activities and have not learned to find enjoyment in the demands and challenges placed on them by the adult world, they concluded that transitional activities appeared to offer a bridge between free and structured kinds of experiences.[32]

Trends in Adolescent Leisure Pursuits

Linda Caldwell points out that a national study of over 46,000 sixth through twelfth grade students identified both positive influences in adolescents' lives and countervailing influences, which included

> . . . such things as being alone at home, hedonistic values, television overexposure, drinking parties, physical and sexual abuse, and social isolation. In each grade . . . the *majority* of students report at least two out of ten countervailing influences.[33]

aldwell summarizes research findings showing that high-risk behavior that potentially limits the future psychological, physical, or economic well-being of students is prevalent. Twenty at-risk indicators, including frequent alcohol use or "binge" drinking, tobacco use, illegal drug use, sexual involvement, depression/suicide, or other forms of antisocial or deviant behavior, were examined.

In 1992, the Surgeon General of the United States emphasized the link between youthful drinking and teen suicides, drowning and vehicle deaths, the commission of serious crimes including rape, and other youth problems. A 1995 study by the Parents Resource Institute for Drug Education showed a significant increase in the use of marijuana, cocaine, LSD, inhalants and other illicit substances among eighth graders and a similar rise in the drinking of beer and wine coolers by children in the sixth to eighth grades.

Teenage gambling has been growing steadily since the legalization of casino gambling, state lotteries, riverboat games, and similar forms of play over the past two decades. Pam Belluck writes:

> Teenagers are gambling everywhere: in schools, on ball fields, at racetracks, in casinos . . . [one California authority] estimates that there are seven million teenagers—one in four nationwide—gambling today and that more than one million of them are at risk of becoming compulsive gamblers.[34]

In 1993, the International Planned Parenthood Federation reported that the United States had the highest rate of teen pregnancies among western developed nations, with a total of more than 600,000 unintended pregnancies a year. Other reports show that the percentage of sexually active teenage girls who have several partners has risen sharply, with a growing number of girls under the age of 14 reporting sexual involvement. Many children as young as 10 or 11 today are involved in mutual masturbation, oral sex, and similar activities as precursors to intercourse.[35]

On a more positive note, however, 1999 reports by the U.S. Department of Health and Human Services and the National Center for Health Statistics indicated that the nation's teenage birth rate had fallen to near-record lows and that there was a clear decline in illicit drug use by young people in the late 1990s.[36]

Influence of Mass Media   As was the case with younger children, there is widespread concern about the influence of movies, television, mass media, and music on the values and behavior of teenagers. First, there is the conviction that excessive television watching may have serious outcomes. The thousands of hours that children and youth spend in passive contemplation of the screen during their formative years are hours "stolen" from the time needed to learn to relate to others and gain usable and enjoyable skills of active participation. It is believed that intensive exposure to television stifles creative imagination and encourages a passive outlook toward life.

Beyond this, there is mounting evidence that television actually encourages violent and criminal youth behavior. As early as 1969, the National Commission on the

Causes and Prevention of Violence concluded that violence on television had to be reduced because it encouraged imitation and strengthened "a distorted, pathological view of society." Studies have repeatedly documented lowered inhibitions of aggressive behavior after exposure to violence on television, and there have been numerous examples of crimes committed shortly after similar crimes were shown on television.

Boredom and the Need for Excitement   Since the last decades of the nineteenth century, the perceived need to provide positive recreation programs and facilities for children and youth has been based on the belief that constructive free-time alternatives not only keep youngsters off the street, but also help prevent the kinds of delinquent play that otherwise might result from boredom. Again and again, adolescents apprehended for criminal activity use the excuse that they were bored, that there was nothing else to do, or that their delinquent actions were a form of fun. Often, however, such forms of thrill-seeking play end in tragic episodes of violence, clashes between different ethnic groups, drug- and alcohol-fueled accidents, or other self-destructive experiences.

Challenges Facing the "Fast Forward" Generation

Even without such factors, there is the reality that adolescents of today are growing up in a turbulent, unpredictable, and often insecure world. Examining a high-school senior class in 1993, Tanya Barrientos wrote:

> . . . [T]here is a new generation inside this and all high schools across the nation. It's the Fast Forward generation. Raised on CNN, DOS and MTV. Schooled in limits by recession, AIDS, and ozone holes. Hardened to parents' divorces. Impatient with unfulfilled ideals. A generation both enraged about the mess its elders have made and pragmatically determined to deal with it. These are the babies of the Boomers, a new set of rebels with no cause but survival.[37]

Barrientos describes the lives of the new generation of teenagers who have learned to live with "mix-and-match" families, a bewildering array of stepfathers and stepmothers, half-brothers and step-sisters, and single parents' live-in lovers.

At the same time, a report by the Carnegie Council on Adolescent Development suggests that the period between the ages of 10 and 14 is the least understood and "most neglected phase of the life span from conception to senescence." Young teens' mental and physical growth is accelerated, with puberty coming two years earlier than it did a century ago. It is argued by feminists that, because schools and society favor boys, adolescent girls seriously suffer from a lack of self-esteem. It has been documented that adolescent girls can be vulnerable to depression, eating disorders, and other addictions. Yet boys make up 85 percent of special-education students with such diagnoses as learning disabled or behavior disordered. They get lower grades and more punishment, commit suicide at a higher rate, and get into far more problems of delinquency than do girls.

Given such problems, it is ironic that more than half of all adolescents will spend at least part of their lives in a single-parent family and that the total time that American children spend with their parents has decreased by at least one-third over the past 30 years. The Carnegie Council report concludes that the United States is neglecting its adolescent population.

Positive Teenage Trends

At the same time that national concern is focused about many of the difficulties facing adolescents today, there is evidence that many hold conservative views and have traditional lifestyles. A nationwide poll reported in 1998 by the *New York Times* and *CBS News* found that teenagers today are worldly, shaped by exposure to a culture that has dropped many of its inhibitions. However, Goodstein and Connelly write:

> . . . [I]n some ways they are as wholesome and devoid of cynicism as the generation that wore saddle shoes. They trust their government, admire their parents, and believe it is possible to start out poor and become rich. Ninety-four percent say they believe in God. Strong majorities say they never drink alcohol and never smoke cigarettes or marijuana.[38]

ADULT LEISURE NEEDS AND INVOLVEMENTS

The adult population in modern society, defined as those in their late teens to their early or mid-60s, may logically be subdivided into several age brackets or lifestyle patterns. These include, among others, young single adults (those who attend college and those who do not), those who remain single throughout their lives, adults who marry and raise families, adults in their middle years, and elderly adults.

Continuity in Leisure Interests

A number of research studies have examined the relationship between recreational interests developed during childhood or adolescence and those enjoyed during later adult life. Scott and Willits, for example, in a longitudinal study, gathered data from 1,298 subjects during their high-school years and compared it to information taken from the same group in their early fifties. They found that, despite the 37-year time interval, there was a significant degree of continuity in the recreational pursuits of those studied.

Refuting the assumption that participation in active forms of play declines through the years of adulthood, Rodney Warnick summarizes research statistics showing that both 25-to-34-year-olds and 35-to-44-year-olds maintained higher rates of participation in a variety of outdoor recreational pursuits than did younger adults aged 18 to 24. He writes:

> [P]articipation rates were higher for 24- to 34-year-olds than for 18- to 24-year-olds in such activities as bicycling, swimming, fresh water fishing, salt water fishing, hiking, cross-country skiing, health club membership . . . This trend carried over to the . . . middle-aged adult segment in activities such as salt water fishing, health club membership, and travel. . . .[39]

Young Single Adults

This population, extending from late teens to early or mid-thirties, has expanded over the past two decades. In the mid-1970s, *Newsweek* commented that there were 48 million single adults over the age of 21 in the United States. In the past, the term "single" usually meant a lonely person, a "loser" whose solitary status was a temporary sidetrack on the way to happy matrimony. But, in the decade of the "Me Generation," with its emphasis on narcissistic pleasure and self-fulfillment, singlehood came to be regarded as a happy ending in itself—or at least an enjoyable prolonged phase of postadolescence.

The findings of a 1980 Study of American Families, an 18-year intergenerational study of several hundred American families, showed that both young people and their parents had begun to see the single life as a legitimate alternative to marriage. When this trend became obvious, a vast number of singles-only institutions sprang up to meet the needs of this newly recognized population with an estimated $40 billion of annual spending power. Singles apartment complexes, bars, weekends at resort hotels, "ex-married" clubs, rap groups at local churches, cruises, and a variety of other leisure programs or services emerged—including computer dating services and other techniques for helping singles to find each other.

Young Adults Attending College

As a subgroup of the young adult population, college students are usually strongly influenced in their choice of leisure activities by their status as students. Students living at home are likely to have relatively little free time, often holding jobs and traveling back and forth to school, and they often find much of their recreation with friends in their neighborhoods. Students living on college campuses generally take part in social or religious clubs, athletic events, fraternity or sorority parties, college union programs, entertainment, or cultural activities.

Many young college students regard their first experience in living away from home for a sustained period of time as an opportunity to engage in hedonistic forms of play without parental supervision. In part, this appears to be a response to the stress that challenges many first-year college students. A January 2000 national survey reported by researchers at the University of California at Los Angeles revealed that both male and female beginning students suffered from higher levels of anxiety than in past generations—with almost twice as many women as men reporting severe levels of stress.[40]

Despite efforts at education and discipline, the College Alcohol Study by the Harvard School of Public Health found that binge drinking in American colleges continued at a high level in the late 1990s, with about two out of every five students currently involved in drinking to excess.

Despite the serious problems attached to alcohol and drug abuse, the majority of young adults are able to use their leisure time in positive and constructive ways. Particularly for those who have finished school and are financially independent, travel, participation in sports or fitness clubs, social clubs or forms of popular entertainment, and involvement in hobbies and creative activities enrich the lives of young single persons—both in colleges and in community settings.

Married Adults and Family Recreation

While millions of men and women have joined the trend toward a continuing single lifestyle, a majority of young American and Canadian adults today accept marriage and family life as a preferred option. Leisure behavior is markedly affected when people marry and have children. Social activities tend to center around the neighborhood in which the couple lives, and the home itself becomes a recreation center for parent and child activities. The family takes part in social programs sponsored by religious agencies, civic and neighborhood associations, or PTAs. As children move into organized community programs, parents begin to use their leisure time for volunteer service as adult leaders for Scout groups, teachers in cooperative nursery schools, Little League coaches and managers, or in similar positions.

Research by Orthner and Mancini confirms the value of shared recreation involvement in contributing to family satisfaction, interaction, and stability.[41] Other studies by Madrigal, Havitz, and Howard illustrate the importance of specific recreational experiences (i.e., family vacations) in enhancing marital relationships, although vacation-taking styles may vary considerably according to whether marriages are traditional or contemporary in terms of the roles of the male and female partners.[42]

Leisure Limitations   The group in this age bracket that is most deprived of leisure consists of single parents who often must work, raise a family under difficult economic and emotional circumstances, and still try at the same time to find needed social outlets and recreational opportunities for themselves. A limited number of municipal and school recreation agencies provide day-care or after-school programs to assist such single parents; in addition, some commercial and voluntary recreation agencies sponsor baby-sitting services in order to permit mothers of young children to take part in their programs during the day.

Middle Adult Years

This age group, which includes individuals ranging from the mid-thirties through the fifties, consists heavily of so-called *baby boomers*—people born during the population surge after World War II or, more particularly, from 1946 to 1964. Paul Light comments that the baby boomers were remarkably homogeneous in terms of the widely accepted social values prevailing in their early childhoods. However, in the following turbulent period of social change, the members of this young generation shifted abruptly from the values of their parents and grandparents. Light writes:

> They may love their parents, but when it comes time to talk about politics, marriage, drugs, or sex, the baby boomers respectfully disagree. From questions on the government's role in creating jobs, religion in the schools, war and peace, political trust, and race, to questions on AIDS, homosexuality, drugs, pornography, and women's rights, the baby boomers maintain their distance from their parents and grandparents.[43]

Studies show that baby boomers have immense diversity in their lifestyles as well. Some are devoted to their families; others remain unattached. Some "boomers" are sports-minded or wilderness-oriented, while others are committed to the arts, hobbies, or literary pursuits. Growing numbers of this age group have begun to place a high value on the creative satisfaction found in work or devote a fuller portion of their time to family and personal involvements.

Effect of Family Changes For parents in the middle adult years, patterns of leisure involvement begin to change as children become more independent. Many nonworking mothers, in particular, who have devoted much time and energy to the family's needs, begin to find these demands less pressing. They have more available time, as well as a need to find a different meaning and fulfillment in life through new interests and challenges.

Middle Age as the Prime of Life In 1999, a portrait of the midlife years based on a 10-year study of nearly 8,000 Americans conducted by the MacArthur Foundation concluded that:

> Far from being a time of turmoil, for most people the midlife years appear to be a time of psychic equanimity, good health, productive activity, and community involvement. . . . Between ages 35 and 65, and in particular between 40 and 60, people report increased feelings of well-being and a greater sense of control over many parts of their lives [with] just a third [describing the period] as a time of personal turmoil brought about by the realization that they were aging.[44]

Strikingly, in the late 1990s, the American Association of Retired Persons reported that most baby boomers in the midlife years were optimistic about retirement and were planning for it financially. However, 80 percent of individuals surveyed by the American Association of Retired Persons (AARP) have indicated that they plan to keep working in some capacity well after the traditional retirement age of their parents.

Gail Sheehy, in her 1995 book, *New Passages: Mapping Your Life Across Time*, suggests that middle age has been extended to a much later point in the life span, and that Americans can now look forward to what she calls the "Flourishing Forties," the "Flaming Fifties," and the "Age of Integrity" in their sixties.

Numerous research studies have documented the importance of recreation and leisure during the middle and later years of life. Valeria Freysinger found that leisure had various connotations; it provides: (1) an agent for change and an opportunity for exerting personal choice and freedom; (2) an opportunity for relaxation, enjoyment, and rejuvenation; (3) a means of affiliation and interaction with others; (4) an area for self-expression and gaining feelings of mastery and accomplishment; and (5) a time for maintenance of friendships and affirming family values.[45]

RECREATION AND THE ELDERLY

In a 1998 report, the United Nations Population Fund concluded that, while overall population growth has been steadily declining, there will be an unprecedented increase in older persons—from 10 percent of the population at century's end to 31 percent in 2150.

In recent years, our view of the aging process has changed dramatically. We used to think of the aging process as "an inexorable slide into illness, impotence and immobility." It was recognized that the extended family—in which older people once lived with their children and grandchildren, maintaining significant relationships—had all but disappeared. More and more communities have developed in which there are few older persons, just as there are many sections of older cities in which there are large numbers of the elderly—often living alone in residential hotels, in SROs (single-room-occupancy units), or in institutions for aging persons.

It is now popular to assert that elderly persons are far more active, vigorous, economically secure, and happy than we had assumed in the past. With improved financial support and pension plans, a much higher percentage of older persons are relatively well-to-do and able to enjoy a far longer period of retirement. Research has shown that many elderly individuals continue to enjoy sexual relations and to maintain active and creative lives well into their seventies and eighties.

Many older persons do tend to withdraw from meaningful contact and involvement with others. One group of sociologists explained this phenomenon by a theory of disengagement, viewing withdrawal from social interaction as a normal process of aging. The "disengagement" theorists held that gradual withdrawal from meaningful human contacts and involvement was a necessary and inevitable process preceding death, which the aging chose for themselves, and which others should accept. This theory has generally been rejected, and most authorities today believe that older people do not withdraw by choice but because of a feeling of exclusion.

Recreation and leisure assume a high priority in the lives of most elderly persons, particularly for those in their late sixties and beyond who have retired from full-time jobs. Without work to fill their time and often with the loss of husbands, wives, or friends, such persons find it necessary to develop new interests and often to establish new relationships. Loneliness can be devastating to the aging. One study showed, for example, that the mortality rate rose dramatically for older men who had been widowed.

The lives of elderly persons have changed dramatically over the past three or four decades. Not only can they expect to live much longer, but their living circumstances are likely to be radically different from those of past generations in terms of familial roles, social activities, economic factors, and other important conditions.

Changes in Family Structure   In the past, it was common for several generations of family members to live together. Older persons continued not only to receive the affection and support of their children and grandchildren, but also to play meaningful roles in family life. With the shift toward living in urban and suburban apartments and small one-family homes, increasing numbers of elderly persons must now live separately; often they become isolated, ill, and unable to care for themselves—and wind up prematurely in long-term care facilities.

A second shift in the family structure is found in the growing number of cases where elderly grandparents are forced to take responsibility for young children because their own children—the parents—are alcoholic, drug dependent, or otherwise unable to maintain a stable household.

Positive Changes for Elderly Persons

Even though these negative trends must be acknowledged, the reality still is that most older persons are living longer, happier, and healthier lives than in the past.

Indeed, there is striking new evidence that the very old are enjoying remarkably good health in comparison to other age groups. The average annual Medicare bill for people who live to be quite elderly—that is, into their late eighties and nineties—is significantly lower than that for those who die sooner. Part of the reason is that very elderly persons tend to be relatively robust. Cancer and heart disease, the two chief killers for retired persons in the younger age brackets, tend not to affect the very old, and Alzheimer's disease also attacks slightly younger men and women.

Today, there are more and more *centenarians*—people who have made it to their 100th birthday—an estimated 30,000 to 50,000, according to demographers, and a sharp increase from the 1980 estimate of 15,000.

There is growing evidence that aging need not be accompanied by mental deterioration. Although some losses in memory or other aspects of mental performance do commonly occur, studies have shown that from 20 percent to 30 percent of people in their eighties who volunteer for cognitive testing perform as well as volunteers in their thirties and forties, who are presumably at the peak of mental performance.

Scientists have recently discovered that the adult brain can generate new cells even well into old age and that the network of connections among brain cells can strengthen over time. They conclude that intellectually challenging work boosts cognitive skills in older adults even more than in younger people:

> Not only can most healthy people function well mentally until the end of life, says the director of George Washington University's Center on Aging, Health and Humanities, but "they can do even better by staying mentally, physically, and socially active."[46]

With improved medical care, people are not just living longer, healthier lives, but they are living them differently. Particularly in the so-called retirement states of New Mexico, Arizona, Nevada, and Florida, with fast-growing populations of elderly men and women, they are engaging in active sports, volunteering, going back to school, and developing new networks of friends and relationships.

Surprisingly, however, recent census reports indicate that only a small fraction of older persons—about one in 10—move at all when they retire. Of that number, about half remain in their home states. In many cases, as younger adults leave farming areas in search of jobs and cultural opportunities elsewhere, elderly men and women remain in rural districts of Nebraska, Iowa, Kansas, and the Dakotas and strive to maintain vital communities in these settings.[47]

Specific Contributions of Recreation and Leisure

Research confirms that recreational involvement meets a number of important physical, emotional, and social needs of elderly persons. Numerous studies have shown that regular physical exercise has immense health-related value for older persons within a range of specific benefits that include preventing heart disease, stroke, cancer, osteoporosis, and diabetes; assisting in weight reduction; improving immunity against common infections; reducing arthritic symptoms; countering depression; and even helping to improve memory and the quality of the older individual's sleep.

In terms of social benefits, one of the key problems affecting the elderly is that they tend to become isolated and lose a sense of playing a significant role in family life or in the community at large. One of the most useful leisure activities for the elderly therefore involves community service and volunteerism. In fact, volunteerism is frequently conceptualized as a satisfactory substitute for paid work for older persons.

Elderly persons gain an important sense of recognition and self-worth through volunteerism. It provides a structure in their lives in terms of regular time commitments and offers social contacts that often lead to friendship and other group involvement.

Another important leisure pursuit for the elderly consists of continuing education—either on a fairly casual basis with classes or workshops in nearby after-school or community center programs or on a more formal basis in noncredit courses taken through Elderhostel or other college-sponsored programs. Robert Hopp writes:

> The hundreds of thousands of "Elderhostel alumni" reflect a positive, motivated, participatory attitude that directly refutes North America's attitude of "used-up elders." Elderhostel is an inexpensive, uncomplicated, and highly accessible experience, promising interaction with peers and interesting travel opportunities. The programs [involving varied cultural, historical, and creative subjects] are usually affiliated with universities, relying on them for residence hall and cafeteria space, as well as instructors, for some of their classes.[48]

Linked to such involvements, a growing number of older persons are traveling the "information superhighway," learning computer skills and exploring the Internet. Still others break new ground by entering a new period of creative development in the arts, writing, social service, or hitherto unknown kinds of personal involvement. Much of today's increased life expectancy has been added, it seems, not to the *end* but to the *middle* of our lives—extending the opportunity for "late bloomers" to realize their dreams.

Many leisure activities of older persons are relatively simple close-to-home pursuits, such as reading for pleasure, talking on the telephone, gardening or raising plants, watching television, socializing with friends and family, and carrying on individual hobbies. Other activities may be more active and demanding, such as sports, outdoor recreation, fitness classes, and dancing. These may be enjoyed with people of all ages or in special senior citizens groups, golden age clubs, or retirement communities.

SUMMARY

Beyond the familiar motivations of seeking fun, pleasure, or relaxation, people engage in leisure pursuits for a host of different reasons. Recreational motivations include personal goals such as the need for companionship, escape from stress or the boredom of daily routine, and the search for challenge, a sense of personal accomplishment, physical fitness, or emotional release. In addition to being based on widely shared motivations, leisure involvement is also influenced by the age, gender, race, or other characteristics of participants, as well as by the unique nature of the play activities themselves.

The outcomes of recreational involvement may be classified under five major headings: physical, emotional, social, intellectual, and spiritual. This chapter summarizes the findings of a number of formal research studies that document the values of recreational experience and cite evidence derived from anecdotal accounts of the personal outcomes of recreation. While the outcomes are separately described, the text stresses that each type of outcome is closely integrated with the others as part of a holistic view of personality.

Age and family status represent key factors that affect the recreational needs and interests of individuals throughout life. Human development experts have outlined a sequence of age groupings extending from infancy through old age, and recreational authorities have developed guidelines for program planning for each group based on the developmental characteristics at each stage.

Today, changes in family life and social environment have altered traditional models of development with significant implications for recreation programmers. The chapter points out that children today grow up much earlier and are subjected to influences that they would have been shielded from in the past. Youth in affluent families often have lavish recreational goods and abundant opportunities for structured play, while children in poverty settings frequently lack recreation facilities or programs. This pattern continues into adolescence, which is marked today by higher rates of teenage drinking and drug abuse, irresponsible sexual activity, and varied forms of delinquency or antisocial play.

The chapter also discusses adult life, pointing out that while a higher percentage of individuals remain or become single than in the past, the majority tend to marry and raise families, with much of their recreation centering around the home and family unit. For the middle-aged and elderly, who represent a steadily increasing proportion of the population, many of the negative stereotypes of the past no longer apply. People today live longer and tend to be more independent and active in the varied forms of recreation that promote their overall well-being and life satisfaction.

QUESTIONS FOR CLASS DISCUSSION OR ESSAY EXAMINATIONS

1. The physical benefits of exercise have been well documented. Vigorous use of exercise machines and treadmills, running, swimming, and bicycling all contribute greatly to cardiovascular health. Why is it desirable to approach such activities as recreation rather than as prescribed exercise carried on for fitness purposes alone? In addition to cardiovascular benefits, what other important health outcomes have been identified?

2. The chapter describes some of the specific contributions of recreation to emotional or mental health. What are they? On the basis of your own experience, can you describe some of the positive emotional outcomes resulting from recreational involvement?

3. We generally regard sports as a valuable means of achieving positive personal development, including encouraging elements of socialization and promoting self-discipline, team loyalty, acceptance of rules, and good sportsmanship. How valid are these expectations? What are some of the less desirable aspects of sport that have been discussed in recent years?

4. Select one of the following age groups: children, teens, or adults. What are their special needs for recreation in modern society, and what barriers or problems do they

face in the appropriate choice of satisfying leisure activity? If you wish, you may deal with a subgroup of the overall category, such as "young single adults."

5. The elderly make up a rapidly growing segment of the American and Canadian populations. How have we traditionally thought of the aging process and of the role of older persons in community life? What new views have developed in recent years? What are the implications of these changes for recreation practitioners working with elderly persons?

ENDNOTES

1 Pam Belluck, "Parents Try to Reclaim Their Children's Time," *New York Times* (13 June 2000): A-18.

2 Rick Crandall, "Motivations for Leisure," *Journal of Leisure Research* (Vol. 12, No. 1, 1980): 45–54.

3 John Kelly, "Leisure Styles and Choices in Three Environments," *Pacific Sociological Review* (Vol. 21, 1978): 178–208.

4 P. Bolla, D. Dawson, and M. Harrington, "Women and Leisure: A Study of Meanings, Experiences, and Constraints," *Recreation Canada* (Vol. 51, No. 3, 1993): 223–226.

5 P. Clough, J. Shepherd, and R. Maughan, "Motives for Participation in Recreational Running," *Journal of Leisure Research* (Vol. 21, No. 4, 1989): 305.

6 Simon Priest et al., "Functions of Privacy in Canadian Wilderness," *Journal of Applied Recreation Research* (Vol. 17, No. 2, 1992): 234–254.

7 D. Williams, R. Schreyer, and R. Knopf, "The Effect of the Experience Use History on the Multidimensional Structure of Motivations to Participate in Leisure Activities," *Journal of Leisure Research* (Vol. 22, No. 1, 1990): 36–54.

8 Daniel Haney, "Overweight Teens, Poor Health Linked," *Associated Press* (5 November 1992).

9 L. Summerfield and L. Priest, "Using Play as Motivation for Exercise," *Journal of Physical Education, Recreation, and Dance—Leisure Today* (October 1987): 24.

10 Leonard Wankel, "Personal and Situational Factors Affecting Exercise Involvement: The Importance of Enjoyment," *Research Quarterly for Exercise and Sport* (3rd Quarter 1985): 275–282.

11 S. E. Iso-Ahola and E. Weissinger, "Leisure and Well-Being: Is There a Connection?" *Parks and Recreation* (June 1984): 40–44.

12 M. Chubb and H. Chubb, *One Third of Our Time: An Introduction to Recreation Behavior and Resources* (New York: John Wiley and Sons, 1981): 51.

13 Natalie Angier, "The Anatomy of Joy," *New York Times Good Health Magazine* (26 April 1992): 50.

14 Abraham Maslow, "A Theory of Psychological Motivation," *Psychological Review* (July 1943): 370–396.

15 Alexander Reid Martin, "Leisure and Our Inner Resources," *Parks and Recreation* (March 1975): 10-a.

16 M. Wilderson and R. Dodder, "What Does Sport Do for People?" *Journal of Physical Education, Recreation, and Dance* (February 1979): 50–51.

17 J. Frey and J. Massengale, "American School Sports Enhancing Social Values Through Restructuring," *Journal of Physical Education, Recreation, and Dance* (August 1988): 40.

18 K. Boccella and S. Bengali, "In Youth Sports, Parental Outbursts Turning Violent," *Philadelphia Inquirer* (16 July 2000): A-1.

19 R. Thomas Jr., "You Want to Play, Not Pay? Listen Up," *New York Times Education Life* (8 January 1995): 23.

20 Jodi Wilgoren, "Quality Day Care, Early, Is Tied to Achievements as an Adult," *New York Times* (22 October 1999): A-16.

21 N. R. Kleinfield, "Executive Fun and Games," *New York Times Business World* (8 June 1986): 1.

22 C. F. McDowell, "Leisure Integrating a Wellness Consciousness," in B. Riley, J. Shank, and S. Nichols, eds., *Therapeutic Recreation: A Holistic Approach* (Durham, N.H.: New England Therapeutic Recreation Consortium, 1987): 22.

23 Daniel Goleman, "Decline of the Nice-Guy Quotient," *New York Times* (10 September 1995): 6-E.

24 B. McCormick, C. White, and F. McGuire, "Parents' Perceptions of Summer Camp for Campers with Mental Retardation," *Therapeutic Recreation Journal* (Third Quarter 1992): 27–37.

25 G. Sheehy, "Am I an Adult Yet?" *Utne Reader* (May–June 1996): 62.

26 S. Millar, *The Psychology of Play* (Baltimore, Md.: Penguin, 1968): 178–184.

27 Lynn Barnett, Developmental Benefits of Play for Children," *Journal of Leisure Research* (Vol. 22, No. 2, 1990): 138–153.

28 Anna Mulriner, "What's Your Favorite Class?" *U.S. News and World Report* (1 May 2000): 50.

29 Marie Winn, "The Loss of Childhood," *New York Times Magazine* (8 May 1983): 18.

30 Claudia Wallis, "The Kids Are Alright," *Time* (5 July 1999): 56.

31 Beth Kivel, "Adolescent Identity Formation and Leisure Contexts : "A Selective Review of Literature," *Journal of Physical Education, Recreation, and Dance* (January 1998): 36.

32 D. Kleiber, R. Larson, and M. Csikszentmihalyi, "The Experience of Leisure in Adolescence," *Journal of Leisure Research* (Vol. 18, No. 3, 1986): 175.

33 Linda Caldwell, "Research Update: On Adolescents and Leisure Activities," *Parks and Recreation* (March 1983): 19.

34 Pam Belluck, "Starting Too Young, Getting In Too Deep," *Philadelphia Inquirer* (16 August 1992): A-1.

35 Anne Jarrell, "The Face of Teenage Sex Grows Younger," *New York Times* (2 April 2000): ST-1.

36 Marc Lacey, "Teenage Birthrate in U.S. Falls Again," *New York Times* (27 October 1999): A-16.

37 Tanya Barrientos, " '93 Class Looks Anxiously Ahead: The Fast Forward Generation," *Philadelphia Inquirer* (21 March 1993): A-1.

38 L. Goodstein and M. Connelly, "Teenage Poll Finds a Turn to the Traditional," *New York Times* (30 April 1998): A-20.

39 Rodney Warnick, "Recreation and Leisure Participation Patterns Among the Adult Middle-Age Market from 1975 to 1984," *Journal of Physical Education, Recreation, and Dance* (October 1987): 49.

40 Jodi Wilgoren, "Freshman Year as Stress Test," *New York Times* (30 January 2000): WK-2.

41 D. Orthner and J. Mancini, "Leisure Impacts on Family Interaction and Cohesion," *Journal of Leisure Research* (Vol. 22, No. 2, 1990): 125–137.

42 R. Madrigal, M. Havitz, and D. Howard, "Married Couples' Involvement with Family Vacations," *Leisure Sciences* (Vol. 14, 1992): 287–301.

43 Paul Light, *Baby Boomers* (New York: W. W. Norton and Co., 1988): 28.

44 Erica Goode, "New Study Finds Middle Age Is Prime of Life," *New York Times* (16 February 1999): D-6.

45 Gail Sheehy, *New Passages: Mapping Your Life Across Time* (New York: Random House, 1995).

46 Laura Tangley, "Aging Brains Need Fresh Challenges to Stay Agile," *U.S. News and World Report* (5 June 2000): 90.

47 Sara Rimer, "Rural Elderly Create Vital Communities as Young Leave Void," *New York Times* (2 February 1998): 1.

48 Robert Hopp, "Experiencing Elderhostel as Lifelong Learners," *Journal of Physical Education, Recreation, and Dance* (April 1998): 27.

CHAPTER 6

GENDER AND RACIAL/ETHNIC FACTORS AFFECTING LEISURE

◆ ◆ ◆

The Nova Scotia Sport and Recreation Commission, in cooperation with its partners, will work to create a provincial environment in which all girls and women see themselves and are recognized by others as participants, athletes, players, coaches, officials, managers, decision makers, and leaders in sport, recreation, and active living; where resources and opportunities are equitably distributed to meet the needs of girls and women, and where all girls and women have reasonable access to a full range of opportunities in safe and welcoming environments.[1]

Growing ethnic diversity is particularly striking in a city [Minneapolis] that was 93 percent white as recently as 1970. During the 1980s, the minority population rose to 21 percent, and the trend is continuing in the 1990s. The public school enrollment is now 68 percent nonwhite. The number of children for whom English is not a native language has tripled since 1990, with students now speaking some 70 languages in the city's schools. And more than 1 in every 10 schoolchildren is Asian-American, compared with less than 1 percent in 1970.[2]

◆ ◆ ◆

INTRODUCTION

This chapter deals with two demographic factors that affect personal leisure values and involvements today: gender and racial or ethnic identity.

It summarizes past practices of leisure-service agencies with respect to gender and the related area of sexual lifestyles. Progress in this field has been striking with respect to expanded recreational opportunities for girls and women in sport and outdoor recreation. While chief concern has been expressed about females and leisure, the role of boys and men in contemporary leisure has also been problematic.

Racial and ethnic identity has also limited many individuals from full participation in organized recreation in the past and continues to influence the leisure involvement not only of African-Americans, but also that of the growing number of Hispanic-Americans and those of Asian background. With continuing waves of immigration from other parts of the world, religion linked to ethnic identify will pose new policy questions as Muslims as well as other new Americans who are neither Christian nor Jewish become part of the national landscape.

GENDER FACTORS INFLUENCING LEISURE

Beyond the issue of one's age group, a second factor that plays an important role in leisure has to do with sexual or gender identity and values.

A distinction should be made between the two terms *sex* and *gender*. Although they are often used interchangeably, social scientists have generally accepted the principle that the term *sex* should be used to identify one's biological or physical classification in terms of the structure and functions that are possessed by one sex or the other. In contrast, the word *gender* is used to describe a broad range of characteristics, roles, or behaviors that society usually attaches to males and females. Stated simply, the words *male* and *female* apply to one's sex, while the words *masculine* and *feminine* are descriptive adjectives applying to gender traits.

Throughout history, distinctions between males and females have been made that extend beyond the procreative functions. These distinctions encompass family or marital roles, educational status, career opportunities, political influences, and all other aspects of daily life. In some societies, women have held considerable power, for example, women worshiped as gods or where they headed nations. For the most part, however, women have been subordinate to men in many societies.

Among younger children, play has served to reinforce gender-related stereotypes. Little boys were given toy guns or cowboy outfits and encouraged to playact in stereotypically masculine roles—like doctors, firefighters, or airline pilots. Girls were given dolls or play equipment designed to encourage stereotypically feminine roles, like caring for babies, cooking, and sewing, or dramatic play as nurses or airline hostesses. Only after the resurgence of the feminist movement following World War II did we begin to question these roles and assumptions and challenge such sexist uses of play in childhood.

Recreation Program Planning Differences

Throughout the development of organized recreation and park programs in the United States and Canada, agency planners typically responded to prevailing societal attitudes regarding appropriate leisure activities for the sexes by developing community recreation programs that supported the traditional stereotypes.

Foster Rhea Dulles points out that during the early decades of this century, leadership roles and activities assigned to girls and women, as well as the expectations regarding their ability to work well in groups, reflected past perceptions of women as weak and inferior in skills and lacking drive, confidence, and the ability to compete and persevere. Victorian prudery and misconceptions about physical capability and health needs also limited programming for girls and women.[3]

Discrimination based on gender was most vividly demonstrated in the field of athletics at this time. Bill Gilbert and Nancy Williamson documented in 1973 the widespread prejudice against females in sport in the United States:

> There is no sharper example of discrimination today than that which operates against girls and women who take part in competitive sports, wish to take part, or might wish to if society did not scorn such endeavors. No matter what her age, education, race, talent, residence or riches, the female's right to play is severely restricted. The funds, facilities, coaching, rewards, and honors allotted women are grossly inferior to those granted men. In many places absolutely no support is given to women's athletics, and females are barred by law, regulation, tradition, or the hostility of males from sharing athletic resources and pleasures.[4]

IMPACT OF FEMINIST MOVEMENT

A number of important social trends were responsible for bringing about major changes with respect to women's roles in recreation and leisure. First, there was the evolving independence of women in terms of family status and work-related roles. With the dramatic increase in divorce, millions of women became single parents and heads of households. Following their counterparts of World War II, who enlisted in the armed forces and worked in war plants by the millions, this new generation of women was determined to assume greater responsibilities. They wanted to break through the accepted patterns of gender-related discrimination that limited their employment in the past.

The feminist movement, which in earlier periods of American history resulted in women obtaining fuller legal and political rights, was revived with a stronger thrust toward obtaining equality with men in a wide range of societal roles. This movement led to the creation of militant women's organizations and support groups and was responsible for legislation and court decisions that broke down the walls of gender discrimination in the 1970s and 1980s.

Emphasis on Sports and Physical Recreation

Recreation and leisure help the feminist movement achieve key goals today. This is particularly true in sports and outdoor recreation, in which relatively few girls and women had been encouraged to participate in the past. Historically, M. Deborah Bialeschki writes, the

> domination of sport by men and their exclusion of women had been one among many forms of male control of women's bodies. This control had been ideological in the form of cultural denigration of women's athletic ability and the myth of female frailty. . . . Through sports and fitness, many women gain a sense of self-definition and self-determination for learning the lesson "I can." Facing a challenge heightens a woman's sense of vitality and the awareness of her individuality. . . .[5]

Women in Sports and Outdoor Recreation

By the millions, girls and women today take part in varied sports, such as volleyball tournaments in New York City, or Texas high school girls basketball state finals. Some organizations, like Adventures in Good Company, sponsor backpacking outings designed exclusively for women members.

Women have increasingly become engaged in a wide range of individual and team sports, achieving a higher participation rate in secondary school and college competitive programs. As professional athletes or international competitors in such sports as tennis, golf, gymnastics, and skiing, they have been successful. Beyond this, many highly skilled women have achieved success as race-car drivers, horse-racing jockeys, dogsled racers, and triathletes. These changes have occurred not only in schools and colleges and at professional levels of sports participation, but also in many community-based programs. In part, this has occurred because of challenges to the exclusion of females from programs that have historically been restricted to male participants.

For example, in baseball programs for children and youth, girls were not permitted to join Little League until 1974. At that time, thanks to civil rights suits throughout the United States (including some supported by the National Organization for Women), Little League changed its charter to incorporate girls. However, at the same time, it organized a softball league. Although softball is not legally restricted to girls, few boys join this program. And, although some girls do play hardball, they are extremely rare. Thus, segregation by gender continues on a voluntary basis, although it is legally possible to cross the line.

In some cases, public recreation and park authorities have been forced to take action to eliminate sex-based discrimination in sports. In Philadelphia, for example, in 1985 the Fairmount Park Commission revoked the ballfield permits of a community sports association that sponsored several baseball leagues with hundreds of youth participants because they refused to let a single girl play hardball in her local league. In the same year, in Canada, a 12-year-old Toronto girl's effort to play on an all-boy hockey team in a city league governed by the provincial Ontario Hockey Association led to a trial before the Ontario Supreme Court.

Title IX, the section of the 1972 federal law that prohibits sex discrimination in education, has had an immense effect—primarily in college—in terms of providing fuller support for women's teams in varied sports. Greater numbers of participants and athletic scholarships, improved facilities, coaching and transportation arrangements have all been part of this picture, although a report issued in the late 1990s by the National Collegiate Athletic Association confirms that equity in women's collegiate athletic programs is still a decade or more away.[6]

On another level, growing numbers of girls and women have been taking part in such formerly male pursuits as rugby, ice hockey, boxing, and even tackle football. With the emergence of women's professional basketball and soccer leagues, the breakdown of gender-based barriers gathered momentum in recent years.

Continuing Patterns of Exclusion

In other leisure-related areas, there are growing efforts to break down long-established patterns of gender-based exclusion. An interesting example has been the effort to open up exclusive private clubs in many of the nation's cities to female membership. While, nominally, these are social groups that should have the right to restrict their memberships, they are also places where influential people meet to do business and where exclusively male memberships mean that women are placed at a marked career disadvantage.

Golf clubs in particular have stubbornly resisted opening their full memberships and playing schedules to women golfers. However, in December 1999, in a case rattling clubs around the country,

> . . . women members of the Haverhill Golf and Country Club in Massachusetts won a stunning jury verdict of $1.9 million in damages for being systematically denied full memberships and equal access to the golf course in prime playing times. The award, and the prospect that the court might now take control of the club, is sure to make clubs around the country review their policies.[7]

In many other areas of outdoor recreation and sports, gender-based policies of exclusion are coming under challenge. As a vivid example, although there are millions of women anglers today, they are routinely discouraged from competing in the big-money Bassmasters Classic and other tournaments promoted by the Bass Anglers Sportsmen Society—an important element in the nation's $60 billion fishing industry.

In terms of employment, growing numbers of women in the 1970s and 1980s rose to executive positions in major public recreation and park agencies and nonprofit organizations. In the late 1980s, after protracted legal challenges, the Boy Scouts of America agreed to let women become scoutmasters and hold all other leadership positions—a long-resisted policy change. And, in May 1995, California's Disneyland adopted a comprehensive unisex "casting" approach for all of its rides.

At the same time, some of the entertainment-oriented activities that portrayed women as sex objects have been removed or modified in recent years. After years of commercial success, the Playboy bunnies gradually went out of style, and the Atlantic City Miss America Pageant, which began as a bathing beauty contest, now requires its contestants to demonstrate performing talents and to speak out on a significant social issue or platform.

Constraints on Women's Leisure

Another limitation on women's enjoyment of leisure stems from their work responsibilities. Firestone and Shelton summarize research showing that, for the most part, women in the paid labor force were responsible for household labor, with men's contribution to household tasks being relatively unresponsive to shifts in their wives' labor force participation. They write:

> Even when employed full time, women are more likely to be responsible for household and child care. Whether the result of socialization, wage discrimination, or different aptitudes, the result is a "double day" that comes at the expense of other activities.[8]

In a similar vein, Harrington and Dawson conducted a study of over 1,500 adult females in Ontario, Canada, in three categories: those employed full-time, those employed part-time, and homemakers not employed outside the home. Homemakers in particular felt they lacked needed leisure skills and confidence, had weak self-images and leisure concepts, and tended to agree that certain leisure activities were clearly "only for men."[9]

A less-subtle barrier to women's participation—particularly in varied forms of outdoor recreation—has to do with the constant threat of physical aggression, mugging, or outright sexual assaults by male predators.[10] In some cities, girls and women have been terrorized, groped, stripped, and raped by "wilding" males, sometimes in or around swimming pools, and, more recently, by crowds of drunken men in parks during parades and festivals. Such extreme forms of abuse often stem, Brent Staples writes, from the long-standing acceptance of schoolyard and playground harassment in which, too often, such behavior is regarded as harmless male "fun."[11]

Another constraint to female participation in varied forms of active recreation has been based on the widely shared assumption that girls and women are fragile creatures with the likelihood of severe damage to their reproductive organs that might be caused by overactive or aggressive play. Such "frailty myths" have been largely discredited in recent years, although some activities, such as competitive gymnastics, may have negative consequences (see page 204).[12]

MEN AND LEISURE

Although most of the professional literature and research studies dealing with gender in recreation and leisure focuses on past discrimination against girls and women and the efforts made to strengthen their opportunities today, it is essential to examine the changing role of males in this area as well. Generally, men have been portrayed as the dominant sex within most areas of community life and have been seen as responsible for denying women access to a full range of leisure pursuits and professional advancement. However, it would be misleading to assume that men's lives are invariably richer and more satisfying than those of women.

Andrew Kimbrell points out that, in addition to having a markedly shorter life span than women, men have four times the suicide rate, three times the alcoholism rate, and substantially higher rates of drug dependency and imprisonment than their female counterparts. Kimbrell continues:

> Men are also a large part of the growing crisis in the American family. . . . Men are increasingly isolated from their families by the pressures of work and the circumstances of divorce. In a recent poll, 72 percent of employed male respondents agreed that they are "torn by conflict" between their jobs and the desire to be with their families.[13]

Rather than view them as the invariably favored sex, we should perhaps note that many men lead relatively powerless, subservient lives in the factory or office, and that they are pressured by the fictional depiction of daring "macho" men in the mass media of entertainment to embrace an unrealistic and unrewarding masculine lifestyle.

Other social critics have reinforced this view of the challenges facing many men in contemporary society. Carlin Romano summarizes the views of Susan Faludi, known as a forceful feminist author:

> The more, Faludi writes, that she considers "what men have lost—a useful role in public life, a way of earning a decent and reliable living, appreciation in the home, respectful treatment in the culture—the more it seems that men [at the end of the twentieth century] are falling into a state oddly similar to that of women at mid-century.[14]

In the late 1990s, workshops, conferences, and a growing number of articles and books began to call attention to the woes of boys in current American culture. Psychotherapists point out that four boys are diagnosed as mentally disturbed for every one girl and that there are six boys diagnosed with attention-deficit/hyperactivity disorder for every girl. Many young boys appear to face a crisis when they are faced with pressures to conform to cultural constructions of masculinity and are forced to strike out on their own when they would rather be still clinging to their mothers' legs. Too often, to show vulnerability or sensitivity is to bring instant ridicule by others.

Shifting Masculine Identities

Boys and men respond in varied ways to such challenges. A growing number today strive to create powerful body images of themselves through relentless weight training. The image of the ideal male has been transformed, as illustrated in the shift from the relatively slender G.I. Joe (Barbie® doll's male counterpart) of 1964 to the immensely muscled G.I. Joe Extreme of 1998. Surprisingly, some men today are taking the opposite tack and doing battle with anorexia—resisting the image of the all-powerful male.[15]

Still other men cheerfully take part in war games to affirm their masculinity. Dressed in camouflage gear and war paint, reeking of bug spray, and armed with rifles and ammo, they replay the games of childhood. Jane Gross describes a typical scene:

> From behind bunkers and thick trees, their escape slowed by gopher holes and knee-high grass, two teams fired gooey pellets of paint at each other. The "dead" left the field with carbon dioxide–powered guns raised over their heads in surrender, then compared welts with those who had fallen before them. . . .[16]

In comparison to women, many men find it difficult to have close friends who provide support. Their inability to feel or show emotion or sympathy is illustrated in the episode of a Minnesota sales engineer who was laid off from a new position after only six weeks on the job and only two days after his wife announced that she wanted a divorce. When his co-workers at the elevator company agreed to take a pay cut so that he could be rehired, he made it a point to shake everybody's hand on his first day back, saying gratefully that

> [their generosity] was a personal high. It shows an incredible amount of heart. If I wasn't a man, I'd be emotional about the whole thing.[17]

Many men are now making a strenuous effort to come to grips with their need to share with others, to get a better sense of their masculine identities, and to become warmer, more expressive individuals. Robert Bly's book, *Iron John*, has encouraged men to join drumming groups and wilderness retreats where they explore their past relationships with their fathers and their own roles as fathers and providers.

The "Million Man March" held in Washington, D.C., in the fall of 1995 stressed themes of responsibility, brotherhood, and commitment to family values for African-American men. Extending this effort, there is a growing "responsible fatherhood" movement around the nation that is uniting vastly different groups around the effort to help noncustodial fathers play a larger role in their children's lives.

In contrast to the findings of Firestone and Shelton cited earlier, some recent studies show that more men *are* beginning to take on child-care responsibilities, for reasons ranging from rising day-care costs to the growth in the number of working women. A late-1990s study by the Families and Work Institute in New York indicates that men are spending substantially more time on household responsibilities and in carrying on activities with their children than in the past.[18]

Implications for Leisure

What are the implications of these trends in masculine identity and lifestyle values for recreation and leisure? In the first place, many boys and men who formerly felt pressured to be involved heavily in sports, both as participants and as spectators, may now feel free *not* to conform to this traditional masculine image. Further, growing numbers of males are increasingly likely to take part in domestic functions or hobbies, the creative arts, or other leisure pursuits that in the past might have raised questions about their degree of "maleness."

This new freedom to engage in leisure pursuits once considered inappropriate for men also extends to attitudes toward women. Increasingly, many parents are becoming sensitive to the way they permit their sons to behave toward girls.

At the same time, many males are rebelling against the notion that all men are "evil" oppressors. Male "bashing," Lance Morrow writes, has become a popular pastime, with men viewed as sexual oppressors, business cheats, and political phonies. Popular culture, in the form of movies, television sitcoms, video games, and sensational talk shows, perpetuates and exaggerates this image and inflames hostility between the sexes.

Men are resisting this distorted image of their character and, within the broad range of recreation and leisure pursuits, are exploring healthier areas of personal expression and masculine identity. Some men are even beginning to argue that *they* are being oppressed, as in the case of Title IX lawsuits filed by male student-athletes at Drake University and the University of Illinois. They claim that men are now being subjected to reverse sex discrimination in college athletic programs.

With respect to *both* sexes, it is important to note that many of the barriers that separated males and females in the past have been broken down in recent years. For example, a number of leading youth organizations, which formerly were separate in terms of membership, have now joined forces, as in the case of Boys and Girls Clubs of America.

In other cases, national organizations like the Young Men's Christian Association not only have substantial numbers of members who are girls and women, but in some communities are directed by women executives and division heads.

HOMOSEXUALITY AND LEISURE

Closely linked to any consideration of the role of gender in determining one's leisure choices and behavior must be an awareness of a substantial and increasingly visible group that pursues alternative sexual lifestyles—*gays*, *lesbians*, *bisexuals*, and *transsexuals*—as they are usually referred to in the popular press.

In the past, throughout much of the Western world, homosexuality was condemned by religious and civil authorities. Until recently, it was categorized as a form of mental illness by the psychiatric establishment and as a crime subject to prosecution by law enforcement agencies. Being identified as gay or lesbian meant that one was barred from employment in many occupational fields. Thus, most homosexuals hid their identity "in the closet." Despite this background, scholars point out that there was a pattern of gays and lesbians sharing a social life in dance halls, nightclubs, and resorts; living in specific neighborhoods of large cities; and often clustering in artistic or creative occupations throughout much of the early twentieth century.

However, during the 1930s and 1940s, a backlash developed against gay forms of entertainment, with state assemblies barring the performance of plays dealing with sexual "degeneracy" and Hollywood agreeing not to depict homosexuality in movies. State liquor authorities closed many bars that catered to gay personnel, arrests for homosexual solicitation rose dramatically, and, in the 1950s, gay government employees lost their jobs because it was assumed that they could be easily blackmailed into spying for other countries on the basis of their hidden identities.

In the 1960s and 1970s, the effect of the Stonewall riot in New York City (a mass protest against police persecution of gays), the impact of the counterculture movement with its emphasis on sexual freedom, and the militant action of other gender or racial minorities all converged to help homosexuals gain a greater measure of public acceptance.

Growing Acceptance

With research into the causes of homosexuality—including new evidence suggesting that it has a genetic or biological base—the psychiatric profession withdrew its classification of homosexuality as a form of mental illness. Beyond this, homosexuality began to gain visibility on the national scene:

- Numerous universities began to employ openly homosexual faculty members; to institute courses and curricula in gay, lesbian, and bisexual studies; and to approve student organizations that sponsored publications, events, and other programs that were homosexual-oriented.
- Gay and lesbian community centers were established in a number of cities to promote homosexual causes and concerns. School curricula and textbooks were adopted that

provided information about homosexuality, gay and lesbian families, and related issues of prejudice and discrimination.

- Gay and lesbian lifestyle issues began to appear more positively in popular culture with homosexual-related themes in books, theater, dance, and fine arts events. Many gay rights groups began to openly take part in public events and celebrations from which they had been barred in the past.

However, on a number of other levels, gay liberation remained a highly contentious issue, as conservative religious and political factions resisted the increasing acceptance of homosexuals in public life. It is worth noting that in Canada, human rights legislation prohibits any form of anti-gay discrimination.[19]

Continuing Resistance to Homosexual Acceptance

In some cases, state legislation or local initiatives have been approved that would nullify civil rights laws or policies giving homosexuals the same freedom from discrimination as women, racial minorities, the aging, or those with a disability. On the national level in the United States, efforts to pass a federal antidiscrimination bill were abandoned in the face of the conservative congressional tide of the mid-1990s.

In a number of public school systems, strong opposition was mounted to the adoption of textbooks providing favorable descriptions of gay or lesbian families. In other cases, teachers were dismissed for distributing novels in literature classes that depicted homosexual characters sympathetically and boards of education have banned gay and lesbian clubs in school systems.

In the armed forces there has been an ongoing struggle between those who seek to eliminate the Pentagon's "don't ask, don't tell" policy—essentially a ban on self-identified gays and lesbians serving in the military—and those opposed to this proposed policy change.

A number of religious denominations, including the Presbyterian Church, the Southern Baptist Convention, and the United Methodist Church, have debated issues relating to the ordination of homosexual members of the clergy, same-sex marriages, or their overall stance with respect to homosexuality. The Catholic Church in particular has been vigorous in its resistance to any lessening of its opposition to homosexuality—calling it an objective "disorder" and comparing it to mental illness.

As evidence of the battle lines that have been drawn, during the Vatican's Holy Year 2000, about 300,000 gays and lesbians held the first worldwide gay pride celebration in Rome to protest the Catholic Church's policy.

Implications for Leisure Policy

How have these trends affected recreation and leisure-service organizations designed to serve the full range of community members? In the past, most public and nonprofit organizations did not deal with such issues or simply accepted gay or lesbian participants as part of their total membership without recognizing or making a point of their sexual orientation. In some cases, however, they have openly refused to employ homosexual staff members in leadership roles with young people or to permit gay or lesbian individuals to continue as program members.

n one such case, a Superior Court judge in New Jersey ruled against a gay Eagle Scout and assistant scoutmaster who brought a discrimination suit against the Boy Scouts of America for expelling him. The judge found

that the state's Law Against Discrimination, which was amended in 1991 to cover "affectional or sexual orientation," did not apply to the distinctly "private" Boy Scouts. . . .

In his decision [the judge] equated homosexuality with sodomy, which was illegal in New Jersey until 1979, and noted that "all religions deem the act of sodomy a serious moral wrong." As such, homosexuality was incompatible with the Boy Scouts, which he called a "moral organization."[20]

Ultimately, this case came before the U.S. Supreme Court, which ruled in June 2000 that the Boy Scouts had the right to exclude homosexuals—a decision that gave rise to a storm of protest and retaliatory action around the nation.

In contrast, a number of recreation, park, and leisure-service educators have vigorously promoted the idea of enriched recreation services for gay and lesbian youth. Pointing out that there are an estimated 7.2 million such individuals in the United States who are often stigmatized and isolated because of their identity, Arnold Grossman suggests that many of these young people are at risk for dropping out—or being forced out—of school, losing their homes, abusing alcohol and drugs, getting AIDS, or committing suicide.[21]

In an example of such special services, a nonprofit agency, the Lavender Youth Recreation and Information Center (LYRIC), and the San Francisco Recreation and Park Department have joined together to promote comprehensive recreation and social activities for gay, lesbian, and bisexual youth in a safe and positive social environment. Preliminary studies of gay and lesbian youth suggest that leisure may have special meaning for such individuals because of the link to issues of sexual identity, accessibility, and safety.[22]

Programs in Other Settings

Beyond services provided by public or nonprofit organizations, the gay and lesbian community itself has established leisure-linked organizations by forming recreation clubs, sports leagues, outdoor recreation associations, and other groups that have functioned on local, state, national, and even international levels. For example, the Gay Olympic Games have involved several thousand participants from 19 countries in 17 different sports. To illustrate, Brenda Pitts conducted a study of over 130 organizations providing organized sports or outdoor recreation for primarily gay and lesbian participants. She found that these groups offered a total of 57 different activities, including camping, bicycling, backpacking, snow skiing, volleyball, swimming, cruises, bowling, sailing, travel, running, mountaineering, and tennis.[23]

Through the 1980s and 1990s, such sports and cultural programs increased steadily in participation. Hollander writes:

The 1982 San Francisco Gay Games had 1,350 athletes and a budget of $125,000, while the 1994 New York Games had 11,000 athletes and a budget of $6.5 million. Both numbers are expected to be much higher for the 2000 Games in Sydney, Australia . . . . [For many gays and lesbians] the increasing visibility of the Gay Games made competing in sports a welcome alternative to a social scene that consisted mainly of bars and clubs.[24]

There are literally thousands of gay-oriented resorts, travel services, tours, events, cruises, and other tourist attractions serving this market today. As an example of this trend, the Greater Miami Convention and Visitors Bureau and other Dade County, Florida, tourist and resort associations are now making a concerted attempt to woo the nation's gay and lesbian travel market. Over the 1995 Memorial Day weekend, Miami Beach treated 17 journalists from the European gay press to an all-expense-paid, four-day tour of Dade County in the hope that these nicely treated junketeers would then promote tourism in Florida by European gays and lesbians.

Nonetheless, homosexuality continues to represent a controversial issue in terms of public policy. In 1998, for example, a gay charter cruise was denied landing rights at the Cayman Islands because the territorial government concluded that the visitors could not be counted on to "uphold standards of appropriate behavior." Instead, the cruise ship went on to dock at Belize—a better site for scuba diving.

In another instance of disputed public policy, the city of San Francisco closed bathhouses in the late 1980s, during the height of the AIDS epidemic, in an effort to control anonymous, casual, and unsafe sex. In the late 1990s, a movement emerged to allow the reopening of bathhouses where men might meet and have sex in private cubicles—under guidelines that might promote safer behavior.

While it seems probable that a substantial segment of American society will continue to resist social advances for homosexuals in the years ahead, it is also probable that growing numbers of recreation and leisure-service agencies will recognize the need to serve this population more effectively as part of their social mandate to meet the leisure needs of the nation's overall population.

INFLUENCE OF RACE AND ETHNICITY

In addition to the factors of age and gender, a third major demographic element is of key importance in determining leisure values and behaviors. A succession of past research studies shows that recreational involvement is heavily influenced by one's racial or ethnic identity. The provision of public, nonprofit, and other forms of recreation facilities and programs is also affected by these demographic factors, and the broader fields of popular culture—including the sports and entertainment worlds—continue to reflect their impact.

Meaning of Race and Ethnicity

Before examining the actual influence of race and ethnicity on recreation and leisure, it is helpful to clarify the meaning of the two terms. Although they are often used interchangeably, social scientists do distinguish between them. *Race* has been defined as follows:

> A race is considered to be a statistical aggregate of people who share a composite of genetically transmitted *physical* traits, such as skin pigmentation, head form, facial features, stature, and the color, distribution, and texture of body hair . . . . Estimates of racial types range from three—Caucasoid, Mongoloid, and Negroid—to thirty or more.[25]

In contrast, *ethnicity* involves having a unique social and cultural heritage that is passed on from one generation to another. Ethnic groups are often identified by patterns of language, family life, religion, recreation, and other customs or traits that distinguish them from other groups.

It is important to recognize that the systems used to classify people into different racial categories, and even the concept of race itself, have been under attack. At a 1995 meeting of the American Association for the Advancement of Science, biological anthropologists argued that race is no longer a valid way of distinguishing among people and that, instead, it is

> a social construct derived mainly from perceptions conditioned by events of recorded history, and it has no basic biological reality.[26]

A recent statement by the American Association of Physical Anthropologists, which is intended to provide a guideline for UNESCO and other international organizations in dealing with racism around the globe, states in part that:

> Pure races in the sense of genetically homogeneous populations do not exist in the human species, nor is there evidence that they have ever existed in the past history of the human family.
>
> Hereditary potentials for overall intelligence and cultural development do not appear to differ among modern human populations, and there is no hereditary justification for considering one population superior to another.

Increasingly, the U.S. Census Bureau is confounded by the difficulty of classifying multiracial people who represent a blend of two or more family origins. The limited categories of "white," "black," "Asian and Pacific Islanders," and "American Indian or Alaskan native" used in the census cannot begin to convey the differences among different groups of Pacific Islanders or the immense number of markedly different Asian-Americans. The broad category of Hispanic-Americans or Latinos may consist of individuals from the Spanish mainland; those of mixed African, Spanish, and Indian backgrounds; or others from dozens of different geographical and cultural groups.

Within any particular population group, sizable segments of people may prefer to be identified by different labels. Typically, research shows that 44.2 percent of Americans of African origin prefer to be called *black,* whereas 28.1 percent prefer *African-American,* 12.1 percent *Afro-American,* and only 3.3 percent *Negro* and 1.1 percent *colored.* Similar variations of preferred labeling exist within other major racial and ethnic groups. Recent Census Bureau studies confirm that few Americans prefer to describe themselves as *multiracial.*

Race and Ethnicity in Leisure

Many folk traditions are featured in community recreation programs and festivals. Here, Mexican dancers perform in the Cinco de Mayo Celebration in Phoenix, Arizona, while Pueblo Indians in ceremonial costume dance at feast day in Santa Fe, New Mexico. Ukrainian Dancers of Dallas perform at Texas Folklife Festival in San Antonio.

Implications for Recreation and Leisure

Despite the limitations of racial or ethnicity-based identification and its meaning in scientific terms, the reality is that the public continues to accept the concept of race and to apply it in terms of popular stereotypes about one group or the other. This is particularly significant for recreation and leisure because our traditional patterns of facility development and program planning were essentially based on the assumption that the public being served was predominantly a white, middle-class population familiar with the literature, traditions, and customs that came to America from the British Isles.

Now, for the first time, we are seeing the rapid growth of non-European populations in the United States as a consequence of recent immigration and birthrate trends. In a number of major cities throughout the country, nonwhites now outnumber those of European background, with the percentage of African-American, Hispanic-American, and Asian-American children in the schools representing sizable majorities in some cases.

If this population trend continues, it is predicted that Hispanics will become the dominant minority in the United States, with major political, social, and economic implications. Similarly, the number of Asian-Americans has grown from 3.5 million in 1980 to over 7.2 million in 1990 and is expected to climb steadily in the decades ahead.

Another striking trend has involved the growing number of Muslims; today the United States is home to almost four million followers of Islam—five times as many as in 1970. The American Muslim population embraces American-born converts, mostly black, and a swelling immigrant tide from Asia, Africa, the Middle East, and the Indian subcontinent. Muslims are expected to outnumber American Jews, who have leveled off at 5.5 million adherents. In addition, two million Americans identify themselves as Buddhists, and the combined number of Hindus and Sikhs is over one million.[27]

In 1990, a *Time* cover story entitled "Beyond the Melting Pot" made it clear that the rapidly approaching twenty-first century would see racial and ethnic groups in the United States outnumbering whites for the first time, with the "browning of America" transforming every aspect of society. Beyond their sheer numbers, it is evident that growing minority populations are also exerting powerful influences on the nation's cultural scene and recreational life.

Research into Minority-Group Recreation Patterns

Recognizing this trend, in recent decades numerous researchers have conducted systematic examinations of the leisure-related patterns and values of racial and ethnic minority group members. As far back as 1927, Lehman and Witty compared the play activities of African-American and white elementary and secondary schoolchildren and came to the conclusion that African-American youngsters participated much more actively in social forms of play than their Caucasian counterparts. In the 1950s, a striking analysis of the leisure pursuits of middle-class African-Americans was carried out by E. Franklin Frazier. He found that many of the pleasure-seeking activities of the black bourgeoisie were influenced by their feelings of insecurity and inferiority in American society and by their effort to escape from the oppressive circumstances of their lives. Other studies at this time by the Wharton School of Finance and the Outdoor Recreation Resources Review Commission found that there were marked differences between African-American and white families with respect to spending on varied forms of entertainment and involvement in outdoor recreation.

In the 1970s and 1980s, a wave of research studies examined the recreation patterns of African-Americans, Mexican-Americans, Asian-Americans, and other minority group members. Stamps and Stamps, for example, reviewed 17 different studies that analyzed African-Americans' use of leisure in terms of urban-suburban, regional, and social class variables and compared them to the involvement of whites.[28]

Similarly, Floyd, Gramann, and Saenz looked at the influence of ethnic acculturation on the use of public outdoor recreation and park areas by Mexican-Americans in a number of Arizona counties.[29] Allison and Geiger studied the leisure involvements of elderly Chinese-American residents in a southwestern city, finding that their pursuits met a number of their educational, cultural, and personal development needs.[30] McDonald and McAvoy have explored the impact of racism on the outdoor recreation experiences of Native Americans and have summed up the need for further research in this area.[31]

Focus on Ethnic-Related Differences and Constraints

Beyond measuring the differences between or among various racial and ethnic groups in their leisure involvements, researchers have sought to develop a theoretical framework that would explain the reasons for the differences. The most prominent models used to explain such differences as "underparticipation" in varied leisure activities by African-Americans are the *marginality* and *ethnicity* hypotheses. Floyd, Shinew, McGuire, and Noe explain the marginality model in terms of the limited economic resources of and historical patterns of discrimination against African-Americans. Stated differently, they write:

> . . . [B]y occupying a subordinate class position, minorities have had limited access to society's major institutions which negatively affects life-chances and lifestyles, and which is reflected in reduced participation in certain types of activities.[32]

Applied to a specific form of recreation, that is, travel and tourism, the *marginality* hypothesis is illustrated by the centuries-long discrimination against African-Americans and by the relatively lower economic resources of many African-American families.

The *ethnicity* hypothesis essentially says that different racial groups are influenced in their leisure choices by different norms, values, and socialization processes. In the case of African-Americans, these might include a range of recreational pursuits that were influenced by African-American history and cultural development, including activities in the realm of music, dance, or traditional games that stem from African heritage, slavery days, or the era of Reconstruction in the rural South.

In general, both models may serve as partial explanations of the distinctive behaviors of racial and ethnic minority populations—combined with continuing factors of social exclusion and self-segregation.

Without question, past practices of racial injustice and discrimination continue to influence present-day recreational involvements, along with lingering prejudices and conflicts among different ethnic and racial groups. Typically, there was great shock in the United States when three white men in Texas were recently convicted of dragging a black man to his death behind their truck on a country road. Yet, within the memory of millions of African-Americans, lynchings of this kind were commonplace throughout the Southern and border states and were taken for granted by whites both as a harsh form of vigilante "justice" and an accepted means of racial intimidation. Prejudices persist on every level. It was only in 1999 that the Alabama legislature repealed a long-standing law against intermarriage between the races, and South Carolina's unwillingness to take down the Confederate flag from its state capitol building became an important campaign issue in that state in the year 2000.

Each ethnic minority carries memories of past injustices. Japanese-Americans still recall being herded into barren relocation camps during World War II—something that did not happen to German- or Italian-Americans. Hundreds of thousands of American-Indian children were sent to government schools through the years, where they were harshly punished if they attempted to speak their tribal languages or maintain other native traditions. Such experiences tend to set members of minorities aside, along with continuing examples of discrimination.

In terms of racial exclusion in recreation, parks, and leisure programs, Chapter 3 and Chapter 4 outline some of the past injustices that kept black Americans out of most public parks, playgrounds, swimming pools, and similar facilities. Until the civil rights era of the 1950s and 1960s, most youth-serving organizations like the YMCA and YWCA or the Boy and Girl Scouts were rigidly segregated on racial grounds—often with few recreational opportunities for individuals of color. Athletic competition through most of the country barred African-Americans from play in both college and professional ranks.

Continuing Examples of Discrimination

While less obvious, a number of examples of race-based exclusion have continued to the present day. Well into the 1990s, a major chain of commercial health and fitness clubs covertly sought to exclude or discourage African-American members, believing that their presence would have a negative effect on white club members. Major restaurant chains have similarly discriminated against black patrons or potential employees, as revealed in recent major court cases and settlements. Private-membership golf clubs had systematically excluded African-American or other minority group members until forced to accept them by public pressures relating to the sponsorship of major tournaments—an ironic circumstance when Tiger Woods (actually a mix of several racial strains, but a young man who would clearly have been perceived as black and barred from most golf clubs a decade before) emerged at century's end as a record-breaking golf champion—and possibly the greatest of all time. Woods's success was particularly interesting because, contrary to a widely shared stereotype about many black athletes that they owe their success to their physical gifts, rather than other personal traits, it is widely conceded that he is a brilliant and highly disciplined golfer.

In the realm of professional and college sports, there is strong evidence that, despite the success of African-American athletes in the major team sports of basketball, baseball, and football, they have been disproportionately excluded from the coaching or management positions in these sports. In the early and mid-1990s, many sports commentators and athletes spoke out against such discrimination, and leaders from the baseball, football, and basketball players' unions formed a coalition with the heads of the NAACP, National Urban League, and Southern Christian Leadership Conference to eliminate racist practices in professional sports.

Despite efforts to improve this situation, in 1998, the Chronicle of Higher Education reported that college and university administrators continue to be reluctant to hire African-American sports administrators at a high level:

> Of the 28 black athletic directors in Division I of the National Collegiate Athletic Association, 20 work at historically black colleges. Exclude these institutions, and the proportion of black athletic directors drops to 2.8 percent—eight of 288.
>
> Black athletes, on the other hand, have a large presence in Division I, particularly in the two most lucrative sports—football (52 percent) and men's basketball (61 percent) [and if the number of starting or star players were measured, the figures would be higher].[33]

Similarly, despite the growing number of racial and ethnic minority group athletes in the major professional sports, their representation among coaches and managers continues to be minimal. According to the Northeastern University Center for the Study of Sport, for example, only 20 percent of the players in the National Basketball Association are white, whereas 76 percent of the head coaches are.[34]

However, racial antagonism and rejection represent a two-sided issue. For example, when Marcus Jacoby, a white quarterback, was recruited and won the starting assignment on the football team at Southern University, a historically black institution in Louisiana, he was rejected by the student body and alumni and was ultimately pressured to leave the school—despite a winning record.[35]

Self-Segregation and Comfort Levels

A key thrust of the civil rights movement in the period from the 1950s through the 1970s was to break down barriers to full participation in society and to forge positive links between different ethnic and racial groups. In contrast, the period of the 1980s and 1990s was marked by continuing racial hostility and patterns of self-segregation in many settings.

On many college campuses, minority group students tend to band together in social activities, housing choices, and other areas in which there would be the potential for friendly contact and improved intergroup relations. While this might appear to be simply a matter of preferring to be with friends of one's own background, there has been increased evidence on many college campuses of a growing racial "divide"—with marked friction between African-American, white, and other racial or ethnic group minority students.

Steven Philipp examined this issue in a study comparing African-American and European-American participation in a range of leisure activities. Although the two groups of survey respondents had similar socioeconomic characteristics—in terms of household size, median income, educational background, and gender—there were statistically significant differences in the ratings of "appeal" and "comfort" that they assigned to different activities. Philipp concludes that continuing discriminatory practices in such areas as housing, employment, and education extend also to many recreation and park settings. He continues:

> Viewed from this position, nearly all of the activities in the investigation that showed significantly lower African-American appeal or comfort were located outside of the study area, in public settings located in other areas of the city or beyond: mountains, beaches, zoos, festivals, restaurants, museums, picnic areas, snow skiing resorts, and country clubs. Conversely, all the leisure activities that showed significantly higher African-American appeal or comfort were found in the study neighborhoods. . . . The lower levels of appeal or comfort may be associated with perceptions of present or historic patterns of discrimination and feeling unwelcome in these leisure areas.[36]

The tendency to separate into self-segregated groups is particularly evident on American college campuses. Arthur Levine, president of Teachers College, Columbia University, writes:

> No type of organization is growing more quickly on campuses today than advocacy groups focused on particular student populations, according to a [recent] study of chief student affairs officers at a sample of 270 college and universities. . . . The larger and more selective the college, the greater the number of such groups. Each campus activity [said one administrator] "appeals to smaller pockets of students."[37]

This reality poses a problem for leisure-service program managers in that providing exclusionary attention to the needs and backgrounds of members of different minority groups runs the risk of helping to create a badly fragmented society—with a loss of the nation's uniquely American cultural identity and set of common values. In the early decades of the twentieth century, when the "melting pot" approach to the assimilation of "new" Americans was widely accepted, such conflicts were rare. Today, given the influence of "political correctness" and the vision of America as a "multicultural mosaic," strong support is given to each minority or immigrant group's effort to maintain its traditions and identity.

In some cases, when the religious beliefs, family values, and social customs of a given immigrant population come into sharp conflict with American beliefs or even laws, the conflict may be extremely severe. Particularly with respect to the role of girls and women, for example, members of certain African tribes or those belonging to extreme Muslim sects may hold values and persist in customs that are unacceptable to most Americans. An extreme example would be the forced circumcision in some tribes of girls entering puberty, without anesthesia and often done with great pain and high risk of infection—apart from its implications with respect to female subordination in society.

Obviously, such issues go beyond the kinds of problems that recreation and park professionals should be expected to face. However, within the total field of intergroup relations, it is essential that leisure-service managers plan programs that will contribute to intergroup understanding and favorable relations. This may be done through community celebrations, holidays, ethnic and folk festivals, friendly sports competition, and a host of other program activities. It is also essential that leisure-service managers continue to strive to overcome the long-standing patterns of prejudice and racial discord that linger in many communities today.

A FINAL CONCERN: WHITES AS MINORITY GROUP MEMBERS

No discussion of racial and ethnic influences on leisure would be complete without recognizing that the majority population in the United States and Canada still consists of whites of European ancestry.

Historically, many individuals from the same European background have tended to band together in sports or gymnastic societies or in folklore groups, sometimes in connection with churches that continue to stress the particular national language and customs to second- or third-generation members of their congregations. Often, public recreation and park departments may assist such groups by providing facilities for their meetings or sponsoring large festivals that showcase their traditional arts.

In some regions or cities, members of a particular national group may still tend to cluster in certain neighborhoods, where the stores, churches, or other community-service organizations continue to meet their specialized needs.

A final concern for recreation and leisure authorities must be white Americans who are increasingly falling into the category of the economically disadvantaged. Although racial and ethnic minority populations—particularly those who are nonwhite—have tended to fall disproportionately into the lower socioeconomic brackets, with the crime, welfare, substance abuse, educational, and other statistical imbalances traditionally associated with poverty, the majority of poor Americans are of European descent.

There is increasing evidence that, with changing economic conditions, more and more white Americans are slipping from the middle socioeconomic group into the lower income brackets, with higher statistics of children being born out of wedlock, unemployment, and similar problems. The term "underclass" has generally been applied to urban or rural members of racial or ethnic minorities who have remained in poverty through successive generations. Today, it is increasingly being applied to whites. Charles Murray writes:

> The [growing] white underclass will begin to show its face in isolated ways. Look for certain schools in the white neighborhoods to get a reputation as being unteachable, with large numbers of disruptive students and indifferent parents. Talk to the police; listen for stories about white neighborhoods where the incidence of domestic disputes and casual violence has been shooting up. Look for white neighborhoods with high concentrations of drug activity and large numbers of men who have dropped out of the labor force.[38]

As an illustration of this trend, when a memorial service was held in South Boston in the mid-1990s for young men who had died—in many cases, from gunshot wounds, beatings, drugs, or suicides—it was noteworthy that they were of Irish, Italian, Lithuanian, or Polish descent. All but a few were white.

Beyond such trends, it is also a reality that, as many larger cities become increasingly dominated by African-American or Latino populations and political control, whites are literally becoming minority group members.

The illusion that it is only members of nonwhite racial or ethnic minorities that are economically depressed and require special social support is just that—an illusion. Today, members of all population groups may well be at risk and in need of the specially designed kinds of recreation and human-service programs that are described in later chapters of this text.

PROGRESS IN THE NEW MILLENNIUM

While this chapter has dealt in detail with many of the past limitations that have affected members of gender or ethnic minorities with respect to recreation and leisure, it must also be stressed that immense progress has been made over the past several decades.

Both women and members of sexual minorities are treated today with far greater respect and have achieved impressive levels of public support and access to a wide range of recreational opportunities that were not accessible to them in the past. Women, in particular, have made great gains in such areas as sports and outdoor recreation with the certainty that such gains will continue in the decades ahead.

In terms of race, similar gains have been achieved—particularly for African-Americans—since World War II. Certain injustices and forms of discrimination continue, particularly within the law enforcement and criminal justice system, where minority group youth and drug offenders are treated far more harshly than white offenders. However, overall, African-Americans at century's end had progressed markedly with respect to education, employment, home ownership, and similar measures.

Beyond these advances, a July 2000 Urban League report stresses that America's blacks are clearly divided into two classes, (1) those who have successfully entered the middle- and upper-socioeconomic groups and (2) a large, depressed underclass. The Urban League report also focuses on the interplay between racial and gender factors—

> . . . gulf between black men and black women in educational attainment. The number of blacks in college has surged by 43 percent since the 1970s. But black women have far outpaced black men in both undergraduate and graduate school settings [and hold twice as many advanced degrees]. . . . The implications are far-reaching. If few black men enter higher education, they will continue to be rare in corporate boardrooms and other spheres of power.[39]

In many cities, particularly in such states as Florida, Texas, and California, large Hispanic-American populations have begun to achieve economic success and a degree of political power. Among the nation's "first Americans," although the majority of tribes still suffer from extreme levels of poverty, unemployment, and other social ills, many Native-Americans have experienced an unexpected wave of prosperity stemming from successful tribal casinos. Gambling revenues have helped a number of American-Indian tribes establish successful new businesses and in some cases give all tribal members generous annual allowances.

In a striking illustration of such casino-based wealth, the Florida Seminoles, who pioneered the American-Indian gambling business in the late 1970s, earned about $110 million in 1997 from gambling. The Seminoles' chief, James Billie, owns a 47-foot yacht and Oklahoma oil wells and has at his disposal a $9 million jet and three helicopters.

Positive Public Attitudes

Strikingly, racist attitudes appear to have declined sharply among young Americans. A 1997 *Time*/CNN poll shows that a significant group of teenagers, both black and white, have moved "beyond their parents' views of race." These young people

> . . . say race is less important to them, both on a personal level and as a social divide, than it is for adults. [Whereas many still consider it a problem in America] a startling number of black teens call it a "small problem" or "not a problem at all." Indeed, nearly twice as many black kids as white believe "failure to take advantage of available opportunities" is more of a problem for blacks than discrimination.[40]

Supporting such views, a *New York Times*/CBS News Poll found that most Americans supported the goals of affirmative action, although they opposed numerical quotas based on race or gender. Instead, they favored policies linked to economic need in such areas as employment or college admissions that might help to eliminate bias in these fields.[41]

Finally, in a best-selling, late-1990s book, sociologist Alan Wolfe concludes that Americans are *not* deeply divided by disputes over race, gender, and cultural issues.[42] Instead, he argues, based on a comprehensive study in eight communities across the nation, the vast majority of Americans make up a single nation dominated by a set of middle-class values that are moving toward consensus on such matters as welfare, immigration, and family values.

SUMMARY

Major influences on recreation and leisure in contemporary society are the demographic factors of gender and race. This chapter defines these terms and shows how they have affected recreational participation in the past and continue to do so today.

As the chapter notes, women and girls have historically been denied many of the leisure opportunities open to men and boys. However, the feminist movement has succeeded in urging colleges, school systems, and community recreation agencies to provide more support to female participants in a wide range of sports and physical activities. This also helps women to develop positive self-images and feelings of empowerment. In addition, many women have overcome barriers to professional advancement in various types of agencies in the leisure-service field. Women are also being admitted to business and social groups that had excluded females in the past.

The status of males with respect to recreation and leisure is also discussed. In the past, many men were pressured to adopt stereotypical "macho" roles in leisure activities. Today, they are being encouraged to play a more open, sensitive, and creative role in their recreational pursuits, as well as in domestic life and their relationships.

The issue of homosexuality is dealt with as well. The chapter points out that, although much progress has been made in terms of acceptance, many organizations continue to resist gays and lesbians in professional roles. In turn, homosexuals have developed a wide range of recreational groups and are beginning to be courted as patrons by different sectors of the commercial recreation fields.

A second major section of the chapter deals with race and ethnicity. America's history of racial and ethnic discrimination is reviewed, along with the progress that has been made in serving minority populations and in developing a multicultural approach to recreation programming. Recent research examining the differences among various racial and ethnic groups in terms of leisure interests and values is examined, along with the theories that have been offered to explain these differences. In an era of increasing hostility on many levels, it is essential that organized recreation service contribute to positive intergroup relations in community life.

QUESTIONS FOR CLASS DISCUSSION OR ESSAY EXAMINATIONS

1. How have women's roles with respect to recreation and leisure differed from those of men, in terms of societal attitudes and constraints, throughout history? How have they changed from the past? As a class, have male and female students analyze and compare their gender-related patterns of leisure interests and involvement.

2. Why is the area of sport and active physical recreation particularly important to girls and women from a feminist perspective? What has been the impact of legislation, court cases, and similar factors in terms of programming policies and other leisure-related areas?

3. Although there is still significant resistance to considering homosexuals as a minority population comparable to women or racial minorities, there has been major progress in terms of their legal standing and status in community life. What issues do you perceive as critical in terms of involving gays and lesbians as identifiable groups in community recreation programs—and what policies would you support in this area?

4. The United States has traditionally regarded itself as a leading example of democracy. With respect to racial prejudice and discrimination, has this actually been the case? Specifically, how have racial or ethnic minorities been treated in terms of recreation and leisure? What progress has been made recently—and what problems continue to exist?

5. In terms of the general cultural scene, members of different racial and ethnic minorities have gained prominence in recent years in film, television, and other artistic or literary areas. What images are generally presented?

ENDNOTES

1 *Gender Equity Statement*, Sport and Recreation Commission, Province of Nova Scotia, Canada (March 1997).

2 Dirk Johnson, "Ethnic Change Tests Mettle of Minneapolis Liberalism," *New York Times* (18 October 1997): 1.

3 F. R. Dulles, *A History of Recreation: America Learns to Play* (New York: Appleton-Century-Crofts, 1965): 96.

4 B. Gilbert and N. Williamson, "Sport Is Unfair to Women," *Sports Illustrated* (28 May 1973): 85.

5 M. Deborah Bialeschki, "The Feminist Movement and Women's Participation in Physical Recreation," *Journal of Physical Education, Recreation, and Dance* (January 1990): 45–47.

6 Tarik El-Bashir, "Equity a Decade Away, A Study of Title IX Shows," *New York Times* (29 April 1997): B-16.

7 "Equality on the Golf Course," *New York Times Editorial* (29 December 1999): A-24.

8 J. Firestone and B. A. Shelton, "A Comparison of Women's and Men's Leisure Time: Subtle Effects of the Double Day," *Leisure Sciences* (January–February 1994): 45.

9 M. Harrington and D. Dawson, "Who Has It Best? Women's Labor Force Participation, Perceptions of Leisure, and Constraints to Enjoyment of Leisure," *Journal of Leisure Research* (Vol. 27, No. 1, 1995): 4–24.

10 L. Whyte and S. Shaw, "Women's Leisure: An Exploratory Study of Fear and Violence as a Leisure Constraint," *Journal of Applied Recreation Research* (Vol. 19, No. 1, 1994): 5–21.

11 Brent Staples, "Playing 'Catch and Grope' in the Schoolyard," *New York Times* (26 June 2000): A-16.

12 Mary Duffy, "Frailty Myth Haunts Women in Sports," *New York Times* (27 April 1999): F-7.

13 Andrew Kimbrell, "A Time for Men to Pull Together," *Utne Reader* (May–June 1991): 66.

14 Carlin Romero, review of Susan Faludi, *Stiffed: The Betrayal of the American Male*, *Philadelphia Inquirer* Book Section (3 October 1999): 8.

15 Erica Goode, "Thinner: The Male Battle with Anorexia," *New York Times* (25 June 2000): MH-8.

16 Jane Gross, "Male Bonding, But No Strippers," *New York Times* (7 July 1998): B-1.

17 Ann Morrill, "A Very Down Week," *Minneapolis Star-Tribune* (11 October 1994): 1-D.

18 Tamar Lewin, "Men Assuming Bigger Share at Home, New Survey Shows," *New York Times* (15 April 1998): A-18.

19 James Brooke, "In Canada, Gay Pride Can Be Part of Scouts' Honor," *New York Times* (3 July 2000): B-1.

20 Chris Conway, "Scornful Judge Rejects Gay Scout's Bias Claim," *Philadelphia Inquirer* (10 November 1995): B-1.

21 Arnold Grossman, "Until There Is Acceptance," *Journal of Physical Education, Recreation, and Dance—Leisure Today* (April 1995): 47.

22 "San Francisco to Offer Recreation Programming for Gay, Lesbian Youth," *Dateline: NRPA* (July 1994): 2.

23 Brenda Pitts, "Beyond the Bars: The Development of Leisure Activity Management in the Lesbian and Gay Population in America," *Leisure Information Quarterly* (Vol. 15, No. 3, 1988–1989).

24 Sophia Hollander, "Competition and Camaraderie for Gay Athletes," *New York Times* (25 June 2000): SP-4.

25 P. Rose, *They and We: Racial and Ethnic Relations in the United States* (New York: Random House, 1964):7–8.

26 Robert Hotz, "Scientists Say Race Has No Basis in Biology," *Los Angeles Times* (20 February 1995): A-2.

27 Mary Rourk, "Many Keep the Faith(s) in 'New' U.S.," *Los Angeles Times* (5 July 1998).

28 S. M. Stamps and M. B. Stamps, "Race, Class, and Leisure Activities of Urban Residents," *Journal of Leisure Research* (Vol. 17, No. 1, 1985): 40–55.

29 M. Floyd, J. Gramann, and R. Saenz, "Effects of Accultunation and Structural Assimilation in Resource-Based Recreation: The Case of Mexican-Americans," *Journal of Leisure Research* (Vol. 25, No. 1, 1993): 6–21.

30 M. Allison and C. Geiger, "Nature of Leisure Activities Among the Chinese-American Elderly," *Leisure Sciences* (Vol. 15, 1993): 309–319.

31 D. McDonald and L. McAvoy, "Native Americans and Leisure: State of the Research and Future Directions," *Journal of Leisure Research* (Vol. 29, No. 2, 1997): 145–166.

32 M. Floyd, K. Shinew, F. McGuire, and F. Noe, "Race, Class, and Leisure Activity Preferences: Marginality and Ethnicity Revisited," *Journal of Leisure Research* (Vol. 26, No. 2, 1994): 159.

33 Jim Naughton, "Black Athletic Directors Remain a Rarity in NCAA's Division I," *Chronicle of Higher Education* (1 July 1998): A-29.

34 Gerald Eskenazi, "Study Faults Teams' Efforts in Hiring Minority Coaches," *New York Times* (25 February 1998): C-2.

35 Ira Berkow, "The Minority Quarterback," *New York Times* (2 July 2000): 1.

36 Steven Philipp, "Race and Leisure Constraints," *Leisure Sciences* (Vol. 17, 1995): 109–120.

37 Arthur Levine, "The Campus Divided, and Divided Again," *New York Times* (11 January 2000): WK-17.

38 Charles Murray, "The Emerging White Underclass," *Philadelphia Inquirer* (15 November 1993): A-15.

39 "Report on Black America Finds a College Gender Gap," *Associated Press* (25 July 2000).

40 Christopher Farley, "Kids and Race," *Time* (24 November 1997): 89.

41 Sam Verhovek, "In Poll, Americans Reject Means but Not Ends of Racial Diversity," *New York Times* (14 December 1997): 1.

42 Alan Wolfe, *One Nation, After All* (New York: Viking Press, 1998).

CHAPTER 7

SOCIAL FUNCTIONS
OF COMMUNITY RECREATION

◆ ◆ ◆

The benefits of parks and recreation seem to pervade practically all domains for human behavior and performance—mental and physical health and wellness; family and community relations; increased pride in one's community and nation; maintenance of ethnic identities; formation of social networks and systems of social support; spiritual renewal; enhanced environmental stewardship; [assistance to] at-risk youth; and national, regional, and local economic development, growth, and stability.[1]

◆ ◆ ◆

INTRODUCTION

As Chapter 2 shows, earlier definitions of recreation suggested that it served to restore participants' energy for renewed work, but did *not* seek to achieve other, extrinsic purposes. Today, it is quite clear that this is no longer the case. Contemporary recreation programs and services—whether sponsored by public, nonprofit, educational, therapeutic, or other types of agencies—are goal-oriented and intended to achieve constructive outcomes for both participants and the community at large.

These outcomes range from improving the quality of life for all community residents and reducing antisocial and destructive uses of leisure to promoting the arts, serving special populations, and protecting the environment. This chapter outlines the societal benefits of organized recreation service in detail and provides a strong rationale for supporting recreation as an essential community function.

NEW EMPHASIS ON COMMUNITY BENEFITS

Thus far in this text, recreation and leisure have been described conceptually as important aspects of human experience. We now examine their contribution to community well-being on a broader scale. The term *community* is used here to mean a significant clustering of people who have a common bond, such as the residents of a city, town, or neighborhood. It may also refer to other aggregations of people, such as the employees of a company or those who live and work on an armed forces base.

Until recently, there was little concerted effort to identify the values and outcomes of community recreation. However, beginning with the period of fiscal austerity that affected many units of government and nonprofit social agencies during the 1980s, it became necessary to document the positive benefits derived from organized recreation programs and services in order to secure support for them.

Over the last several years, a number of major reports have been issued that present the demonstrated outcomes of organized recreation. One report by the Parks and Recreation Federation of Ontario, Canada, and several cooperating Canadian organizations concluded that the benefits of community recreation fell under four major headings: personal, social, economic, and environmental.[2]

In a detailed text in the early 1990s, Driver, Brown, and Peterson outlined the overall benefits of organized recreation services, with an emphasis on recreation and park functions.[3] Similarly, a major study supported by the National Institute on Disability and Rehabilitation Research of the U.S. Department of Education summarized hundreds of research reports showing the benefits of therapeutic recreation—chiefly in a medical or rehabilitative context.[4] And, in the mid-1990s, a task force affiliated with the National Recreation and Park Association initiated a systematic analysis of the social functions of community recreation in dealing with major community needs—including problems involving ethnic or racial relations, the environment, disability, family life, and poverty.[5]

It is important to recognize that, while many of the benefits and outcomes of recreational experience are defined in personal terms—that is, positive effects for individuals—they must also be understood as contributing to the common welfare. Dustin and Goodale write that personal benefits *must* be seen in this light:

> Our leisure services profession can play an important part in drawing people out of themselves and into the world of others. Especially throughout public and quasi-public programs aimed at youth-at-risk, the poor, and other disenfranchised groups, we can help provide the social glue that is necessary to sustain community—to sustain democracy. We can help foster . . . a sense of neighborliness, a commitment to place, a feeling of responsibility for the good of our towns and cities and regions, an affection for the creatures that share the land with us, and a higher regard for spiritual values than for material achievements.[6]

Given this understanding, we now examine 10 major areas of recreation's contribution to community life, drawing documentation from formal research studies and from anecdotal or qualitative evidence. In several cases, the benefits cited are similar to those presented in preceding chapters dealing with the personal values of recreation. However, here they apply to broader community needs and benefits.

DID YOU KNOW?

YMCAs...

■ serve all incomes, all ages and all abilities

We serve 16.9 million people in diverse communities nationwide. YMCAs this year raised $571 million for scholarships, subsidies and other community services. YMCAs are open to everyone and bring together the poor and not-so-poor, young and old, men and women, all faiths and all backgrounds.

■ reach 9 million children in non-school hours

Children and their families find a wide range of activities at the Y including community service projects, gang prevention programs, literacy tutoring, kids clubs and sports leagues. The values of caring, honesty, respect and responsibility are woven into every Y activity.

■ provide child care nationwide

YMCAs are collectively the nation's largest child care provider. Ys offer quality, affordable infant, pre-school and after-school child care programs. Approximately half of the children in YMCA child care come from households with annual incomes of less than $25,000.

■ partner with neighborhood organizations

400 YMCAs work with juvenile courts - 300 with public housing developments - 1,550 with elementary schools - 1,033 with high schools - and 700 with colleges or universities.

■ encourage volunteers

YMCAs are volunteer founded, volunteer based and volunteer led. We wouldn't exist without our volunteers. Ys mobilize more than 580,000 volunteers every year, and our Commitment to Volunteers campaign recruits more every day.

■ live their mission every day

Founded almost 150 years ago, today YMCAs together make up the largest not-for-profit community organization in America. All 2,283 independent YMCAs are guided by the common mission, "To put Christian principles into practice through programs that build healthy spirit, mind and body for all."

Y

YMCA
We build strong kids,
strong families, strong communities.

Organizations like the Ys, Scouts, Boys and Girls Clubs, and Police Athletic League, along with public recreation and park departments, provide important child-care, citizenship development, vocational, educational, counseling, and other services to children and youth throughout North America.

FUNCTION NO. I: Enriching the Quality of Life

PURPOSE: to enrich the quality of life in the community setting by providing pleasurable and constructive leisure opportunities for residents of all ages, backgrounds, and socioeconomic classes.

Recreation's most obvious value is the opportunity that it provides for fun, relaxation, and pleasure through active participation in sports and games, social events, cultural pursuits, and a host of hobbies and leisure involvements. Throughout all of society—particularly in larger cities, which often tend to be impersonal and cold—people need meaningful ways to make contact with each other in direct, open, and friendly situations. Janet MacLean has written:

> In a . . . hurried, noise-bombarded, harried, compacted, technological society, the opportunity for identity, positive self-image, social interaction, creative expression, and even the intellectual or physical stimuli to maintain physical and mental health may come in exciting leisure opportunities or not at all.[7]

For many individuals, one's quality of life would be directly linked to one's level of happiness. Here, psychologist Mihaly Csikszentmihalyi contends that creative experiences involving discovery contribute to one's zest for life and sense of well-being:

> When people are given a list and asked to choose the best description of what they enjoy about doing what they enjoy most—reading, climbing mountains, playing chess—the answer most frequently chosen is "designing or discovering something new." At first, it seems strange that dancers, rock climbers, and composers all agree that their most enjoyable experiences resemble a process of discovery. But the evidence suggests that at least some people . . . enjoy discovering and creating above all else.[8]

Parks provide a vivid illustration of the social value of leisure. During the warmer months of the year, they provide outdoor living spaces that are used by people of all ages and backgrounds. In swimming pools, zoos, playgrounds, nature centers, and sports facilities, community residents enjoy vigorous and sociable forms of group recreation. In community centers, children and adults can join clubs and special interest groups, take courses in a variety of enriching hobbies or self-development skills, and find both relaxation and challenge. Thus, in many ways, organized leisure service contributes significantly to the overall quality and enjoyment of community life.

A number of research studies have examined the degree to which recreation and leisure contribute to residents' satisfaction with community life. Lawrence Allen, for example, demonstrated the importance of recreation by citing evidence to show that, out of seven dimensions of community life, recreation was the best predictor of overall satisfaction among residents surveyed.[9] In their view, recreation, parks, and leisure services make an important contribution to the quality of life in their communities.

FUNCTION No. 2: Contributing to Personal Development

PURPOSE: to contribute to a person's healthy physical, social, emotional, intellectual, and spiritual development, as well as to family cohesion and well-being.

As earlier chapters in this text illustrate, recreation does far more than simply provide fun or pleasure for participants. It also makes an important contribution to their growth and development at each stage of life. While we often tend to focus on such obvious goals as improving physical fitness or social adjustment, recreation participation also can help people to reach their full potential as integrated human beings. For example, psychologists point out that many individuals have vivid memories of sports experiences in their childhood. Such experiences often play a key role in developing positive self-concepts and, beyond this, help to strengthen the bonds between parents and their children. In addition to providing benefits for children, these experiences may also contribute to the parent's own sense of well-being and mental health.

Varied types of community-sponsored recreation programs provide a rich setting in which children and youth are able to explore and confirm their personal values, experience positive peer relationships, discover their talents, and achieve other important personal benefits. Organized camping represents a useful example of the role of recreational experiences in the personal development of children and youth. As an intensive, sustained experience, Marta Moorman writes, it

> . . . provides a creative, recreational and educational opportunity in group living in the outdoors. It uses trained leadership and the resources of the natural surroundings to contribute to each camper's mental, physical, social, and spiritual growth.[10]

Writing in the *New York Times*, Roger Rosenblatt expresses the concern that many young people today are growing up in a "moral vacuum." He describes the "character education" movement that is striving to fill this gap: a number of boards of education have developed programs designed to inculcate positive core values that relate to such issues as self-respect and responsibility, loyalty, self-discipline, good citizenship, stereotyping and prejudice, and family values.[11]

Camp Fire Boys and Girls, for example, states that its fundamental purpose is to provide, through a program of informal education (which includes camping, recreation, and service projects), opportunities for youth to realize their potential and to function effectively as caring, self-directed individuals, responsible to themselves and to others. It continues:

> To achieve this purpose, Camp Fire works with individuals, communities and society as a whole to encourage the development and preservation of spiritual and ethical values; the realization of the dignity and worth of each individual; and the elimination of human barriers which prejudge individuals. . . . [12]

Similarly, the Girl Scouts of the U.S.A. strives to help young girls grow up in a healthy and positive way, able to face the stresses and challenges that threaten all children and youth today. Many of its program activities promote self-knowledge, creative thinking and problem-solving, feelings of self-worth, skills in relating to people, and other important areas of personal growth. Illustrative of its mission with respect to the emotional and social development of its members is the Contemporary

Issues Series of leadership manuals published by the Girl Scouts. The series contains such titles as:

Tune In to Well-Being, Say No to Drugs: Substance Abuse
Staying Safe: Preventing Child Abuse
Girls Are Great: Growing Up Female
Into the World of Today and Tomorrow: Leading Girls to Mathematics, Science and Technology
Reaching Out: Preventing Youth Suicide
Caring and Coping: Facing Family Crises
Decisions for Your Life: Preventing Teenage Pregnancy
Valuing Differences: Pluralism[13]

How effective are such programs? While it is difficult to demonstrate their effectiveness through rigorous experimental research studies, there is a wealth of information regarding the positive benefits of membership in youth organizations. A 1994 report by the Boy Scouts of America is particularly convincing in this regard. Summarizing the results of three surveys conducted by Louis Harris Associates of several thousand men and boys, including present and former adult Scout leaders and nonleaders as well as boy members and nonmembers, the report found that there was powerful evidence of the value of scouting. Overall, the study compared the values, standards, and life experiences of men and boys of different ages, racial and ethnic backgrounds, and geographic locations. It found that, within a national pattern of declining ethical and moral standards in such areas as cheating, shoplifting, carrying a gun to school, drinking and using drugs, and similar activities, both former and present scouts reported higher standards for personal behavior than did nonscouts.

Similarly, a detailed study of the outcomes of youth involvement in a Boys and Girls Club in a large city in the Southwest showed that this agency was able to meet important youth development needs. Carruthers and Busser point out:

> . . . [I]n the past few decades, the well-being of children has come to be regarded narrowly as the responsibility of the family and select child welfare agencies, rather than all citizens and socializing institutions within a community. [However,] the healthy development of youth is dependent on the broad support of a rich and varied network of constructive relationships and environments within the family and community. [It is also recognized that] the after-school hours, when children are not under the direct supervision of parents and schools [represent] a potentially dangerous time for youth.[14]

Systematic evaluation showed that the club that was studied made important contributions within several core areas, including cultural enrichment, developing conflict resolution skills, citizenship and leadership development, accepting positive adult role models, and resisting negative or antisocial forms of play.

FUNCTION NO. 3: Making the Community a More Attractive Place to Live

PURPOSE: to improve the physical environment and make the community a more attractive place to live by providing a network of parks and open spaces, incorporating leisure attractions in the redesign and rehabilitation of run-down urban areas, and fostering positive environmental attitudes and policies.

Saving Lives :

— measuring the impact of Boys & Girls Clubs.

BOYS & GIRLS CLUBS
OF AMERICA

④ Involving **Parents** in Drug Prevention

A Three-year Longitudinal Study in Boys & Girls Clubs, Pennsylvania State University, 1997

"Boys & Girls Clubs in this study had positive reputations in their communities as **safe places where young people participated in constructive activities.** Parents did not feel threatened and intimidated by the Boys & Girls Clubs as they did by many of the other community organizations or agencies such as the housing authority, social welfare, the juvenile justice system, or even the schools. Youths' existing Club involvement **provided an ideal opportunity to reach out to parents in a positive, respectful way** that laid the foundation for developing a trusting relationship over time."

⑤ Club Impact on Communities and Schools

The Center for Youth Development and Policy Research, Academy for Educational Development, 1996

An evaluation of demonstration sites funded by the Kellogg Foundation found Clubs in non-traditional locations were:

- ▶ **a resource for underserved communities**
- ▶ **a safe and supervised place for young people**
- ▶ **an inclusive place for sports and recreation**
- ▶ **a place for low-cost services**
- ▶ **a place for school-age child care**
- ▶ **a support or resource for school**
- ▶ **a place for informal adult interaction**

1-800-854-CLUB
www.bgca.org
© 1999 Boys & Girls Clubs of America

Documenting their impact, Boys and Girls Clubs of America have demonstrated positive benefits for young people in such areas as school performance, self-esteem and leadership skills, drug prevention, and the reduction of delinquency, based on national surveys.

In local governments, the recreation function is closely linked to the management of parks and other open spaces, historical sites, and cultural facilities. Together, they help to make cities and towns more physically appealing as places to live. In the post–World War II decades, it was recognized that many of our cities had deteriorated greatly. Gradually, we have come to realize that we can no longer permit our urban centers to be congested by cars, poisoned by smog, cut off from natural vistas, and scarred by the random disposal of industrial debris, ugly signs, auto junkyards, decaying railroad yards, and burned-out slum tenements. It is essential to protect and grace rivers with trees, shaded walkways, boating facilities, and cafes; to eliminate auto traffic in selected areas by creating pedestrian shopping centers; and to provide increased numbers of malls, playgrounds, and sitting areas that furnish opportunities for both passive and active uses of leisure.

In a number of American cities, once-abandoned freight yards, wharves, waterfront ports, or junk-filled streams winding through inner-city slums have been dramatically transformed into new, attractive open plazas and park-like settings. Frequently with the help of the business community, these eyesores have been rebuilt into condominium housing, offices, up-scale shopping centers, marinas for boating or waterfront play, and outdoor amphitheaters for various forms of entertainment throughout the year. Run-down architectural masterpieces have been restored, and older ethnic neighborhoods have been preserved while adding restaurants, art galleries, and other cultural activities that appeal to tourists. In some cases, cities have been farsighted enough not to have to reclaim their waterfronts. Chicago, for example, thanks to a series of turn-of-the-century lawsuits initiated by A. Montgomery Ward—a leading businessman who was also a strong conservationist—never had to reclaim its priceless lakefront from rotting wharves and warehouses:

> It has preserved the area as practically a 20-some-mile-long park lined with smooth, paved bicycle and jogging paths, marinas, parks, picnic grounds, barbecue pits and beaches whose fair-weather scenes, smells, and patrons provide revealing insights into the ethnic mix of the Midwest's capital. . . . Sport fishing is coming back on [Lake Michigan]. And boating never left. Few cities can rival Chicago's view on summer Sundays when the yellow sun burns brightly on the azure lake, dotted by hundreds of brightly colored sails and pleasure craft on comfortable cruises and in regular regattas.[15]

Over the past two decades, numerous cities throughout the world have adopted ambitious projects of promoting recreation and tourism through the revitalization of their waterfronts—both in the redevelopment of decayed harbor areas and in the recreational uses of formerly polluted rivers.[16]

Beyond recreation's role in helping to maintain and improve the environment in the central cities themselves, it also is a key player in helping to reclaim or protect natural areas within the larger framework of surrounding county or metropolitan regions. Environmental planners and park authorities are collaborating in many communities on remodeling abandoned railway corridors and establishing greenways to permit outdoor play or environmental education, provide hiking trails, or protect historic sites.

In the Sonoran Desert surrounding Phoenix, Arizona, the city's Department of Parks, Recreation, and Library has played a leading role in coordinating a major preservation master plan that incorporates outdoor education and recreation within sound ecological limits.[17]

In Canada, outdoor planners have sought to reconcile conflicting recreational and ecological priorities and are generally supported by the public, which has demonstrated awareness of the need for a multivalued approach to the management of forests and other natural areas.[18]

FUNCTION NO. 4: Preventing Antisocial Uses of Leisure

PURPOSE: to prevent or reduce antisocial or destructive uses of leisure, such as delinquency or substance abuse, by providing challenging programs that offer young people constructive and enjoyable recreational opportunities linked to other needed services.

As Chapter 3 shows one of the major objectives of the early recreation movement in the United States and Canada was to help prevent or reduce juvenile delinquency. Indeed, during the last decades of the nineteenth century and for much of the first half of the twentieth century, it was widely accepted that vigorous group activities were helpful in burning up the excess energy of youth, diverting their aggressive or antisocial drives, and "keeping them off the streets" and sheltered from exposure to criminal influences.

In the United States, there was widespread support for playgrounds, community centers, and other recreation programs for city youth by the police, juvenile court judges, and other youth authorities (see page 83). A number of sociologists pointed out that much delinquent behavior on the part of younger children stemmed from the search for excitement, risktaking, and the need to impress their peers. It was argued that, if other, more challenging forms of constructive play could be offered to youngsters at this stage, it would be possible to divert them from more serious involvement in criminal activities.

On the other hand, some investigators identified play as one of the ways in which delinquency becomes established as a way of life. Tannenbaum located the beginning of the alienation of gang youth from societal controls and values in the random play activities of youngsters:

> In the very beginning, the definition of the situation by the young delinquent may be in the form of play, adventure, excitement, interest, mischief, fun. Breaking windows, annoying people . . . playing truant—all are forms of play, adventure, excitement.[19]

Other investigators pointed out that much juvenile crime was committed for "the hell of it"—apart from considerations of gain or profit. Gradually, however, social workers and other experts on juvenile crime sought other explanations for youth delinquency. One school of sociologists developed psychological theories that emphasized the impact of the child's personality: children from broken homes with unstable, high-impulse behavior patterns, with a need for excitement, and with poor tolerance for delayed gratification were seen as delinquent-prone types. Other behavioral scientists held that juvenile delinquency was a cultural problem whose real roots were in the society itself.

Clearly, poverty and depressed neighborhood social conditions are key factors leading to gang involvement by children at risk. Lobo and Olson write:

> . . . [B]ehind the facade of the promotional material showing children playing on glistening playgrounds in well-groomed parks is another world, a world in which children don't swim in sparkling pools or scamper over clean, bright grass. In the underbelly of every society are children who had little opportunity to personally come to understand

and appreciate leisure and recreation. . . . Children living in the shadow of society subsist in poverty, are targeted with violence, suffer hunger and disease, receive little education, and swing between anger and hopelessness. For these children, adulthood holds few promises. These are children at risk.[20]

For youth in many so-called ghetto areas, membership in a gang becomes a form of survival and a means of protecting oneself against extortion and random violence. Particularly in the barrios of southwestern cities, gang membership involves strong ties of loyalty and brotherhood that may continue through the years of adolescence and become strengthened through stays in correctional youth centers and later criminal activity and prison sentences.

Despite such motivations for gang affiliation, it is also true that a considerable amount of juvenile delinquency is carried out in a spirit of excitement and challenge and in response to what young lawbreakers describe as "boredom—nothing to do" (see page 146). While it may be hard to conceive of mugging, savage gang attacks, or rape as forms of play, they certainly involve risk and a spirit of adventure that might otherwise be found in various forms of thrill-seeking outdoor recreation.

It is important to recognize that deviant behavior is now found across all socioeconomic class lines. Only a portion of today's delinquents are lower-class urban youth involved in gangs. A considerable amount of crime is carried on by teenagers, often of middle- or upper-class backgrounds, in well-to-do suburbs. There has been an increase in amateur shoplifting, auto theft, and vandalism by such youth. Thrill-seeking and joyriding are cited as the primary reasons for car theft by juveniles, and vandalism is obviously motivated by reasons other than economic gain. In addition to such forms of delinquent behavior, many other acts reveal a search for excitement on the part of modern teenagers. Drag-racing or pranks involving desperate risks (like playing "chicken" and risking head-on collisions on highways or in tunnels) are examples of such thrill-seeking stunts.

Linkage Between Recreation and Delinquency

While it is difficult to prove the specific benefits of organized recreation services for at-risk youth through experimental research, a number of other studies have demonstrated positive outcomes.

In an extensive study of the relationship between sports and delinquency, Donnelly noted several research reports that demonstrate the value of athletic participation. One such study, involving several midwestern high schools, found that only 7 percent of the boys who had participated for at least a full year in an interscholastic sport had been apprehended for delinquent behavior, compared with 17 percent of nonathletes.[21]

M. S. Searle documented the effects of youth sports programs in reducing juvenile delinquency in towns in northern Manitoba, Canada, as compared to communities that had not undertaken such programs.[22] Kelly and Baer found that juvenile delinquents who had taken part in Outward Bound programs had a substantially lower rate of recidivism than young offenders who had not been involved in such experiences.[23] Similarly, John Crompton has described a three-year study of several English cities that linked sports and other leisure pursuits with counseling and other probationary or social services for high-risk juvenile offenders. The final report of the British Sports Council, which evaluated the project, concluded that its overall impact was positive, although British confidentiality laws limited the ability to publish actual recidivism rates.[24]

A number of other cities and professional recreation and park societies have taken recent action to overcome the influence of gangs, which have been a leading factor underlying juvenile delinquency.[25] Austin, Texas has experimented successfully with the use of roving leaders, although they have experienced difficulty in some cases in integrating at-risk youth into community recreation centers.[26] The Canadian Parks/Recreation Association has collaborated with the University of New Brunswick in mobilizing a number of federal and provincial agencies to promote stronger initiatives to combat delinquency.[27] The California Park and Recreation Society has developed recommended strategies in this area that involve three approaches: prevention, intervention, and suppression.[28]

Numerous other cities have made use of recreational activities to reach at-risk youth. For example, the Chicago Housing Authority initiated a highly successful Midnight Basketball League designed to serve older youth and young adults by providing exciting league play during the hours of the night when much criminal activity takes place. A number of other cities have begun similar programs, as have county recreation agencies in such places as Prince George's County, Maryland. In some cases, both nonprofit agencies and private organizations have developed "wilderness therapy," borrowing from Outward Bound models, which seek to

> . . . strip away bad habits, build character, and restore self-esteem by forcing teenagers to fend for themselves and one another through a daily routine of hiking, campfire-building, food preparation [and campground responsibilities, along with "survival" and challenge activities].29

Probably the leading example of such at-risk youth programs is to be found in Phoenix, Arizona, where the public Parks, Recreation, and Library Department has sought special funding from a variety of sources to sponsor the following innovative services:

1. Several new teen centers in high-impact crime neighborhoods or public housing projects
2. Numerous special interest clubs to serve adolescents, along with talent shows, sports leagues, dances, tournaments, adventure trips, and similar recreation programs
3. Employment assistance through a Teens-n-Training Project partially funded through the Job Training Partnership Act and including the provision of occupational skills, counseling, and job development services
4. Cultural enrichment activities promoting multicultural awareness, with an emphasis on African-American and Hispanic themes
5. Teen leadership forums, councils, and peer mentorship programs
6. An extensive Juvenile Curfew Program, in which the public recreation agency works with police and other authorities to counsel hundreds of youthful curfew violators

FUNCTION NO. 5: Improving Intergroup and Intergenerational Relations

PURPOSE: to help improve intergroup relations among community residents of different racial, ethnic, or religious backgrounds, and among different generational groups, through shared recreational and cultural experiences.

As Chapter 6 points out, racial and ethnic identity plays an important role in shaping the leisure-related values and behavior patterns of community residents throughout the United States and Canada. Clearly this presents a challenge to recreation and park professionals in terms of the need to provide program opportunities suited to the tastes and traditions of different racial and ethnic groups, while at the same time maintaining a core of shared values and interests.

A related concern involves the need to use recreation as a means of overcoming the hostility and tension that have been building in many communities due to economic competition, negative stereotyping of minority populations, and other social factors that promote bigotry such as the growing use of the Internet to incite prejudice. In the late 1980s, there was considerable evidence that racism was on the rise in American society, with numerous incidents of violence and the revival of hate organizations in different regions of the country. An overwhelming 92 percent of blacks and 87 percent of whites polled by *Time* magazine in 1987 agreed that racial prejudice was still widespread in the United States.

The arts in particular represent a major area of opportunity for sharing cultural traditions and increasing the self-knowledge and pride of different racial and ethnic populations. As an example, the Recreation Department of Prince George's County, Maryland, regularly features performances by choral groups, storytellers, theater companies, and dance and music groups, as well as workshops, festivals, arts and crafts fairs, and similar activities that illustrate the history, traditions, and cultural contributions of African-American and other minority groups.

Karlis and Dawson have examined the role of recreation in helping members of different national groups to maintain their ethnic identity in Canada. In a study of participation in Greek cultural affairs in the city of Ottawa, for example, they analyzed the role of the Hellenic Community Association in serving both newly arrived Greek immigrants and those of an earlier generation who have undergone a process of cultural transition.[30]

In some cases, leisure-service agencies and programs may focus on problems of intergroup hostility and prejudice through meetings, staff training programs, workshops, and similar efforts. Organizations like the YWCA have focused on the elimination of prejudice and discrimination as a key program goal, and in some cases youth camping programs have been established to promote intercultural friendship and understanding. In one such camp, the "Seeds of Peace" camp in Wayne, Maine, hundreds of Arab and Israeli boys and girls designated by their respective governments have come together for several summers to share cultural traditions and begin to build respect and friendship. Many such programs appear to have been successful, as evidenced in the recent findings that racial and ethnic tensions appeared to have declined among many young people (see page 179).

FUNCTION NO. 6: Strengthening Neighborhood and Community Ties

PURPOSE: to strengthen neighborhood and community life by involving residents in volunteer projects or service programs and events to enhance civic pride and morale.

An important tenet of the early recreation movement was that shared recreational experiences helped to strengthen neighborhood and community ties by giving residents of all backgrounds a sense of belonging and common purpose, helping them to maintain social traditions and cultural ties, and enabling them to join together in volunteer service roles. For example, in many Canadian cities during the early decades of the twentieth century, community-based organizations initiated the development of after-school centers and community recreation programs. In Edmonton, Alberta, 10 volunteer community leagues were established that organized and conducted recreational, cultural, and educational programs within their geographical areas.

By the late 1980s, there were 139 individual community leagues in Edmonton, sustained by thousands of volunteers; approximately one-third of the city's population of 600,000 was actively involved in supporting their community leagues and participating in local programs. In many other Canadian and U.S. cities, parents' leagues sponsor youth sports activities, using public sports fields or indoor gymnasiums to schedule instructional or competitive programs year-round. Often they raise funds to rehabilitate or maintain facilities, purchase needed equipment, hire referees, or support such programs in other ways.

For the ordinary community resident, involvement in recreation programs often provides a means of developing a sense of acceptance and identity. Many communities sponsor neighborhood block parties or community festivals as a means of getting to know each other better and strengthening their feelings of unity, as well as for fund-raising purposes. Sometimes such events are even sponsored by the police. For example, a Police Open House and Community Day sponsored in North Philadelphia combined entertainment such as puppet shows, police wagon rides, children's games, and displays of police, fire, and National Guard equipment, with the obvious purpose of building favorable relations between the police and local community residents.

In the same city, residents in depressed neighborhoods have joined together to revive and rebuild drug-ridden, trash-filled, vandalized, and graffiti-covered recreation centers in cooperation with the Philadelphia Recreation Department—building a sense of civic responsibility and community pride.

In Phoenix, Arizona, the Parks, Recreation, and Library Department coordinates a wide range of volunteer programs in such areas as park maintenance and trail-building, library operations, and human services. It also works closely with The Salvation Army and AmeriCorps Vista in Project Hope, an outreach program for homeless individuals and families.

The unique role of recreation in helping to boost community "togetherness" and morale is illustrated in Toms River, New Jersey, which has suffered from an inordinately high rate of cancer among its children. In what some say is a response to this tragedy, parents in Toms River have given tremendous support to the tiny town's Pop Warner football teams and Little League baseball teams—winning national championships in both sports.[31]

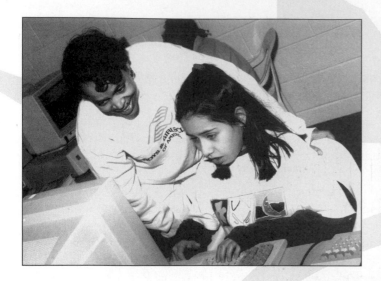

Youngsters learn computer skills and enjoy sports programs in Boys and Girls Clubs, while Police Athletic League sponsors a wide range of sports, social, hobby, and citizenship activities—including this National Archery Tournament in Ohio. Teenagers take part in intergroup human relations workshop in Phoenix, Arizona.

Fun

Where can you go horseback riding, rock-climbing or play tennis, take a nature hike, make pottery *and* serve your community? Or dance, play music, travel and go shopping? Fun and adventure know no bounds. Girl Scouts do it all!

Friends

One of the great things about Girl Scouting is that it grows with you. Younger girls enjoy hobbies like crafts and discovering nature. As you grow older, you will explore opportunities to make decisions about your future. And best of all, you will do all these things with your friends and you will make lots of new friends as a Girl Scout!

and Discovery

Girl Scouts Encourage Diversity

Girl Scouting promotes valuable social learnings, along with recreational satisfaction. To build racial and ethnic diversity, the brochure of this Pennsylvania-based organization includes enrollment appeals in Spanish and three different Asian languages.

In many other communities, recreational projects related to sports, the environment, the arts, disabled persons, and similar concerns serve to promote civic pride and neighborhood cooperation. In some cases, municipal recreation and park departments have mobilized community volunteers to provide emergency relief and survival assistance at times of disaster, such as hurricane or tornado situations.[32]

In a more formal way, citizens can assist recreation and park programs by serving on legally established boards and commissions or on district or neighborhood advisory councils. A *Parks and Recreation* editorial points out that citizen leaders, whether they serve as elected or appointed officials, and whether they are policymakers or advisors, have great influence in improving and expanding recreation and park programs, facilities, and services:

> Concerned citizens . . . can forward programs that will serve the leisure needs of the people; they can support those efforts designed to improve and expand the recreation and park profession as an enhancement of public service; and they can shape the parks and recreation program as an integral part of the community.[33]

Unselfish involvement in such civic-betterment activities is particularly important today, when many Americans see the signs of a spreading social and moral breakdown around them. At such a time, it is critical that every means be explored to develop a true sense of community, of sharing and mutual support in neighborhood life. Clearly, volunteerism and the kinds of projects just described do help to promote such values and positive interactions among community residents.

FUNCTION NO. 7: Meeting the Needs of Special Populations

PURPOSE: to serve special populations like those with physical or mental disabilities, both through therapeutic recreation service in treatment settings and through community-based programs serving individuals with a broad range of disabilities.

While all people need diversified recreational opportunity, those with disabilities find it especially difficult to meet these needs in constructive and varied ways, partly because their physical or mental impairments limit their participation and partly because of society's reluctance to help them engage in activity to their full potential. Yet, recreation is of even greater importance to many disabled persons. A study published by the federal government's General Accounting Office in the late 1980s revealed that although an estimated 10 percent to 15 percent of the nation's 2.7 million disabled workers were capable of paid employment, less than 1 percent of those who receive job training actually go back to work. This report, which illustrates the difficulty that the Social Security Administration has had in rehabilitating disabled workers, makes it clear that great numbers of disabled individuals do *not* work and have overwhelming amounts of free time—and thus have a critical need for appropriate leisure programming.[34]

In the past, many recreation and park departments barred disabled persons from their programs claiming that to serve the disabled would require specialized leadership that their agencies could not afford to provide. The stigma that society attached to disability often caused administrators to fear that the presence of blind, retarded, or orthopedically disabled participants would be distasteful to the public at large, who might then cease to use the facilities. Sometimes parents or relatives sheltered the disabled excessively, and often the disabled person's lack of skill or fear of rejection by others limited his or her recreational participation.

Today, a number of factors have combined to make this function an increasingly important one for recreation, park, and leisure-service agencies. First, public agencies have been barred by law, through Title II of the Americans with Disabilities Act of 1990, from refusing to provide disabled individuals with equal opportunities to participate in or benefit from their programs simply because of their disabilities. Secondly, while the initial thrust of therapeutic recreation was to use leisure-based programs as a treatment tool in hospitals or rehabilitation settings, today an equally important goal is to provide adequate recreational opportunities to disabled persons living in the community. The emphasis has essentially been shifted toward "mainstreaming" or integrating such individuals into programs with nondisabled persons.

In January 2000, the official policy of the National Recreation and Park Association affirmed that diversity was a cornerstone of American life, and made it essential that including people with disabilities in the fabric of society strengthens both the community and its individual members:

> Inclusive leisure experiences encourage and enhance opportunities for people of varying abilities to participate and interact in life's activities together with dignity. It also provides an environment that promotes and fosters physical, social, and psychological inclusion of people with diverse experiences and skill levels . . . enhancing individuals' potential for full and active participation in leisure activities and experiences.[35]

To coordinate the various types of agencies that serve people with disabilities, some communities have formed special committees or task forces to promote or sponsor leisure-service programs. Often representatives of wheelchair sports associations, local branches of the Easter Seal Society, service clubs, fraternal organizations, the Boy Scouts and Girl Scouts, and similar organizations are members of such bodies.

Throughout this process, it is essential that disabled persons themselves be involved in determining needs and in planning programs, so that they are no longer kept in a dependent or subordinate role but are empowered to take a degree of control over their own lives.

FUNCTION NO. 8: Maintaining Economic Health and Community Stability

PURPOSE: to maintain the economic health and stability of communities by acting as a catalyst for business development and a source of community or regional income and employment and by keeping neighborhoods desirable places to live.

Recreation has become a major focus of business investment and an essential element in the total national economy. Some cities have set out deliberately to transform themselves into centers of entertainment and sports. San Jose, California, for example, has built a huge new downtown arena that has housed circuses, ice shows, concerts, amateur and professional sports (including the city's professional ice hockey team, the San Jose Sharks), tractor pulls, and numerous expositions. It is now moving ahead on the development of varied arts institutions, including a symphony, opera company, civic light opera company, repertory theater, and art, technology, and children's museums—all designed to breathe new life and appeal into a formerly dull and charmless city. In other cases, cities depend on a single major recreational event, carried on year after year, to stimulate economic activity. For example, the Calgary Stampede in Canada, held each July for 10 days,

> is big business, drawing almost two million visitors annually to a raucous party that turns the entire city into a western theme park featuring rodeo events, chuckwagon racing, a huge agricultural fair, and even Las Vegas-style casinos and star-studded performances.[36]

For many American Indian tribes, tourism, gambling casinos, and outdoor recreation have proven to be important economic assets. Programs administered by tribal governments on about 56 million acres of Indian land from Maine to California and from Florida to Alaska help to meet the growing demand for outdoor recreation experiences, including hunting, hiking, horseback riding, biking, and such winter sports as snowmobiling:

> Tribal fish, wildlife and other natural resources support millions of recreational use days annually. Indian pow-wows, fiestas, fairs and religious ceremonies—many featuring traditional dancing, dress and foods—draw additional millions of visitors, including many from foreign countries. Indian museums, cultural centers, heritage displays, and arts and crafts shops are popular attractions.[37]

Interest in wildlife and nature has become a powerful attraction for many regions of the country. Even as specialized a hobby as bird-watching (actually, one of the most popular forms of outdoor recreation) sends millions of amateur ornithologists out on expeditions—some from as far away as New Zealand, South Africa, Japan, and Argentina. Often they come to see the migration of hundreds of different species—hawks, songbirds, and water fowl—through coastal areas of New Jersey. The economic benefits to host communities are surprising:

> . . . [B]irders represent the most visible and most lucrative segment of the state's growing ecotourism industry. A recent study released by the Cape May Bird Observatory, which is affiliated with the New Jersey Audubon Society, found that birders visiting Cape May County spend more than $31 million there each year, on food, lodgings, gifts, souvenirs, art, photography supplies, and even birdhouses.[38]

Similarly, aquariums have become an important lure to tourists, with a growing number of major cities building elaborate new aquariums, often along with new sports stadiums, museums, and performing arts centers. Edwin McDowell writes that this trend reflects the ability of aquariums to attract visitor dollars (attendance over the past decade has soared from 23 million to 36.6 million) and their importance in helping to regenerate run-down or abandoned urban areas:

> Moreover, aquariums, like zoos, have benefited not only from visitor curiosity about sea creatures, but also from the growing interest in wildlife conservation and the environment. No longer just collections of fish, mammals, or other marine life in tanks, modern aquariums often offer the aquatic equivalent of petting zoos, as well as interactive

musical entertainment, seminars for adults, story times for children, movies and slide shows, intern programs, and posted feeding times.[39]

Sometimes the benefits of expensive new projects, such as elaborate new sports stadiums, which are often subsidized by states and cities, may be exaggerated. John Crompton has critically analyzed the economic impact assumptions that are frequently made with respect to such ventures, and other experts—particularly economists—have concluded that government subsidies almost never are justified in sheer dollar terms.[40]

What is less easily measured is the importance of such elements as cultural attractions, outdoor recreation opportunities, sports teams, and similar leisure-related features in terms of attracting middle-class homeowners to cities—or persuading them to resist the lure of suburban life. Having major professional sports teams, for example, is believed to contribute to the image and overall morale of many communities and to make them more exciting places in which to live.

Summing up, evidence shows that public, private, and commercial leisure attractions and resources of cities are key elements in their economic health and stability, not only in bringing tourism revenues but also in the positive picture they present to potential residents and companies that are seeking to relocate.

FUNCTION NO. 9: Enriching Community Cultural Life

PURPOSE: to enrich cultural life by promoting fine and performing arts, special events, and cultural programs and by supporting historic sites, folk heritage customs, and community arts institutions.

It is generally recognized that the arts provide a vital ingredient in the culture of nations. Through the continued performance and appreciation of the great works of the past, in the areas of symphonic and choral music, opera, ballet, theater, painting, and sculpture, or through contemporary ventures in newer forms of expression, such as modern dance or experimental art forms, people of every age and background gain a sense of beauty and human creativity. Although America generally lagged far behind Europe in its support for the arts, after World War II public interest and participation increased dramatically.

During the 1970s and 1980s, many public recreation and park departments assumed fuller responsibility for sponsoring or assisting programs in the arts. Such cities as Indianapolis, Seattle, Detroit, and Los Angeles began to offer extensive arts programs—including directly sponsoring music, dance, and theater performances, maintaining fine arts centers, assisting independent arts organizations, and sponsoring arts festivals and summer workshops.

However, in the late 1980s and early 1990s, the performing and fine arts fields began to suffer a dramatic decline in support. With tighter municipal and educational budgets, many communities reduced the financial support they had given to music, dance, and theater companies, while boards of education eliminated classes and performances in the arts.

At the same time, conservative political leaders and religious factions joined together to attack the National Endowment for the Arts, which had been responsible for funding both major arts institutions and tiny, grass-roots companies and performers throughout the United States. With a declining level of support from foundations, corporations, and private funding as well, many orchestras and other performing companies have been forced to cut back on their seasons or slash the pay and employment schedules of performers and staff members.

In general, Canadian provinces and cities have not seen such assaults on the arts and have given substantial support to varied cultural programs. In Vancouver, British Columbia, for example, community public art projects are seen as providing important social, personal, and educational benefits. Varied art projects, including artist-in-residence programs, exhibitions, neighborhood murals, "memory quilts," banners and tiling projects, and innovative art installations, have all received public funding support in Vancouver.

Concern about "Popular" Culture Excesses

Within this overall picture, growing concern has been raised about another aspect of the arts—the "popular" culture that is provided by the mass media of entertainment and communication. There is a growing consensus that television, movies, and much rock and rap music are contributing to a national climate that encourages crime and immorality. Elizabeth Kolbert writes:

> Americans have a starkly negative view of popular culture and blame television more than any other factor for teenage sex and violence. . . . These are among the findings of a *New York Times* poll [in August 1995] examining Americans' attitudes about the influence of popular culture. The results of the poll suggest that Americans are deeply ambivalent about their own diversions. Although the average adult in the United States watches television for more than four hours a day, a little more than half of the adults polled could not think of a single good thing to say about television or about movies or popular music. Instead, nine out of ten mentioned too much sex, violence and vulgar language . . . bias and just plain stupidity.[41]

Such dissatisfaction with many of the aspects of popular culture makes it all the more imperative that community agencies, both public and nonprofit, play a stronger role in presenting programs in the arts that improve the level of popular taste and provide an opportunity for direct personal expression through music, dance, theater, and arts and crafts. One such program is found in Vero Beach, Florida, where a major Center for the Arts has been established in the city's Riverside Park. Backed by extensive community support, successful fund-raising activities, and cooperation from hundreds of volunteers and civic groups, this center's primary goal is to provide opportunity for the public's cultural enrichment, through:

Exhibition of the highest accomplishments of all cultures in the visual arts, with an emphasis on American art and Florida artists in particular

Explorations in the humanities through programs of lectures and seminars by eminent scholars and cultural leaders and offerings in the musical, cinematic, and dramatic arts by recognized artists and performers

Professional studio and classroom instruction in the arts for students of all ages

The collection, preservation and presentation of important art with emphasis on American art and Florida artists in particular

As evidence that growing numbers of Americans are taking advantage of such opportunities to become more directly involved in varied forms of cultural expression, the National Research Center for the Arts has documented growing amateur involvement in such activities as photography, painting, etching and drawing, choral singing, ballet and modern dance, ceramics, and creative writing.

Finally, some communities have directly linked the arts to current social needs, such as serving at-risk youth or promoting racial and ethnic pride among varied subcultural groups. Jana Ransom writes:

> Tucked into a corner of one of Long Beach's more colorful historic buildings is Homeland Neighborhood Cultural Center. Founded as a center for cultural preservation for the people of Long Beach's ethnically rich Anaheim Corridor provides opportunities in support of artists from traditions centuries old to those who make up contemporary subcultures, like those currently arising out of prisons.[42]

In the tension between mass-produced, commercially dominated forms of entertainment and leisure experience and more authentically involving kinds of personal expression, such artistic ventures and projects play an important role.

FUNCTION NO. 10: Promoting Health and Safety

PURPOSE: to promote community heath and safety by offering needed services and programs, including leadership training and certification courses and supervision or regulation of high-risk activities.

A little recognized but extremely important value of community recreation is its role in promoting public health and safety. As shown in Chapter 5, its most obvious value is the effect that its varied programs of sports and other physical activities have in promoting fitness. A wealth of recent studies have shown the value of systematic exercise in combating cardiovascular disease, obesity, and even some forms of cancer. There is striking evidence that athletically active women cut their risk of breast and uterine cancer in half and risk of diabetes by two-thirds; another study shows that exercise reduces the risk of colon cancer.[43]

Increasing recognition is being given to recreation's role as a health-related field of service. A special issue of *Leisure Today* in April 1994 was devoted to the theme of "Enabling Healthy Lives Through Leisure," and the U.S. Surgeon General's Report in 1996 on Physical Activity and Health has made a major impact on the public's consciousness.

Payne, Orsega-Smith, Spangler, and Godbey have defined the role of public recreation and park agencies in promoting healthy lifestyles, with special emphasis on senior wellness programs,[44] and Leonard Wankel confirms that what individuals do in their leisure time has major implications for their physical and mental health and ultimate longevity.[45]

Under federal and provincial leadership, many Canadian communities have developed cooperative programs to promote active lifestyles with input from recreation and park agencies, business, environmental and educational bodies, and various health and social-service organizations. Similarly, the supervision by public departments of organized sports leagues, ice skating, sledding, or other carefully directed activities helps to prevent many injuries and deaths. Many departments offer courses in boating skills, riflery, camping, or even—in Vancouver—a driving skills program for young children that has a miniature car facility complete with traffic lights, intersections, and police officers.

In terms of popular activities like swimming, which remains a leading cause of accidents for children, hundreds of thousands of youngsters ages three to five receive water safety and skills instruction today. In addition to discussing the role of public recreation and park departments in this area, Johnston, Bruya, and Langendorfer describe the work of numerous nonprofit organizations:

> Over the past decade, numerous preschool aquatic programs have emerged. The YMCA of the U.S.A. organized the Y Skippers in 1987, the American Red Cross established the Infant and Preschool Aquatics Program (IPAP) in 1988; the American Swimming Coaches Association started their Swim American preschool program in 1987; and most recently, the National Safety Council published the Learn to Swim program, which is endorsed by the National Recreation and Park Association, in 1993.[46]

In numerous other ways, public, private, and nonprofit agencies are working to reduce the injuries and deaths that frequently result from high-risk recreational activities. For example, many state commissions today regulate the use of boats—requiring that children or adults operating them have boating safety certificates—govern the use of jet skis, and maintain strict controls by prohibiting the use of alcohol while boating. Twenty-seven states have skiing safety acts that define skiers' and ski area operators' responsibilities on the slopes. Commercial companies and business associations provide safety education and guidelines along with training programs in such areas as scuba diving, roller-blading, skate-boarding, and other popular forms of outdoor play.

At the same time, it is necessary to recognize that many accepted, even traditional, activities contain a high-risk component. The tragic collapse of a giant woodpile being built by students at Texas A & M University as preparation for the Thanksgiving weekend football game against rival University of Texas resulted in the death of 12 students and critical injuries to many others. This bonfire ritual was a highly valued custom at the university.[47] However, like many other such activities, it raised questions of responsibility, supervision, and the ultimate purpose of student-run programs.

At a lesser level of risk, other physical pursuits carried on at an intensive level also pose dangers for participants. For example, while all athletes risk injury, the danger is particularly great for young female gymnasts whose growing bodies are especially vulnerable. Writing in *The New England Journal of Medicine*, medical authorities point out:

> Girls' intense training [for as much as 45 hours per week] suppresses estrogen production, delaying puberty and causing 18- and 19-year-old Olympians to resemble 12-year-olds. The lack of estrogen keeps their bones thin and puts them at risk of osteoporosis. . . . Many gymnasts and former gymnasts have a high incidence of back deterioration, wrist, and knee problems that can be quite debilitating and limit their activity as adults.[48]

On the positive side, many organized recreation programs help to divert or channel the drive that young people in particular often have for extremely dangerous forms of unsupervised or informal play into controlled or supervised programs. While the formal recreation system in the community can never fully satisfy these urges to dare and risk, it can and often does provide physically demanding and exciting alternatives in which the danger of serious accidents is much lower.

The challenge to the organized recreation movement is to offer other types of experiences that provide the same kinds of rewards or satisfactions as riots or other acts of gratuitous violence, but without their devastating social consequences. It must be recognized that this is a complex process. The easy assumption that competitive team sports provide an automatic safety valve for anger and aggression is not always valid. Under some circumstances, sports may simply provoke greater hostility and violent explosions if the participants' needs are not met. This suggests that we need to explore a wide range of pursuits—including many hazardous and active outdoor recreation activities—particularly in providing programs for those who are most violence-prone.

NEED FOR A COHERENT PHILOSOPHY OF SERVICE

This chapter has presented 10 major areas of social concern in which community recreation may satisfy important needs, constituting a strong justification for providing socially oriented recreation programs and facilities. However, if such programs and facilities are not based on a sound philosophy of service, they may not achieve the desired ends. Chapter 12 discusses a number of issues or problems facing this field today and suggests guidelines for developing a coherent philosophy for solving these issues.

SUMMARY

Far from simply providing casual or superficial amusement, organized recreation services help to satisfy a number of significant community needs, including the following:

1. *Quality of Life.* Constructive and enjoyable leisure for people of all ages and backgrounds contributes significantly to their quality of life and satisfaction with their communities.
2. *Personal Development.* As described in Chapter 5, organized recreation promotes healthy personal development in physical, emotional, social, intellectual, and spiritual terms—thus contributing to overall community well-being.
3. *Environmental Attractiveness.* Recreation and park agencies maintain parks, nature reserves, riverfronts, and other natural areas and may assist in rehabilitating or sponsoring historic and cultural settings.
4. *Combating Juvenile Delinquency.* As an important element in the community's educational, social, and other services for youth, organized recreation assists in preventing or reducing delinquency and other deviant forms of play.
5. *Improving Intergroup Relations.* Recreation serves as a useful tool in promoting ethnic or racial pride and intergroup understanding and cooperation. It also assists in positive intergenerational programming.
6. *Strengthening Community Ties.* Volunteerism and taking part in neighborhood efforts to improve the community environment, assistance programs for children or disabled persons, and similar involvements help to build civic togetherness.
7. *Needs of Special Populations.* In both treatment settings and in the community at large, therapeutic recreation service promotes mainstreaming and independence for persons with physical, mental, or social disabilities.

8. *Maintaining Economic Health.* As a growing form of business enterprise, recreation employs millions of people today. By helping to attract tourists, industries that are relocating, or new residents, it also provides income and promotes community stability.

9. *Enriching Cultural Life.* Many public and nonprofit leisure-service agencies today assist or sponsor programming in the various artistic and cultural fields, strengthening this important dimension of community life.

10. *Promoting Health and Safety.* Increasingly, recreation is recognized as a health-related discipline by helping individuals to maintain sound lifestyles and by helping to promote safety in outdoor recreation and other risk-related leisure pursuits.

QUESTIONS FOR CLASS DISCUSSION OR ESSAY EXAMINATIONS

1. This chapter presents 10 different areas in which recreation, parks, and leisure services contribute to community life. If you had to present a positive argument for establishing or expanding a community recreation and park department, which of these areas would you emphasize, and why?

2. Prevention of juvenile delinquency has been a long-standing purpose of many public and voluntary leisure-service agencies. Recognizing that there is limited research evidence to support the effectiveness of recreation in this area, could you sum up the evidence that exists, search for other research findings, and make a logical case for recreation's anti-delinquency role?

3. Explain and discuss the importance of community recreation within one of the following areas: (1) economic contribution; (2) health-related benefits; (3) promoting the cultural arts; or (4) improving intergroup relations among residents of different socioeconomic, racial, or cultural backgrounds.

ENDNOTES

1 Bev Driver, summarized from "The Benefits Are Endless . . . But Why?" *Parks and Recreation* (February 1998): 26, 28.

2 Ontario, Canada, Parks and Recreation Federation, *The Benefits of Parks and Recreation.* See Programmers Information Network, National Park and Recreation Association (Vol. 4, No. 4, 1993): 1.

3 B. L. Driver, P. Brown, and G. Peterson, eds., *Benefits of Leisure* (State College, Pa.: Venture Publishing, 1991).

4 C. Coyle, W. W. Kinney, and J. Shank, *Effect of Therapeutic Recreation and Leisure Lifestyle on Rehabilitation Outcomes and on the Physical and Psychological Health of Individuals with Physical Disability* (Philadelphia, Pa.: Temple University and U.S. Department of Education, Office of Special Education and Rehabilitative Services, 1993).

5 "New Study Reveals Recreation, Parks' Impact on Serious Social Issues," *Dateline: NRPA* (December 1994): 1–2.

6 D. Dustin and T. Goodale, "The Social Cost of Individual 'Benefits'," *Parks and Recreation* (July 1997): 22.

7 Janet MacLean, "Leisure and the Quality of Life," in Timothy Craig, ed., *The Humanistic and Mental Health Aspects of Sports, Exercise, and Recreation* (Chicago: American Medical Association, 1975): 73–74.

8 Mihalyi Czikszentmihalyi, "Happiness and Creativity: Going with the Flow," *The Futurist: Special Report on Happiness,* n.d.

9 Lawrence Allen, "Benefits of Leisure Attributes to Community Satisfaction," *Journal of Leisure Research* (22, 1990): 183–196.

10 Marta Moorman, "Satisfaction in Organized Camping," *Parks and Recreation* (April 1999): 41.

11 Roger Rosenblatt, "Teaching Johnny to Be Good," *New York Times Magazine* (20 April 1995): 36–41.

12 *The Fire We Light Is the Fire Within,* (Kansas City, Mo.: Camp Fire Boys and Girls Brochure, 1995).

13 *Contemporary Issues: Reaching Out* (New York: Girl Scouts of the U.S.A. Brochure, 1992).

14 C. Carruthers and J. Busser, "A Qualitative Outcome Study of Boys and Girls Club Program Leaders, Club Members and Parents," *Journal of Park and Recreation Administration* (Spring 2000, Vol. 18, No. 1): 50–67.

15 "The Midwest's Brawny Capital," *New York Times* (5 May 1985): X-14.

16 S. Craig-Smith and M. Fagence, eds., *Recreation and Tourism as a Catalyst for Urban Waterfront Redevelopment* (Westport, Conn.: Praeger, 1995).

17 *Sonoran Preserve Master Plan* (Phoenix, Ariz.: Department of Recreation, Parks, and Library, Open Space Report, 1998).

18 D. Robinson and J. Zeiger, "Come Together, Right Now," *Parks and Recreation* (September 1999): 137.

19 Frank Tannenbaum, *Crime and the Community* (New York: Columbia University Press, 1938): 17–20.

20 F. Lobo and E. Olson, "Leisure Services and Children at Risk: Against All Odds," *Journal of Park and Recreation Administration* (Spring 2000, Vol. 18, No. 1): 5.

21 Peter Donnelly, "Athletes and Juvenile Delinquents: A Comparative Analysis Based on a Review of the Literature," *Adolescence* (Summer 1981): 415.

22 M. S. Searle, *Synthesis of the Research Literature on the Benefits of Recreation: A Technical Report* (Winnipeg, Manitoba: University of Manitoba, 1989).

23 See Stacey McKay, "Research Findings Related to the Potential of Recreation in Delinquency Prevention," *Trends* (Vol. 30, No. 3, 1993): 27.

24 John Crompton, "Rescuing Young Offenders with Recreation Programs," *Trends* (Vol. 30, No. 3, 1993): 23–26.

25 S. Battin, K. Hill, R. Abbott, R. Catalano, and J. D. Hawkins, "The Contribution of Gang Membership to Delinquency . . . ," *Criminology* (November 1998): 93.

26 J. Baker and P. Witt, "Backstreet Beacons: Austin's Roving Leaders," *Journal of Park and Recreation Administration* (Spring 2000, Vol. 18, No. 1): 87–105.

27 *Impacts and Benefits of Physical Activity and Recreation in Canadian Youth-at-Risk,* Special Report, Interprovincial Sport and Recreation Council and Health Canada, 1997.

28 *Phoenix Report,* California Park and Recreation Society (1995).

29 Michael Janofsky, "Deep in the Wilderness, a Growth Industry is Blooming," *New York Times* (11 December 1999): A-12.

30 G. Karlis and D. Dawson, "Ethnic Maintenance and Recreation: A Case Study," *Journal of Applied Recreation Research* (Vol. 15, No. 2, 1990): 85–99.

31 Jon Stenzler, "Town's Triumphs, Tragedy, May Be Linked, Some Say," *Philadelphia Inquirer* (30 January 2000): A-1.

32 Sheila Franklin, "Operation Recreation Relief," *Parks and Recreation* (October 1999): 78.

33 L. W. Gahan, "Citizen Involvement," *Parks and Recreation* (July 1982): 24.

34 "Study: Few Disabled Go Back to Work," *Philadelphia Inquirer* (23 February 1988): 7-B.

35 *National Therapeutic Recreation Society Report* (Vol. 25, No. 1, January 2000): 19.

36 Suzanne Carmichael, "What's Doing in Calgary?" *New York Times* (18 June 1995): 10XX.

37 Gary Rankel. "Few Know Extent of Outdoor Recreation in Indian Country," *Recreation Executive Report* (October 1994): 1–16.

38 Bill Kent, "The Birding Business," *New York Times* (14 September 1999): NJ-1.

39 Edwin McDowell, "A Big Boom Underwater," *New York Times* (21 April 1999): 8.

40 John Crompton, "Economic Impact Analysis of Sports Facilities and Events: Eleven Sources of Misapplication," *Journal of Sport Management* (Vol. 9, 1995): 145. See also: Richard Perez-Pena, "Economists Dispute Value of Spending for Stadiums," *New York Times* (3 August 1997): 29.

41 Elizabeth Kolbert, "America's Despair of Popular Culture," *New York Times* (20 August 1995): H-23.

42 Jana Ransom, "Arts for At-Risk Youth," *Parks and Recreation* (March 1996): 40.

43 Vic Sussman, "No Pain and Lots of Gain," *U.S. News and World Report* (4 May 1992): 86–88.

44 L. Payne, E. Orsega-Smith, K. Spangler, and Geoffrey Godbey, "Local Parks and Recreation for the Health of It," *Parks and Recreation* (October 1999): 72.

45 Leonard Wankel, "Health and Leisure: Inextricably Linked," *Journal of Physical Education, Recreation, and Dance* (April 1994): 28.

46 K. Johnston, L. Bruya, and S. Langendorfer, "Ready to Paddle," *Parks and Recreation* (February 1994): 50.

47 Jodie Morse, "A Good Time Goes Bad," *Time* (29 November 1999): 68.

48 Susan Gilbert, "The Smallest Olympians Pay the Biggest Price," *New York Times* (28 July 1996): E-4.

CHAPTER 8

THE LEISURE-SERVICE SYSTEM:
Governmental, Nonprofit, and Commercial Recreation Agencies

◆ ◆ ◆

Within each park lies a compelling story—a powerful reminder of our nation's origins and destiny. Geology, political science, marine ecology, the Civil War, language, art, music, maritime history, geography, wildlife, the American Revolution, technology—all come to life in our National Park System.

Today, the men and women of the National Park Service are reaching out to the next generation of caretakers, instilling in our children a respect for the land, an understanding of our common American heritage, and an appreciation of parks as places of inspiration.[1]

◆ ◆ ◆

INTRODUCTION

We now turn to a detailed examination of the overall leisure-service system in the United States and Canada at the turn of the twenty-first century. This chapter deals with three major types of recreation providers that share a broad responsibility for sponsoring recreation, park, and related leisure facilities and programs for the public at large; (1) governmental agencies, (2) nonprofit community organizations, and (3) commercial recreation businesses. In each case, the background, mission, and chief program elements of sponsoring agencies are described, with numerous examples drawn from the field that illustrate recreation and leisure services today.

KEY ELEMENTS IN THE LEISURE-SERVICE SYSTEM

A number of respected authors have described the leisure-service system in modern society as consisting of two or three components. This approach is incomplete. Actually, there are 10 different types of leisure-service organizations in modern society, as shown in Table 8.1. Of these, three of the major types that meet a broad range of public needs are described in this chapter, with the other seven in the two chapters that follow.

GOVERNMENT RECREATION, PARK, AND LEISURE SERVICES

In both the United States and Canada, government leisure-service agencies have the following characteristics: (1) they were the first type of agency to be formally recognized as responsible for serving the public's recreation needs and, as such, have constituted the core of the recreation movement; (2) the primary means of support for most government recreation and park agencies has been tax funding, although in recent years other revenue sources have begun to be used more fully; (3) government agencies have a major responsibility for the management of natural resources; and (4) they are obligated to serve the public at large with socially useful or constructive programs because of their tax-supported status.

Federal Government's Role

The federal government's responsibility for managing parks and providing or assisting other leisure services evolved gradually. Reynold Carlson and his co-authors summarized the process as follows:

> In the more than two hundred years of our history as a nation, the attitudes and services of the federal government regarding responsibility for leisure have undergone dramatic changes. In the early years of the republic, the official attitude was one of indifference, even though public lands were used for recreation, particularly fishing and hunting. Later, as public lands were reserved for parks and forests, recreation gained status as one of their important uses. Even though recreation was permitted, however, the federal government held—and still holds—these lands primarily for the protection of natural resources.[2]

Overall, the federal government in the United States has developed a great variety of programs related to recreation in dozens of different departments, bureaus, or other administrative units. Typically, recreation functions evolved in federal agencies as secondary responsibilities. For example, the initial purposes of the Tennessee Valley Authority lakes and reservoirs were to provide flood control and rural electrification; only over time did recreation uses become important.

Direct Management of Outdoor Recreation Resources   The federal government, through such agencies as the National Park Service and the Bureau of Land Management, owns and operates a vast network of parks, forests, lakes, reservoirs, seashores, and other facilities used extensively for outdoor recreation.

TABLE 8.1

TEN MAJOR ELEMENTS IN THE MODERN LEISURE-SERVICE SYSTEM

(Note: The same program elements, facilities, leisure needs, and outcomes may be found in all ten types of agencies. Each column should be read vertically, rather than across the page.)

Types of Recreation Sponsoring Organizations	Assisted by Support Groups and Services	Provide Leisure Programs Consisting of	To Satisfy Public Needs for	Yielding Major Benefits in Four Areas
Government recreation and park agencies	Trade associations	Direct program leadership	Full spectrum of involvement in:	Personal values (health, emotional wellness, mental development)
Nonprofit community organizations	Professional societies	Provision of facilities for undirected public use	Games and sports	
	Special-interest groups		Outdoor recreation	Social and community-based outcomes
Commercial recreation businesses		Education for leisure	Cultural activities	
	Sponsors of special programs or events		Creative arts	
Employee service and recreation programs		Information-referral services	Hobbies	Economic benefits, employment, taxes, other fiscal returns
	Professional preparation institutions		Special events	
Armed forces morale, welfare, and recreation units		Enabling facilitation	Club and other social groups	Environmental values, both natural and urban settings
	Private groups that subcontract leisure functions	Advocacy and leadership in special areas	Other social services	
Private membership organizations			With needs influenced by:	
Campus recreation programs	Other civic agencies and citizen's groups	Jointly sponsored campaigns and events	Age group	
			Gender	
Therapeutic recreation service			Socioeconomic status	
			Racial/ethnic factors	
Sports management organizations			Educational background	
			Residential and regional factors	
Tourism and hospitality industry			Physical and emotional health	
			Family status	

Conservation and Resource Reclamation   Closely related to the preceding function is the government's role in reclaiming natural resources that have been destroyed, damaged, or threatened and in promoting programs related to conservation, wildlife, and antipollution controls.

Assistance to Open-Space and Park Development Programs   Chiefly with funding authorized under the 1965 Land and Water Fund Conservation Act, the federal government has provided billions of dollars in matching grants to states and localities to promote open-space development. Also, through direct aid to municipalities carrying out housing and urban development projects, the federal government has subsidized the development of local parks, playgrounds, and centers.

Direct Programs of Recreation Participation   The federal government operates a number of direct programs of recreation service in Veterans Administration hospitals and other federal institutions and in the armed forces on bases throughout the world.

Advisory and Financial Assistance   The federal government provides varied forms of assistance to states, localities, and other public or voluntary community agencies. For example, many community programs serving economically and socially disadvantaged populations have been assisted by the (then) Departments of Health, Education, and Welfare; Housing and Urban Development; Labor; and others.

Aid to Professional Education   Federal agencies concerned with education and the needs of special populations have provided training grants for professional education in colleges and universities throughout the United States.

Promotion of Recreation as an Economic Function   The federal government has been active in promoting tourism, providing aid to rural residents in developing recreation enterprises, and assisting Indian tribes in establishing recreational and tourist facilities on their reservations. Such agencies as the Bureau of the Census and the Coast Guard also provide needed information for those interested in travel, boating, and similar pastimes.

Research and Technical Assistance   The federal government has supported a broad spectrum of research on topics ranging from outdoor recreation trends and needs and the current status of urban recreation and parks to specific studies of wildlife conservation, forest recreation, or the needs of special populations.

Regulation and Standards   The federal government has developed regulatory policies with respect to pollution control, watershed production, and environmental quality. It has also established standards with respect to rehabilitative service for the ill and disabled and architectural standards to guarantee access to facilities for the disabled.

The first two areas of responsibility are carried out by seven major federal agencies that are either service units or bureaus in cabinet departments or separate authorities. They are the National Park Service, the Forest Service, the Bureau of Land Management, the Bureau of Reclamation, the U.S. Fish and Wildlife Service, the Tennessee Valley Authority, and the U.S. Army Corps of Engineers. Altogether, over 16 billion visitor-hours were recorded at facilities operated by these seven agencies in the mid-1990s.

The National Park Service

One of the leading federal agencies with respect to outdoor recreation is the National Park Service, housed in the Department of the Interior. Its mission has been stated as follows:

> The National Park Service is dedicated to conserving unimpaired the natural and cultural resources and values of the National Park System for the enjoyment, education, and inspiration of this and future generations. The Service is also responsible for managing a great variety of national and international programs designed to help extend the benefits of natural and cultural resource conservation and outdoor recreation throughout this country and the world.

Most of the property administered by the Park Service in its early years was west of the Mississippi, but in recent decades it has added major seashore parks and other areas throughout the country and closer to urban centers. For example, East Coast sites now include the Fire Island National Seashore on Long Island, Acadia National Park in Maine, Assateague National Seashore on the Maryland coast, Cape Hatteras National Seashore in North Carolina, and Gateway East in the New York–New Jersey harbor area.

The national park system generates a huge volume of tourism, with appeal for domestic travelers and foreign visitors and with major benefits for the nation's economy and the balance of trade payments with other countries.

However, in recent years, the National Park Service has been troubled by overcrowding, shrinking or frozen budgets, and Congress's appetite for "pork"—the determination of legislators to have the federal government establish new sites in their states. *U.S. News & World Report* commented in 1995:

> While tight budgets are forcing the park service to defer maintenance, cut staff and programs, and allow environmental problems to fester at many units, Congress has pushed through some 83 new national parks [or other recreational or historic units] in the past 20 years. In the decade ending in 1993, lawmakers ordered almost $1.4 billion worth of projects the Park service didn't want but could not refuse. Once they were established, Congress starved them of operating and maintenance funds.[3]

With a growing wave of public concern about overcrowded, poorly maintained, and deteriorating national parks, the Department of the Interior mounted a number of important initiatives in the late 1990s, including:

Imposition of a range of new and higher fees at many parks to support maintenance and staffing budgets

Stricter policies and regulations to curb off-road recreation vehicle use in parks, including a ban on snowmobiles in many parks

Remodeling or removal of many parking areas, roads, and bridges in such national parks as Yosemite, to reduce traffic

Stronger emphasis on the role of the National Park Service in historical interpretation to reflect the role of women and minorities in national life[4]

Other initiatives at this time included promoting greater use of volunteers and environmental organizations in park operations, new funding grants to local communities to assist in land and water conservation programs, and major projects to protect the nation's fragile shoreline and to restore environmental health to such areas as the Everglades.

The Forest Service

A second federal agency that administers extensive wilderness preserves for public recreation use is the Forest Service within the Department of Agriculture. In contrast to the National Park Service, the Forest Service is responsible not for scenic monuments and historical or geological treasures, but for huge areas of forests and grasslands. Rather than following the National Park Service's single-use concept of preservation and public enjoyment of natural areas, the Forest Service accepts the multiple-use concept of federally owned land under its control; mining, grazing, lumbering, and hunting are all permitted in the national forests.

The recreation function of the Forest Service has continued to grow steadily. In the mid-1990s, it encompassed a total forest system of 191.6 million acres, which included 35 million acres of wilderness as well as major elements of the National Scenic Byways and National Wild and Scenic Rivers Systems, wildlife and fish habitats, and numerous other special-use areas. In the same year, the Forest Service recorded 330.3 million visitor-days and served over 120,000 persons in its human resource programs, as well as permitting extensive commercial uses with respect to timber harvesting, grazing, and mining operations. Its major recreational uses in 1994 were for mechanized travel and viewing scenery; camping, picnicking, and swimming; hiking, horseback riding, and water travel; winter sports; and hunting and fishing.

At the same time, the Forest Service has been forced to carefully review its basic mission, as its extensive logging programs have come under attack by environmentalists. In the late 1990s, the Forest Service moved to promote recreational uses of the wilderness, with research reports that such activities were worth 6 to 10 times the economic value of logging. It also took the initiative to promote reforestation in urban regions in the East and enact a ban on new roads in many forest areas.

Other Federal Agencies

The Bureau of Land Management administers over 270 million acres, chiefly in the western states and Alaska. Its properties are used for a variety of resource-based outdoor recreation activities (including camping, biking, hunting and fishing, mountain climbing, and cycle racing), as well as mining, grazing, and lumbering activities that yield over $800 million a year in revenues—much of it returned to state and local governments.

The federal Bureau of Reclamation is responsible for water resource development, primarily in the western states. Although its original function was to promote irrigation and electric power, it has accepted recreation as a responsibility since 1936.

The policy of the Bureau of Reclamation is to transfer reservoir areas wherever possible to other federal agencies; often these become classified as National Recreation Areas and are assigned to the National Park Service for operation, The emphasis is on active recreational use such as boating, camping, hiking, hunting, and fishing rather than sightseeing.

As in the case of the Forest Service, the Bureau of Reclamation has provided employment opportunities for thousands of young men and women through the Youth

Conservation Corps (YCC) and Young Adult Conservation Corps (YACC), which have cooperated in rehabilitating or building campgrounds and boating facilities at recreation areas throughout the West.

The U.S. Fish and Wildlife Service originally consisted of two federal bureaus, one dealing with commercial fisheries (which was transferred to the Department of Commerce) and the other dealing with sports fisheries and wildlife (which remained in the Department of the Interior). Its functions include restoring the nation's fisheries, enforcing laws, managing wildlife populations, conducting research, and operating the National Wildlife Refuge System. This system includes 504 units comprising 92 million acres, of which 77 million are in Alaska. In addition to meeting the ongoing needs of hunters and fishermen, the Fish and Wildlife Service has been particularly active in helping to ensure the survival of endangered species, conserving migratory birds, and administering federal aid programs that assist state wildlife programs.

The Tennessee Valley Authority operates extensive reservoirs in Kentucky, North Carolina, Tennessee, and other southern or border states. The TVA does not manage recreation facilities itself, but makes land available to other public agencies or private groups for development.

Visitor-days to TVA lakes within the Tennessee Valley region's more than 1,000 square miles of water surface and 11,000 miles of shoreline were reported to be approximately 80 million a year until 1987, when the TVA discontinued reporting visitation to non–fee-charging areas. Today the visitor-day total is reported to be approximately 14 million a year, but this includes those involved with the more than 30 universities and colleges that participate in resource management, environmental education, and campground operation through a consortium program at the Land Between the Lakes, an outstanding natural facility of more than 170,000 acres located in west Kentucky and Tennessee.

The U.S. Army Corps of Engineers is responsible for the improvement and maintenance of rivers and other waterways to facilitate navigation and flood control. It constructs reservoirs, protects and improves beaches and harbors, and administers over 11 million acres of federally owned land and water impoundments. This includes 460 reservoirs and lakes; the majority of these are managed by the Corps, and the remainder are managed by state and local agencies under lease. Army Corps of Engineers recreation sites are heavily used by the public for boating, camping, hunting, and fishing.

Several other agencies in the Department of Agriculture have important recreation functions. The Agricultural Stabilization Service assists farmers in developing ponds and reservoirs on private land and stocking them with fish. The Farmers Home Administration gives credit and management advice to rural organizations and farmers in developing recreation facilities. The Extension Service aids community recreation planning in rural areas and advises states on outdoor recreation development, working in many states through extension agents at land-grant agricultural colleges.

The Bureau of Indian Affairs exists primarily to provide service to American Indian tribes in such areas as health, education, economic development, and land management. However, it also operates (under civilian control in the Department of the Interior) Indian-owned properties of about 56 million acres with more than 5,500 lakes, which are used heavily for recreational purposes, including camping, museum visits, hunting, and fishing.

Programs in Health and Human Services, Education, and Housing

A number of federal agencies related to health and human services, education, and housing and urban development have provided funding, technical assistance, and other forms of aid to recreation programs designed to meet various social needs in American communities. Within the federal Department of Health and Human Services, such units as the Administration on Aging, the Children's Bureau, and the Public Health Service have been active in this area. For example, the Administration on Aging, authorized by the Older Americans Act of 1965, promotes comprehensive programs for elderly persons and supports training programs and demonstration projects intended to prepare professional personnel to work with older people. It also gathers information on new or expanded programs and services for the aging and supports research projects in this field.

The Rehabilitation Services Administration administers the federal law authorizing vocational rehabilitation programs designed to help persons with physical or mental disabilities gain employment and lead fuller lives, and it has been responsible for special projects in the areas of research, demonstration, and training.

Other federal legislation, such as Section 504 of the Rehabilitation Act of 1975 (often called the "nondiscrimination clause") and the Americans with Disabilities Act of 1990, has been instrumental in pressuring school systems, units of local government, and other agencies to provide equal opportunity for people with disabilities in a wide range of community opportunity fields.

The Federal Department of Housing and Urban Development was established in 1965, with responsibility for a range of federally assisted programs, including urban renewal and planning, public housing, mass transit, and open space. With funding of $7.5 billion for a four-year period, HUD was empowered to provide up to 50 percent of the cost of land acquisition, development, and beautification. Section 705 of the act, known as "the small parks program," authorized grants for extensive planning and development in depressed urban areas. Federal programs under the Model Cities Program, Metropolitan Development Act, and Neighborhood Facilities Program provided matching funds to help local governments develop parks, playgrounds, and other facilities, particularly in disadvantaged urban areas. During the mid-1970s, a number of such programs merged into the Community Development Block Grants program.

Arts and Humanities Support

Another area of federal involvement in leisure pursuits in the United States has reflected the growing public interest in the arts and a wide range of cultural activities. Created as an independent federal agency in 1965, the National Foundation on the Arts and the Humanities supports and encourages programs in the arts (including dance, music, drama, folk art, creative writing, and the visual media) and humanities (including literature, history, philosophy, and the study of language).

In the 1980s, the National Endowment for the Arts and its advisory Federal Council provided grants of over $180 million a year to help individuals and nonprofit, tax-exempt organizations in the arts, dance, literature, music, and theater. Aid has been given not only to established arts organizations, but also to unconventional and innovative arts programs in communities throughout the United States.

Although there was strong conservative resistance to such programs in the 1990s, they continued through the decade, and the public, when polled, indicated its strong support for federal assistance to the arts.

Physical Fitness and Sports Promotion

Another recreation-related federal program has been the President's Council on Physical Fitness and Sports. Created in 1956 to help upgrade the fitness of the nation's youth, and broadened in 1968 to include the promotion of sports participation, the Council has operated to encourage public awareness of fitness needs and to stimulate school- and community-based sports and fitness programs. It has conducted nationwide promotional campaigns through the media and has sponsored many regional physical fitness clinics.

This effort continued through the 1990s, with a President's Challenge Physical Fitness Program providing for state and federal goals and guidelines, school "championships," and participant fitness awards. Along with community school systems, many local recreation and park agencies and professional groups have assisted in such fitness programs.

RECREATION-RELATED FUNCTIONS OF STATE GOVERNMENTS

The role of state governments in recreation and parks has generally rested upon the Tenth Amendment to the Constitution, which states, "The powers not delegated to the United States by the Constitution, nor prohibited by it to the States, are reserved to the States respectively, or to the people." This amendment, commonly referred to as the "states' rights amendment," is regarded as the source of state powers in such areas as public education, welfare, and health services.

Outdoor Recreation Resources and Programs

Each state government today operates a network of parks and other outdoor recreation resources. The programs may vary in nature, but generally include the following types of facilities and areas:

Wilderness areas, which may be left nearly untouched in order to retain their primitive character

State reserves or *natural preserves,* which are usually set aside for their specific cultural, natural, or scientific value and sometimes because they contain unique natural specimens or topographical features

Historical monuments or *cultural preserves,* which may include locations of important historical significance or of special archaeological or other cultural interest

Recreation areas, which are intended for active recreational use and which may include camping areas attached to larger preserves, smaller wayside campgrounds and wayside rests, and beaches, lakes, ski areas, vehicular recreation areas, underwater recreation areas, forests, and other locations for backpacking and various leisure uses

During the 1960s and early 1970s, most state governments expanded their recreation and park holdings, primarily with funding assistance from the Land and Water Conservation Fund—but also through major bond issues totalling hundreds of millions of dollars in many cases. Open space and natural beauty were widely supported catchwords, and the public enthusiastically supported programs of land acquisition and water cleanup.

Even with the economic constraints of the last two decades, a number of state governments have continued to upgrade their park and recreation operations. For example, in Pennsylvania in 1993 the state legislature approved a funding plan based on a $50 million bond issue and revenues to be derived from the state's real estate transfer tax. Supported by over 60 environmental, cultural, and recreational organizations, the plan was designed to provide a permanent source of funding for maintenance needs and capital improvements at state and local parks, libraries, public zoos, historic sites, and museums. In July 1999, the New Jersey legislature approved a plan to dedicate more than $1 billion in state funds to preserve as much as one million acres of open space over the next decade—following approval of the plan by a statewide voter referendum.[5]

Other State Functions

An important function of state government is to assist and work with local governments in environmental efforts. Just as no single municipality can clean up a polluted stream that flows through a state, so in the broad field of urban planning, recreation resource development, and conservation, problems *must* be approached on a statewide or even a regional basis. In such planning—as in many other aspects of federal relationships with local communities—the state acts as a catalyst for action and as a vital link between the national and local governments.

Many state governments have offices or sponsor arts councils that distribute funds to nonprofit organizations and performing groups or institutions in various areas of creative and cultural activity. A unique aspect of state-sponsored or assisted recreation is the state fair. This term covers a wide variety of fairs and expositions held each year throughout the United States and includes carnivals and midways, displays and competitions of livestock and produce, farm equipment shows, and a host of special presentations by corporations of every type. The majority of such fairs are run by nonprofit organizations that are publicly owned and operated—including a number of bona fide state agencies. Attended by about 160 million persons each year, they promote civic and state boosterism, offer a showcase for agricultural and other regional industries or attractions, and provide varied forms of entertainment.

An important function of state governments is to promote all aspects of leisure involvement that support economic development. Many states assist or coordinate outdoor recreation ventures, tourism campaigns, regional recovery projects, and other efforts to attract visitors and revive local economies. Typically:

Nevada urges gamblers to stay an extra day to see the desert; New Jersey, too, has persuaded its casino operators to push the state's other entertainment possibilities. Connecticut has divided itself into 19 tourism districts, each with its own appeal. Wisconsin offers free coffee and racks of tourist literature at booths along the interstates. New England has toll-free telephone numbers where prospective leaf gawkers may learn of the advance of autumn colors. States advertise in newspapers and magazines, on radio and television; New York, which more or less started the whole thing with its "I Love New York" TV ad campaign a decade ago, now spends $15 million a year to promote itself.[6]

Therapeutic Recreation Service   Each state government provides direct recreation services within the institutions or agencies it sponsors, such as mental hospitals or mental health centers, special schools for mentally retarded persons, and penal or correctional facilities. Many of the largest networks of facilities that employ therapeutic recreation specialists are tax-supported state mental health systems or similar organizations, although their overall numbers have been reduced because of deinstitutionalization policies.

Promotion of Professional Advancement   While states promote effective leadership and administrative practices in recreation and parks by developing personnel standards and providing conferences and research support, their major contribution lies in the professional preparation of recreation practitioners in state colleges and universities. Of the colleges and universities in the United States with professional recreation and park curricula, a substantial majority are part of state university systems.

Many state agencies also assist professional development by conducting annual surveys of municipal and county recreation and parks departments and publishing their findings on facilities, fiscal practices, and personnel.

Development and Enforcement of Standards   States also have the function of screening personnel by establishing standards and hiring procedures, or by requiring Civil Service examinations, certification, or personnel registration programs in recreation and parks.

Many states also have developed standards relating to health and safety practices in camping and similar settings. State departments enforce safety codes, promote facilities standards, ensure that recreation resources can accommodate persons with disabilities, regulate or prohibit certain types of commercial attractions, and in some cases carry out regular inspections of camps, pools, or other facilities.

THE ROLE OF COUNTY AND LOCAL GOVERNMENTS

While federal and state governments provide major forms of recreation service in the United States, the responsibility for meeting year-round leisure needs belongs to agencies of local government. These range from counties, special park districts, and townships (which embrace larger geographical areas) to cities, villages, and other political subdivisions.

For recreation and parks in the United States, all powers that are not vested in the federal government belong to the states. In turn, local governments must get their authority through enabling laws passed by state legislatures or through other special charter or home-rule arrangements.

Of all branches of government, the local government is closest to the people and therefore most able to meet the widest range of recreation needs.

County and Special Park District Programs

As an intermediate stage between state and incorporated local government agencies, county or special district park and recreation units provide large parks and other outdoor recreation resources as a primary function. They may also sponsor services for special populations—that is, programs for the aging or disabled—as well as services for all residents of the county, such as programs in the fine and performing arts.

During the early decades of the century, county governments had relatively limited functions. However, since World War II, the rapid growth of suburban populations around large cities has given many county governments new influence and power. Counties have become a base for coordinating and funneling numerous federal grants-in-aid programs. As a result, county park and recreation departments expanded rapidly.

Dade County, Florida   As an example of leading county agencies, the Metropolitan Dade County Park and Recreation Department operates an outstanding network of 16 parks, beaches, gardens, auditoriums, and camping areas, as well as 5 golf courses and 3 large tennis centers. It offers four miles of sandy ocean beaches, atoll pools in Biscayne Bay, and five marinas offering wet and dry docks. In all, Dade County has 8,000 acres of carefully planned and developed park and recreation facilities serving more than 18 million visitors and residents each year. Vizcaya, a 70-room Italian villa built by a prominent industrialist and now owned by the county, serves as a magnificent museum and garden attraction. The Crandon Park Zoo, Dade County Auditorium, and other facilities are important elements in this recreation-oriented metropolitan area, which depends heavily on its tourists. In addition, the Dade County department promotes numerous other privately owned or nonprofit attractions and leisure facilities—such as an impressive array of art museums, galleries, and collections in the metropolitan area that are sponsored by universities, individuals, and civic groups.

Regional and Special Park Districts

Several states, including California, Illinois, Oregon, and North Dakota, have enabling legislation that permits the establishment of special park and recreation districts. Illinois has 345 such districts, including forest preserve and conservation districts. North Dakota has 225 park districts and California 118, while Oregon has 17 park and recreation districts.

Many special recreation and park districts are in heavily populated areas; in some cases, they may encompass a number of independent, separate counties and municipalities in a single structure. Frequently, special park districts and counties are able to carry out vigorous programs of land acquisition in a combined effort or to impose other means of protecting open space. Many counties have enacted laws requiring home developers to set aside community recreation areas. One such example is Anne Arundel County, Maryland, which since 1957 has required all developers to allocate 5 percent of the land to be developed as park areas. Some county governments are establishing permanently protected green belts to halt the tide of construction. Strengthened zoning policies and more flexible building codes that permit cluster zoning of homes with larger and more concentrated open spaces are also helpful.

MUNICIPAL RECREATION AND PARK DEPARTMENTS

Municipal government is the term generally used to describe the local political unit of government such as the village, town, or city that is responsible for providing the bulk of direct community service such as street maintenance, police and fire protection, and education. Most areas depend on municipal government to provide many important recreation and park facilities and program opportunities, in addition to those provided by voluntary, private, and commercial agencies.

With the widespread recognition of this responsibility, municipal recreation and park agencies expanded rapidly in the United States during the period following World War II, with a steady increase in the number of departments, amount of acreage in park and recreation areas, number of full- and part-time or seasonal personnel, and total expenditures.

Functions and Structure of Municipal Agencies

Until World War II, many American communities had two or more leisure-service agencies existing side by side, such as a separate *park* department managing parks and other physical resources for outdoor recreation and a *recreation* department responsible for playgrounds and varied year-round programs. In the 1950s and 1960s, most such departments merged into single administrative entities, and new departments formed in other cities usually were structured as joint recreation and parks agencies.

Other municipal agencies may also sponsor special leisure services that are linked to their own missions. They may include: (1) police departments, which often operate youth-service centers or leagues; (2) welfare departments or social-service agencies, which may operate day-care centers or senior centers; (3) youth boards, which tend to focus on out-of-school youth or teen gangs; (4) health and hospital agencies, which sometimes operate community mental health centers or similar services; (5) public housing departments, which sometimes have recreation centers in their projects; (6) cultural departments or boards, which frequently sponsor performing arts programs or civic celebrations; and (7) school systems and local community colleges.

Programs of Municipal Agencies

Municipal recreation and parks departments operate programs within several categories of activity: games and sports, aquatics, outdoor and nature-oriented programs, arts and crafts, performing arts, special services, social programs, hobby groups, and other playground and community center activities.

In addition, public recreation and parks departments often sponsor large-scale special events such as holiday celebrations, festival programs, art and hobby shows, and sports tournaments.

These departments also assist other community agencies to organize, publicize, and schedule activities. Frequently, sports programs for children and youth, such as Little League or American Legion baseball, are cosponsored by public departments and associations of interested parents who undertake much of the actual management of the activity, including coaching, fund-raising, and scheduling. Similarly, many cultural programs, such as Civic Opera or Little Theater associations, are affiliated with and receive assistance from public recreation departments.

The arts are an important part of community recreation. In Vero Beach, Florida, all ages take part in creative activities in the city's Center for the Arts and Children's Theatre program. In Westchester County, New York, children learn instruments at the county's summer Blue Mountain Music Camp. Ballet is popular with youngsters in Montgomery County, Maryland.

Varied Program Emphases

Cities tend to have different emphases in their recreation and park operations. Omaha, Nebraska, for example, has a well-established department that operates a major auditorium and stadium complex, extensive boating facilities, and other unusual physical facilities, including an outstanding indoor tennis complex and a trap-and-skeet shooting facility. With revenues from these sources, it is able to support a substantial portion of its overall recreation operations.

Vancouver, British Columbia, has given high priority to developing and maintaining an extensive network of parks, beaches, pools, golf courses, conservatories, ice rinks, community centers, and an outstanding zoo in famed Stanley Park. This landmark, established more than 100 years ago, has a remarkable seawall promenade, a zoo, an aquarium, outstanding sports facilities, and other sites for leisure participation. A section of Stanley Park was named a Heritage Park Site in 1980, and its meadows and forests are carefully preserved as magnificent examples of relatively untouched natural environments.

Indianapolis, Indiana, is an excellent example of a city that has combined vigorous expansion of its sports and cultural facilities and programs with a sound public recreation and parks program to enhance its appeal to new businesses, residents, and tourists. Once viewed as a less-than-lively midwestern town, Indianapolis is fast becoming known as the amateur sports capital of the nation. In addition to its famed Indianapolis 500 auto racing event, the city now has two major league sports teams, the Pacers and the Colts. It has built seven major sports facilities, including the Hoosier Dome and other stadiums, velodromes, and natatoriums. Ten national sports associations have moved their headquarters to Indianapolis, including the Amateur Athletic Union, the U.S. Rowing Association, and the American College of Sports Medicine. In addition, the city boasts new art galleries, theaters, museums, and performing companies.

Fitness Programming   Many cities have undertaken special programs to promote health, fitness, and sport. This effort has been assisted by the Fitness Coalition, a joint effort of the National Recreation and Park Association and the President's Council on Physical Fitness and Sports. The Coalition has sought to develop model community programs to enlist the wide-scale support of municipal recreation delivery systems. It has also called upon major corporations in the United States to help promote exercise, health, and nutrition—particularly asking for support from companies involved in manufacturing food, medicine, recreation and athletic equipment, and health products, as well as companies selling life insurance programs.

Linked to this program emphasis is the recent trend by many city and county recreation departments to build outstanding new aquatic facilities that include extensive exercise and sport components. Prince William County, Virginia, for example, has constructed the outstanding Chinn Aquatics and Fitness Center, with such features as an 8-lane, 40-yard competitive swimming pool, a leisure pool, whirlpools, saunas, fitness rooms, a large gymnasium, racquetball courts, a youth center, and childcare facilities. Built at a cost of $10.4 million, this state-of-the-art facility is designed to be self-supporting financially and relies on charges of up to several hundreds of dollars for annual family memberships.

Aquatics & Fitness fun for Everyone at

CHINN AQUATICS & FITNESS CENTER

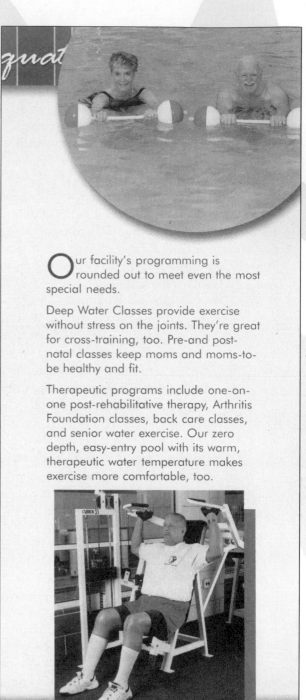

Our facility's programming is rounded out to meet even the most special needs.

Deep Water Classes provide exercise without stress on the joints. They're great for cross-training, too. Pre-and post-natal classes keep moms and moms-to-be healthy and fit.

Therapeutic programs include one-on-one post-rehabilitative therapy, Arthritis Foundation classes, back care classes, and senior water exercise. Our zero depth, easy-entry pool with its warm, therapeutic water temperature makes exercise more comfortable, too.

Many cities have built outstanding facilities for public recreation such as this impressive aquatic and fitness center operated by the Prince William County, Virginia, Park Authority.

Human-Service Functions   Many local recreation and park agencies have moved vigorously into the area of programming to meet human and social-service needs.

The Human Services Department of the city of Gardena, California, for example, offers the following services in addition to traditional recreation programs: (1) youth services, including individual, family, and group counseling; tutoring workshops; and alcohol and drug abuse programs; (2) family services, including health-care and immunization clinics, emergency food and shelter programs, and child abuse or battered women's programs; (3) manpower and employment training, including youth job-readiness sessions, displaced homemaker workshops, and placement referral services; and (4) senior citizen activities, including health and welfare counseling, Social Security and Medicare assistance, daily lunch and Meals on Wheels programs, escort services, and homemaker referrals, along with tax and legal assistance.

A trend of the last two decades has been to develop multiservice departments in which recreation and park programs play a leading role. Thus, a merged department of community services might have responsibility for beaches, parking meters, special housing units, libraries, and other special public facilities or programs. Larger urban recreation and park departments may include management responsibilities for stadiums, convention centers, piers and marinas, or even municipal airports.

Fee-Based Programs

In response to the period of fiscal austerity described in Chapter 4, fee-based programs have gained popularity with recreation and park departments.

A 1988 study of fees and charges in almost 500 municipal recreation and parks departments in eight Great Lakes region states by James Brademas and Julie Readnour found that 85 percent of all responding departments had increased fees in the 1986–1987 fiscal year, and that 73 percent anticipated doing so in the following year. The most widely found fees were charges for participating in program activities (97 percent), rentals (88 percent), user fees (72 percent), and sales (70 percent). The mean operating budgets of all responding departments was $1.78 million, and mean reported income from fees and charges was $542,947—almost one-third of the total budget of each agency. And, despite the possibility that increased fees might have reduced participation, 74 percent of the responding Great Lakes recreation and park directors found that the number of participants in their programs had increased.[7]

The trend toward imposing substantial fees for many program elements or facilities membership in public recreation and parks has been firmly established over the past three decades. Those who favor it argue that it provides a logical means of developing rich programs and services and strengthens the role of the recreation and agency in community life. Realistically, they point out that it is part of the thrust toward a more businesslike approach in city management—indeed, a logical outcome of the 1990s emphasis on "reinventing government."

On the other hand, some critics argue that placing heavy reliance on fee structures discriminates against children and youth, the elderly, disabled persons, and the poor generally, who cannot afford to pay significant fees for participation in public recreation programs. As such, it represents a retreat from the fundamental mission of public recreation and leisure programs. In some cases, cities or other public recreation and park agencies have provided fee discounts or "scholarships" or variable pricing policies to enable participation by poorer families.

While such policies are generally acceptable in well-to-do towns or suburban areas, they are obviously not workable in socially and economically disadvantaged inner-city neighborhoods or in less affluent communities. Some cities have developed models in which they assess the social priority that should be attached to recreation facilities or programs and base fee-charging policies on this assessment, as shown in Table 8.2.

TABLE 8.2

DEPARTMENTAL SERVICE MODEL, OKLAHOMA CITY, OKLAHOMA, PARKS AND RECREATION MARKETING PLAN, 1995

Basic	Enhanced	Specialized
Benefits all citizens. Totally supported through tax base. Non-fee programs.	Benefits all citizens, with participants receiving most benefit. Partial costs recovered by fees.	Benefits participants only. Self-supporting or mostly self-supporting through fees.
After-school youth centers	Adaptive programs	After-school fun clubs
At-risk youth programs	Athletic fields (baseball, rugby, soccer, softball)	Athletic leagues
Basic classes for kids		Building rentals
Beautification efforts	Community center classes	Concessions
Gyms—regular hours	Crystal Bridge @ Myriad Botanical Gardens	Equipment rentals
Basic horticulture programs		Golf
Maintenance	Fishing classes and tournaments	Myriad Botanical Gardens gift shop
Myriad botanical gardens (outdoor)	Garden center	Myriad Botanical Gardens rentals
Open tennis courts	Leased facilities	Rose garden weddings
Outdoor recreation	Martin Park tours	Special events, i.e., trout fish out
Self-taught classes at community centers	Permitted lake activities, i.e., fishing, boating	Summer day camp
Senior citizens center programs—regular hours	Special events, i.e., Easter egg hunt	Swimming lessons
	Special senior classes at community centers	Swimming pool rentals
Trails		Tennis centers
Unreserved picnic facilities at parks and lakes	Youth athletic leagues	

Innovative Developments in Larger Cities

As earlier chapters in this text have shown, problems related to inadequate budgets, increasing crime, and declining infrastructure and maintenance services tend to be most severe in older cities with limited public, nonprofit, and commercial leisure resources. Yet, even in these communities, recreation and park administrators are working to expand and improve leisure facilities, programs, and maintenance. New York City, which had experienced major cuts in recreation and park operations during the 1980s, has been able to mount aggressive campaigns to improve the care of its major parks, such as Central Park and Prospect Park, through the contributions of thousands of businesses and individual residents who joined park foundations or conservancy organizations.

New York has also successfully moved ahead with plans to develop its waterfront areas, as other cities like Baltimore have done, with mixed public, private, and commercial recreational uses. With the state's approval, four huge piers jutting into the Hudson River, which had been built in the early 1900s to accommodate a generation of giant ocean liners, have been converted into a major sports and entertainment complex. While continuing to ensure public access to the waterfront, this $100 million project, known as the Chelsea Piers, has already constructed

> back-to-back ice rinks [where the city's youth and adult amateur hockey leagues, which had to travel to suburban rinks, can now practice and play], a golf-driving range, a huge gymnastics center, and two outdoor roller rinks. The rest of the project [will have] a sprawling fitness center with an indoor sand volleyball court, a rock-climbing wall, and a quarter-mile running track that is billed as the world's longest indoor track, as well as restaurants . . . sound stages, a photography studio, and offices.[8]

Extending such efforts, New York continued to develop popular and heavily used parks along the Hudson River, repairing Civil War–era seawalls, and, in June 2000, received approval from the federal government to create a five-mile riverfront park in lower Manhattan. In another example of recreation's role in the recovery of older, major cities, the Boston, Massachusetts, harbor area is undergoing an $11 billion transformation, which will include water-based recreation in the city's newly clean seaport and bay waters.[9]

Along with such environmental and marketing-based efforts, many municipal recreation and park agencies have also moved vigorously in the direction of benefits-based programming as a means of documenting and providing direction to their overall services.

PUBLIC RECREATION AND PARKS IN CANADA

Although this text focuses primarily on recreation and leisure in the United States, Canada's history and present development of recreation and parks should be noted. As early as the 1760s, local communities set aside open space for recreation use. A century later, the Public Parks Act of Ontario led to the development of municipal public parks throughout Canada, and the federal government established Rocky Mountain Park in Banff to promote tourism.

Since these early efforts in the 1880s, Canadian provinces and cities have roughly paralleled American government programs in the development of parks and playgrounds and support given to public recreation needs. Today, the federal and provincial governments play a vigorous role in promoting outdoor recreation opportunities, culture and the arts, tourism and travel, sports and physical recreation, and similar areas. Searle and Brayley write that, as of the 1980s, 64 federal government agencies were significantly involved in the provision of park, recreation, and leisure services. They continue:

> These include the Fitness and Amateur Sport Branch, Environment Canada (National Parks and Historic Sites), Industry, Science and Technology (Tourism), and Secretary of State (Arts and Culture). Corrections Canada, Health and Welfare, the Department of External Affairs, and the Department of Consumer and Corporate Affairs also have areas of responsibility related to public leisure services.[10]

The importance of these services is emphasized in the development of a national business plan for Parks Canada, covering the period from 1995 to 2000. The Executive Summary of this plan outlined new fiscal and management strategies for the national park system, marine conservation areas, and historic sites, emphasizing both the image-related and economic importance of recreation and parks:

> The national parks and national historic sites recognize, protect, and give expression to the key natural and cultural features of Canada. A 1994 poll confirmed that national parks and historic sites ranked equally with the Canadian flag and the national anthem as symbols of the country. For this reason they are key images in federal, provincial, and private-sector marketing campaigns and in many regions are the backbone of local and regional tourism offerings.[11]

While transfer payments between federal, provincial, and municipal governments were cut back sharply during the 1990s, as a result of an economic slump at this time,[12] government park and recreation programs continued to flourish. On the provincial level, emphasis has been placed on giving strong support to multicultural and gender-based needs, sports and fitness, the needs of aboriginal—Indian and Inuit (Eskimo)—populations, heritage programs, and youth-related priorities. In general, such provinces as British Columbia, Ontario, Nova Scotia, and Alberta have aggressively promoted such efforts through conferences and forums, grants, leadership training, and research.

A number of Canadian cities, including Vancouver, Calgary, Toronto, Kamloops, Saskatoon, and North York, have established impressive reputations for their innovative municipal recreation and park operations.

NONPROFIT ORGANIZATIONS: THE VOLUNTARY SECTOR

While government recreation and park agencies are responsible for providing a floor of basic leisure services for the public throughout the United States and Canada, a major segment of recreational opportunities is sponsored by nonprofit organizations—often called *voluntary* agencies. These consist of several different types of youth-serving, special-interest, and charitable organizations.

Organizations in this category may be completely independent or may be part of national or regional federations. Often they are described as "quasi-public" or "public/private." In some cases, they must meet government-imposed standards as charitable organizations to retain tax-exempt status. They tend to share the following characteristics:

1. Usually established to meet significant social needs through organized citizen cooperation, community organizations represent the voluntary wishes and expressed needs of neighborhood residents. Thus, they are voluntary in origin.
2. Governing boards of directors or trustees are usually public-spirited citizens who accept such responsibilities as a form of social obligation. Thus, membership and administrative control are voluntary.
3. For funding, voluntary agencies usually rely on public contributions, either directly to the agency itself or to Community Chest, United Way, Red Feather Campaign, or similar shared fund-raising efforts. Contributed funds are usually supplemented by membership fees and charges for participation. In recent years, many voluntary organizations have also undertaken special projects for which they receive government funding.
4. Leadership of voluntary agencies is partly professional and partly voluntary. Management is usually by directors and supervisors professionally trained in social work, recreation, or education. At other levels, leadership is by nonprofessionals, part-time or seasonal personnel, and volunteers.
5. In some cases, nonprofit organizations in the overall leisure-service system do not sponsor recreation activities directly, but represent organizations that do or that manufacture equipment or provide services, often on a for-profit basis. However, as in the case of educational institutions or professional societies in this field, they are nonprofit and tax exempt.

Nonprofit voluntary agencies regard recreation as part of their total spectrum of services, rather than their sole function. Typically, they recognize the importance of creative and constructive leisure and see recreation as a threshold activity that serves to attract participants to their agencies. In addition, they see it as a means of achieving significant social goals, such as building character among youth, reducing social pathology, enriching educational experience, strengthening community unity, and similar objectives. In general, even though voluntary agencies do not describe themselves as recreation agencies, this often tends to be the largest single component in their programs.

Nonprofit but Fee Charging

Many voluntary organizations, though they are nonprofit and interested in meeting important social goals, may charge substantial fees. For example, YMCAs or YWCAs in suburban areas are likely to have fees that are as high as several hundred dollars a year for full family memberships and charge impressive sums for varied program activities. However, such fees are intended simply to help the organization maintain financial stability, *without* making a profit, and are frequently used to subsidize other services to disadvantaged or disabled populations who cannot afford to pay fees for membership or participation.

Because of the word "voluntary," some assume incorrectly that such agencies are staffed solely by volunteer workers. The reality is that, although some nonprofit organizations like the Boy Scouts and Girl Scouts rely heavily on volunteer leaders, all of them have full-time, paid professionals in their key management or supervisory posts.

It was estimated in 1986 that nonprofit organizations employed 7.2 million people—approximately one in 16 working Americans—and that the number would rise to 9.3 million in 1995. Salaries for professional employees of such bodies as Boy Scouts and Girl Scouts, the YMCA and YWCA, Junior Achievement, and Big Brothers/Big Sisters of America have all risen steadily in recent years. Indeed, during the early and mid-1990s, a wave of public criticism was directed at the executives of some major nonprofit, charitable organizations who had received exorbitant salaries and benefits.

TYPES OF NONPROFIT YOUTH-SERVING AGENCIES

While voluntary nonprofit organizations fit under many headings—including the arts, education, health, and social service—the largest segment of such groups with strong recreational components is generally youth-oriented. Included in this segment are (1) nonsectarian youth-serving organizations; (2) religiously affiliated youth-serving or social agencies; (3) settlement houses and independent community centers; and (4) special-interest organizations in such fields as sports, outdoor recreation, and travel.

Nonsectarian Youth-Serving Organizations

Nationally structured organizations that function directly through local branches, nonsectarian youth-serving groups have broad goals related to social development and good citizenship and operate extensive programs of recreational activity. There are hundreds of such organizations; many of them are junior affiliates of adult organizations, whereas others are independent. Sponsorship is by such varied bodies as civic and fraternal organizations, veterans' clubs, rural and farm organizations, and business clubs. Several examples follow.

Boy Scouts of America Founded in the United States in 1910, the Boy Scouts of America is a powerful and widespread organization. In January 2000, its youth membership consisted of 4.9 million individuals, ranging from Tiger Cubs to Venturers. Together with adult leaders, a total of 6.2 million were involved in Boy Scouts of America in 144,800 packs, troops, and other units, directed by a professional staff of 3,700.

In addition to its membership in the United States, Boy Scouts of America is part of a worldwide scouting movement involving more than 100 other countries. The program emphasizes mental and physical fitness, vocational and social development, and the enrichment of youth hobbies and prevocational interests, relying heavily on adventure and scouting skills and service activities.

The Boy Scouts of America has been regarded as a middle-class organization in American society and as a small-town or suburban rather than a big-city phenomenon. However, beginning in the mid-1960s, the Scouts became more active in inner-city neighborhoods. In 1968, the Boy Scouts of America announced a nationwide campaign of expansion in city slums and impoverished rural areas in order to attract greater numbers of youth. The original focus on outdoor adventure and skills was broadened to include urban activities. Today, scouts may earn badges in urban conservation and cleanup or block renewal.

Girl Scouts of the U.S.A.   The largest voluntary organization serving girls in the world, the Girl Scouts of the U.S.A. is open to girls between the ages of 6 and 17 who subscribe to its ideals as stated in the Girl Scout Promise and Law. It is part of a worldwide association of girls and adults in 104 countries through its membership in the World Association of Girl Guides and Girl Scouts. Its membership in the mid-1990s consisted of 2.6 million members in five age categories (Daisies, Brownies, Juniors, Cadettes, and Seniors) and 827,000 adults, including volunteers, board members, and staff specialists.

Founded in 1912, the Girl Scouts of the U.S.A. provides a sequential program of activities centered around the arts, the home, and the outdoors, with emphasis on character and citizenship development, community service, international understanding, health and safety. Senior Girl Scouts in particular may take on responsibilities in hospitals, museums, child care, or environmental programs. Like the Boy Scouts of America, the Girl Scouts of the U.S.A. today conducts special programs for the poor; those with physical, emotional, or other disabilities; and similar populations.

While the national Girl Scout organization has taken no stand on the women's liberation movement, self-worth and self-realization have become important goals, and proficiency badges today stress life skills for girls and young women. Where once the Girl Scout emphasis was on categories like "dressmaker" and "hostess," now badges are awarded for "aerospace" and "business."

Boys and Girls Clubs of America   The Boys and Girls Clubs movement is the fastest growing youth-serving organization in the United States today. Originally composed of two separate organizations, the merged club movement holds a U.S. Congressional Charter and is endorsed by 21 leading service, fraternal, civic, veteran, labor, and business organizations.

Today, the Boys and Girls Clubs movement serves three million youth members in 2,260 club locations, with a staff of 9,500 full-time trained professionals and over 200,000 adult volunteers. Programs include sports and games, arts and crafts, social activities, and camping, as well as remedial education, work training, and job placement and counseling. The national goals of the Boys and Girls Clubs of America include the following: citizenship education and leadership development; health, fitness, and preparation for leisure; educational-vocational motivation; intergroup understanding and value development; and enrichment of both family and community life.

With the help of special funding from corporations, foundations, and government agencies, the organization has developed program curricula for several key projects in the social services area. While each club is an independent organization, with its own board and professional staff, the national headquarters and seven regional offices provide essential services to local clubs in such areas as personnel recruitment and management training, program research and development, fund-raising and public relations, and building design and construction assistance.

The movement is geared to serving disadvantaged and at-risk youth. In 1986, fewer than 40 clubs operated in public housing settings. By the mid-1990s, some 270 Boys and Girls Clubs were located in low-income public housing projects, reaching more than 100,000 young people, with 53 percent of the organization's youth membership coming from single-parent families and 54 percent from minority families.

Police Athletic Leagues   In hundreds of communities today, law enforcement agencies sponsor Police Athletic Leagues (PAL). Operating in poverty areas, the league programs rely primarily on civilian staffing and voluntary contributions for support, although they sometimes receive technical assistance from officers on special assignment from cooperative municipal police departments. In a few cities, men and women police officers provide the bulk of full-time professional leadership in PAL programs. Police Athletic Leagues typically provide extensive recreation programming, indoor centers, and summer play streets, with strong emphasis on sports and games, creative arts, drum and bugle corps, and remedial education. Many leagues also maintain placement, counseling, and job-training programs and assist youth who have dropped out of school.

The Police Athletic League is one of the few youth organizations that continue to resist juvenile delinquency as a primary thrust. One of its principal purposes has been to promote favorable relationships between young people and the police in urban settings, and it has been markedly successful in this effort. Like other voluntary agencies, Police Athletic Leagues rely on varied funding sources, including United Way, independent fund-raising campaigns, contracts with government, and often partial police department sponsorship.

Camp Fire Boys and Girls   Founded in 1910 under the name Camp Fire Girls, this organization has been concerned with character building through a program of outdoor recreation, community service, and educational activities. Beginning in the 1970s, the membership of the Camp Fire Girls declined sharply from a high of more than 600,000 to approximately 325,000 in the early 1980s. The organization responded to this challenge by changing its name to Camp Fire Boys and Girls and embracing a coeducational membership diverse in racial, ethnic, religious, and economic terms.

With over 6,500 volunteer and paid leaders, the staff and board members work extensively in cooperation with local schools in conducting child-care programs. Many Camp Fire programs also sponsor day and resident camping programs for young people from kindergarten age to 21. Like other youth-serving groups, Camp Fire serves as a strong advocate for youth in such areas as juvenile justice, child abuse, AIDS, and teen suicide.

Church and Synagogue Recreation Programs

Many religious organizations sponsor youth programs with recreational components today, including both activities sponsored by local churches or synagogues and activities sponsored by national federations that are affiliated with a particular denomination.

Recreation programs provided by local churches or synagogues tend to have two broad purposes: (1) to sponsor recreation for their own members or congregations in order to meet their leisure needs in ways that promote involvement with the institution, and (2) to provide leisure opportunities for the community at large or for a selected population group in ways that are compatible with their own religious beliefs. Typical activities offered by individual churches and synagogues may include the following:

Day camps, play schools, or summer Bible schools, which include recreation along with religious instruction

Year-round recreation activities for families, including picnics, outings, bazaars, covered-dish suppers, carnivals, single adult clubs, dances, game nights, and similar events

Programs in the fine and performing arts, including innovative worship programs involving dance and folk music

Fellowship programs for various age levels, including discussion groups on religious and other themes

Varied special-interest or social-service programs, including day-care centers for children, senior citizens clubs or golden age groups, and recreation programs for disabled persons

Sports activities, including bowling and basketball leagues, or other forms of instructional or competitive participation

National Youth Organizations

On a broader level, such organizations as the Young Men's Christian Association (YMCA), Young Women's Christian Association (YWCA), the Catholic Youth Organization (CYO), and the Young Men's and Young Women's Hebrew Association (YM-YWHA) provide a network of facilities and programs with diversified recreation, education, and youth-service activities. Although their titles include the words "young" or "youth," they tend to serve a broad range of children, youth, adult, and aging members.

YMCA *and* YWCA   Voluntary organizations affiliated with Protestantism in general rather than with any single denomination, the Ys are devoted to the promotion of religious ideals of living and view themselves as worldwide fellowships "dedicated to the enrichment of life through the development of Christian character and a Christian society." However, the actual membership of the Ys is multireligious and multiracial. One out of four members of the YMCA is a girl or woman; and a 1960s study showed that the religious affiliation of Y members was 75.2 percent Protestant, 18.9 percent Roman Catholic, and 3.3 percent Jewish. In the United States, racial discrimination was formally banned by the National Council of YMCAs in the 1960s, and by the early 1970s almost all Ys, in both the North and the South, had integrated membership rolls and facilities.

In many communities, the YMCA offers the best facilities and leadership for indoor aquatics, sports and games, physical fitness, social and cultural programs, and family-centered programs. These activities are usually aggressively marketed and bring in substantial revenues. Both the YMCA and YWCA derive funding from varied sources: membership fees, corporate and private contributions through United Way, fund-raising drives, and government and foundation grants.

In some cases, private health club owners have initiated lawsuits to force YMCAs onto the tax rolls, claiming that they actually function as businesses in competition with commercial businesses and do not deserve tax-exempt status.[13]

In addition to meeting recreational needs, the YWCA in particular has changed its image from a traditional, predominantly white conservative organization to one more directly concerned with social needs and problems. This new attitude is illustrated by the list of courses, clinics, and workshops offered by many YWs today: Assertiveness Training for Women, Career Development, Personal Finance, Living Single, The Marriage Contract, Sexual Consciousness Raising, Focus: Women Over Forty, Survival in the City, Women's Self-Expression Workshop, Know Your Body, and The Divorce Experience. Almost 200 YWCAs have initiated programs for battered women, and the National YWCA has initiated national conferences and workshops on domestic violence. Hundreds of YWCAs provide career-planning and employment programs.

Catholic Youth Organization   The leading Catholic organization concerned with providing spiritual, social, and recreational services for young people in the United States is the Catholic Youth Organization. CYO originated in the early 1930s, when a number of dioceses under the leadership of Bishop Sheil of Chicago began experimenting with varied forms of youth organizations. It was established as a national organization in 1951 as a component of the National Council of Catholic Youth. Today, the National CYO Federation has an office in Washington, D.C., as well as many citywide or diocesan offices. The parish, however, is the core of the Catholic Youth Organization, which depends heavily on the leadership of the parish priest and the services of adult volunteers from the neighborhood for direction and assistance.

Within its religious context, CYO is clearly recognized as a leisure program, meeting its goals through projects and activities operated through local clubs. The following official CYO statement illustrates its view of recreation as a means of rejecting negative or antisocial forms of leisure:

> The most vulnerable period in the lives of our young people are [sic] the leisure-time hours when they are on their own, away from the positive influences of family, school, and church. The values and standards of these significant institutions can then be challenged by the growing impulse for self-assertion and the natural instincts of pleasure seeking and self-indulgence. This sensitive situation encompasses nearly half the lifetime of the preteen and teenager, and it is the mission of the Catholic Youth Organization to "move in" on these idle hours to an extension of the family, church, and school with recreation, spiritual, apostolic, social, and cultural programming that will give the youngster attractive alternatives to the appealing excitement of the "offbeat" activities that are the root of delinquency.

Young Men's and Young Women's Hebrew Association   Today, there are 250 YM-YWHAs, Jewish Community Centers, and camps serving one million members throughout the United States and Canada. Like the YMCAs and YWCAs, the Jewish Ys do not regard themselves primarily as recreation agencies, but rather as community organizations devoted to social service but with a strong Jewish cultural component. Specifically, the YM-YWHA has defined its mission in the following way:

To meet the leisure-time social, cultural, and recreational needs of its membership, embracing both sexes and all age groups

To stimulate individual growth and personality development by encouraging interest and capacity for group and community participation

To teach leadership responsibility and democratic process through group participation

To encourage citizenship education and responsibility among its members and, as a social welfare agency, to participate in community-wide programs of social betterment

Customarily, leaders of the Jewish Community Center movement identify a set of priorities at five-year intervals, with specific implications for local community centers and for the Jewish Welfare Board, which serves to coordinate and assist both centers and Ys. Responding to changing demographic and social conditions, for example, the goals set for the 1990–1995 period included the providing of services that strengthen the Jewish family, provide outreach to community newcomers and immigrants, strengthen Jewish education, and develop new leadership for the Community Center movement.

Special-Interest Organizations

Numerous other types of voluntary nonprofit organizations can best be classified as special-interest groups, concerned with promoting a particular area of activity or social concern. Their functions may include leadership training, public relations, lobbying and legislation, establishing national standards or operational policies, or the direct sponsorship of program activities.

Special-interest organizations may be free of commercial involvement or may represent manufacturers of equipment, owners of facilities, schools, or other businesses that seek to stimulate public interest and support and, ultimately, improve their own business success.

Conservation and Outdoor Recreation

There are numerous organizations that seek to educate the public and influence governmental policies in the areas of conservation and outdoor recreation. In some cases, they lobby, conduct research, and sponsor conferences and publications. In others, their primary thrust is to mount projects and carry out direct action on state or local levels.

Sierra Club   Founded in 1892 and headed initially by the famous naturalist John Muir, the Sierra Club has sought to make Americans aware "of what we have lost and can lose during 200 years of continuing exploitation of our resources for commodity purposes and failure to realize their value for scenic, scientific, and aesthetic purposes." In recent years, the Sierra Club has become known for its battles to protect major natural resources threatened by commercial exploitation. However, its activities are not restricted to conservation; it is also the nation's largest skiing and hiking club, operating a major network of ski lodges and "river runners," numerous wilderness outings, and ecological group projects.

Appalachian Mountain Club   This organization has a regional focus; its purpose when founded in 1876 was to "explore the mountains of New England and adjacent regions . . . for scientific and artistic purposes, and . . . to cultivate an interest in geographical studies." Since its inception, it has explored and mapped many of the wildest and most scenic areas in Massachusetts, New Hampshire, and Maine, in addition to promoting such sports as skiing, snowshoeing, mountain climbing, and canoeing.

Although practical conservation remains a primary concern of the club, it has also acquired various camp properties, published guides and maps, and maintained hundreds of miles of trails and a network of huts and shelters throughout the White Mountains for use by its members. It promotes programs of instruction and leadership training in such activities as snowshoeing, skiing, smooth and white-water canoeing, and rock climbing.

National Outdoor Leadership School   A number of other national nonprofit organizations teach outdoor leadership skills and promote sound environmental practices in the wilderness. The National Outdoor Leadership School sponsors a variety of courses in backpacking, mountaineering, rock climbing, sea kayaking and other outdoor adventure activities in settings throughout the western states, Alaska, and such foreign countries as Australia, Mexico, Patagonia, and Kenya. Other organizations offering programs concerned with environmental education, personal growth, and outdoor adventure recreation include the Wilderness Education Association, the Outward Bound National Office, and the Association for Experiential Education. Woodswomen, Inc., located in Minneapolis, Minnesota, is the oldest and largest women's adventure travel organization.

Organizations Promoting Youth Sports and Games

There are thousands of national, regional, and local organizations promoting and regulating sports of every kind. While many of these govern professional play or high-level intercollegiate competition, others are concerned with sports and games on a purely amateur basis. One example of such organizations follows.

Little League   Founded in Williamsport, Pennsylvania, in 1939, this is the largest youth sports program in the world today. In its various leagues, it serves more than three million players each year. As an example of its popularity, it fields 196,000 teams in 91 nations; 7,000 teams were in the tournament leading up to the 1995 Little League Baseball World Series, with 16,000 tournament games being played in six weeks.

Little League operates an impressive headquarters complex and stadium in Williamsport, where camps, conferences, and the annual World Series are held. It has standardized rules of play, requirements for financial operation and fee structures, insurance coverage, approved equipment, and other arrangements for member leagues and teams. Little League also conducts research into youth sports and carries out a great variety of training programs for league officials, district administrators, umpires, managers, and coaches, as well as parent-education activities and publications. More than 750,000 adult volunteers are involved in running Little Leagues.

Youth sports in general are assisted by national organizations that set standards and promote effective, values-oriented coaching approaches, such as the National Youth Sports Coaches Association, the National Association of Youth Leagues, and the National Clearinghouse for Youth Sports Information. Examples of organizations that are particularly concerned with individual sports include Youth Basketball of America, the Young American Bowling Alliance, and the United States Tennis Association. The latter organization has mounted a vigorous campaign to promote tennis to children and youth through the schools and public recreation agencies—including a National Minority Participation Committee that seeks to increase participation by racial and ethnic minorities in tennis as a lifetime sport.

Arts Councils and Cultural Organizations

Another major area of activity for voluntary agencies is the arts. In addition to nonprofit schools and art centers that offer painting, drawing, sculpture, and similar programs, there are literally thousands of civic organizations that sponsor or present performing arts. These include symphony orchestras, bands of various types, choral societies, opera or operetta companies, little theater groups, ballet and modern dance companies, and similar bodies.

In many communities, special-interest organizations in the arts are coordinated or assisted by umbrella agencies that help to promote their joint efforts. For example, the varied community arts organizations in the Province of British Columbia are assisted by the Community Arts Council of Vancouver. Founded in 1946 as the first such organization in North America, this council's purpose has been to stimulate awareness and support of the various arts in community life. Working closely with universities, museums, performing groups, and other public and voluntary agencies, the Vancouver Arts Council has succeeded in achieving a favorable climate for all of the arts.

Service and Fraternal Clubs

Another category of nonprofit organizations that provide recreation for their own membership and sponsor programs for other population groups is community service clubs and fraternal organizations.

These include service clubs such as the Kiwanis, Lions, or Rotary clubs, which represent the business and professional groups in the community and which have as their purpose the improvement of the business environment and contributing to social well-being. A number of organizations established specifically for women—such as the Association of Junior Leagues, the General Federation of Women's Clubs, and the Business and Professional Women's Club—have similar goals.

The goals of such groups may include publicizing environmental concerns or issues, promoting the arts and other cultural activities, helping disadvantaged children and youth, and providing programs for disabled persons. For example, many Kiwanis organizations are involved in providing camping programs for special populations.

Promotional and Coordinating Bodies

A final type of nonprofit organization in the recreation, parks, and leisure-service field consists of associations that serve to promote, publicize, or coordinate activities within a given recreational field. In bowling, for example, the American Bowling Congress is composed of thousands of individuals whose careers or livelihoods depend on bowling and who therefore seek to promote and guide the sport as aggressively as possible—including setting standards and regulations and sponsoring a range of major tournaments each year.

There are hundreds of such nonprofit organizations in the fields of travel, tourism, entertainment, and hospitality, covering the range from associations of theme park or waterplay park management to associations of tour directors or cruise ship operators. As an example, the Outdoor Amusement Business Association works to upgrade standards and services throughout the carnival and outdoor show industry. Its membership consists chiefly of manufacturers and distributors of trailers, tents and tarps, games supplies, and similar materials, as well as operators of many different kinds of traveling shows, concessions, and carnivals.

Similarly, the International Association of Amusement Parks and Attractions conducts market studies, publishes standards and guidelines, and sponsors huge conventions and trade shows for thousands of companies worldwide in the tourism, entertainment, and amusement field.

Within local communities, there are often several types of coordinating groups that serve to exchange information, conduct studies, identify priorities, develop planning reports, provide technical assistance, train leadership, and organize events related to recreation and leisure. In some cases, these include councils of social agencies, including religious, health care, youth-serving, and social work groups.

SIGNIFICANCE OF NONPROFIT ORGANIZATIONS

Without question, agencies in the nonprofit sector make a major contribution to recreation and leisure-service programming in the United States and Canada. They differ from government organizations in the recreation field in a number of respects.

First, their goals are broader in that voluntary and special-interest organizations tend to have a variety of social goals and purposes, rather than recreation alone. At the same time, they usually serve a membership group restricted by age level, religious or other demographic characteristics, or special-program interest.

Organizationally, they tend to be more flexible in determining goals and objectives and in changing priorities and programs as social conditions warrant. From a financial point of view, they are less secure than government agencies, which can usually count on continued support from year to year. Instead, voluntary agencies are heavily dependent on membership fees and dues and on community giving either through United Fund, Red Feather, Community Chest, or similar campaigns or through their own fund-raising efforts.

Those voluntary agencies that are part of national federations or associations must frequently conform to goals, standards, and policies established by the larger body. On the other hand, since they are usually governed by local boards or trustees and must work directly with advisory groups, volunteers, and other community representatives, they must also respond fully to local needs.

COMMERCIAL RECREATION

We now turn to the type of recreation sponsor that provides the largest variety of leisure opportunities in the United States and Canada today—commercial, profit-oriented businesses. Such organizations have proliferated in recent years, and they run the gamut from small "mom-and-pop" operations to franchised programs and services; large-scale networks of health and fitness clubs, theme parks, hotel and casino businesses; manufacturers of games, toys, and hobby equipment; and various other entertainment ventures.

The Nature of Commercial Recreation

Commercial recreation is easily defined. John Bullaro and Christopher Edginton write:

> A commercial leisure service organization can be thought of as a business, the primary purpose of which is to serve people while at the same time making a profit. [It] has two basic characteristics. First, it creates and distributes leisure services; second, it has as its primary goal, profit.[14]

The profit motive distinguishes a recreation business from any other type of leisure-service sponsor. While public or voluntary agencies may charge for their services and may seek to clear a profit on individual program elements—or at least to run them on a self-sustaining basis where possible—their overall purpose is to meet important community or social needs. But the commercial recreation organization has as a *primary* thrust the need to show a profit on the overall operation.

In the past, there was considerable concern about the extent to which profit-minded entrepreneurs were attracting the public in their programs. During the early decades of the century, commercial sponsors were viewed as unscrupulous, and their offerings were often seen as destructive to society. Today, it is taken for granted that, without commercial businesses that provide a host of important and high-quality leisure experiences, our recreational opportunities would be sharply diminished.

Commercial recreation sponsors today have the following characteristics: (1) they must constantly seek to identify and capitalize on recreational interests that are on the rise in order to ensure a constant or growing level of participation; (2) they are flexible and independent in their programmatic decisions and are not subject to the policy strictures of a city or town council or an agency board of trustees; (3) they constantly seek to promote and create a climate of desirability by packaging a product that will appeal to the public, by systematic marketing research and by clever advertising and public relations; and (4) to be successful, they depend on effective entrepreneurship—a creative and aggressive approach to management that is willing to take risks in order to make gains.

Categories of Service

Commercial recreation services may be classified under several major headings, including the following:

1. Admission to facilities, either for self-directed participation (as in the use of a rented tennis court or admission to an ice-skating rink or billiard parlor) or for participation with some degree of supervision, instruction, or scheduling (as in admission to a ski center with use of a ski tow).
2. Organized instruction in individual leisure activities or areas of personnel enrichment, such as classes in arts and crafts, music, dance, or other hobbies.
3. Membership in a commercially operated club, such as a for-profit tennis, golf, or boat club.
4. Provision of hospitality or social contacts, ranging from hotels and resorts to bars, singles clubs, or dating services, which may use computers, videotaping, telephone contacts, or other means to help clients meet each other. At the socially less acceptable end of this spectrum of services are "escort services," "massage parlors," and sexually oriented telephone conversation operations.
5. Arranged tours or cruises, domestic or foreign, which may consist solely of travel arrangements or which may also include a full package of travel, housing accommodations, meals, special events, side trips, or guide services.
6. Commercial manufacture, sale, and service of recreation-related equipment, including sports supplies, electronic products, boats, off-road vehicles, toys, games, and hobby equipment.
7. Entertainment and special events, such as theater, rock concerts, circuses, rodeos, and other such activities, when they are sponsored by a for-profit business, rather than a nonprofit, tax-exempt group.

Several of these types of commercial recreation businesses are described in the concluding section of this chapter. Others, such as sports and games or travel and tourism, are presented in Chapter 10.

Outdoor Recreation

The broad field of outdoor recreation—defined as leisure pursuits that depend on the outdoor environment for their special appeal or character—represents an important area of commercially sponsored services. While a major portion of outdoor recreation is carried on in government-managed settings, many activities are provided by for-profit enterprises.

At the end of the 1990s, the U.S. Fish and Wildlife Service reported that 77 million Americans age 16 and older fished, hunted, and watched wildlife each year, including

> . . . 35.2 million anglers and 14 million hunters, numbers that remained unchanged from the previous survey. . . . [F]ishing-related spending, adjusted for inflation, rose 37 percent [over a five-year period, while] hunters' time afield increased only 10 percent, but their spending jumped 43 percent.
>
> Despite [shrinking numbers] wildlife watchers spent an additional 25 percent. The three groups spent $100 billion on equipment, travel, and items such as publications and membership dues.[15]

Commercial recreation in the outdoors takes many forms, including hunting preserves and guide services; charter fishing and other private fishing operations; marinas and other boating services; and the provision of ski centers and schools, paintball centers, and numerous other pursuits.

In many cases, a single company, such as Pocono Outdoor Adventure in Jim Thorpe, Pennsylvania, may offer several different types of adventure activities, such as river rafting, family biking excursions, or paintball, at different seasons of the year. Numerous hunting businesses throughout the United States and Canada offer the opportunity to shoot big game and in some cases exotic species imported from other continents. Both inland and ocean fishing represent another huge industry. Boating alone represents a major segment of the outdoor recreation market, with annual retail sales in the early 1990s estimated at over $17 billion.

Health Spas and Fitness Clubs

Through the 1980s and 1990s, commercial fitness centers and health clubs constituted a major source of leisure spending in the United States and Canada.

Although those who join such facilities may have varying kinds of motivations, ranging from actual health concerns to a cosmetic concern with one's appearance, the reality is that health spas often offer an attractive social setting—particularly for single men and women.

This overall field includes a variety of program emphases, such as aquatic and fitness centers with varied pool facilities, exercise-equipment rooms, aerobics and Jazzercise classes, yoga or Oriental exercise groups, conditioning counseling or remedial services, and similar options with annual fees that may range up to thousands of dollars.

As a variation of such health-connected services, many nonprofit hospitals or long-term care facilities have established for-profit subsidiary companies that offer a wide range of exercise programs, physical therapy, aerobic classes, and innovative techniques that include hypnosis, pain management, acupuncture, and other alternative forms of treatment serving the public at large. They may also focus on holistic and homeopathic treatment, including meditation groups, clubs dealing with specific forms of illness, such as arthritis, "overeaters anonymous," "living with loss," and massage and "reflexology" methods.

The "Learning Studio" Approach

A trend over the past two decades has involved businesses that offer a range of short-term learning experiences for adults dealing with such varied personal concerns as home buying; investment strategies; career development; health and wellness; computer skills; hobbies, sports, and games; creative writing; arts and crafts; home repairs; cookery and wine expertise; stress management; scuba diving; and other forms of social enrichment.

Through clever marketing, the use of well-known and highly skilled experts as instructors or presenters, and the ability to zero in on appealing and catchy subjects ("how to flirt," "how to write a book in 3 weeks or less," "find your true career through your handwriting," "establish yourself as an expert," "how to make the big money," or "stop aging before it stops you"), such adult personal development offerings seem likely to expand as a unique form of commercial leisure business in the years ahead.

Family Fun Centers

Another recently evolved for-profit recreation enterprise includes family fun centers that combine children's play activities and equipment, video games, and other computerized activities with refreshments.

These businesses developed as an outgrowth of such "kiddie exercise" programs as Playorena, Gymboree, or Discovery Zone, which expanded as franchised chains that were usually situated in shopping malls in the 1960s and 1970s. To broaden their appeal, many entrepreneurs added more family-slanted activities, such as miniature golf or other indoor games, and packaged them with fast-food options, such as pizza, hot dogs, and soft drinks for birthday party and other group visits. One such operation, Chuck E. Cheese Entertainment, Inc., has 332 centers in 44 states, with annual revenues of over $450 million.

Other For-Profit Ventures

Beyond the examples just cited, commercial recreation today includes a host of other kinds of social and hobby activities and amusement or entertainment ventures.

Private golf or tennis clubs, bowling alleys and billiard parlors, contract bridge or chess clubs, night clubs and dance halls, and even dating services and gambling casinos are all part of this picture. In a sense, movies, television, video games, book publishing, and music CDs are all aspects of popular culture that represent forms of commercialized leisure.

In addition, both amateur sports participation and professional spectator sports and travel and tourism involve huge elements in the commercial recreation field and are discussed in detail in a later chapter.

DIFFERENCES AND SIMILARITIES AMONG AGENCIES

This chapter has described the provision of organized recreation services today by three types of organizations: public or governmental, nonprofit or voluntary, and commercial recreation businesses. Clearly, each of these types of leisure-service organizations plays a different role in the overall recreational system, while at the same time interacting with and supplementing the other types.

Public recreation and park agencies, for example, have a major responsibility for maintaining and operating outdoor resources such as parks, forests, playgrounds, sports and aquatic facilities, and, in many cases, indoor centers, performing arts, conference or convention halls, stadiums, and similar facilities. Their obligation is to serve the public at large, including individuals and families at all socioeconomic levels and without regard to ethnic, religious, or other demographic differences. However, given the intensified use of marketing-based fees and charges for many recreation programs, many government recreation and park agencies today are *not* reaching community groups with limited economic capability.

Nonprofit voluntary agencies are generally most concerned with social values and with achieving constructive outcomes either for the community or for specific population groups. They see recreation both as an end in itself and as a means to an end and are generally respectful of the environment and sensitive to gender- and race-related issues. Particularly in terms of serving young people and special recreation interests, they are able to offer richer programs than many public agencies.

Of the three types of sponsors, commercial recreation sponsors provide by far the greatest range of recreational services and opportunities today, and they represent a steadily growing sphere of organized leisure programming. In some ways, profit-oriented businesses are similar to public and nonprofit recreation and park agencies in terms of their offerings and the leisure needs they satisfy. What distinguishes them is their ability to commit substantial sums to developing facilities and programs that will attract the public. Huge corporations that are able to design and build theme parks, aquatic complexes, stadiums, health and fitness clubs, and other types of specialized equipment or programs obviously have a tremendous advantage in appealing to those who are able to pay the necessary fees and charges. Commercial recreation sponsors have harnessed technology and industry in creating spectacular environments for play and have used the most subtle and sophisticated public relations and advertising techniques to market their products successfully.

Social Values in Recreation Planning

It would be wrong to assume that commercial recreation businesses are entirely free to provide any sort of leisure activity without considering its social impact.

Health clubs, camps, theaters, dance halls, gambling casinos, taverns, and a host of other facilities are subject to regulation under state, county, and municipal laws. These may include provisions regarding the sale of liquor, sanitary conditions, service to minors, safety practices, hours of operation, and similar restrictions. Many enterprises that require licenses may have these withdrawn if the operators do not conform to approved practices. Similarly, trade associations often influence practices, even though they may not have the legal power to enforce their rulings.

Public attitudes—as expressed in the press; through the statements of leading citizens, civic officials, or religious organizations; or through consumer pressures—are often able to influence the operators in desired directions. For example, when Time-Warner was sharply criticized in the press for its promotion of violent, racist, and sexist "rap" music products, it divested itself of the involved recording label.

The competition of other organizations and products is another key factor in the management of commercial recreation agencies. Often, better products and services within a branch of the industry will serve to drive out inferior competitors. The entire field of recreation service and participation may be viewed as a marketing system in which the economic forces of supply and demand work so that, as a new product or service appears, existing products and services are threatened. Within this framework, there is a constant pruning and reshuffling of recreation enterprises as competing sponsors seek to maintain public interest and attendance.

PARTNERSHIPS AMONG MAJOR LEISURE-SERVICE AGENCIES

Although public, nonprofit, and commercial leisure-service agencies are dealt with separately in this chapter, it is important to emphasize that in actual practice they often join together in cooperative ventures. For example, a survey of over 100 cities found that almost all municipal recreation and parks departments conducted programs with other agencies and organizations; more than half of the respondents had 10 or more synergetic programs during the year. They worked closely with voluntary agencies, schools and colleges, service clubs, and business and industry to promote sport, cultural, and other types of events and projects.

During the 1990s, in an era of reinventing government, many recreation and park managers turned to partnerships to maximize the use of limited tax dollars in order to meet expanding public demands for high-quality recreation experiences. Typically, this is often done through coalitions of several different public agencies.

Today, there are numerous examples of such linkages among government departments, as well as partnerships with private groups of citizens, corporations, and other types of educational or leisure-service agencies. In Durham, North Carolina, for example, more than 40 public, nonprofit, and commercial organizations have joined together in a common effort to reduce juvenile delinquency. Two historic parks in Connecticut—Hartford's Bushnell Park and New Haven's Green Park—have been fully restored and are being maintained through the efforts of well-organized public-private partnership groups—a pattern found in hundreds of cities in which businesses or civic groups have taken on responsibility for managing or maintaining parks and playgrounds, sponsoring youth programs, or conducting major sports or cultural events.

Often, contractual relationships are established between public authorities and private or commercial businesses to operate major sectors of a community's recreation program. For example, in Dallas, Texas, the city's Park and Recreation Department has contracted for years with a private operator to manage five major tennis centers under an arrangement in which

The park and recreation board approves court fees and policies.

The [private] managers operate the facilities, keep them clean, and are responsible for other expenses associated with the tennis business (labor, marketing, equipment, and office supplies fall in this category).

The city is responsible for utilities, court, building and grounds repair, and maintenance costs, and site renovation or expansion expenditures.

With this partnership agreement, the Department's revenues have increased annually and its expenditures have been reduced, while a high-quality tennis program has been maintained at the same time that other services have been cut back.

Numerous examples may also be shown of partnerships in the areas of open-space acquisition and environmental recovery. Burde, Kraft, and Beck describe the collaboration of several federal and state government agencies in a wetland restoration and wildlife refuge program in Illinois.[16] In an unusual alliance of two groups that frequently are opposed—cattlemen and environmentalists—an alliance was formed to preserve valuable, threatened wildlands in Colorado.[17]

Similarly, nonprofit organizations are frequently involved in collaborative program efforts. Typically, Boy and Girl Scout troops often work closely with churches and religious organizations or with school boards. The Young Men's Christian Association encourages numerous partnership arrangements with local park and recreation departments, schools and colleges, public housing boards, hospitals, and even correctional institutions. A 1997 survey of such projects states:

> The YMCA offers child care programs; senior, teen, and youth programs; parenting skills programs; drug, gang, pregnancy, and violence prevention programs; and wellness programs, to name a few, as part of these collaborative efforts.
>
> In addition to establishing partnerships and programs, YMCA collaborations include resource sharing. Buildings, gyms, parks, sports fields, and swimming pools are among the facility resources involved in collaborations. The sharing of equipment purchases, program funding, and staff salaries exemplify the maximization of financial resources within such alliances.[18]

In many cases, colleges and universities also work closely with other agencies— such as government units, nearby communities, and nonprofit organizations—in partnership ventures. For example, the Recreation, Parks, and Tourism Science Department of Texas A & M University, through the Sea Grant College Program and the Texas Cooperative Extension Service, assists small communities and rural areas in developing coastal tourism and recreation resources. The University of Northern Iowa and the University of Oregon have each conducted highly successful day and resident camping programs at U.S. Army Air Force bases in the United States and Korea, under contract with the Department of Defense.

Other examples of partnerships have involved both public and private agencies in "land-swapping" deals that have benefited both commercial and environmental interests. The most dramatic example of such cooperative efforts occurred in 1994 when the state of Washington and a privately held lumber corporation exchanged more than 100 separate parcels of forest and special-interest natural resource lands, totaling more than 20,000 acres, under an agreement enthusiastically supported by environmental groups.

Finally, professional societies have been successful in initiating a number of partnerships, particularly in the area of youth sports. The National Recreation and Park Association, for example, has joined the American Coaching Effectiveness Program (ACEP) to develop a comprehensive education program for youth sports administrators. In addition, NRPA has developed joint ventures with the United States Tennis Association, the National Football League's Flag Football program, and the Hershey Track and Field youth program to reach millions of children and youth through these sports. Collaborative arrangements of this type are growing in number and variety and are helping to build a climate of mutual assistance among the different elements that comprise the leisure-service system.

SUMMARY

Government's role with respect to organized leisure services is a diversified one. On the federal level, government is concerned with the management of outdoor recreation resources, either as a primary function or within a multiple-use concept, through such agencies as the National Park Service, U.S. Forest Service, Bureau of Land Management, and TVA. The federal government also assists the states and local political units through funding and technical assistance for programs serving children and youth, those with disabilities, the elderly, and similar groups.

State governments operate major park systems and play an important role in promoting environmental conservation and outdoor recreation opportunities. They also set standards and pass enabling legislation that defines the role of local governments in the area of recreation and parks. In addition, states have traditionally maintained networks of state hospitals and special schools for those with disabilities, although this function has been reduced in recent years as a result of deinstitutionalization trends toward placing many such individuals in community settings.

The chief sponsors of government recreation and park programs are on the local level—city, town, county, and special district government agencies. They operate varied facilities and generally offer a wide range of classes, leagues, or special events in sports, the arts, social activities, and other leisure areas. They also provide or assist in many programs in the human-services area. While many municipal departments have expanded their revenue-source operations, departments in other larger and older cities suffer from depleted staff resources and have limited program and maintenance potential.

Voluntary agencies place their greatest emphasis on using leisure to achieve positive social goals. Several types of youth-serving organizations are described, including both sectarian and nonsectarian groups. Such agencies rarely consider themselves to be primarily recreation organizations; instead, they generally prefer to be regarded as educational, character-building, or youth-serving organizations. However, recreation usually does constitute a sector of their program activities.

A second type of nonprofit leisure-service agency consists of special-interest groups, which usually promote a particular area of activity in outdoor recreation, sports, the arts, or hobbies. Such groups, while they may include many enthusiasts as members, are often formed to promote business interests within the particular leisure specialization.

Commercial recreation businesses offer an immense amount of public recreational opportunities today in such areas as travel and tourism, outdoor recreation, sports, popular entertainment and the mass media of communication, hobbies, and crafts and toys. Their primary goal is to make a consistent profit; and, in many cases, they are huge and highly diversified operations, such as the Walt Disney organization with its theme parks; resorts; and television, movie, and popular music components. From a social perspective, while many for-profit businesses offer constructive, high-quality programs, in some cases—as in sectors of the entertainment industry—they are believed to contribute to youth violence, sexism, and racial hostility.

QUESTIONS FOR CLASS DISCUSSION OR ESSAY EXAMINATIONS

1. Review the major recreation and park functions of *either* the federal government *or* state governments, identifying key agencies and their leisure-related roles. Apart from managing resources for outdoor recreation, what are the other important activities of these two levels of government?

2. Municipal recreation and park departments, including city, town, or other types of local public agencies, provide a diverse range of leisure opportunities for community

residents today. What are some of the major trends in municipal-recreation programming in recent years, and what problems have affected such departments as a result of fiscal austerity?

3. Discuss the concept of partnership arrangements among governmental and other types of nonpublic community organizations, in terms of recreation programming. What are the values and what are several examples of such partnership arrangements?

4. What are the major differences between voluntary nonprofit agencies and government departments providing recreation facilities and programs? Compare goals and objectives, funding, individuals or groups served, and program elements.

5. Define commercial recreation agencies and indicate several of the major categories of leisure services provided by such businesses. Select one major area of commercial recreation, such as outdoor recreation or travel and tourism, and describe trends in this field, the nature of service offered, and problems or issues connected to that particular recreation.

ENDNOTES

1 President William Clinton, excerpt from *National Park Week Proclamation* (1995).

2 R. Carlson, J. MacLean, T. Deppe, and J. Peterson, *Recreation and Leisure: The Changing Scene* (Belmont, Calif.: Wadsworth, 1979): 117.

3 Mitchell Satchell, "Trouble in Paradise," *U.S. News and World Report* (19 June 1995): 25–26.

4 See for example Evelyn Nieves, "Interior Department Plans to Reduce Traffic in Yosemite," *New York Times* (28 March 2000): A-14.

5 David Kocieniewski, "New Jersey Dedicates More Than $1 Billion to Land Preservation," *New York Times* (1 July 1999): B-7.

6 Andrew Malcolm, "As Other Industries Fade, States Set Their Sights on Tourism," *New York Times* (6 September 1987): E-1.

7 J. Brademas and J. Readnour, research presented at NRPA Congress (October 1988).

8 Paul Goldberger, "Giving New Life to Abandoned Old Piers," *New York Times* (17 November 1995): C-1.

9 Carey Goldberg, "Boston Leading a Renewal of Old Northern Cities," *New York Times* (3 November 1998): 1.

10 M. Searle and R. Brayley, *Leisure Services in Canada: An Introduction* (State College, Pa.: Venture Publishing, 1993): 77.

11 *Parks Canada National Business Plan: 1995–2000* (Ottawa, Canada: Parks Canada, 1995).

12 Mary Janigan, "Dustup Over Dollars," *Macleans* (19 May 1997): 20.

13 Mary Janco, "Exercised by Y, Club Sues Under New Law," *Philadelphia Inquirer* (31 July 1998): A-1.

14 J. Bullaro and C. Edginton, *Commercial Leisure Services: Managing for Profit, Service, and Personal Satisfaction* (New York: Macmillan, 1986): 17.

15 Robert Winkler, "Wildlife Participation Is Holding Steady," *New York Times* (8 February 1998): SP-13.

16 J. Burde, S. Kraft, and R. Beck, "Partnerships in Wetland Restoration," *Parks and Recreation* (February 1998): 34–43.

17 James Brooke, "Rare Alliance in the Rockies Strives to Save Open Space," *New York Times* (14 August 1998): A-1.

18 Myrtis Meyer, Study Director, *Collaboration Study Report* (Chicago, Ill.: YMCA, 1997): 1.

CHAPTER 9

SPECIALIZED LEISURE-SERVICE AREAS

◆ ◆ ◆

Inclusive recreation has swept the country. Individuals with disabilities and their families are more aware of their right to inclusion than ever before. More agencies are including children, teens, and adults with disabilities in programs along with people without disabilities. This right has resulted in a dynamic change in the way public recreation agencies provide leisure services.[1]

In the light of drawdowns and base closures, one might conclude that the military morale, welfare, and recreation arena would be headed for a decline as well. However, just as surviving bases can expect an influx of inhabitants and thus an expansion of their program, other military services represent an untapped growth opportunity.

Depending on your base location, your MWR facilities and staff may encounter a varying number of Army and/or Air National Guardsmen and women. Morale and retention are just as important to these populations as they are to active-duty Department of Defense personnel [in terms of] quality of life, namely, fitness centers, hospitality, and other areas of recreation.[2]

◆ ◆ ◆

INTRODUCTION

Having examined three areas of organized leisure services that are designed for the public at large, we now turn to five categories of recreation sponsors that serve more specialized needs and interests. These five areas—namely, therapeutic recreation, armed forces morale and welfare services, employee services, campus recreation, and private-membership groups—each serve a specific type of population or organization with goals and program elements geared to meeting its specific needs.

Throughout the analysis of these five leisure-service areas, emphasis will be placed on the dynamic changes they are going through in the transition from the traditional models that evolved in the twentieth century to more innovative forms of service in the new millenium.

THERAPEUTIC RECREATION SERVICE

Over the past 50 years, there has been increased recognition of the value of recreation as a means of treatment or rehabilitation for individuals with serious illnesses or impairments and of the need to provide special or adapted recreational opportunities for persons with disabilities in community settings.

Early Development of Therapeutic Recreation

The history of past centuries provides a number of examples of the use of recreation in the treatment of psychiatric patients, in both Europe and America. The fullest impetus for therapeutic recreation, however, came in the twentieth century in three types of institutions: (1) hospitals and rehabilitation centers for those with physical disabilities; (2) hospitals for mentally ill persons; and (3) special schools for those with developmental disabilities.

After both World War I and World War II, there was a wave of concern about the need to rehabilitate veterans who had sustained major physical injuries or psychological trauma while in service. As a consequence, Veterans Administration and military hospitals developed comprehensive programs of rehabilitative services, including physical and occupational therapy, psychotherapy, social service, vocational training, guidance, *and* recreation. In such settings, recreation was perceived as being one of several techniques that contributed to patient recovery.

At the same time, recreation gained recognition as a form of allied or adjunctive service within such civilian institutions as special homes or schools for individuals with mental retardation or other disabilities, nursing homes and long-term care institutions, or state or private psychiatic hospitals or mental health centers. Gradually, *therapeutic recreation*—as it came to be known rather than the earlier term *recreation therapy*—gained acceptance in the health-care field. Colleges and universities initiated major curricula or degree options in this field, and professional societies developed standards for practice and accreditation and certification procedures for practitioners.

Federal legislation promoting the rights of special populations, particularly with respect to education, included recreation as a form of related or supportive service. For example, in 1976, Congress enacted the Education for All Handicapped Children Act, which resulted in dramatically increased programs for children with disabilities, including physical and occupational therapy and recreation (identified as important "related services" for the disabled). Section 504 of the Rehabilitation Act of 1973, often called the "nondiscrimination clause," made it illegal to bar otherwise qualified individuals who were disabled from any program or activity receiving federal funding. Numerous federal agencies, such as the Bureau of Education for the Handicapped of the Office of Education, the Division of Mental Retardation of the Rehabilitation Services Administration, and the Administration on Aging, have funded training and research programs, as well as ongoing services, within different categories of disability.

Emerging Models of Therapeutic Recreation

With growing interest in this field of professional practice, educators and practitioners sought to clarify its identity and essential functions. In the mid-1970s, for example, Gerald O'Morrow identified five models of service that reflected different approaches in the field:

Custodial Model: Recreation programs are provided in long-term care settings in which little effort is made to provide rehabilitation or meaningful educational or other needed services. Recreation is primarily employed to lighten the atmosphere and improve the morale of the institution; it may also be part of the reward-and-punishment system, or may be a useful means of creating a favorable public relations image for the outside world.

Medical-Clinical-Model: In most treatment settings, this has been the dominant pattern. Recreation is viewed as an important element in the treatment plan, and is designed to help treat illness, under medical direction. It has been most widely found in psychiatric institutions or physical rehabilitation settings.

Therapeutic Milieu Model: Also found predominantly in programs for the mentally ill or socially deviant, this approach stresses the need to create a healthy environment, or therapeutic community in which all staff members and patients or clients themselves act as therapeutic agents. Recreation becomes a useful medium for group living, planning and carrying out projects, and the development of daily living skills.

Education and Training Model: This is a goal-oriented approach, often used with the mentally retarded; it places heavy emphasis on occupational therapy, remedial education, vocational training, and similar modalities. Recreation is used to teach basic cognitive or social skills, and may also be used as part of behavior modification programs with the disturbed or socially deviant.

Community Model: This describes the type of therapeutic recreation service that is provided in the community at large. Often, it has been the goal of institutional personnel to help equip their patients or clients to return to community life and function successfully; in many cases, beginning contacts and involvements have been made while they are still under care in the treatment setting.[3]

In an effort to clarify the appropriate focus and philosophy of therapeutic recreation service, in the early 1980s, the National Therapeutic Recreation Society (NTRS), a branch of the National Recreation and Parks Association, developed a comprehensive definition of the field. NTRS identified three services that should be offered as part of a comprehensive approach to therapeutic recreation. These are: (1) *therapy,* (2) *leisure education,* and (3) *recreational participation.* In any given situation, the therapeutic recreation specialist should be ready to provide any or all of these services:

The decision as to where and when each of these services would be provided would be based on the assessment of client need. Different individuals have a variety of different needs related to leisure utilization. For some clients, improvement of a functional behavior or problem (physical, mental, social, or emotional) is a necessary prerequisite to meaningful leisure experiences. For others, acquiring leisure skills, knowledge, and ability is a priority need. For others, special recreation participation opportunities are necessary, based on place of residence or because assistance or adapted activities are required.[4]

The NTRS statement is based on a principle known as "progressive patient care." It implies that at each stage of a patient's illness and recovery (or a client's involvement over a period of time with a service agency), program experiences are provided that are geared to achieving maximum benefit for the subject appropriate to that stage and helping the individual move along constructively to the next stage.

What came to be known as the "Leisure Ability Model" was based on a number of assumptions about the role of leisure in every individual's lifestyle and about important characteristics and needs of persons with disability. Charles Sylvester, for example, cited a fundamental principle that extended beyond a narrow concern with helping an individual in the recovery process or contributing to his or her functional behavior. This broader view, he writes, was summed up in the NTRS's 1982 *Philosophical Position Statement:*

> All human beings, including those individuals with disabilities, illnesses, or limiting conditions, have a *right* [emphasis added] to, and need for, leisure involvement as a necessary aspect of the human experience. The purpose of therapeutic recreation service is to facilitate . . . an appropriate leisure lifestyle for individuals with limitations. . . .[5]

Other elements in the rationale for providing therapeutic recreation for persons with illnesses or disabilities had to do with the psychological nature and behavior of many persons with disabilities. Stumbo and Peterson sum up a number of these, having to do with such attributes as "learned helplessness," the need for "intrinsic motivation," and a sense of "personal causality" and "freedom of choice"—all factors affecting the disabled individual's ability to lead a full and satisfying life.[6]

It was recognized that persons with disabilities had special needs with respect to leisure and recreation. While all individuals need diversified recreational outlets, those who have a significant degree of disability frequently find it especially difficult to meet their needs in constructive and convenient ways. In part, this is because serious physical impairments, emotional difficulties, or cognitive limitations may legitimately constrict the potential range of participation by persons with disabilities.

Much of the recreational deprivation of disabled individuals, however, is caused by society's failure to assist them, or even *permit* them, to engage in activity to the full extent of their potential. Many communities and organizations in the past did not make the design adaptations that would permit disabled persons to use their facilities. In some cases, recreation and park departments have barred disabled persons from their programs, arguing that they did not have staff members who were skilled in working with special populations or that serving the disabled would impose the risk of accident lawsuits and increased insurance costs. In other cases, administrators have felt that the presence of blind, retarded, or orthopedically disabled participants would be distasteful to the public at large, which might then cease to use the facilities. Sometimes parents or relatives have tended to shelter them excessively, and often their lack of skill or fear of rejection by others has caused persons with disabilities to limit their recreational participation.

Expansion of Field   Due both to the legislation cited earlier and to growing public awareness and support for such programs, institutions and organizations providing leisure services for persons with disabilities proliferated in the 1970s and 1980s. They included:

1. Hospitals of all types, serving those with every form of illness or disability in active treatment programs

2. Nursing homes and long-term or intensive care facilities, serving chiefly the infirm or disoriented aging person but also persons in other age categories who have had major trauma (strokes or disabling injuries) and cannot live independently

3. Schools or residential centers for those with developmental disability, severe learning disability, or emotional disturbance

4. Special schools, treatment centers, or penal institutions for those with social deviancy

5. Residential centers for aging persons who, while not requiring full-time nursing care, cannot safely live independently

6. Centers for physical medicine and rehabilitation, which provide programs of physical, psychological, and vocational rehabilitation

7. Programs provided by public recreation and park agencies

8. Programs provided by voluntary agencies, including both organizations concerned with a particular disability and its varied service needs and organizations designed to provide recreation and related social services to those with different categories of disability

9. Aftercare and other sheltered environments or workshop programs that assist persons with disability living in the community

Contrasting Emphases in the Field   Gradually it became apparent that, while the NTRS Leisure Ability statement presented an idealized model of what therapeutic recreation seeks to accomplish, it does not realistically describe *all* present-day practices. Many recreation specialists in treatment centers continue to provide essentially diversional programs, while others who work in the community simply provide modified recreation programs for groups of disabled individuals, without clearly rehabilitative purposes.

In light of these practices, it would appear that two distinctly different approaches to serving disabled persons in modern society with recreation may be identified. The first of these may be called the *clinical approach* and the second *special recreation*.

Clinical Approach

This model of service is clearly designed to carry out significant goals of rehabilitation within the overall treatment program. It is found in most therapeutic recreation textbooks and curricula today and is the basis for national and regional workshops dealing with hospital or rehabilitation-centered programs.

The practice of therapeutic recreation under this model has become increasingly sophisticated. In February 1994, the National Therapeutic Recreation Society approved the following revised definition of therapeutic recreation:

> Practiced in clinical, residential, and community settings, the profession of therapeutic recreation uses treatment, education, and recreation services to help people with illnesses, disabilities, and other conditions to develop and use their leisure in ways that enhance their health, independence, and well-being.[7]

Following this statement, the NTRS Standards of Practice Committee published a detailed set of standards, criteria, and operational guidelines for practitioners in this field, covering the following elements of service: (1) scope of service; (2) mission and purpose, goals and objectives; (3) individual treatment and program plan; (4) documentation; (5) plan of operation; (6) personnel qualifications; (7) ethical responsibilities; and (8) evaluation and research.

he detailed nature of these Standards of Practice is indicated by the criteria used to support the guidelines for development and implementation of recreation services under *Standard I, Scope of Service*. These are as follows:

a. There is a plan for assessing and identifying goals and objectives, client leisure needs, interests, competencies, and capabilities. This is sometimes referred to as a needs assessment or benefit-based management.

b. Opportunities are available for clients to provide input into the development of their recreation experiences.

c. Barriers to client participation are identified, considered, and accommodated for in the planning and implementation of recreation activities. These can include architectural, financial, transportation, communication, and/or attitudinal barriers.

d. Plans are developed for each client to participate at his/her optimal level of ability and to progress according to interests, competencies, and capabilities.

e. Planned activities are age and developmentally appropriate and modified through the use of accommodations, including adaptive equipment and techniques.

f. Recreation services are planned and implemented to accommodate the client's cultural, social, educational, and economic background.

g. Recreation services are planned to encompass the normal rhythm of life and attempt to align with normalization principles and the promotion of integration and inclusion.

h. Persons who deliver recreation services are qualified by holding a current certificate as Certified Therapeutic Recreation Specialist (CTRS), Certified Leisure Professional (CLP), and/or Certified Leisure Associate (CLA).

i. Recreation services are planned and integrated within the agency to achieve maximum use of available resources.

j. Program plans, protocols (procedures), and risk management policies exist, and risks and potentials for risk are identified for the client prior to recreation participation.

k. Essential eligibility criteria are established for all activities.

l. There is an initial client orientation, with assistance provided to the available recreation programs, facilities, and resources to achieve maximum mobility and independence.

m. There is a plan for homebound/bedside activities, when needed.

n. There is a plan for client feedback regarding program effectiveness.

o. There is periodic evaluation of the recreation services program plan.

The provision of clinical therapeutic recreation, like that of other adjunctive services like occupational therapy or physical therapy, must depend on financial reimbursement through third-party payments from an insurance company or health-care plan to the hospital or other agency providing care. Charles Bullock writes:

> Currently many TR services are provided in clinical settings. Improving functional ability is generally the primary component of TR service provision in the health-care arena and these services are reimbursable by a third-party payor. Leisure education, when used to improve a client's functional ability, might also qualify as a reimbursable TR service. Recreation participation, however, is not considered a reimbursable service.[8]

Realistically, recreation services provided for persons with disabilities in community settings rarely meet the detailed Standards of Practice just cited. Consequently, although community-based programs are included in the NTRS definition of therapeutic recreation, they cannot be considered forms of clinical service. Instead, they have typically been described under the heading of *special recreation*.

Shift to Special Recreation in Community Settings

While the primary thrust of the organized therapeutic recreation field continued to be on the clinical approach in formal treatment programs, there was a pronounced growth of concern about persons with disabilities in community settings. This shift was in part a response to the deinstitutionalization of hundreds of thousands of mentally ill or mentally retarded individuals that took place very widely in the 1960s and 1970s. For the first time, great numbers of such individuals were no longer shut up in long-term care in isolated custodial institutions, but lived in the community, receiving services in local mental health centers and residing in independent or semi-independent environments.

Realistically, many of the community programs and services that were planned for such individuals were not provided or were seriously underfunded. As a consequence, numerous reports in the 1990s indicated that large numbers of mentally ill or retarded persons were homeless or in prisons and jails, rather than safe residential settings.[9]

Nonetheless, there was a great surge of interest in providing community-based leisure opportunities for persons with disabilities throughout the United States and Canada. It was recognized that far greater numbers of persons with disabilities lived in the community than in residential treatment centers, and that they had equally strong needs for recreation. Municipal recreation and park agencies began to assume a higher degree of responsibility for providing special programs for the disabled—usually rather limited activities for groups with a particular type of impairment, such as blind, physically disabled, or mentally retarded persons. Voluntary agencies also gave fuller emphasis to programming social activities, adapted sports, or camping for special populations.

The term generally applied to such programs is *special recreation*. Dan Kennedy and his co-authors write:

> The term *special recreation* has recently emerged to describe recreation and leisure provisions that accommodate recreation participation by members of special population groups, and particularly by persons with disabilities. . . . [They] allow participation by individuals who have disabilities that necessitate special accommodations (modifications of activities, altered environments, personal assistance, etc.) above and beyond the kinds of accommodations generally provided.[10]

While they do not deliberately gear programs to achieving specific treatment or rehabilitative goals within a clinical framework, those providing special recreation do have important purposes. They value recreation as an important life experience for persons with disabilities and seek to achieve positive physical, social, and emotional outcomes, making whatever adaptations in programming, facilities, equipment, or leadership methods that are appropriate.

In an attempt to gain an overview of community-based special recreation programs, the Prince George's County, Maryland, Department of Parks and Recreation carried out a survey of 18 county or municipal programs serving persons with disabilities throughout the United States. It revealed a wide range of program trends and positive developments in the field of special recreation, but also uncovered problems in such areas as competition for funding, recruitment and placement of volunteers, changing community attitudes, and educating both persons with disabilities and their families as to the importance of recreation and their basic rights.

Expansion of Sports and Outdoor Recreation Participation

At every level, people of all ages with physical or mental disabilities who previously had been unable to engage in active forms of play are now taking part in varied forms of sports, camping, and outdoor recreation pursuits. Many of these activities are promoted by Wheelchair Sports, USA (formerly the National Wheelchair Athletic Association), a multisport organization for disabled athletes who compete annually in regional, national, and international games. Included among the competitive events for both men and women are archery, athletics (track and field, pentathlon, road racing), basketball, quad rugby, shooting, swimming, table tennis, tennis, and weightlifting. Thousands of young athletes also participate in Special Olympics events, while many others compete in marathons, bowling leagues, and other individual or team sports.

In terms of outdoor recreation, since the 1950s, camping and outdoor adventure programs have become increasingly geared for individuals with disabilities. Michael Kelley points out that numerous research studies have confirmed the positive effects of outdoor adventure activities, such as wilderness backpacking, canoeing, mountaineering, white-water rafting, and other Outward Bound–type programs for emotionally disturbed or chronically mentally ill individuals.[11]

Use of Technology and Assistive Devices

Sophisticated technology is also being brought into play to permit persons with disabilities to participate successfully in different leisure activities. For several decades, various modified instruments or pieces of equipment have been used to help disabled individuals take part in card and table games, arts and crafts, team and individual sports, and other pursuits. For example, the kinds of equipment used for blind persons in sports and games include:

(1) guide ropes that enable blind individuals to run at top speed without fear, holding a short rope attached to a ring that slides along a wire without interference; (2) audible goal detectors (consisting of a motor-driven noisemaker that makes clicking sounds at a constant rate); (3) audible balls for modified ball games, such as kickball, that have

either a battery-operated beeper or bell placed inside; and (4) a portable aluminum rail for use in bowling that is movable from lane to lane and orients the blind bowler.[12]

Aerodynamic wheelchairs are now being used by disabled racers, and carbon-fiber prosthetic feet enable amputee athletes to run almost as fast as able-bodied athletes. Research into the use of electrodes to jolt the leg muscles of persons with spinal cord injuries promises ultimately to help them "walk," while numerous other devices are being invented each year to facilitate independent functioning for disabled persons. Electronic devices such as "aura interactor" strap-on vests enable deaf people to dance, without straining to hear the music, and help blind videogame players to feel laser beams "bouncing" off the screen.

Cooperative Networks of Agencies

Because many community and nonprofit organizations lacked the staff resources or special facilities required to provide comprehensive leisure-service programs for disabled persons, the 1980s and 1990s saw a trend toward developing cooperative networks of such agencies.

In such structures, two or more public or nonprofit human-service organizations— or a combination of both types—share their funding and facilities to provide needed recreation programs in a number of locations. For example, there are over 20 independent Special Recreation Associations (SRAs) in northern Illinois, with budgets ranging from $50,000 to $1.5 million annually, based on revenue generated from special direct property taxes. All SRAs are coordinated by boards representing the cooperating communities. They interface with municipal recreation and park departments and offer programming for persons with all types of disabling conditions in both integrated and segregated groupings.

In another example of jointly operated programs, the South East Consortium for Special Services has been established in Westchester County, New York, to serve nine towns, cities, and villages with a wide range of special recreation activities and services. Since the bulk of its funding (apart from contributed facilities and staff resources) is received from the State Office of Mental Retardation and Developmental Disabilities, it focuses on individuals with autism, cerebral palsy, epilepsy, mental retardation, and neurological impairment or multiple disabilities and provides services in a variety of integrated and separate groupings.

Throughout the country, numerous independent nonprofit organizations, such as RCH, Inc., in San Francisco, have established facilities and programs that are designed to meet varied life needs—recreational, social, educational, and vocational—of people in different categories of disability.

New Emphasis on *Inclusion*

In the late 1990s, instead of the term *special recreation*, professional organizations began to use the term *inclusion*—meaning simply the involvement and full acceptance of disabled persons in a wide range of community settings. In 1998, for example, a National Recreation and Park Association survey team conducted an intensive study of the inclusion practices of 900 public recreation and park agencies. It analyzed the types of services provided and the categories of individuals served, the accommodations that were made in terms of facilities and equipment, and the problems and staff training needs in the communities that were surveyed.[13] In September 2000, a major National Institute on Recreation Inclusion was held in Deerfield, Illinois, bringing together representatives from many different kinds of agencies and highlighting the outstanding programs that were being developed in this area.

Impact of Health-Care Management Trends

In a sense, this broad-based shift to community programs serving disabled persons is a response to dramatic changes that have taken place within the nation's health-care system. First, as indicated, deinstitutionalization was responsible for closing down or cutting back many of the large state hospitals or special schools that had formerly employed thousands of therapeutic recreation professionals. Beyond this, many residents or patients who remained in such settings tended to be so ill or limited in their capabilities that it was difficult to develop meaningful programs for them.

In communities, generally, the entire health-care system has been in a state of crisis over the past decade. Many hospitals, with reduced Medicare funding and with insurance companies and managed care administrators slashing their approved services, have been forced to merge, eliminate emergency care operations, or reduce staffs and lengths of patient stays. Similarly, nursing homes, especially commercially operated chains, have also experienced economic pressures that have compelled them to reduce services, barely meeting state-imposed standards.[14] All of these factors have pressured clinically based therapeutic recreation specialists to develop new program-delivery strategies and to conduct evaluation and research studies that confirm the value of their services.

Examples of Efficacy Research

A key element in the maturing of therapeutic recreation as a field of professional service—particularly in clinical settings—has been the increased emphasis given by educators and practitioners to the evaluation of therapeutic recreation program outcomes. The most comprehensive compilation of efficacy study findings was carried out by Coyle, Kinney, Riley, and Shank as part of a study at Temple University. Supported by the National Institute on Disability and Rehabilitation Research of the federal Department of Education, this report compiled the positive findings of hundreds of research studies on therapeutic recreation's impact from a medical perspective.[15]

Beyond this, numerous articles have appeared in the *Therapeutic Recreation Journal* documenting the positive outcomes of therapeutic recreation services, based on research and demonstration projects with patients ranging from those with spinal cord injuries to regressed geriatric patients. Still others have urged broadening the scope of therapeutic recreation to such other areas of need as HIV-AIDs patients, working with at-risk youth and in correctional settings, or with pathological gamblers, a growing problem.

In a summary of the changes that have taken place that have affected this field of service, Riley and Skalko describe the demographic shifts, dynamics of the health-care industry (including cost containment and expansion of outpatient services), and changing nature of the workplace—all of which pose challenges for professionals. They predict that future therapeutic recreation professionals will work with a far greater range of individual and social problems:

Therapeutic recreation specialists will market their skills and talents . . . across delivery settings . . . and will increasingly capture service-delivery roles in home health, homeless care, domestic abuse, substance abuse, at-risk youth services, transplant units, adult day services, partial hospitalizations, retirement services, and care for the frail elderly.[16]

Whether the acceptance of therapeutic recreation as a meaningful service in such areas comes to pass and whether young practitioners-to-be elect to enter such difficult and specialized areas of social service that appear to be remote from the way recreation is popularly conceived remain open questions.

ARMED FORCES RECREATION

For many years it has been the official policy of the military establishment to provide a well-rounded "morale, welfare, and recreational program" for the physical, social, and mental well-being of its personnel. During World War I, Special Services Divisions were established to provide social and recreational programs that would sustain favorable morale, curb homesickness and boredom, minimize fatigue, and reduce AWOL (absent without leave) and venereal disease rates.

Today, each branch of the armed forces has its own pattern of recreation sponsorship, although they are all under the same Morale, Welfare, and Recreation Program (MWR), which is administratively responsible to the Office of the Assistant Secretary of Defense for Manpower, Reserve Affairs, and Logistics. They serve several million individuals, including active duty, reserve, and retired military personnel and their dependents; civilian employees; and surviving spouses of military personnel who died in active duty. In addition, MWR services are also provided to Coast Guard personnel, who are *not* part of the Department of Defense.

Goals and Scope of Armed Forces Recreation Today

Lankford and DeGraaf have succinctly presented the rationale justifying armed forces recreation programs:

> The purpose of military recreation is to provide facilities and programs to enhance the physical and mental well-being of service men and women and their families. . . . To better support the armed forces mission of readiness, the primary objectives of MWR are tied to fitness, unit and community cohesion, family well-being, quality of life, and recreation awareness and outreach.[17]

In the early 1990s, they summarized the scope of armed forces recreation, pointing out that it served more than 2.1 million active military personnel; more than 2.7 million family members ranging from infants to retirees; and more than 1.4 million National Guard and Reserve members who are eligible for recreation programs. While the number of armed forces bases and personnel has been substantially reduced over the past decade, military recreation and its related services continue to constitute an immense worldwide operation.

Program Elements

MWR programs include an extensive range of sports, fitness, social, creative, outdoor recreation, travel, entertainment, and hobby leisure pursuits. In the Air Force, for example, an extensive program of sports activities has typically included six major elements: (1) *instruction* in basic sports skills; (2) a *self-directed* phase of informal participation in sports under minimum supervision or direction; (3) an *intramural* program, in which personnel assigned to a particular base compete with others at the same base; (4) an *extramural* program, which includes competition with teams from different Air Force bases or with teams from neighboring communities; (5) a *varsity* program, which involves high-level competition with players selected for their advanced skills who compete on a broader national or international scale; and (6) a program for *women* in the Air Force.

In addition to such programs attached to individual services, the armed forces promote an extensive range of competitive sports programs. Through interservice competition in such sports as basketball, boxing, wrestling, track and field, and softball, all-service teams are selected; armed forces teams are then chosen to represent the United States in international competition.

Hundreds of Army, Air Force, Navy, and Marine bases have adopted the popular *Start Smart Sports Development Program*, which helps children as young as age three in learning basic motor skills that progress to organized sports involvement—and in which parents become heavily involved in leadership roles.[18]

Fitness Programs   Health and wellness have become a major focus of armed forces recreation. To improve fitness levels of personnel, the Air Force has installed Health and Wellness Centers (HAWC) on each base; these centers are well-equipped and are staffed with leaders qualified to provide the following services: fitness and health risk assessments, exercise programming and weight counseling, stress management and smoking cessation assistance, and similar activities.

On some military bases, fitness is promoted through well-publicized and challenging special events. At the Marine Corps Base at Camp Lejeune, North Carolina, the Lejeune Grand Prix Series features a number of competitive events that involve hundreds of service personnel in a European Cross Country race over natural terrain; a Tour d'Pain, a grueling endurance cycling race; a Masters Swim Meet; a Davy Jones Open Ocean Swim; a Toughman Triathlon; and other types of races.

Outdoor Recreation   Often, outdoor program activities are keyed to the location of a base. For example, Fort Carson, Colorado, sponsors an extensive ski program that features an annual Ski Expo, with over 150 vendors and representatives of ski areas and average attendance of more than 5,000 skiing enthusiasts. Responding to widespread interest in mountain climbing and rock climbing, this Army base has constructed a 17,400-square-foot outdoor recreation center that features a 32-foot-high indoor climbing wall, with the look and feel of natural rock, and climbing routes geared to different skill levels. Other bases offer instruction, equipment, and facilities for such water-based activities as fishing, wind-surfing, jet skiing, scuba diving, and similar pastimes.

Family Recreation   The Department of Defense has become increasingly aware of the need to provide varied family-focused programs to counter the special problems that may affect the spouses and children of military personnel. Particular emphasis is given to the need to serve military youth. Steven Waller and Asuncion Suren write:

> Adolescents residing in military installations are confronted with the same range of social problems that occur within society as a whole. Crime, violence, substance abuse, the social environment, and the unproductive use of leisure time are critical issues that confront military youth.[19]

As one response to this challenge, MWR planners have developed a Drug Demand Reduction Task Force, a program designed to combat substance abuse affecting at-risk youth on military bases and in communities where the bases are located. This program employs structured recreation activities including athletics and high-risk outdoor pursuits, day and residential camps, and other counseling and educational programs designed to build self-esteem, self-discipline, and leadership among youth—particularly in Marine and Navy base settings.

The Defense Department focused during the 1990s on improving child-care services in the military, in the effort to remake a program known as the "ghetto" of child care—marked by long waiting lists, uneven leadership, and high costs. After creating an expanded network of child-care centers, after-school programs, and referral services, the military tripled the number of children being served and was hailed by the National Women's Law Center, a nonprofit research and advocacy group, as "a model for child-care reform nationwide" in May 2000.[20]

For older youth, the Defense Department's concern led to the development of a Strategic Youth Action Plan by the Office of Family Policy. Some of the pressing issues related to military youth and the positive outcomes of different model programs—many of which were conducted by Morale, Welfare, and Recreation personnel—are summarized on page 351. Special emphasis was placed in this plan on strengthening family relationships.

Community Relations   Many military bases in the United States and overseas place a high priority on establishing positive relationships between armed forces personnel and nearby communities. Civilian MWR personnel working around the globe in such settings as Europe, Korea, and Central America, and even Saudi Arabia, Turkey, and Africa, seek to provide a wealth of outdoor recreational experiences and positive intercultural experiences with local residents:

> Activities for family members [overseas] may include living aboard a tall ship for a few days and learning how to work together and sail the coast of Holland or backpacking in the Swiss Alps. Soldiers and airmen learn teamwork, leadership, communication skills, and technical skills . . . from a ropes course, playing paintball, rock climbing, kayaking, or rafting down an Austrian river. . . . [Our mission is also to] bridge the cultural gap and introduce the Americans to their new—albeit temporary—homeland by integrating activities and resources with those of the host nation.[21]

On just one such distant base, on the island of Sasebo, Japan, Navy MWR specialists provide a huge range of leisure services, including travel tours to scenic locations and festivals in the region, fitness and outdoor recreation activities, hobby shops,

COMMANDER FLEET ACTIVITIES SASEBO

MORALE, WELFARE & RECREATION

In armed forces recreation, the Sasebo, Japan, Naval Base offers a wide range of activities, facilities, and services, including an extensive set of social programs for single sailors and marines.

professional entertainment, holiday events, extensive youth programs, library services, varied sports tournaments, and even such unusual services as a "pet-holding" facility for military families going on vacation. Although such varied programs are not typical of *all* military installations, the Sasebo MWR operations offer leisure opportunities that far excel those in many stateside, civilian communities.

Fiscal Support of Armed Forces Recreation

Military recreation has traditionally depended on two types of funding: *appropriated funds*, which are tax funds approved by Congress, and *nonappropriated funds*, which are generated on the military base through a combination of post exchange profits and other revenue from fees, rentals, and other recreation charges. The Navy Personnel Command in the Department of Defense defines the different types of recreation funds generated by Navy personnel and their dependents to help provide financial support for their recreation activities. Specifically, these are

> monies received from Navy exchange profits, fees and charges placed on the use of recreation facilities and services or other authorized sources for the support of Navy recreation programs. Unit Recreation Funds are those which serve the recreation needs of individual ships, shore stations and other Navy activities. Composite Recreation Funds are those which serve two or more activities which share the same recreation facilities. Consolidated Recreation Funds are those which serve the recreation needs of several separate installations within a geographical area.[22]

In the late 1980s, the Department of Defense classified all MWR activities as either *mission-sustaining activities*, such as overseas entertainment, physical fitness centers, or temporary lodging facilities; or *business activities*, such as amusement machine centers, bingo, golf courses, marinas, and rod-and-gun clubs. Guidelines suggested that there be higher levels of fiscal support for more critical services and lower support levels for purely recreational activities that have the potential for being self-sustaining.

Since this time, with growing budget cutbacks and the need to maximize revenues from clubs, messes, post exchanges, and varied forms of commercial sponsorship or partnerships, MWR planners have initiated a range of new fiscal strategies. The effort has been to reduce the costs of operations, standardize procedures, and eliminate redundant programs or personnel. The Navy, for example, has established 10 major regions to simplify the planning and supervision of programs, has increasingly encouraged public-private projects, and has established new planning processes to "reinvent" facility development and other projects.

Through much of its ongoing operations, Morale, Welfare, and Recreation stresses that it serves several million individuals in the world's "largest leisure-delivery system." In promotion for a major trade show for suppliers and other commercial concerns doing business with the military—1998 MWR EXPO—it itemized dozens of different kinds of equipment and services used by the armed forces, stating:

> This industry is an untapped market in that many suppliers do not even know it is out there. With over 7,000 military food service and club activities, annual sales will be well over $6 billion—over 2 percent of the entire U.S. food service market.

More than 1,000 individuals from the Services' MWR organizations will attend the 1998 MWR EXPO to buy products and services with the objective to continue providing cost effective and recreational services to our U.S. Armed Forces.[23]

Through the 1990s, as base closures and budget cuts continued, military recreation professionals sought to develop an even more business-oriented approach to their services. Pat Harden, director of Navy recreation training at Patuxent River, Maryland, pointed out that two prevailing orientations have generally guided armed forces recreation: (1) the quality of life approach that sees MWR recreation and club services essentially as an amenity, although deserving of Department of Defense support; and (2) the businesslike marketing approach that urges that all recreation services be viewed primarily as a commodity to be merchandised, with a minimum of social and mission support goals or constraints.

Instead, Harden argues, it is essential to define the important mission of MWR programs within the overall Department of Defense structure and to work effectively to achieve the goals related to this mission. He quotes a Defense Department official as follows:

> Readiness is the cornerstone of this administration. A ready-to-fight force is linked intrinsically to the morale, sense of well-being, commitment, and pride in the mission of each Service and family member. Our Morale, Welfare, and Recreation programs play a direct role in developing and maintaining these characteristics within our force and are more important than ever during this time of transition, when profound changes are taking place that are having a powerful impact on Service members and their families.[24]

EMPLOYEE SERVICES AND RECREATION PROGRAMS

A third important area of specialized recreation programs involves the role of business and industry in providing recreation and related personnel services to employees and in some cases their families or other community residents.

Background of Company-Sponsored Programs

Employee recreation (formerly called "industrial recreation") began in the nineteenth century, but did not expand rapidly until after World War II. In 1975, *The New York Times* reported that 50,000 companies were spending $2 billion a year on recreation-related programs. Recent reports indicate that 4,000 businesses and other types of institutions are affiliated with the National Employee Services and Recreation Association (NESRA), with a substantial number belonging as well to the Association for Worksite Health Promotion.

While the providers of employee services and recreation originally were manufacturing companies and other industrial concerns, today many different types of organizations also sponsor employee activities. They include such diverse groups as food market chains, airline companies, insurance concerns, hospitals, and government agencies.

Goals of Employee Recreation

The major goals of the institutions providing such programs and services include the following.

Improvement of Employer-Employee Relations   Earlier in America's industrial development, there was considerable friction between management and labor that often resulted in extended and violent strikes. A major purpose of industrial recreation programs at this time was to create favorable employer-employee relationships and instill a sense of loyalty among workers. Today, with relative peace in most industries, this remains a significant goal of employee recreation. It is believed that such programs tend to create a feeling of belonging and identification among employees, and that group participation by workers at various job levels contributes to improved worker morale, increased harmony, and an attitude of mutual cooperation.

In the intense competition that characterized many businesses in the early and mid-1990s in a period of company downsizing and mergers, these goals became particularly important as a way of strengthening employee work morale and performance. Jerry Junkins, Chairman and Chief Executive Officer of Texas Instruments Inc. in Dallas, Texas, expresses this view:

> We see employee services and recreation as one part of a total package that includes competitive salaries, benefits, and health promotion services and activities. All of these are designed to let our people know we value them, and we view them as the key contributors to our company's success. . . . We've tried to design our ES & R programs to address the total well-being of our employees and their families by providing them with programs that can enhance their physical, mental, and emotional health.[25]

Directly Promoting Employee Fitness and Efficiency   Corporations large and small today have become concerned about maintaining the health of their employees. One reason may be the skyrocketing costs of health insurance. It was reported in 1988 that General Motors alone was spending some $2 billion annually on medical care coverage for its 2.3 million employees and retirees and their dependents. Beyond this, it costs huge sums for companies to replace middle- and upper-level managers who suffer heart attacks or other fatal illnesses that could be avoided by appropriate programs.

Numerous reports from varied company sources document the effectiveness of recreation and fitness programs in achieving health and productivity-related goals:

> At General Electric in Cincinnati, exercisers [in company-sponsored fitness programs] were absent from work 45 percent fewer days than nonparticipants.
>
> General Mills found that participants in its employee fitness program had a 19 percent reduction in absenteeism compared to a 69 percent increase in nonparticipants.
>
> Toronto Life Assurance found that employee turnover during a 10-month period was substantially lower for program participants than for nonparticipants—1.5 percent versus 15 percent.[26]

Such justifications for expanded programs of employee services and recreation became increasingly important in the last years of the 1990s and the beginning of the new century. National prosperity and a record-breaking rate of employment meant that many companies had to use new strategies to recruit new employees and to retain their present workers.

Recruitment-Retention Appeal

An attractive program of recreation and related personnel services that can meet the needs of both the employee and his or her family is a persuasive recruitment weapon. Crompton, Love, and More have documented the role of recreation, parks, and open space in many companies' decision-making process, with respect to decisions about relocation.[27] Outlining a number of strategies for effective personnel recruitment, Amy Berger writes:

> As you promote your department and its offerings, you send a message to current and future employees that your department is what makes your company a great place to work. Promotional campaigns are most successful when all of your company's departments join forces to educate employees on the services available and encourage their involvement on an individual basis.[28]

In terms of retention, many companies find that successful employee programs help reduce job turnover. Litton Laser Systems in Apopka, Florida, for example, credits its low employee turnover and high morale to its Social Activities Committee (SAC), a group of employees who manage social, recreational, and sports events and other services for all company members and their families.

Company Image and Community Role

An important part of the recreation and services function involves external relations—the company's external, community-based role. Barbara Altman comments that in the mid-1990s, many companies sought to redefine the idea of corporate citizenship. Research showed that

> . . . pressures in the business and social environment were prompting issues in community relations practice. Executives were struggling with how to operationalize community responsibility, how to respond to their multiple communities, and how to explain the linkage between community involvement and business strategy.[29]

At Litton Laser Systems, one expression of this concern was found in the organized employee giving program, which resulted in large sums being raised each year for United Way, the American Heart Association, American Red Cross, and a special "Loaves and Fishes" Charity program. In many cases, company recreation programs and facilities serve community groups, and, in others, the director of the employee services and recreation program is also given responsibility for numerous community-relations activities of the company. The employee services coordinator for the M. D. Anderson Cancer Center at the University of Texas in Houston, Texas, recruits

> employees for community events such as the Houston/Tenneco Marathon and the University of Texas Health Science Center Sportathon. We sponsor health fairs and guest lectures during the Texas Medical Center Wellness Week. We promote cultural events in Houston throughout the workplace with the Council for the Visual and Performing Arts.
>
> We maintain seasonal special events, such as our Employee Christmas Dinner, Christmas decorating contest, National Hospital Week, Savings Bond drive, United Way, etc. . . . We handle discount programs for employees dealing with sporting and cultural events and various coupon books. We maintain our institutional bulletin

Racing is a popular sport in many forms. In Westchester County, New York, boys and girls compete in relay races, while in Orlando, Florida, Navy Morale, Welfare, and Recreation program sponsors track meet. In Pennsylvania, CoreStates Bank schedules major annual bike race.

board which publicizes our programs and those from other departments. We are also in charge of the monthly Outstanding Employee Award program.[30]

In other settings, the employee services program provides a means through which company executives can move purposefully to transform the business's internal and external image. As a vivid example, the Coors Brewing Company in Colorado, which had long had a reputation for conservative policies and funding right-wing political groups, sought deliberately to change its image, encouraging sensitivity training for its diverse workforce and shifts in its national identity as well. It sponsors 10 "resource councils" representing gays, women, and Native Americans, among others, and supports programs ranging from a marathon gay dance party in Miami to the first large-scale corporate mammography program in the country.

Program Activities and Services

In a 1980s analysis of the overall operation of such employee programs, activities were classified under four main headings as shown in Table 9.1.

Many companies have established extensive and well-equipped recreation and fitness centers and staffed them with qualified personnel. The Texins Activity Center in Dallas, serving employees of Texas Instruments, contains a multi-use gymnasium; strength and cardiovascular exercise areas; conference rooms; child-care rooms; club rooms; and a Natatorium with a six-lane, 25-lap pool, two aerobic studios, an indoor running track, and varied outdoor facilities.

TABLE 9.1

ELEMENTS IN COMPANY SERVICES AND RECREATION PROGRAMS

Physical Programs	% Response	Service Programs	% Response
Softball	64.5	Discount service/tickets	73.5
Bowling	57.8	United Way drive	63.4
Golf	48.4	Blood drives	59.2
Basketball	42.9	Award/recognition program	58.9
Volleyball	35.5	Discount service/products	54.4
Tennis	30.3	First aid/CPR training	50.2
Fitness program	30.0	Employee assistance program	28.6

Social/Cultural Programs		Facilities Operated	
Picnics	64.5	Ball diamond	19.9
Christmas parties	60.0	Fitness facility	18.8
Dinner/theater outings	28.6	Basketball court	16.0
Travel program	24.0	Activities field	15.3
Adult education (non-job-related)	20.9	Activities building	13.2
Drama/theater	19.2	Employee park	9.4
		Fitness trail	9.4

Wellness Programs and Fitness Centers The largest single thrust in employee service and recreation programs is toward providing health and wellness activities. Beyond simply offering exercise equipment or classes, wellness programs may include activities that promote physical, emotional, social, environmental, and even spiritual health. Kondrasuk and Carl have listed the varied components that are typically found in many company-sponsored wellness programs today:

Screenings, health risk appraisals (HRA): Blood pressure, weight, body fat, pulse, diabetes, AIDS, cardiovascular diseases, cancer and mammography, lifestyle and environmental questionnaires.

Exercise programs: Endurance/cardiovascular/aerobics, strength training, flexibility.

Education/awareness and possible interventions: Stress reduction, smoking cessation, obesity/weight control, lipid control, back pain, blood pressure/hypertension reduction, retirement and pre-retirement counseling, pre- and post-natal education, employee/family counseling on emotional issues, relaxation programs/meditation, producing healthier environments (like health food in vending machines).

Developing healthful skills, behaviors: First aid, CPR use, back injury prevention, increasing seat belt use.[31]

Administrative Arrangements

There are various approaches to the management of employee service and recreation programs. In some, the company itself provides the facilities and leadership and maintains complete control of the operation. In other organizations, the company provides the facilities, but an employee recreation association takes actual responsibility for running the program. Other companies use combinations of these approaches. Frequently, profits from canteens or plant vending machines provide financial support for the program, as does revenue from moderate fees for participation or membership. Many activities—such as charter vacation flights—are completely self-supporting; others are fully or partly subsidized by the company.

Some companies restrict participation in recreation programs to employees and their families, while others make them available to the surrounding community. For example, the Flick-Reedy Corporation designed its main building for the recreational use of the entire community, with thousands of children and adults using its gymnasium, auditorium, or dining room for special banquets and events each year.

Scheduling Flexibility: Off-Shift Programming

Employee service and recreation managers must adapt to the special circumstances of their organizations and the changing needs of the employees they serve. Often this may involve providing a wide range of special courses designed for vocational or career development, cultural interest, or personal enrichment. Some large corporations seek to meet the needs of their employees who work second and third shifts by scheduling facilities like health clubs or weight rooms to be available at odd hours of the day and night. For example, Phillips Petroleum and Pratt and Whitney schedule morning and midnight softball and bowling leagues for off-shift workers and make gyms, tennis courts, and other facilities, as well as discount ticket operations, available to them at convenient times.

Innovation and Entrepreneurship

Just as in other sectors of the leisure-service field, employee service and recreation practitioners have experienced the need to become more fiscally independent by generating a fuller level of revenues through their offerings and by demonstrating their value in convincing terms.

The purposes of adopting businesslike values and strategies are: (1) to enable employee programs to become less dependent on company financial support; and (2) to ensure that funds allocated to them by management yield significant, quantifiable benefits. A number of employee service and recreation directors in major corporations have been quite innovative in developing revenue sources based on businesslike ventures. Hauglie cites an example of such ventures:

> *Employee Stores.* At Control Data Corporation in Minneapolis, Minnesota, a business plan was developed for an employee store, including a needs assessment, marketing strategy, profit-and-loss projections, and start-up funding requirements. Following approval, which included a business loan from the company, the project was set in motion. By the early 1990s, three employee stores were operating successfully, and Control Data's initial investment was paid back within the first year of the program's operation.[32]

Changes in Professional Association

Over the past two decades, the primary professional organization in this field, the National Employee Services and Recreation Association, has seen a steady broadening of the responsibilities of its member companies. Today, while recreation continues to be a major function in such human-resource departments, there are 10 important elements within their overall operations. As defined in January 2000, when the organization changed its title to the Employee Services Management Association, they include the following: (1) employee stores, (2) community services, (3) convenience services, (4) recreation programs, (5) special events, (6) voluntary benefits, (7) dependent care assistance, (8) recognition and awards programs, (9) travel services, and (10) wellness/fitness programs.[33]

In promoting these services, the ESM Association publishes a magazine and buyer's guide; maintains an E-mail service and membership directory; holds an annual conference and exhibit; sponsors an Awards of Excellence Program and a certification program; and conducts varied continuing education, information, and research projects. In promoting high standards of performance in the employee services and recreation field, it maintains two kinds of memberships: (1) *organizational members,* who are actually employed in companies with management or leadership responsibilities; and (2) *associate members*, who provide services, equipment, or supplies to company employee programs.

CAMPUS RECREATION

The nation's colleges and universities provide a major setting for organized programs of leisure services involving millions of participants each year in a wide range of recreational activities. While their primary purpose is to serve students, on many campuses, faculty and staff members may also be involved in such programs.

All institutions of higher education today sponsor some forms of leisure activity for their resident and commuter populations. Many of the larger colleges and universities have campus unions, departments of student affairs, nor student centers that house a wide range of such activities. Frequently, a dean of student life is responsible for overseeing these programs, although intramural and recreational sports may often be administratively attached to a department or college of physical education and recreation or to a department of intercollegiate athletics.

The diversified leisure-service function may include operating performing arts centers (sometimes in cooperation with academic departments or schools in these fields), planning arts series, film programs and forums with guest speakers, and similar cultural events. Student union buildings may include such specialized facilities as bowling alleys, coffee houses, game rooms, restaurants, bookstores, and other activity areas.

Rationale for Campus Programs

Several logical reasons for sponsoring college and university recreation programs may be cited. Discussion of some of these follows.

Leisure as Cocurricular Enrichment   Not all of the learning that takes place in higher education is provided in the classroom or laboratory. Many special interests of students can be explored to the fullest only by cocurricular (nonclass) experiences, ranging from the journalism major who works on the staff of the campus newspaper or literary magazine to the botany major who becomes involved in wilderness backpacking or camping. Often such programs are carried on with the express cooperation of the campus department most directly involved with the leisure interest.

Maintaining Campus Control and Morale   Historically, American and Canadian colleges acted *in loco parentis;* that is, they were obligated to maintain a degree of control over the private lives of their students in areas such as drinking, gambling, sexual behavior, or the general domain of health and safety. For centuries, they therefore maintained codes of behavior, rules for on-campus living, curfews, and numerous other restrictions that controlled various forms of leisure behavior.

During the 1960s and 1970s, many campuses relinquished their responsibility for supervising students' private lives, particularly in areas related to personal morality. They did so at a time when students were forcibly demanding fuller rights of participation in campus governance, freedom from restrictive campus rules, and less structured academic curricula. However, during the 1980s, many institutions not only reintroduced curriculum requirements, but also became aware of the necessity to maintain fuller control over the social lives of their students.

The need for such supervision became evident in the mid- and late 1980s. In a series of feature articles, the *Chronicle of Higher Education* documented the striking growth in student drinking and drug abuse, including deaths stemming from forced drinking in hazing; increased incidents of drunken driving; and wild, mob-like behavior during spring breaks in Florida and on the Texas Gulf Coast.

If anything, these problems became more acute during the 1990s, with continuing reports of binge drinking in colleges, dangerous hazing practices, and even an ugly rise in racial tensions and incidents on a number of campuses.[34] As a consequence, the *New York Times* reported in March 1999 that in a revolution of new rules for college students, many campuses were turning full circle. Ethan Bronner writes:

> Reflecting a range of societal changes—consumerism, litigiousness, a shift in intergenerational relations, and increased fears about campus drinking—colleges are offering and students are often demanding greater supervision of their lives.[35]

At this time, many colleges began to take concrete steps to change the culture of drinking on their campuses—some banning alcohol entirely, cracking down on underage drinking, or limiting the use of liquor in fraternity houses.[36]

In general, it is now believed by many that colleges must play a larger role in guiding the lives of students outside of the classroom. While few administrators are seeking a return to the days of single-sex dormitories, dress codes, curfews, and other rigid rules, a consensus has grown that many of today's college students lack the responsibility to handle their newfound freedom sensibly and that it is necessary to establish and enforce some guidelines for students' social behavior.

Beyond being part of the effort to control negative kinds of behavior, campus recreation promotes positive student growth throughout the college experience. At a number of eastern colleges, students are drawn into outdoor recreation or community-service projects beginning with their freshman orientation period. At Lehigh University and Lafayette College, for example, new students are drawn into overnight canoe and backpacking trips and begin to make new friends immediately. Similarly, entering students at Bryn Mawr College are assigned one-day service projects with the Philadelphia Zoo, the Children's Hospital of Philadelphia, and Habitat for Humanity.

Enhancing the University's Image   Particularly in an era in which colleges and universities must compete for the enrollment of high-quality students, maintaining an appealing and impressive institutional image is critical. Probably the best-known vehicle for doing this is by fielding teams that play glamorous schedules in such popular sports as football or basketball. However, there are many other ways of building a positive image—through academic distinction, by winning prizes and awards, by having outstanding orchestras or theater companies, by having a distinguished university press, and through the accomplishments of alumni.

Certainly, having attractive recreational facilities and campus leisure programs also helps to build a positive image—particularly for potential students who visit a campus and are considering whether they want to live there for the next four years. Higher education appeals to a number of values and needs: not the least of these is the student's desire for an exciting and interesting social life.

Contributing to Student Development   Beyond enriching a student's formal academic experience, involvement in noncurricular experiences contributes significantly to his or her overall personal growth. In an article on academic productivity, Judith Bryant and James Bradley cite a Harvard University report, *Teaching, Learning, and Student Life*, which stresses that out-of-classroom activities relate directly to higher grades and to social integration. Furthermore, a study of recent alumni of the University of Tennessee found that participation in intramural sports was an important factor in several areas of personal growth.[37]

Range of Campus Recreation Experiences

Campus recreation programs today are becoming more diversified, including a wide range of recreational sports, outdoor activities, entertainment and social events, cultural programs, activities for persons with disabilities, and various other services.

Recreational Sports   During the 1970s and 1980s, both intramural leagues and sports clubs expanded rapidly in many institutions, with a growing emphasis on lifetime sports and on coeducational participation. Due in part to changed sex-role expectations and the effect of Title IX, many more girls and women are involved in sports today than in the past. More and more colleges and universities are providing varied facilities for sports and games, including aquatic facilities, boxing/martial arts and exercise rooms, saunas and locker rooms, extensive outdoor areas with night lighting for evening play, and other special facilities for outdoor hobbies and instruction.

An outstanding example of college sports programming is found at Virginia Commonwealth University in Richmond, Virginia, which sponsors a host of recreational sports activities and events and fitness programs in six impressive campus facilities (see Figure 9.1). Programs include a huge range of instructional, club, and intramural activities in such areas as individual, dual, and team sports; aerobics; dancing; yoga; martial arts; aquatics; and social programs. Participation in all programs and facilities is free for students through the general student fee. Spouses, staff, and faculty members pay modest annual fees.

Similar sports programs are offered throughout the United States and Canada. At the University of Victoria in Canada, for example, emphasis is placed on many coeducational leagues and tournaments, fitness and lifestyle activities, leader certification courses, and aquatics and informal recreational play.

FIGURE 9.1

An exciting two day fitness event presented by the VCU Wellness Committe
October 19-20, 1995 10:00 am to 4:00 pm
On the Business Building Lawn.

Recreational Sports VCU

Just a few events you might want to try!

√The Jeep Eagle Rock Climbing Wall and Sports Challenge

√Plymouth Bungee Run and Human Bowling

√BACCHUS Alcohol IQ Test

√Rebok Mountain biking Challenge

√Sure Fit Dorm Room

√Lipton Brisk Ladder Climb

√The Gladiator Duel,Bouncy Boxing & Sumo Wrestling Challenges

√Discover Card Velcro Fly Wall

Novelty Programming at Virginia Commonwealth University

Along with traditional sports and fitness programs, this campus recreation service sponsors occasional special events, featuring such competitions as "bungee runs" and "human bowling," an "Alcohol IQ Test," a "Velcro Fly Wall," and "sumo wrestling."

Outdoor Recreation   Outdoor recreation, which includes clinics, clubs, and outings, may involve hiking, backpacking, camping, mountain climbing, scuba diving, sailing, skiing, and numerous other nature-based programs. These are often sponsored by campus outing clubs, which may in turn be affiliated with national organizations or federations. Gary Nussbaum points out that a well-developed outdoor recreation program may yield positive benefits in student achievement and satisfaction, and suggests that such programs should be used to enrich the intramural programs at many colleges and universities. In addition to actual sponsorship of such activities, campus recreation directors may provide varied support and information services. Examples might include

> the inexpensive rental of backpacking and camping gear . . . the provision of information including resource data, the location of clothing/equipment outfitters, and a directory of other clubs, organizations, and commercial enterprises offering outdoor recreation services. . . . [and] Outdoor literature (e.g., "how-to" books, periodical works) may be a joint provision of the intramural office and the university library.[38]

Southern Illinois University, for example, offers a diversified range of appealing trips and outings, clinics, and classes, including rock climbing and backpacking, spelunking (cave exploration), canoeing, biking, and Earth Day events (see Figure 9.2).

Special Events: Entertainment and Cultural Programs   Many campuses sponsor large-scale entertainment events and cultural series. Typically, singers, rock bands, and comedians are booked to entertain students in stadiums, field houses, and campus centers. The college or university's own departments of music, theater, and dance may provide performing companies that present concerts or other stage presentations, along with other kinds of specialized programs.

Large-scale special events that students plan and carry out themselves—such as sports carnivals or other major competitions—are highlights of campus social programs. They involve both intimacy of interaction among leaders and participants and an intense outpouring of energy as people share fun in a crowded school or college setting. Similar excitement may be noted at major musical events like rock concerts, although such programs often require supervision to assure adherence to campus policies regarding alcohol and drugs.

Services for Special Populations   Students with disabilities are being encouraged and assisted to participate in general campus recreation programs whenever possible. However, for those students whose disabilities are too severe to permit this, or who have not yet developed the needed degree of confidence and independence, it has been necessary to design special programs using modified facilities and adapted instructional techniques or rules.

Outstanding examples of such programs are those offered by the University of Illinois, which provides special teams in the areas of football, softball, basketball, swimming, and track and field for physically disabled students. Other activities, such as archery, judo, swimming, bowling, and softball, have been adapted for such special groups as the visually impaired.

Office of Intramural-Recreational Sports
Instructional Programs
The health millennium...making it happen at the Rec

Personal
Training

SIU
Southern Illinois University
Carbondale

Office of Intramural-Recreational Sports
Instructional Programs
*The health millennium...
making it happen at the Rec*

Racquet Sports

Fall 2000

Student Recreation Center

SIU
Southern Illinois University
Carbondale

Meditation
Yoga
And
Fitness
Energizers

Fall 2000

Office of Intramural-Recreational Sports
Instructional Programs
*the health millennium...
Making it happen at the Rec*

SIU
Southern Illinois University
Carbondale

Office of Intramural-Recreational Sports
Instructional Programs
"The Health Millennium...Making it happen at the Rec"

Kung-Fu
fall 2000

Youth & Adult Programs

Student Recreation Center

SIU
Southern Illinois University
Carbondale

Adult & Youth Swim Programs
Student Recreation Center

FALL 2000

Aquatics

SIU
Southern Illinois University
Carbondale

As an example of campus recreation, the Office of Intramural-Recreational Sports at Southern Illinois University at Carbondale presents numerous instructional, club, and intramural activities, including diversified outdoor adventure programs.

Community Service Projects   Many students also become involved in volunteer community projects such as repairing facilities, working with the elderly, or providing "big brother" or tax assistance services. Such efforts are important for two reasons: (1) they illustrate how student-life activities may include a broad range of involvements beyond those that are clearly recognizable as recreational "fun" events; and (2) they serve to blend academic and extracurricular student experiences, increasing the individual's exposure to life and enhancing his or her leadership capability. Findings of the Cooperative Institutional Research Program at the University of California at Los Angeles show that the more students are involved in their education, the more likely they are to remain at an institution: "The most successful students . . . are those who live and work on their campuses, participate in college activities and academic programs outside of their classes, and interact with faculty and staff members."

Overview of Campus Recreation

Campus recreation provides students with practical experience within a wide range of functions that supplement and enrich their academic programs. For example, many students may gain administrative or business skills, often on an advanced level. The Associated Students' Organization of San Diego State University in California provides a setting for such learning experiences. This multi-million-dollar corporation, funded by student fees, operates the Aztec Center, the college's student union building. Among its services are a successful travel agency, intramurals and sports clubs, special events, leisure classes, lectures, movies, concerts, an open-air theater, an aquatics center, campus radio station, child-care center, general store, campus information booth, and other programs. The bulk of its recreational activities are operated directly by the Recreation Activities Board, a unit within the overall Associated Students' Organization.

Such experiences illustrate the important contributions made by campus recreation programs, along with other student noncurricular activities, to the college or university experience. They involve the whole student in meaningful and creative ways and thus provide a meaningful transition to adult life and potential career opportunities.

While the term *campus recreation* is usually applied only to higher education settings, recreation also is closely linked to other levels of educational experience. Many elementary and secondary school systems also provide recreation facilities and programs that meet significant leisure needs.

School District Programs

Throughout the twentieth century, many school districts established extensive programs of extra- and cocurricular activities for students, including clubs, sports, music and drama groups, and similar types of leisure involvement. While budget restraints of the 1980s and 1990s have compelled many districts to reduce such offerings, they still provide an opportunity for school-centered recreation in many communities. Beyond this, a growing number of school systems now provide impressive adult education classes on a fee basis; these may include both remedial or diploma-oriented options and offerings relating to varied hobby interests, such as language, arts and crafts, sports skills, literary and musical topics, investment planning, fitness, and other similar self-enrichment subjects.

In other settings, this cooperation may take the form of shared responsibility for constructing and maintaining facilities that are used jointly by schools and municipal authorities. Frequently, such facilities become multiservice community centers that blend educational, recreational, and social services. For example, in New Brighton, Minnesota,

> the Mounds View School District owns 12,500 square feet of the parks and recreation department's 70,000-square-foot Family Service Center, which the district uses for its early childhood and family education program. The park department also is renting an additional 1,000 square feet to the school district for the adult education component of its program and 1,000 square feet to the nonprofit Northwest Youth and Family Service, a teen counseling group.[39]

Similarly, in Sunnyvale, California, the City of Sunnyvale, in cooperation with the elementary school district, constructed a $3.5-million addition to its Columbia Middle School in the mid-1990s. The AMD Sports and Service Center (named after Advanced Micro Devices, a local company that contributed $1 million to the project) includes a gymnasium, counseling rooms, and a health center. The gymnasium is used by the school during the day and by the city during nonschool hours.

PRIVATE-MEMBERSHIP RECREATION ORGANIZATIONS

A significant portion of recreational opportunity today is provided by private-membership organizations. As distinguished from commercial recreation businesses—in which any individual may simply pay an admission fee to a theme park, for example—private-membership bodies usually restrict use of their facilities or programs to individual members and their families and guests.

Within the broad field of sport and outdoor recreation, there are many organizations that offer facilities, instruction, or other services for activities such as skiing, tennis, golf, boating, and hunting or fishing. While some private-membership organizations are commercially owned and operated, others exist as independent, incorporated clubs of members who own their own facilities, with policy being set by elected officers and boards and with the actual work of maintenance, instruction, and supervision being carried out by paid employees.

An important characteristic of many private-membership organizations has been their social exclusiveness. Membership policies often have screened out certain prospective members for reasons of religion, ethnicity, or other demographic factors.

It is important to recognize that although the ostensible function of such private organizations is to provide sociability as well as specific forms of leisure activity, the clubs also provide a setting in which the most powerful members of American communities meet regularly to discuss business or political matters and often reach informal decisions or plans for action. Those who are barred from membership in such clubs are thus excluded also from this behind-the-scenes, establishment-based process of influence and power.

In the late 1970s and early 1980s, such organizations received more public scrutiny, as the U.S. Senate Banking Committee initiated an investigation of the payment of employee membership dues to private clubs and social organizations by financial institutions. It was found that women as well as blacks and other ethnic minorities were frequently excluded from private clubs.

In a number of cases, national membership organizations have been compelled to open their membership rolls to minority-group members because of lawsuits that have threatened them with withdrawal of tax-exempt status. However, as recently as the late 1980s and early 1990s, some organizations, such as Rotary International, continued to do battle in the courts to maintain their sexually discriminatory policies and have expelled member clubs that have yielded on the issue. In 1987, at a time when women made up 44 percent of the workforce and 37 percent of managers and executives, *U.S. News & World Report* commented that to exclude them from an organization designed for business promotion seemed no longer justifiable.

Yet, only in the late 1990s did many private golf clubs begin to admit more than "token" numbers of members of racial or religious minority background—or grant full membership privileges to women as a result of costly lawsuits penalizing them for gender discrimination.

Continuing Efforts to Discriminate

Despite such changes, many private-membership organizations continue to represent exclusive enclaves of the rich and powerful. Country clubs, as indicated, are generally of two types: (1) nonprofit "equity clubs," owned and operated by members; and (2) commercially owned, for-profit clubs. Over 70 such clubs are owned by Club Corporation International; surprisingly, this organization has frequently been sued by its members for not being exclusive *enough,* and for permitting too many nonmembers to use its facilities as paying guests. Private, they argue, should mean *private.*[40]

Residence-Connected Clubs

Other types of private-membership recreation organizations continue to flourish—particularly in connection with new forms of home building and marketing. Many real estate developers have recognized that one of the key selling points in home development projects is the provision of attractive recreational facilities. Thus, tennis courts, golf courses, swimming pools, health spas, and similar recreation facilities are frequently provided for the residents of apartment buildings, condominiums, or one-family home developments whether the residents are families, "singles," or retired persons.

An important trend in American society has been the rapid growth of housing developments in the suburbs, with community associations that carry out such functions as street cleaning, grounds maintenance, security, and the provision of leisure facilities such as tennis courts, golf courses, and swimming pools. Once found chiefly in the Southwest, such developments and community associations have now spread throughout the United States. In 1970, there were 10,000 such associations. But in 1990, they numbered 130,000, with the prediction that there would be over 200,000 by century's end.

Although such real estate developments tend to be expensive and thus intended chiefly for affluent tenants or homebuyers, there are exceptions. For example, a giant apartment development in Brooklyn, New York, known as Starrett City, was constructed in the mid-1970s to serve middle-income tenants drawn from varied ethnic populations—approximately half were of black, Hispanic, and Asian origin. Its thousands of residents enjoy a huge clubhouse with meeting rooms, hobby, craft, and dance classes, and an extensive pool program and tennis complex, as well as numerous classes, teams, and special events through the year.

In some cases, large condominium-structured apartment buildings also have extensive leisure facilities and programs. For example, in Philadelphia, one such building with 776 residential units has a bank, restaurant, 10 stores, doctors' and dentists' offices, garages, and two swimming pools, all under one roof. It also has a library, card room, fitness center, and numerous clubs and committees, including a welcoming committee, Weight Watchers, a writers' club, book club, and computer club.

Vacation Homes

A specialized form of such residence-connected recreation is often found in vacation home developments. During the 1960s and 1970s, direct ownership and time-sharing arrangements for such homes became more popular, often in large-scale developments situated close to a lake or other major recreational attraction.

The baby boom, with millions of couples reaching the age and financial status at which they are able to afford vacation homes, has led to a rapid rise in the number of such developments. According to demographic researchers, some 4.8 million U.S. households owned vacation homes or time-share condominiums in 1994, with the expectation that the population group most likely to buy—35 to 54-year-olds with no kids at home—could double by the year 2000.

Typically, time-sharing apartments or condominiums in attractive vacation areas today cost as much as $15,000 to $20,000 for the right to use the facility one week each year. While this may seem expensive, it is minimal compared to the cost in vacation areas where the "jet set"—the wealthy elite of American society—enjoy their vacations. Illustrating the tendency to seek privacy in exclusive surroundings, a number of millionaires and billionaires who formerly enjoyed their vacations in Aspen, Colorado, left that area when it became too well known and popular. Today they fly their own jets to a stunningly beautiful mountain hamlet in Wyoming known as Saratoga. Members of the Old Baldy Club live in "cottages" that would be considered mansions anywhere else. When asked how much it cost to join the Old Baldy Club, a local resident received the reply, "If you have to ask, you can't afford it."

Retirement Communities

Similarly, large retirement villages offer recreation and social programs for their residents; often they are actually called "leisure villages." A vivid example may be found in Sun City, Arizona. Established in 1960, this community has about 45,000 residents. Marla Dial writes:

> At the Sundial—one of seven multimillion-dollar recreation centers here—residents can participate in everything from swimming and weight training to sewing, ceramics, or art classes. The building also houses a mineral museum, photo lab, and shuffleboard facilities. Eleven golf courses have been built over the years, and designers are making each one tougher, as they find that retirees are better golfers than they first thought.
>
> "You can do as little as you want to, you can do as much as you want to," said [one long-term resident]. "That's the life here. It keeps us moving, keeps us young."[41]

So successful has the Sun City formula been that in the 1980s and 1990s, two additional communities were developed in the area—Sun City West and Sun City Grand. With many younger, earlier retirees, these communities not only feature the traditional

Retirement Community Recreation

Many retirement communities offer extensive recreation facilities and programs, and encourage residents to attend cultural events in the surrounding area, as in this Sun City West brochure. Others, as in Sarasota, Florida's Pelican Cove, have uniquely beautiful natural surroundings, including a marina with easy access to open bay waters.

FACILITIES OPEN TO SUN CITY WEST RESIDENTS

Recreation Centers	4	Tennis Courts	27
Golf Courses	9	Tennis Platforms	8
Mini Golf Courses	2	Swimming Pools	6
Bowling Lanes	30	Shuffleboard Courts	5
Table Tennis Tables	7	Racquet/Handball Courts	2
Billiard/Pool Tables	30	Fitness & Dance Rooms	5
Softball Field	1	Lawn Bowling Rinks	32
Walking Tracks	3	Bocce Ball Courts	14

* 7,000 seat Sundome Center for the Performing Arts
* 300 seat Kuentz Theater
* West Valley Art Museum
* Sun Cities Symphony Orchestra & Chorus
* City park at Beardsley with bandstand and ramadas
* Nearby shopping mall with 14 movie theater complex
* 3,300 RV Storage Compound
* 40,000 volume R.H. Johnson Library

Physical Activities Outdoor/indoor walking tracks and swimming pools, regulation and platform tennis, regulation and mini golf, lawn bowling, Bocce, volley ball, fitness rooms, therapy pools, shuffleboard, table tennis, racquet ball, handball, bowling, softball, horseshoes, ballroom dancing, square dancing, and line dancing.

Crafts, Hobbies, and Games Almost 100 chartered clubs, many state clubs, professional woodshop and metalshop facilities, card rooms and space allotted for hobbies and crafts such as lapidary, silk flower creations, sewing, ceramics, silversmithing, pottery, leather tooling, stained glass, painting, calligraphy, model railroading, and others.

pastimes of the elderly, but also such newer or more demanding activities as weight training, rollerblading, and rock climbing. Growing numbers of semiretired residents continue to volunteer, do part-time work, or even start their own businesses—and in some cases accept such challenges as training for triathlons or helicopter hiking in the remote Canadian Rockies.[42] In numerous other retirement communities, such as Leisure World in Laguna Hills, California, such recreational facilities as pools, tennis courts, and riding stables are often found.

Significantly, the time-shares section of the vacation-homes market has grown dramatically, vaulting the industry from a modest $300-million business in 1978 to an estimated $3.5-billion operation in 1999.[43]

COMPARISONS AMONG SPECIAL-FOCUS AGENCIES

There are both differences and similarities among the five different types of leisure-service organizations meeting special needs that are described in this chapter.

Therapeutic recreation is obviously concerned chiefly with meeting the needs of persons with disabilities in American and Canadian society, as well as using recreation as a purposeful tool to achieve goals of habilitation or rehabilitation. While its major emphasis is on providing both clinical and community-based recreation programs for disabled persons, the strong thrust today is toward mainstreaming and integration of disabled individuals within the larger population. As such, it shares many common program elements and facilities with the overall community recreation system.

Armed forces recreation involves a huge, sprawling, worldwide operation. It is essentially made up of hundreds of smaller individual programs on both domestic or foreign bases or on shipboard. Uniquely, it is governed by a bureaucratic structure and specific policies that originate within the Defense Department, while at the same time responding to the special needs and resources of different branches of the military services and to local capabilities and interests. Its services and programs also range from businesslike and commercialized approaches to entertainment or hospitality to purposeful, social-service activities meeting the needs of children and youth or dependent families.

Employee recreation service differs from other special branches of the leisure-service system in that it has become just one of ten important functions designed to improve the quality of life in the work environment and to contribute to the effective operation of its sponsoring companies. Within this spectrum of service, recreation has the unique responsibility of upgrading company morale and human relationships, as well as promoting the positive image of the overall enterprise. As in both therapeutic and armed forces recreation, employee programs must be concerned with achieving important agency goals and with documenting their worth in concrete, measurable terms.

Campus recreation, whether primarily concerned with sports programming or with broader cultural and curriculum-connected activities, is today seen as an integral element in the overall higher education structure. Particularly in colleges and universities in which older adolescents and those just entering adulthood are faced with the challenge of their first real social independence, it is critical that campus recreation help students develop positive lifestyle values and patterns of leisure choices. As part of this purpose, campus activities should serve as an attractive counterbalance to less desirable leisure involvements.

Finally, private-membership leisure-service organizations are heavily influenced by socioeconomic factors, in that they tend to be provided for individuals and families who are relatively elite in financial and demographic terms. Although they have been undergoing a gradual process of democratization, many such groups continue to be exclusive and focus on a narrow range of recreational interests. One exception is found in the growing number of retirement communities, which often sponsor a considerable variety of recreational programs, particularly for younger individuals and couples who are entering such communities.

SUMMARY

Five specialized areas of leisure-service delivery described in this chapter illustrate the diversity of agencies that provide organized recreation opportunities today. In each case, they have their own goals and objectives, populations served, and program emphases. Yet they are important elements within the overall leisure-service system and represent attractive fields of career opportunity for recreation, park, and leisure-service students today.

Therapeutic recreation service, in its two areas of professional emphasis—clinical or treatment service and community-based special recreation—is probably the most highly professionalized of all the separate disciplines in the leisure-service field. It has a long history of professional development, with separate sections of state and national societies, early emphasis on registration and certification (as Chapter 11 will show more fully), numerous specialized curricula, and a rich literature and background of research. With the possibility of lessened support being given to clinical therapeutic recreation in an era of costcutting, hospital retrenchment, managed patient care, and deinstitutionalization, it is probable that community-based special recreation, with its emphasis on mainstreaming, will constitute an increasingly important element in therapeutic recreation.

Armed forces recreation professionals serve a distinct population, composed both of large numbers of relatively young service men and women—often single and away from home—and of families and dependents with special needs prompted by the military setting. Morale, fitness, and mission accomplishment are important armed forces recreation goals, and these are reflected in an increasingly businesslike approach to planning, marketing, and evaluating programs. With reduced budgets caused by downsizing and a greater emphasis on fiscal self-sufficiency, military recreation has undergone major transformations in recent years; yet it continues to offer a wide range of attractive program opportunities and often has excellent facilities, both stateside and abroad.

Employee recreation and services today have gone far beyond their original emphasis on providing a narrow range of social and sports activities designed to promote company-worker relationships. They are carried on in many different kinds of organizations and include varied health- and fitness-related program elements, as well as such other personnel services as discount programs, company stores, community relationships, and other benefits-driven functions—all necessarily provided within a business-oriented framework that demands productivity and demonstrated outcomes.

Campus recreation is carried on within an educational setting with relatively little interaction with the overall recreation and parks field. At the same time, it has important responsibilities in terms of promoting the overall well-being of students, helping to reduce negative or destructive forms of play, extending and enriching academic learnings, and contributing to other college and university goals.

The last type of organization described in this chapter, the private-membership association, includes a wide range of country clubs, golf clubs, yacht clubs, and other social or business membership groups that often tend to be socially exclusive. They represent a growing trend in the United States today, with millions of families now living in residential developments that have their own community associations to provide services, including recreation. This tends to limit their interest in or dependence on public, tax-supported recreation services.

QUESTIONS FOR CLASS DISCUSSION OR ESSAY EXAMINATIONS

1. What are the major goals of recreation in the armed forces? Describe some of the key programming areas and indicate how military recreation planners have adapted to problems posed by cutbacks in military bases and personnel and fiscal restraints.

2. One of the chief emphases in employee services and recreation programs involves health and fitness. Using examples taken from the chapter, what forms of services are provided and what documented evidence is there to support their value?

3. Campus recreation has a number of important values for colleges and universities today. Identify and describe these and then focus in detail on the *in loco parentis* function of institutions of higher education. What does this principle involve and why is it particularly important today? Applied to your own institution, how does the administration provide a degree of control over students' lives and what part does campus recreation play in this effort?

4. Describe the two major thrusts in therapeutic recreation service today. In terms of special recreation, explain the current thinking with respect to mainstreaming individuals with disabilities. What limitations, if any, should be applied to the integration of persons with disabilities in all ongoing community recreation programs?

5. What is the unique role of private-membership organizations and what are some of the examples of this type of leisure-service sponsor? How do they differ from governmental, voluntary nonprofit, and commercial recreation agencies? Indicate some of the social issues that center around such private organizations.

ENDNOTES

1 *National Institute on Recreation Inclusion Brochure* (Deerfield, Ill.: September 2000).

2 "MWR Directors: Don't Let Your Guard Down," *Military Clubs and Hospitality* (October 1997): 24.

3 Adapted from Garald O'Morrow, *Therapeutic Recreation: A Helping Profession* (Reston, Va.: Reston Publishing, 1976): Chapter 7.

4 See *Statement of Philosophy of Therapeutic Recreation* (Arlington, Va.: National Therapeutic Recreation Society, 1982).

5 Charles Sylvester, "Therapeutic Recreation and the Right to Leisure," *Therapeutic Recreation Journal* (2nd Quarter 1992): 10.

6 N. Stumbo and C. Peterson, "The Leisurability Model," *Therapeutic Recreation Journal* (2nd Quarter 1998): 82–96.

7 *Standards of Practice in Therapeutic Recreation Service* (Arlington, Va.: National Therapeutic Recreation Society, 1994): i.

8 Charles Bullock, "The Leisurability Model: Implications for the Researcher," *Therapeutic Recreation Journal* (2nd Quarter 1998): 105.

9 Michael Winerip, "Bedlam in the Streets," *New York Times Magazine* (23 May 1999): 42.

10 D. Kennedy, D. Austin, and R. Smith, *Special Recreation: Opportunities for Persons with Disability* (Philadelphia: Saunders Publishing, 1987): 31.

11 Michael Kelley, "The Therapeutic Potential of Outdoor Adventure: A Review with Focus on Adults with Mental Illness," *Therapeutic Recreation Journal* (2nd Quarter 1993): 110–121.

12 Ladd Colston, "The Expanding Role of Assistive Technology in Therapeutic Recreation," *Journal of Physical Education, Recreation, and Dance* (April 1991): 15.

13 *NTRS Report* (Vol. 23, No. 3, May–June 1998): 8–9.

14 Harold Brubaker, "Nursing Homes' Era of Profits Dashed by Debt," *Philadelphia Inquirer* (9 July 2000): E-1.

15 C. Coyle, W. B. Kinney, B. Riley, and J. Shank, *Benefits of Therapeutic Recreation: A Consensus View* (Philadelphia: Temples University and National Institute on Disability and Rehabilitation Research, 1994).

16 B. Riley and T. Skalko, "The Evolution of Therapeutic Recreation," *Parks and Recreation* (May 1998): 69.

17 S. Lankford and D. DeGraaf, "Strengths, Weaknesses, Opportunities, and Threats in Morale, Welfare, and Recreation Organizations: Challenges of the 1990s," *Journal of Park and Recreation Administration* (Vol. 10, No. 1, 1992): 31–32.

18 "Start Smart Popular on Military Bases Worldwide," *Parks and Recreation* (December 1998): 27.

19 S. Waller and A. Suren, "Recreation and Military Youth," *Journal of Physical Education, Recreation, and Dance—Leisure Today* (April 1995): 22.

20 Elizabeth Becker, "Child Care in Military Is Praised As a Model," *New York Times* (17 May 2000): A-19.

21 Gail Howerton, "American Armed Forces Overseas: The Few, the Proud, the Creative," *Parks and Recreation* (December 1994): 57.

22 See R. Kraus and J. Curtis, *Creative Management in Recreation and Parks* (St. Louis, Mo.: Mosby, 1982): 206–207.

23 *MWR Expo Brochure* (Long Beach, Calif.: MWR, 1998).

24 Carolyn Becraft, quoted in Pat Harden, "Armed Forces Recreation Services Our Hallowed Ground Raison D'Etre," *Parks and Recreation* (December 1994): 24.

25 "NESRA's Employer of the Year," *Employee Services Management* (May/June 1991): 17.

26 Steven Blair, "Worksite Health Promotion 'Bottom-Line' Facts and Figures," *Employee Services Management* (May/June 1995): 31–33.

27 J. L. Crompton, L. L. Love, and T. A. More, "An Empirical State of the Role of Recreation, Park and in Companies' (Re)Location Decisions," *Journal of Park and Recreation Administration* (Vol. 15, No. 1, Spring 1997): 37–58.

28 Amy Berger, "Advertise Your Company as an Employer of Choice by Promoting Your Employee Services Department," *Employee Services Management* (October 1999): 24–25.

29 Barbara Altman, "Corporate Community Relations in the 1990s: A Study in Transformation," *Business and Society* (June 1998): 221.

30 "Member Success Profile," *Employee Services Management* (September 1991): 13.

31 J. Kondrasuk and C. Carl, "Wellness Programs: Present and Future," *Employee Services Management* (December/January 1991–1992): 9.

32 Joe Hauglie, "Adopting an Entrepreneurial Attitude," *Employee Services Management* (May/June 1991): 14.

33 *Employee Services Management Brochure* (Oakbrook, Ill.: Spring 2000).

34 "New Hampshire Campuses Address Rise in Racial Tensions," *Associated Press* (29 November 1998).

35 Ethan Bronner, "In a Revolution of Rules, Campuses Go Full Circle," *New York Times* (3 March 1999): A-1.

36 Carolyn Kleiner, "Schools Turn Off the Tap," *U.S. News and World Report* (30 August 1999).

37 J. Bryant and J. Bradley, "Enhancing Academic Productivity: Student Development and Employment Potential," *NIRSA Journal* (Fall 1993): 42.

38 Gary Nussbaum, "Adventures in Intramural Outdoor Recreation Programming," *Journal of Physical Education, Recreation, and Dance* (February 1987): 58.

39 "Family Service," *Athletic Business* (October 1995): 32.

40 Diana Henriques, "Bickering in the Clubhouse," *New York Times* (14 June 1998): B-1.

41 Marla Dial, "At 35, A Model Retirement Community Finds Life Still Golden," *Associated Press* (8 January 1995).

42 Joseph Shapiro, "No Sunset for Sun City," *U.S. News and World Report* (28 June 1999): 78.

43 Edwin McDowell, "A Few Weeks to Call Your Own," *New York Times* (29 January 2000): C-1.

CHAPTER 10

TWO MAJOR LEISURE-SERVICE COMPONENTS:

Sports and Tourism

◆ ◆ ◆

*Many people desire spectator sport opportunities, and professional and ama-
teur sports organizations have created substantial sporting events to fulfill
that niche. [Many others] seek more active participation, and leisure professionals have attempted to create recreation sport opportunities for them, [in]
public and private, nonprofit and for-profit, college and university, and
employee-service recreation settings.*[1]

*Orlando is hotter than ever. Its insatiable appetite for new and expanded fun
zones—more than 80 now exist in and around the city—and white-hot
competition between its two theme-park giants, Disney and Universal, has
experts drooling with anticipation. . . . Meanwhile, attendance is going
through the roof. Amusement Business magazine says six of the eight largest
theme parks in North America last year were in Orlando. Disney World
sold nearly 43 million tickets.*[2]

◆ ◆ ◆

INTRODUCTION

Having examined eight major sectors of organized leisure services, we now turn to two
forms of involvement that not only have close links to other types of agencies but also
represent full-fledged fields of recreational participation in their own right.

Sports on various levels, travel, and tourism represent major areas of recreational
programming today and constitute powerful economic forces through their attraction
for people of every age and background. Uniquely, they have strong links to each other
through the growing field of sport tourism and also overlap heavily with outdoor recreation attractions. This chapter presents an overview of both sport and tourism, emphasizing their roles within the leisure spectrum, their rapid expansion over the past several decades, and their prospects for the years that lie ahead.

SPORTS AS POPULAR RECREATION

Although some athletes or social commentators may demean their importance, the reality is that sports represent far more than trivial amusement or childish play in American society. Any activity or enterprise that involves hundreds of billions of dollars in equipment and facilities, personnel costs, admissions charges, television fees, and other forms of expenditure must be based on more than superficial appeal. Of all types of leisure involvement, it seems likely that sports command the highest degree of personal interest and emotional involvement—both for those who participate actively in them and those who are part of a vast army of fans of school, college, and professional teams.

Sports are generally defined as physical activities demanding exertion and skill, involving competition, carried on with both formal rules and general standards of etiquette and fair play. Some authorities describe them more concisely as (1) activities with clear performance standards; (2) involving competition through physical exertion; (3) governed by norms defining role relationships; (4) typically performed by members of organized groups; (5) with the goal of achieving a reward; (6) through the defeat of other participants.

Clearly, sports activities, in terms of both participation and spectator involvement, represent key leisure interests for most youth and adults today. Apart from amateur, school, and college play, there are professional sports, which have clearly become a form of big business. They are moneymakers, sponsored by powerful commercial interests and promoted by advertising, public relations, television, radio, magazines, and newspapers—and bolstered by the loyalty of millions of fans who identify closely with their favorite teams and star athletes.

In 1986, a new magazine of the sports business, *Sports Inc.*, reported that the sports industry had become the nation's twenty-fifth biggest form of enterprise. Among the key spending areas measured by Wharton Economic Forecasting Associates were

> leisure-and-participant sports, ranging from $4.3 million in Babe Ruth baseball team fees to $1.1 billion in ski-lift tickets, $3.9 billion in greens fees, and $4.9 billion in health-and-fitness clubs. Equipment, clothing, and footwear for players generated an additional $15 billion in revenues.[3]

Beyond these figures, gate receipts for college and professional sports brought in $3.1 billion, vendor sales amounted to $1.9 billion, sports-related advertising in print media cost $3.6 billion, and corporations sponsored $800 million worth of sports events. These figures attested to the tremendous popularity of sports in the United States and Canada, both as a form of active recreation for all ages and as spectator entertainment.

In the 1990s, the sports field continued to grow, with the expansion of professional sports leagues, the emphasis on youth sports programs, and the spread of typically American sports such as baseball, football, and basketball to many other nations of the world. However, as sports have become more commercialized, with professional players receiving astronomical salaries and team franchises skipping from city to city, many fans have become disillusioned with the changing nature of sport.

Although sports are obviously an important form of free-time activity, in many ways they do not conform to the traditional view of leisure. Rather than relaxed activity carried on within a context of casual free choice, sports are often highly structured, purposeful, and disciplined, with elaborate rules and rich rewards. At the same time, sports represent an important social institution, recognized as such not only in the United States but around the world.

PATTERNS OF SPORTS INVOLVEMENT

Some forms of sport, such as baseball, ice hockey, and football, are primarily masculine in participation and interest, whereas others are geared to feminine interests, and still others are gender-neutral. In terms of age levels, many active sports are most popular during the teenage or young adult years, although some games and active outdoor pursuits actually increase in participation among those in older age brackets.

With respect to income level, participation is usually highest for those in the $35,000 to $49,999 income brackets, although sports such as golf, soccer, downhill skiing, and tennis have their highest rate of involvement in the over-$50,000 bracket.

The most popular sports activities, in terms of participation, are identified in Table 10.1. As indicated earlier, a number of the pastimes listed might better be described as outdoor recreation pursuits, such as exercise walking or camping. Others, such as skiing, swimming, or even fishing, are usually engaged in as noncompetitive recreation, although they also are often part of school or college competition or large-scale tournaments.

LEVELS OF SPORTS COMPETITION

Sports are engaged in at several levels of competitive skills and intensity, ranging from informal neighborhood play through youth sports leagues or school and college play and extending to professional competition and even international play in the Olympics and other large-scale events.

In addition to school, college, and professional leagues, millions of sports participants are served by municipal, county, or special-district recreation and park departments, nonprofit youth organizations (many of which focus on a single sport, such as Little League or Pop Warner football leagues), country clubs, and military recreation services. In general, the management of sports events, the setting of standards and rules for play, and similar functions are carried out by national organizations that govern competition and promote instructional programs for youth.

The spectator aspect of sport is vividly shown in the immense sums paid by television networks for the right to broadcast college and professional contests. In 1998, the ABC, CBS, and Fox networks agreed to collectively pay $17.6 billion for the rights to broadcast National Football League games for the next eight years—the richest deal in television history.

Sums ranging as high as $700 million or $800 million were paid to purchase baseball or football franchises, and individual stars in sports such as basketball have been paid $12 million or $15 million a year. It has been estimated that Tiger Woods will— if he continues at his present pace—earn as much as one billion dollars in golf tournament winnings and advertising commercials over his competitive lifetime.[4]

TABLE 10.1

PARTICIPATION IN SELECTED SPORTS ACTIVITIES

(Number of persons over age of 7 participating at least once in previous year, in thousands)

Activity	All Persons			Sex	
	Number	Rank	Male	Female
Total	237,745	(X)	115,443	122,301
Aerobic exercise	24,119	11	5,314	18,805
Backpacking	11,469	22	7,240	4,229
Badminton	6,084	28	2,909	3,175
Baseball	14,823	18	11,610	3,213
Basketball	33,281	9	22,375	10,906
Bicycle riding	53,342	3	28,595	24,747
Billiards	34,477	8	21,841	12,636
Bowling	42,895	6	22,579	20,316
Calisthenics	10,064	25	5,023	5,041
Camping	44,695	5	24,102	20,593
Exercise walking	73,307	1	26,666	46,641
Exercising with equipment	47,823	4	22,200	25,622
Fishing, freshwater	40,208	7	27,160	13,048
Fishing, saltwater	11,045	23	7,926	3,119
Football, tackle	8,219	27	7,436	783
Football, touch	11,645	20	9,603	2,042
Golf	23,082	12	18,219	4,863
Hiking	26,457	10	14,465	11,992
Hunting with firearms	19,251	15	16,317	2,933
Martial arts	4,673	30	3,286	5,251
Raquetball	5,582	29	3,768	1,814
Running/jogging	22,239	13	12,320	9,919
Skiing, downhill	10,466	24	6,277	4,188
Skiing, cross-country	3,385	21	1,820	1,566
Soccer	13,876	19	8,626	5,251
Softball	19,873	14	10,837	9,035
Swimming	60,223	2	29,145	31,078
Table tennis	9,542	26	5,907	3,635
Target shooting	15,695	17	11,097	4,598
Tennis	11,486	21	6,381	5,105
Volleyball	18,535	16	8,970	9,565

Source: *Statistical Abstract of the United States* (1999) and National Sporting Goods Association.

TABLE 10.2

SELECTED SPECTATOR SPORTS ATTENDANCE: 1985–1996

Sport Category	Unit	1985	1990	1996
Baseball Major League Attendance	1,000	47,742	55,512	61,665
Basketball—NCAA				
Men's colleges		753	767	866
Attendance	1,000	26,584	28,741	28,225
Professional		24	27	29
Attendance	1,000	11,534	18,586	21,797
Football—NCAA				
Colleges		509	533	566
Attendance	1,000	34,952	35,330	36,083
National Football League attendance	1,000	14,058	17,666	
National Hockey League attendance	1,000	12,774	13,786	17,105

Source: *Statistical Abstract of the United States* (1999).

To illustrate the popularity of spectator sports, attendance at major college and professional league games rose during most of the 1980s and 1990s (see Table 10.2), although, as this chapter will show, there was some decline in interest during the last years of the twentieth century.

RELIGIOUS IMPLICATIONS OF SPORTS

So fervent is the public interest in college and professional sports that many scholars have concluded that they have become America's newest folk religion. One such observer, Professor Charles Prebish of Pennsylvania State University's religious studies program, states:

> For growing numbers of Americans, sport religion has become a more appropriate expression of personal religiosity than Christianity, Judaism, or any of the traditional religions. [Prebish cited] terms that athletes and sportswriters regularly use: *faith, ritual, ultimate, dedicated, sacrifice, peace, commitment, spirit.*[5]

Russell Chandler points out that football is often used as a metaphor for religious faith. He describes how a young Texas Baptist, Jarrell McCracken, wrote and recorded a script that equated football with *The Game of Life*. In the record, which led to a multi-million-dollar music and publishing business:

> Jesus was the head coach, and "Average Christian" was the quarterback. The bottom line of the sermonizing allegory was that if Christians followed their heavenly blockers and skirted the evil defenders, they made it safely to the big end zone in the

sky. . . . More recently, a country singer recorded a hit song that pleaded: "Drop kick me, Jesus, through the goal posts of life."[6]

Over the past several years, numerous athletes have attested their religious faith through membership in the Fellowship of Christian Athletes. Often players hold prayer circles on the field, and many teams in varied sports are accompanied by chaplains who counsel and inspire them.

In a stirring pregame sermon before Florida State University's football team played an important game, the team's chaplain preached:

> I want to talk to you today about Jesus Christ when he spoke to his team at the Last Supper. He told them he was proud of them but they'd have to play the game without him. . . . This is like Coach Bowden telling you what you have to do on offense and defense. Now remember, your coaches love you. The greatest thing you can do for them is to play the best you can and then say: "God made that tackle, not me . . . and give glory to God."[7]

At another level, the importance of sport in modern society has been illustrated by the immense support given by nations—particularly Iron Curtain countries during the Soviet era—to their athletes in international competition. So fervent has such support been that it once caused an armed conflict—the so-called "Soccer War" between two Central American nations. During the 1980s and 1990s, international competition led to a number of deadly riots—several of them instigated by Great Britain's "soccer thugs."

HISTORICAL EVOLUTION OF SPORTS

Although sports have had a long history of acceptance in earlier civilizations, during much of the Renaissance and early Industrial period they tended to be disapproved by moral authorities throughout Europe and the North American continent. Often, they had an unsavory reputation because of their linkage with drinking and gambling. Rader describes the metropolitan "sporting fraternity" of the late nineteenth century:

> The saloon keepers especially courted those interested in politics, sport, and gambling. There, the two extremes of society—young "dissolute" men of some means and the workingmen—could meet to review the latest sport gossip, schedule sporting events, and take bets. . . . Without ties to wives or traditional homes, many [bachelors] sought friendship and excitement at the brothels, gambling halls, billiard rooms, cock-pits, boxing rings, or the race tracks.[8]

In time, team sports gained respectability in England and America as the concept of "muscular Christianity" entered the literature and began to be heard in religious sermons. Churches, YMCAs, and educators all encouraged sports as a means of achieving physical fitness and self-discipline and as an alternative to other forms of dissipation in play. Gradually, sports became dominated by commercial interests, and the manufacture of sporting goods evolved into a successful industry.

SPORTS AS A SOURCE OF MORAL VALUES

It was widely believed that sports had several important values: (1) contributing to health and physical fitness, as a form of rigorous training, conditioning, and exercise; (2) building personal traits such as courage and perseverance, self-discipline, and sportsmanship; (3) social values linked to obeying rules, dedication to team goals, and providing a channel for social mobility, especially for individuals from disadvantaged backgrounds; and (4) serving as a force to build group loyalty, cohesiveness, and positive morale in schools and colleges and in communities throughout the nation.

Beyond these values, sports obviously have immense appeal, both for participants and for the vastly large audience of fans who often attach themselves to their favorite teams, wearing their colors or uniforms, cheering them enthusiastically, traveling to spring practice or "away" games, and contributing as loyal alumni to the recruitment or support of star athletes. This very fervor and degree of commitment to sport has led inevitably to a number of major abuses or problems affecting sports on all levels.

ABUSES AND PROBLEMS OF SPORTS COMPETITION

Sports for children have too often been influenced by adult pressures to win at all costs. As a result, youngsters often feel excessive pressure to compete and to win, and the experience is no longer fun for them. Studies have shown that many children about to enter their teen years quit organized sports at this point or shift to a much more relaxed, recreational approach to games.

Linked to such pressures, adults frequently encourage overaggressive and violent play, as well as tactics that ignore sportsmanship and condone rule breaking. In extreme cases, parents may verbally or physically abuse players, parents, or coaches of rival teams and even attack officials who have made decisions ruling against them.[9]

On secondary school levels, the influence of high-pressure college sports begins to make itself felt, as promising young players attend special camps financed by manufacturers of sports equipment or clothing. In many cases, parents and college coaches are no longer the primary influences in helping young players make decisions about their future. Instead, Bollinger and Goss write:

> . . . [A] network of summer basketball camps bankrolled by shoe companies has taken over the recruiting process. Hoping to attract the loyalties of players with star potential, the companies spend more than $5 million a year on these summer programs. The young men in this system sometimes play 80 to 100 games outside of the high-school season.[10]

As early as high school, players may be wooed by agents, given free merchandise, and treated to other benefits that are prohibited at the college level. Such abuses become more extreme in college competition in which, especially in high-visibility sports like basketball and football, there has been a long history of academic violations. Players are too often recruited with faked course records or doctored school transcripts and are academically coddled as long as they remain eligible to compete—to the point that they accomplish little real college work and leave without degrees.

Again and again, there have been scandals and investigations involving gambling on college sports—often with players themselves betting on games—or having to do with the criminal behavior of athletes. In professional sports, conflicts between players and owners, the sudden departures of favorite athletes, or the transfer of sports franchises have all strengthened the public perception of sports as "just a business," and have eroded fan loyalty and attendance in many cities.

Other problems surrounding sports on all levels have involved physically dangerous and even life-threatening conditioning practices and hazing in sports like ice hockey or football that has included physical, emotional, and even sexual abuse.[11]

Finally, the wave of building expensive new stadiums with costly skyboxes and the often-added charges to season-ticket purchasers for the right to buy tickets have dramatically escalated the financial costs for fans. In many cases, the middle-class or blue-collar audience that has traditionally supported professional sports, particularly in large, older cities, is no longer able to do so. As a result, there is disturbing evidence that the fan base for professional sports is declining and that many members of the public are instead transferring their loyalties to local, minor-league teams, in part because of nostalgic affection for sport "as it used to be."

Corruption in International Sports

On the international scene, even the Olympics, traditionally viewed idealistically as amateur sport at its best, were revealed in 1999 as having involved widespread bribery in the awarding of the 2000 Summer Olympics to Sydney, Australia, and the 2002 Winter Olympics to Salt Lake City.[12]

Beyond corruption at this level, the constant disclosure of prohibited performance-enhancing drugs and "blood doping" being used in international sports has helped to destroy public confidence in such events as the major bicycling event, the Tour de France, and other competitions.[13] Championship boxing matches have been shown to be under the control of criminal elements, and fixed soccer games have threatened the integrity of international competition at the highest level.[14]

DECLINE OF PUBLIC INTEREST

As indicated earlier, the late 1990s began to show a decline in public interest and support for major forms of spectator sport. Reports in the late 1990s showed that the television ratings for professional football broadcasts, as well as the April 2000 NCAA men's basketball championship series and the National Basketball Association's television ratings, had all dropped off sharply.

Dan McGraw writes in *U.S. News and World Report* that the middle class seems to be increasingly disenchanted with the commercialization of professional sports and by the notion that the sports pages seem increasingly to resemble the financial section—if not the police blotter:

> Now, fed-up fans may be exacting their revenge. The sports leagues have long viewed them as a bottomless money pit, but there are signs that the fans are close to being tapped out. That could spell major-league trouble not just for professional sports but

also for TV networks forced to shell out increasingly exorbitant amounts to broadcast the games.[15]

Despite such signs, a growing number of cities entered a race to build expensive new sports stadiums in order to prevent their professional sports teams from going elsewhere. By century's end, it was estimated that some $24 billion worth of already approved sports facilities would be built in the United States by 2005, with 70 percent to 80 percent of the funds to come from public money—much of this financed by tax-free bonds, which in turn cost the federal government substantial income.

From an academic perspective, critics have questioned both the effect of the spiraling costs that are making the entire big-league sports structure unworkable and the assumption that publicly supported sports stadiums justify themselves financially. Dennis Howard, for example, has concluded that many teams with new venues are now saddled with staggering debt burdens and an overdependence on luxury seating and are pricing themselves out of the market.[16]

FUTURE TRENDS IN SPORT

Whether or not such negative trends accelerate, sports managers and participants on all levels will need to deal with the problems that have been presented in this chapter. Clearly, the continuing expansion of professional sports has reached a point of diminishing returns. If team owners and league policy makers are to retain—or regain—fan loyalty, it will be necessary to curb the growing costs of sports attendance, which are clearly tied to the astronomical salaries being paid to star players and the greediness of team owners.

Sport as Active Play

In general, sport as a recreational pursuit appears to be on a healthier footing. Some critics complain that children and youth are excessively scheduled in athletics—as well as other free-time activities—and that organized play has driven out the kinds of spontaneous, neighborhood games that children used to play. However, the reality is that the major national organizations in baseball, softball, basketball, football, and soccer, as well as many others in individual and team sports, have been successful in providing opportunities for play for many millions of young participants.

In terms of the need to control overemphasis on winning, excessive parental pressures, or the kinds of coaching physical, emotional, and even sexual abuse of participants that have received publicity in recent years, a number of leading national organizations have mobilized to improve youth sports. Such private, nonprofit organizations as the Sports Coaches Association in West Palm Beach, Florida, and Parents and Coaches in Sports in Park City, Utah, have all developed ongoing campaigns to enlighten parents and promote positive coaching approaches.

Organizations representing individual sports, such as Little League Baseball, the American Youth Soccer Organization, or the United States Tennis Association, have not only developed guidelines and regulations for the same purposes but have also initiated

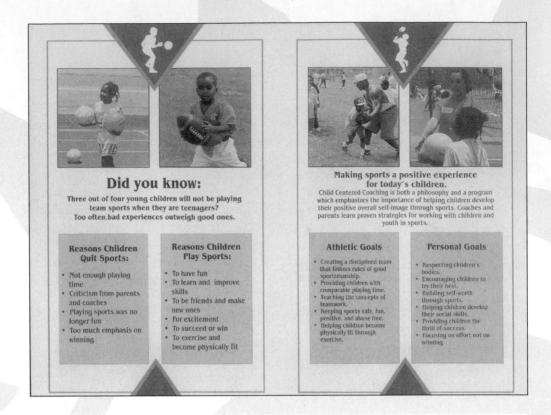

Did you know:

Three out of four young children will not be playing
team sports when they are teenagers?
Too often, bad experiences outweigh good ones.

Reasons Children Quit Sports:

- Not enough playing time
- Criticism from parents and coaches
- Playing sports was no longer fun
- Too much emphasis on winning

Reasons Children Play Sports:

- To have fun
- To learn and improve skills
- To be friends and make new ones
- For excitement
- To succeed or win
- To exercise and become physically fit

Making sports a positive experience for today's children.

Child Centered Coaching is both a philosophy and a program
which emphasizes the importance of helping children develop
their positive overall self-image through sports. Coaches and
parents learn proven strategies for working with children and
youth in sports.

Athletic Goals

- Creating a disciplined team that follows rules of good sportsmanship.
- Providing children with comparable playing time.
- Teaching the concepts of teamwork.
- Keeping sports safe, fun, positive, and abuse free.
- Helping children become physically fit through exercise.

Personal Goals

- Respecting children's bodies.
- Encouraging children to try their best.
- Building self-worth through sports.
- Helping children develop their social skills.
- Providing children the thrill of success.
- Focusing on effort not on winning.

Nonprofit, voluntary organizations promote varied sports for children and youth
throughout the United States and Canada. The National Institute for Child-
Centered Coaching in Park City, Utah, offers coaching manuals and clinics, parents' handbooks, and other materials and services to improve sports for youth. In
Brooklyn, New York, the New York Junior Tennis League has built an outdoor
facility in a crowded inner-city neighborhood to make the sport more accessible
for children and youth.

campaigns to prevent drug use among youth and to encourage fuller participation by minority-group children and in inner-city areas.

In Canada particularly, city and provincial youth and sports authorities in Nova Scotia, Saskatchewan, Alberta, and British Columbia, among others, have promoted guidelines to ensure fair and safe play, encourage fuller participation by girls, eliminate barriers, and build bridges among community organizations to sponsor sound sports programs. All of these efforts are particularly important, given the marked decline in the support of physical education—including sports instruction and sponsorship—in many elementary and secondary schools throughout the United States. As a result of shifting educational priorities and economic pressures, many school physical education programs have been sharply cut back. Deborah Tannehill writes:

> Generally, the trend has progressed from daily required physical education for all children to our current status of a limited number of hours per week or credits per year in physical education. In some states, physical education is being eliminated entirely from the required school curriculum.[17]

Recognizing that one aspect of physical education that is taught almost universally across all levels is sports and games, this trend represents a severe threat to the overall health of many young people—an area of concern that is illustrated in recent findings about their lack of fitness generally. Other evidence indicates that sales of sporting equipment have declined in the last several years, reflecting lower rates of involvement by many American youth and adults. Bob Fernandez sums up industry reports:

> Over the last decade, about 30 million people in the United States quit participating in traditional sports such as tennis, racquetball, baseball, volleyball, and softball, according to periodic studies of households. . . . Only soccer, basketball, and ice hockey among team sports—in addition to new sports such as in-line skating—have held their own, according to American Sports Data and other industry sources.[18]

Shifts in Sports Interests

Other reports confirm a growing trend toward other kinds of "alternative" and often extreme forms of physical recreation. Karl Greenfield points out that television has helped promote this trend, with a new band of athletes helping to drive the

> . . . fast-growing world of nontraditional sports to an ever-increasing share of the TV-ad dollar. Emerging sports such as surfing, skateboarding, snowboarding, mountain biking, rock climbing, NASCAR racing, and even bass fishing are gaining increasing TV exposure, providing greater choice for sports fans and advertisers.[19]

At the same time, it is clear that the major team, individual, and dual sports are still a dominant force in North American leisure. Strikingly, recent psychological research confirms the degree to which sports fans are influenced by the outcomes of games. Not only do spectators experience excitement and a sense of community through shared rooting for their teams, but their self-esteem and emotional state rise or fall markedly, depending on their teams' victories or losses.

James McKinley Jr. points out that researchers find that fervent fans experience measurable hormonal surges and other physiological changes while watching games. He continues:

> Our sports heroes are our warriors [states a professor of psychology]. This is not some light diversion to be enjoyed for its inherent grace and harmony. The self is centrally involved in the outcome of the event. Whoever you root for represents you.
>
> Psychologists have long suspected that many die-hard fans are lonely, alienated people searching for self-esteem by identifying with a sports team. But a study at the University of Kansas suggests just the opposite—that sports fans suffer fewer bouts of depression and alienation than do people who are uninterested in sports.[20]

Some authorities speculate that with the decline of such fundamental societal institutions as religion, the family, or political affiliation, sport has emerged to fill the need of many individuals for attachment to a cause. Whether this is the case or not, sports on every level—including both the traditional sports and the more innovative forms of play just discussed—represent a significant segment of today's leisure-service system and will certainly continue to do so.

TRAVEL AND TOURISM

We now turn to a second major area of diversified recreational involvement that is facilitated or sponsored by every type of leisure-service agency: *travel and tourism*. The terms are easily defined. *Travel* simply refers to movement from one location to another. It may be carried on by plane, ship, railroad, bicycle, or other means of transportation. In some definitions, travel is considered to involve trips taken over a minimum distance or from one region or country to another.

Tourism is described by McIntosh, Goeldner, and Ritchie as the activities of persons traveling to and staying in places outside their usual environment for not more than one consecutive year for leisure, businesses, or other purposes. They continue:

> [Tourism is] a vast conglomerate of transportation systems, service providers, recreational facilities, accommodations, consumer products, and specialized services—among many others. Practically everything that you see, touch, hear, and taste has something to do with tourism. You visit national parks, you touch animals at the zoo, you hear a symphony, you eat at a restaurant—all are related to tourism.[21]

A related term, *hospitality*, refers to the vast system of accommodations such as hotels, restaurants, entertainment and shopping facilities, and other services that are part of the overall travel and tourism system.

SCOPE OF TOURISM

Overall, the travel and tourism industry has been described as one of the world's largest businesses. Close to 7 percent of the gross national product in the United States is generated by travel and tourism, according to the U.S. Chamber of Commerce. It is the nation's second largest employer, second only to health services. Worldwide, its impact is immense. In 1999:

> The World Travel Organization reported that 635 million people traveled to a foreign country in 1998, spending US$439 billion. International tourism receipts combined with passenger transportation totaled more than US$504—making tourism the world's #1 export earner, ahead of automotive products, chemicals, petroleum, and food.[22]

Uniquely, many different kinds of organizations provide tourism opportunities. Thousands of commercial sponsors of tourist attractions and transportation services, theme parks and waterplay parks, cruise ships, charter airline operators, group tour managers, hotel chains, and numerous other businesses satisfy the tourism market. Many government agencies manage parks, historical sites, oceanfront areas, and other kinds of events that attract millions of recreational visitors.

Similarly, many nonprofit organizations sponsor sports events, cultural programs, educational tours, religious pilgrimages, and other special travel programs that serve millions of tourists each year. Armed forces Morale, Welfare, and Recreation units offer travel services to men and women in uniform; and industrial and other business concerns frequently schedule charter flights for their employees. Local convention and visitors bureaus facilitate vacation travel and promote regional tourist attractions.

Within this overall structure, the basic tourism industry consists of four key elements: (1) the *tourist,* who is motivated by a variety of motivations and needs, ranging from the search for novelty or excitement to aesthetic or cultural involvement; (2) the *businesses* that provide the bulk of transportation services, as well as the attractions that entertain visitors, along with other nonprofit cultural and environmental groups that maintain zoos, aquariums, botanical gardens, and events; (3) *governments* of host communities that encourage and facilitate tourism programs and attractions, often sponsoring them jointly with other agencies; and (4) *accommodations,* consisting of lodging, food and beverage services, camping sites, and other amenities that facilitate tourist visits.

Role of the Internet

An important development in the late 1990s involved the rapidly growing number of websites developed by different elements in the travel industry to facilitate the overall tourism marketing system. In 1997, *The Futurist* predicted that by 2000 on-line travel sales would reach more than $3 billion annually, a tenfold increase in just five years.

While many longtime travel buyers still look to brochures and travel agencies to provide information and arrange reservations, most new customers now buy travel service via the Web. Robert Schley writes:

> Key benefits of researching travel options through the Internet include: the sheer quantity of up-to-date information available, the convenience of accessing it from your desktop or laptop computer, and the ability to interact with other travelers interested in the same destinations. If you are interested in visiting a particular city, you might find listings of hotels and restaurants and important sights to visit, just like a guidebook . . . complete with colorful photos, current price listings, and menus, as well as a guide to current or upcoming events in that city.[23]

Internationally, it was predicted in 1998 that the number of non-U.S. Internet users would jump to 143 million by 2002, up from 16.4 million in 1997, with global websites making it easier for travelers from abroad to make tourism arrangements. According to later forecasts, it is expected that by the year 2010 almost every adult under 55 in the developed world will have access to the Internet, with travel and tourism representing a key area of consumer on-line involvement. Even today, a single Internet enterprise, Travelocity.com, provides reservation capabilities for 95 percent of all airline seats, more than 40,000 hotels, and more than 50 rental car companies.

MAJOR AREAS OF TOURISM SERVICES

Several major elements in the overall travel and tourism enterprise are now examined, beginning with theme parks and water parks.

THEME PARKS AND WATER PARKS

Closely linked to the growth of tourism as a form of recreation has been the expansion of theme parks like California's famous Disneyland. This major entertainment complex was built at a cost of over $50 million and covers 65 acres in Anaheim, California. Its success led to the construction of a second major Disney complex, Walt Disney World, at Lake Buena Vista, Florida.

Crompton and Van Doren point out that Disney effectively resurrected a dying industry. The outdoor amusement park, once an important form of popular entertainment, had become a cultural anachronism. Disney's contribution, they note, was to emphasize cleanliness, courtesy, and safety, in marked contrast to the traditional amusement park. Furthermore, they write:

> The theology of pleasure is reinforced by promotional messages. The theme park creates an atmosphere in which the visitor is likely to experience fantasy, glamour, escapism, prestige, and excitemen . . . . Once inside the gate, the visitor is completely shut off from the outside world and immersed in an enjoyable recreational experience . . . . The theme park's primary market is the family; theme parks keep a family involved and entertained for a whole day.[24]

New Kinds of Theme Parks

Other entertainment entrepreneurs soon followed the Disney example, and by 1976 at least three dozen parks of similar scale had been built around the United States. Some parks concentrate on a single theme, such as Opryland, U.S.A., in Nashville and the Land of Oz in North Carolina. Others incorporate moving rides through settings based on literary, historical, or international themes; entertainment; and typical amusement park "thrill" rides like rollercoasters and parachute jumps.

Another unusual facility which opened in the early 1980s by Busch Gardens was Adventure Island in Tampa, Florida. This 22-acre water park provides vistas of white sand beaches, glistening waters, palm trees, and tropical plants. Built on varied levels with complex waterfalls, slides, pools, cliffs, and rocks, Adventure Island provides an all-inclusive water experience in which visitors slide down twisting water chutes, ride the waves in the Endless Surf pool, dive from cliffs, and enjoy other forms of aquatic play.

Expansion of Disney Entertainment Empire

However, none of the other chains of theme parks or outdoor play centers could match the diversity and inventiveness of the Disney planners. In 1982, they opened EPCOT (an acronym for Experimental Prototype Community of Tomorrow), an $800-million, 260-acre development that was conceived of as being more than a theme park. Instead, EPCOT was intended to be a place that would offer an environment where people of many nations might meet and exchange ideas. It consists of two sections: (1) Future World, which contains corporate pavilions primarily concerned with technology; and (2) World Showcase, which has international pavilions designed to show the tourist attractions of various nations around the world.

Since then, Disney World has added a number of other spectacular and imaginative attractions, including Typhoon Lagoon, River Country, the Disney MGM Studios, and, in 1995, Blizzard Beach, Florida's first "snow-capped" water park; it is patterned after an Alpine ski resort, with mountain slopes covered with toboggan slides, ski jumps, and slalom runs. In 1983, a new Disneyland opened in Japan, on 202 acres of landfill in Tokyo Bay and featuring the traditional Disney characters and popular rides and attractions. While the new attraction is owned by a Japanese corporation, Disney provided technology and guidance during the construction and operation of Tokyo Disneyland for a share of the gross ticket take. Then, with the opening of Disneyland Paris, otherwise known as Euro Disney, the company created the largest theme park in Europe. While it was initially resisted and had to revise its approach to suit French and European patrons, by 1995 Disneyland Paris began to return its first sizable profits.

Through the 1990s, Disney continued to add new attractions and program features. In 1997, Disney's 200-acre Wide World of Sports offered a 7,500-seat stadium and other facilities to provide a venue for the Atlanta Braves, the Harlem Globetrotters, and the Indiana Pacers—as well as thousands of other competitors on every age level in several different sports. Through a cooperative arrangement with the Amateur Athletic Union, national youth tournaments in baseball, basketball, softball, and tennis, among others, are held at this facility. In 1998, Disney's spectacular Animal Kingdom offered an $800-million "African plain," populated by hundreds of wild animals of every description—with 10 million visitors expected the first year.

Other Parks

In addition to the leading Disney parks, other successful ventures at the end of the 1990s included Universal Studios, Florida, Busch Gardens in Tampa Bay, Six Flags Great Adventure in New Jersey, Knott's Berry Farm and Sea World in California, and Cedar Point in Ohio.

The leading chains feature increasingly spectacular and frightening rides and often characters or settings linked to popular movies or cartoon characters. Universal Studios Florida, for example, offers a 19-day Halloween Horror Nights series in which:

Roving bands of chain saw–brandishing hoodlums pursue fleeing customers through darkened streets. Zombies and demons lunge from every nook and cranny. Shrieks and foul odors emerge from haunted houses. Basically, in the words of one Universal employee, the theme park wants "to try to make you scream until there's no sound left."[25]

Similarly, Universal's new Island of Adventure offers stunning, pummeling rides, with steep, twisting and lurching, and high-speed courses accompanied by 3-D images of destruction on giant screens and spectacular fire and water effects.

However, not all theme parks rely on such forms of entertainment. Dollywood, for example, a complex of shops, rides, shows, craft centers, restaurants, and other theatrical features based on folk themes, is an outstanding tourist attraction in the Great Smoky Mountain National Park Region. Linked to the image of Dolly Parton, the popular movie actress and country music star, Dollywood offers gospel music performances, harvest celebrations, a "showcase" series of well-known performances, and other programs attuned to its traditional Appalachian mountain environment.

Water Parks

A specialized type of theme park today consists of water parks—tourist destinations that feature wave pools, slides, chutes, shows, and other forms of water-based play and entertainment. There are about 1,000 water parks today that provide such outdoor play in the United States, mainly in southern states with warmer climates.

Often these are part of larger theme park operations. In Universal's Islands of Adventure, for example, the Jurassic Park River Adventure, Bilge-Rat Barges, and Poseidon's Fury offer either whirling and steep white-water rides and sluice falls or swirling vortexes that spray riders thoroughly. Each year, dozens of new water parks have been opened, with the latest technology, marketing, and management skills taught to their operators at conventions held by the American Water Park Association.

OTHER FUN CENTERS

In heavily populated metropolitan areas throughout the United States, other entrepreneurs have developed a variety of indoor fun centers, ranging from children's play, gymnastics, and exercise chains to family party centers, video game arcades, and huge restaurants with game areas. Typifying the latter, Dave and Buster's, an immensely successful chain of adult "fun-and-food" offerings in Dallas, Houston, Atlanta, Chicago, and Philadelphia, offers a host of simulated fun experiences: golf, motorcycling, race car driving, space combat, and virtual reality, among others.

Similarly, the new children's and family play centers that have been established in thousands of suburban neighborhoods and shopping malls around the United States offer a combination of computer and video games, billiards and other table games, miniature golf, entertainment by clowns and magicians, music, and popular fast-food refreshments. Offering packaged birthday parties and other family play services, they illustrate commercial recreation's success in providing attractive play activities that have supplanted more traditional home-based and "do-it-yourself" kinds of recreation.

CRUISE SHIPS

Over the past three decades, the growing prosperity of many North Americans has made it possible for greater numbers of vacationers to indulge themselves with more varied forms of travel. Luxury cruise ships are no longer simply a vehicle for getting from one place to another or for extended, leisurely ocean voyages. Instead, they have evolved into floating amusement parks, health spas, classrooms, and nightclubs. The major cruise companies have also developed huge new vessels and are catering to younger and less affluent individuals with relatively inexpensive short-term trips.

Today, more than 200 cruise ship lines offer a remarkable variety of vacation options afloat, ranging from small sail-propelled schooners to giant, luxurious ocean liners. In many cases, their attractions include gourmet meals; early morning workouts; nightlife and, often, gambling; language classes and charm clinics; deck games; and visits to exotic ports. Elsewhere, the author has written:

> The North American cruise industry anticipated breaking the six million–passenger mark for the first time in 2000, having committed itself to building and refurbishing more than 60 ships by 2004. In 1999, 12 new ships—including three by Holland America line—joined the North American fleet, adding more than 17,500 new berths for the 57 million Americans who have indicated their intention to take cruises within the next five years.
>
> North American cruises—including Caribbean, Alaska, Bermuda, and trans-Canada routes—represent the largest portion of money spent on vacation cruises, with short cruises becoming increasingly popular.[26]

A recent report indicated that the total economic impact in the United States of the cruise lines, their passengers, and suppliers reached $11.6 billion annually in the late 1990s and was projected to climb to over $18 billion by 2002. This spending generated over 176,000 jobs, and cruise-related employment was expected to grow to 273,000 jobs by the later year.

Variety of Cruise Experiences

As in the overall tourism field, cruise passengers' motivations and interests take many different forms. While some travelers prefer luxurious, pampered, and relatively inactive trips, others enjoy excursions and activities that are demanding or that provide unusual leisure experiences. For example, Windjammer Cruises, which schedules sailing vacations to over 60 ports chiefly throughout the Caribbean region, offers its passengers such optional possibilities as kayaking and parasailing, deep sea fishing and scuba diving, nature walks and mountain bikes, and cultural and historic tours on a host of island visits.

Other specially designed cruises offer such formats or themes as *nudism* (Bare Necessities sponsors "clothing-optional" trips for "naturists"); *sobriety* cruises (sponsored by Sober Vacations International in California); or *golf*, combining shipboard lessons and lectures with visits to notable links (offered by Wide World of Golf); as well as many other unique travel tours with sea-and-land adventures.

Cruise Vacations

Many cruise ships today have become floating entertainment palaces. Here, Celebrity Cruises Horizon leaves Bermuda, and Carnival's Voyage of the Seas features spectacular three-tiered dining room, which is similar to Elation's towering atrium. In contrast to these architectural monuments, Windjammer Barefoot Cruises offers simpler voyages under full sail on Polynesia and other wind-driven craft.

OTHER TOURISM THEMES

Apart from traveling to theme parks and similar attractions or embarking on vacation cruises, tourists today seek to satisfy a remarkable range of personal interests and motivations.

Cultural and Historical Interests

The term *cultural* may have two possible meanings when applied to tourism motivations. It may suggest interest in attending major performing arts festivals, visiting famous art museums, or having other kinds of aesthetic experiences. Another meaning involves interest in being exposed to new and different cultures.

The arts in general have great appeal for travelers, and many cities in the United States are using them to appeal to tourists. Edwin McDowell points out that even cities like Orlando, Florida, famous for its theme parks and similar attractions, today give growing support to music, drama, and dance events—including major opera performances. He continues:

> From the former mining town of Bisbee, Arizona, which boasts 27 arts galleries, three museums, and its first arts festival . . . to the seaport city of Norfolk, Virginia, which is hoping to stimulate tourism with a $1.9-million, 18-day international arts festival, hundreds of cities and towns across the country have recently discovered that there is money to be made by promoting the arts.[27]

A 1998 report in *Travel and Tourism Analyst* reports that when foreign travelers tour Great Britain, roughly two-thirds of them (62 percent) visit art museums, a third (34 percent) visit art galleries, and a third (32 percent) go to the theater—especially in London.[28] Similarly, studies of tourism in the United States indicate that visiting museums, live theater, and festivals are among the more popular activities of travelers to urban destinations.

In a broader sense, cultural tourism may include exposure to such regional or ethnically different locations as the Amish countryside in Pennsylvania, smaller communities throughout French Canada where the culture is determinedly Gallic, or visits to Indian reservations throughout the West—destinations that have special appeal for many Europeans. It may also involve what Canadian authorities term "heritage tourism," with trips to see old mines, factories, or prisons that have been redesigned to provide today's visitors with a fuller understanding of the past.

Increasingly, festivals or holiday events commemorate famous battles of the past, scenes of the Civil War, or other historic events. Even rodeos, which illustrate the real-life work of cowboys in the American West, or lumberjack contests and similar competitions at state fairs serve as experiences that make this kind of tourism meaningful. Confer and Kerstetter sum up the meaning of heritage tourism:

> It is about the cultural traditions, places, and values that groups throughout the world are proud to conserve. Cultural traditions such as family patterns, religious practices, folklore traditions, and social customs attract individuals interested in heritage tourism, as do monuments, museums, battlefields, historic structures, and landmarks. [It also includes] natural heritage sites—gardens, wilderness areas of scenic beauty, and valued cultural landscapes.[29]

Tourism offers varied attractions. The Renaissance Festival in Sterling Forest, New York, features knightly jousting, Halloween horror shows, falconry displays, and other sixteenth-century entertainment. In Silver Springs Theme Park in Florida, animal shows include giant toads, tarantulas, scorpions, Egyptian fruit bats, and less fearsome creatures. In Santa Fe, New Mexico, Native American handmade crafts are on display for tourists.

Linked to this type of cultural and historic exploration, such organizations as American Youth Hostels or the Elderhostel movement that serves older travelers combine educational and cultural exposures with what are usually short-term stays in foreign lands or distant locations.

Sports Tourism

This area of special interest, which began to arouse scholarly interest only in the late 1990s, encompasses a variety of travel experiences that have as their purpose either engaging directly in a form of sport or attending sports events as a spectator. To illustrate, Americans took 60 million trips in 1998 to attend or take part in a sports event, generating $27 billion and accounting for nearly 6 percent of the 1.2 billion trips that year. *Travel and Tourism Executive Report* continues:

> Local governments aggressively promote tour packages to the events they host, a tactic that's also used by Walt Disney's various sports teams and events through ESPN. The National Football League may develop and sell packages for corporations and [various cities are now hiring] sports marketing specialists.[30]

Typically, it has been reported that about 60 percent of the 1.5 million fans who watch spring-training games in Florida come from out of state chiefly for baseball. Major college and professional tournaments and championships capture huge audiences, along with major boxing matches, golf and tennis events, and even sports like softball, which has brought huge revenues to another little-known city, Lancaster, California.

Heather Gibson points out that other sports places serve as key destination attractions. In a sense, visiting such establishments as the Basketball Hall of Fame in Springfield, Massachusetts; sports museums like the NASCAR Museum in Charlotte, North Carolina; or famous ballfields like Yankee Stadium represent a form of heritage tourism. She continues:

> Another trend . . . has emerged in recent years: meeting famous sports personalities. The cruise industry has been very adept in this area. Theme cruises such as Norwegian Cruise Lines' "Pro-Am Golf Cruise" or the "NBA Basketball Cruise" allow passengers to meet sports personalities on the ship.[31]

Religion-Based Tourism

Centuries ago, one of the motivations spurring international travel consisted of pilgrimages. Today, religion-oriented travel is one of the industry's fastest-growing segments. Tours highlight Christian, Jewish, Muslim, and even Buddhist places of importance. Describing a visit to the Mount of the Beatitudes in Israel, part of a two-week Holy Land church-group trip arranged with the help of the Israel Government Tourist Office, one worshipper commented:

> This is the most joyful day of my life. To think I am standing where Christ preached the Sermon on the Mount, saying his words in this sacred place, is really a fantasy come true.[32]

Although Jerusalem represents the best-known and most popular such destination, other religion-based tours involve trips to Pamplona in Spain, which has appeal for all three major religions, and to ancient synagogues, churches, and cemeteries throughout Europe, the Middle and Far East, and the Americas:

> The dream of spiritual pilgrimage is one travelers are fulfilling in rapidly increasing numbers, making religious tourism a $1-billion-a-year business worldwide and creating a boom for tour companies specializing in religious themes. . . . Trips range from deeply religious programs with prayer services conducted by accompanying clergymen to cultural heritage journeys that bring spiritual connection [exploring a people's past] through historical documentation rather than religious rituals.[33]

Often, such trips are not narrowly denominational but bring members of various faiths together to explore their linked heritages and contrast their present beliefs and practices.

Health-Related Tourism

Recognizing that religious travel is for many persons a means of obtaining spiritual well-being and emotional health, it should be stressed that for many other individuals health needs represent a primary motivation for travel. In Europe, particularly, visits to traditional health spas that are based on natural mineral springs are being gradually replaced by stays at more modern health and fitness centers. These destinations often combine varied forms of exercise, nutritional care, massage, yoga, and other holistic approaches to health care to provide a fuller range of services to visitors. While weight reduction or recovery from alcohol or drug addiction is the primary focus of many such centers, others involve a much broader approach to achieving "wellness."

Ecotourism and Adventure Travel

With the growth of environmental concerns and programs over the past three decades, a form of leisure travel has emerged that is deeply concerned with the preservation and protection of the natural environment. Generally referred to as *ecotourism*, but sometimes as *resource-based tourism*, this approach is closely linked to environmentally sensitive outdoor recreation, in that it implies a strong degree of respect for the environment—both ecological and human. Nora Haenn writes that it is not just a new mode of traveling. Instead, ecotourism is

> . . . a new way for travelers to relate to the places they visit. Any kind of travel adventure can take the tourist to a new place. Ecotourism's distinction is to inspire in the traveler a special kind of connection with the environment. By encouraging respect and appreciation for the environment and people of foreign lands, ecotourism promises the tourist will gain an emotional closeness to [the places visited].[34]

Ecotourism may be carried on at various levels of personal challenge and comfort. In one type of planned journey, travelers were scheduled to stay overnight at a camp deep in the rain forest of Brazil, with other stays on the Amazon River and in a remote jungle hotel, learning about the lives of indigenous people in this region. Later, one of the members of the group commented that "shimmying catwalks, cold showers, pushy monkeys, and killer bees were quite enough for this reluctant ecotourist."

As a variant of this approach, some tourist companies offer the possibility for "action vacations"—offering the traveler the chance to visit foreign lands, not simply to lie on a beach but to take part in an archaeological dig, study wildlife or the local environment systematically, teach English to children, or be involved in health-care projects. With less of a social-service orientation and more of a recreational focus, such vacations may involve high-risk adventure pastimes such as trail rides through wild country, cave diving, hang-gliding, mountain climbing, or white-water rafting on turbulent streams.

Extreme versions of adventure tourism may involve the opportunity to track down tornadoes, offered as a package deal by a number of companies in Midwest or Southwest regions of the United States during the tornado seasons of the year.[35] Most extreme was the tour designed by a Nashua, New Hampshire, company in the mid-1990s, which offered to take thrill-seeking tourists to combat zones in parts of the former Soviet Union and spots on the Indian Ocean. The president of War Tours, Ltd., promised clients

> . . . front-line battle exposure, including being shot at and viewing the effects of heavy artillery. For about $6,000, the war traveler receives a package tour of several danger spots. The price includes boots and body armor, which may be kept as souvenirs . . . and there is no guarantee of personal safety.[36]

Other well-heeled adventurers today embark on expeditions to climb the Matterhorn, fly to the North Pole, break the sound barrier in a Russian MIG 25 fighter jet, or pay deposits to take suborbital rides into space (defined as 62 miles up)—scheduled to be offered by commercial rocket builders beginning as early as 2002.

Hedonistic Forms of Tourism

Still other forms of tourism are designed to provide hedonistic forms of pleasure to participants. Gambling clearly represents the most popular such activity, with millions of individuals traveling each year to major casinos throughout the world or enjoying gaming as a convenient amenity on ocean cruises or major airline flights.

At another level, thousands of young people each year roam through the Far East, including unscheduled, free-wheeling trips through Thailand, Burma, Cambodia, and Nepal—partly to experience their exotic environments, but also to take part in the drug culture that is readily available and inexpensive in these regions. Too often, many of these free spirits end as heavily substance-addicted individuals or simply disappear from sight and are not heard of again.

Finally, a form of pleasure-seeking tourism that has emerged throughout the world involves the search for sex. With the breakup of the Soviet Union, many young women from Russia, Ukraine, and other former Iron Curtain countries have been recruited as prostitutes in regions of Southern Europe and North Africa. And, increasingly, many pedophiles are finding new victims in

> Latin America, where an estimated 2 million kids are homeless after last year's hurricanes [in 1998. Some have been arrested] but others not only continue their predations but actually smuggle children into the U.S. [despite] the 1994 sex-tourism law, which prohibits Americans from traveling abroad for sex with minors.[37]

As an aspect of the overall tourist industry, Sheila Jeffreys points out that the sex industry has become extremely profitable, providing substantial revenues, not only to individuals and the networks involved in trafficking women but to some nations that have come to depend on sex industry profits. Given the increasingly loose standards or expectations of public morality, Jeffreys points out that a growing number of "normalizers" today take the position that sex tourism and other forms of prostitution should come to be seen as a legitimate leisure industry, one in which women and children are literally "men's leisure."[38] Obviously, such issues raise serious questions about the meaning and purpose of leisure within national life, as well as the specific kinds of controls that should be exerted over various forms of play.

MARKETING ADVANCES IN TRAVEL AND TOURISM

Perhaps more than in any other form of recreation, travel and tourism illustrate the increasing sophistication that is used to market leisure experiences today. Within this highly competitive but immensely lucrative field, as M. Uysal has pointed out, it is no longer possible to think of tourists as a large, homogeneous market. Instead, the planning and marketing of travel and tourist destinations must take into account the highly specialized interests of vacationers, their tastes in comfort and service, and their growing awareness of values and costs.[39]

Marketing segmentation studies, Uysal notes, must assess the socioeconomic and demographic variables of potential tourists, as well as product-related variables (having to do with transportation, length of stay, recreation activity, and similar factors); psychographic variables like personal lifestyle and personality traits; geographical variables; and cultural factors such as religion, ethnic origin, and national customs.

New Links Between Public and Commercial Sponsors

It is becoming apparent that both public and commercial agencies have an important stake in promoting successful tourist programs today. In the past, tourism has been regarded as a commercial economic phenomenon rooted in the private business sector. Today, with cities, states, and entire nations competing to attract large numbers of tourists because of their contribution to the overall economy, both government agencies and private entrepreneurs have joined forces in planning and promoting tourist attractions.

In some cases, local park and recreation departments have begun to sponsor packaged vacation trips as part of their overall programs. Crompton and Richardson cite the example of the Jackson County, Missouri, Park and Recreation Department, which has been aggressively programming such tours:

> They . . . operate an expanding year-round travel program, which consists of over 30 long-distance tours to destinations such as Europe, Hawaii, and Canada, 15 one-to-two-day trips, and a series of one-day "look around the town trips." [Included are] five high adventure trips to Canada (with camping, lake fishing, canoeing, and a wilderness black bear hunt).[40]

At another level, as this chapter has shown, many states and local governments have moved vigorously into cooperative ventures to sponsor and promote varied forms of sports and tourist attractions, both to heighten their positive image and to draw needed revenues and bolster local employment.

SUMMARY

Sports management and tourism are similar in that they involve huge sections of the leisure-service field, are provided by many different kinds of organizations, and have developed into complex disciplines in terms of job specializations, academic preparation, professional societies, and career opportunity.

This chapter examines sport on various levels, ranging from familiar games for children and youth to high-level college and professional competition. It outlines the personal and social values that are commonly ascribed to sports involvement and describes a number of the abuses that undermine these values, such as overemphasis on winning in high-pressure youth sports or the corruption that exists in many college athletic programs. Finally, it suggests that overcommercialization and rapidly climbing costs threaten the fan base of professional sports and notes the trend away from some of the most familiar, traditional games in the direction of "extreme" or "alternative" physical recreation activities.

Travel and tourism represent equally diverse forms of leisure activity, with immense economic revenues. This chapter describes some of the most popular forms of tourism, such as visits to theme parks and water-play parks, cruises, or tours of various types—adventure, religious, cultural, or hedonism directed. As in the case of sport, tourism appears to be running the risk of being overbuilt in a number of areas, with the supply of costly attractions exceeding the demand in the decades ahead.

QUESTIONS FOR CLASS DISCUSSION OR ESSAY EXAMINATIONS

1. As class members have observed it, describe the transition from childhood interest and involvement in sport, through adolescence and adult participation or spectator experiences.
2. The chapter points out that sports are often seen as a religion. At the same time, they are widely recognized as a business. How can these two points of view be reconciled?
3. Many cities have recently built or are building expensive new arenas or stadiums to house professional teams—often with substantial subsidies. What is the rationale for their using tax funds for this purpose? Argue the pros and cons of this practice.
4. Tourism may be carried on for many purposes: exploration of different environments, cultural or educational purposes, adventure and risk, or hedonism as a motivation. Give examples of such forms of tourism, based on class members' experiences.
5. Select either theme parks or cruise ship lines, and describe their role today in the tourism industry, including current trends and new formulas for appealing to the public.

ENDNOTES

1 J. B. Lewis, T. R. Jones, G. Lamke, and L. M. Dunn, "Recreational Sport: Making the Grade on College Campuses," *Parks and Recreation* (December 1998): 73.

2 Gregg Zoroya, "Orlando Overload," *U.S.A. Today* (10 May 1999): 1.

3 "Sport Your Economy," *U.S. News and World Report* (7 December 1987): 59.

4 "Woods Is on His Way to a Billion," *Associated Press* (25 June 2000).

5 Charles Prebish, cited in R. Chandler, "Are Sports Becoming America's New Folk Religion?" *Philadelphia Inquirer* (3 January 1987): 1-C.

6 J. Mathiesen, in Chandler, op. cit., p. 5-C.

7 Pat Jordan, "Belittled Big Men," *New York Times Magazine* (10 December 1995): 75.

8 B. Rader, *American Sports from the Age of Folk Games to the Age of Spectators* (Englewood Cliffs, N.J.: Prentice-Hall, 1983): 32.

9 James Kozlowski, "Sport League Held Liable for Brutal Attack on Coach," *Parks and Recreation* (November 1999): 45–52.

10 L. C. Bollinger and T. Goss, "Cleaning Up College Basketball," *New York Times* (5 September 1998): A-11.

11 Joe La Points, "A Hard Winter in Vermont: Hockey Season Canceled Over Hazing," *New York Times* (3 February 2000): D-1.

12 Robert Sullivan, "How the Olympics Were Bought," *Time* (25 January 1999): 38.

13 Michael Lemonick, "Le Tour des Drugs," *Time* (10 August 1998): 76.

14 Jere Longman, "Fixed Matches Are Darkening Soccer's Image," *New York Times* (7 June 1998): 1.

15 Dan McGraw, "NBA Finals Are No Slam-Dunk for TV," *U.S. News and World Report* (1 May 2000): 45.

16 Dennis Howard, "The Changing Fanscape for Big-League Sports: Implications for Sports Managers," *Journal of Sport Management* (Vol. 13, January 1999): 78–91.

17 Deborah Tannehill, "Sport Education," *Journal of Physical Education, Recreation, and Dance* (April 1998): 16.

18 Bob Fernandez, "Seeking a Sporting Chance," *Philadelphia Inquirer* (18 June 2000): E-1.

19 Karl Greenfield, "A Wider World of Sport," *Time* (9 November 1998): 80.

20 J. C. McKinley Jr., "It Isn't Just a Game: Clues to Avid Rooting," *New York Times* (11 August 2000): A-1.

21 R. McIntosh, C. Goeldner, and J. R. Brent Ritchie, *Tourism: Principles, Practices, Philosophies* (New York: John Wiley and Sons, 1995): 2.

22 "A Worldwide TSA: Finally a Way to Measure Tourism's Economic Impact," *Travel and Tourism Executive Report* (Nos. 3 and 4, 1999): 12.

23 Robert Schley, "Travel Planning Online," *The Futurist* (November/December 1997): 12.

24 J. Crompton and C. Van Doren, "Amusement Parks, Theme Parks, and Municipal Leisure Services: Contrasts in Adaptation to Cultural Change," *Journal of Physical Education, Recreation, and Dance—Leisure Today* (October 1976): 45.

25 Edwin McDowell, "Bloodcurdling Capitalism," *New York Times* (31 October 1998): C-1.

26 See Richard Kraus, *Introduction to Leisure Services: Career Perspectives* (Champaign, Ill.: Sagamore Publishing, 2001): 200.

27 Edwin McDowell, "Tourists Respond to Lure of Culture," *New York Times* (24 April 1997): B-1.

28 D. Gilbert and M. Lizotte, "Tourism and the Performing Arts," *Travel and Tourism Analyst* (No. 1, 1998), 82.

29 J. C. Confer and D. L. Kerstetter, "Past Perfect: Exploration of Heritage Tourism," *Parks and Recreation* (February 2000): 28.

30 *Travel and Tourism Executive Report* (Nos. 3 and 4, 1999): 7.

31 Heather Gibson, "The Wide World of Sport Tourism," *Parks and Recreation* (September 1998): 112.

32 Judi Dash, "Journeys of Faith," *New York Times* (4 April 1999): T-6.

33 Ibid.

34 Nora Haenn, "A New Tourist, A New Environment: Can Ecotourism Deliver?" *Trends* (Vol. 3, No. 2, 1994): 28.

35 Dan McGraw, "Whirlwind Tourism," *U.S. News and World Report* (8 June 1998): 58.

36 "Adventure Travel: Bang for the Buck," *New York Times Magazine* (17 September 1995): 24.

37 Timothy Roche, "Tourists Who Prey on Kids," *Time* (15 February 1999): 58.

38 Sheila Jeffreys, "Globalizing Sexual Exploitation: Sex Tourism and the Traffic in Women," *Leisure Studies* (Vol. 18, 1999): 179.

39 M. Uysal, "Marketing for Tourism, A Growing Field," *Parks and Recreation* (October 1986): 61.

40 J. Crompton and S. Richardson, "The Tourism Connection: Where Public and Private Leisure Services Merge," *Parks and Recreation* (October 1986): 44.

CHAPTER 11

CAREER OPPORTUNITIES AND PROFESSIONALISM

◆ ◆ ◆

Recreation programs, as diverse as the people they serve, are offered at local playgrounds and recreation areas, parks, community centers, health clubs, religious organizations, camps, theme parks, and most tourism attractions. . . . Of those who held year-round jobs as recreation workers [in the mid-1990s], about half worked in [public] park and recreation departments. Nearly two out of 10 worked in membership organizations with a civic, social, fraternal, or religious orientation. . . . About two out of 10 were in programs run by social service organizations—senior centers or adult-day-care programs or residential care [or correctional facilities].[1]

A leisure service professional has mastered a body of knowledge . . . related to the behavior of people during leisure, management techniques, and strategies used to provide leisure services. They have a value structure or philosophy that promotes such ends as the wise use of leisure, preservation and conservation of resources, and the promotion of human dignity. Possessing such knowledge, leisure service professionals are, in fact, uniquely equipped to plan, organize, provide, and evaluate the impact of leisure experience.[2]

◆ ◆ ◆

INTRODUCTION

As earlier chapters have shown, recreation, parks, and leisure services have expanded greatly over the past several decades as a diversified area of employment. Today, several million men and women work in different sectors of this field, including amateur and professional sports, entertainment and amusement services, travel and tourism, recreation-related businesses, and government and nonprofit community organizations.

As a distinct part of this larger group, several hundred thousand men and women are directly involved as recreation leaders, supervisors, managers, therapists, planners, and consultants in public, voluntary, commercial, therapeutic, and other types of agencies. These individuals, with a primary concern for the provision of recreation services, are generally regarded as *professionals* on the basis of their job responsibilities, specialized training, and affiliations with professional societies.

The prevailing image of leisure-service professionals has been that of public, governmental recreation, and park employees. The leading professional societies, as well as most textbooks and college curricula, have reinforced this narrowly defined identity.

However, the reality is that vast sectors of employment in recreation and leisure services are *not* government related but, instead, have to do with nonprofit community agencies, company-sponsored, commercial, therapeutic, sports-management, or travel and tourism programs. As such, they have their own professional associations, as well as goals, job functions, and strategies that differ from those of public recreation and park specialists.

RECREATION AS A CAREER

People have worked in recreation for many centuries in the sense that there have been professional athletes and entertainers throughout history. Musicians, tumblers, dancers, huntsmen, park designers, and gardeners were all recreation specialists attending to the leisure needs first of royalty and, ultimately, the public at large. However, the idea of recreation itself as a career field did not surface until the late 1800s, when public parks and playgrounds, along with voluntary social-service and youth-serving organizations, were established.

After the beginning of the twentieth century, courses in play leadership were developed by the Playground Association of America and were taken by many teachers. In the middle 1920s, the National Recreation Association provided a graduate training program for professional recreation and park administrators, and leisure as a distinct area of public service came to be recognized. This recognition increased during the Great Depression of the 1930s as many thousands of individuals were assigned by the federal government to emergency posts providing community recreation programs and developing new parks and other facilities. But it was not until the development of separate degree programs in a handful of colleges that higher education in recreation and parks as a distinct career field came into being.

By the second half of the twentieth century, careers in recreation and parks were seen as a growth area. A nationwide study of workforce requirements in the 1960s concluded that there would be a need for hundreds of thousands of new recreation and park professionals in the years ahead. The U.S. Department of Labor reported widespread shortages of leisure-service personnel in local government, hospitals, and youth-serving organizations. Several factors, such as the federal government's expanded activity in outdoor recreation and open space and the establishment of the National Recreation and Park Association, stimulated interest in this field. In the 1970s, as employment grew, curricula in recreation and leisure service gained increased acceptance in higher education.

Scope of Employment Today

Today, as previous chapters have shown, the kinds of organizations that employ recreation and park personnel are highly diversified. In a comprehensive analysis of the managed recreation system, *Recreation, Sports, and Leisure* points out that the director of a hotel/spa complex grossing $30 million is a managed recreation professional:

> So is a student athletic director and a stadium manager. Also included are health club owners, Jewish community center directors, county fair operators, tennis pros, and dozens of others. Some have MBAs and practically live in vested suits; others couldn't survive without a pair of sneakers.[3]

The report goes on to point out that in every category—from educational background to salary levels or job responsibilities—recreation professionals are a diverse group. Many feel no special professional or emotional kinship with their peers. The element that they share in common is that they are all in the same business—the business of providing recreation and leisure programs in large, competitive environments.

A report on the growing recreation field, published in 1965 by the U.S. Department of Labor, pointed out that it was difficult to determine the exact number of people employed in the recreation field, because so many occupations—such as those connected with travel—are only *partly* based on leisure motivations. Nonetheless, through the years, numerous reports on employment in recreation, parks, and leisure services have been issued.

In 1995, the *Statistical Abstract of the United States* reported that employment totals in various leisure-related fields were as follows: hotels and other lodging jobs: 1.5 million; motion picture industry: 404,000; amusement and recreation services: 1.1 million; and social services (museums, zoos, and membership organizations): 1.9 million.

In separate tables, it reported that positions as amusement and recreation attendants were projected to grow from 121,000 in 1992 to 303,000 in 2005, and that jobs as sports and fitness coaches and instructors were estimated to increase from 260,000 to 355,000 over the same period.

In 1995, government recreation and park employees on all levels (federal, state, and local) totaled 345,000, while those concerned with natural resources numbered 436,000.[4]

Beyond such estimates, millions of men and women today are employed in specialized areas of leisure-related businesses, such as those related to boating, hunting and fishing, fitness and health club settings, educational institutions, entertainment services, and other enterprises. Within each of the 10 areas of organized leisure services

FIGURE 11.1

PERSONNEL PRACTICES, YOUNG MEN'S CHRISTIAN ASSOCIATION

In addition to rallying 515,720 volunteers to lead programs, YMCAs collectively employ more than 20,000 full-time staff and thousands more nationwide. Staff members represent all religions, a range of ages and diverse ethnicities. They work as child care providers, camp counselors, building and pool maintenance technicians, front-desk staff, CEOs, program directors, lifeguards, accountants, public relations managers, community outreach directors, and human resources administrators. The list goes on and on.

The YMCA is dedicated to thorough training of all full-time and part-time staff as well as volunteers. To that end, the YMCA of the USA has established a series of training initiatives for all levels of employees. All full- and part-time employees and volunteers are encouraged—and all directors are required—to attend a one-week training camp that inspires associates to personify the YMCA mission in their lives and YMCA careers. Senior-level staff in program areas undergo an additional management-training program. A leadership institute delivers a comprehensive training in management tools and resources for YMCA CEOs to make them effective leaders in their communities.

Source: YMCA Employment Brochure (2000).

described in earlier chapters, many thousands of individuals are employed. As a single example, Figure 11.1 describes the staffing scope of a leading nonprofit organization, the Young Men's Christian Association.

Examples of Job Titles in Specialized Fields

Rather than such titles as *recreation leader* or *center director*, which would be found in public recreation and park agencies, position titles in sports-related organizations might include *coach, trainer, recruiter, sportscaster* or *announcer, sports medicine* or *fitness specialist, lifeguard* or *pool manager, risk manager* or *insurance specialist, aerobics instructor, health club manager,* or *fund-raiser*. In the tourism field, *chefs* or *food-service managers, front-desk personnel, tour directors, travel agents,* or *customer-service employees,* along with *marketing, sales management,* and *advertising* or *public relations* positions are widespread.

To illustrate the diversity of job titles and functions in nonpublic agency programs, Figure 11.2 shows the variety of positions in Morale, Welfare, and Recreation in a single U.S. Navy base in Sasebo, Japan. Throughout armed forces recreation units around the world, many thousands of civilian employees fill such posts in armed forces recreation programs.

Such examples illustrate a basic point about careers in recreation. Although many texts in this field tend to define other specialized areas such as employee recreation, military recreation, or travel and tourism as *subareas of the overall leisure-service field,* in *their* view, *exactly the opposite is the case*. For example, in employee programs, recreation is just *one* of the services provided. Just as in Figure 11.2, it represents one of many different functions in military programs.

FIGURE 11.2

Working For MWR

MWR has a variety of job opportunities available at any given time. There are full and part-time positions in many vocations. Whether your schedule can afford 40 hours per week or only eight, the following are the most common openings within MWR:

◗ **Bartender**

◗ **Bowling Equipment Worker**

◗ **Cashier**

◗ **Cashier-Checker**

◗ **Club Operations Assistant**

◗ **Child Development Program Ass.**

◗ **Cook**

◗ **Delivery Person**

◗ **Food Service Worker**

◗ **Lifeguards**

◗ **Maintenance Worker**

◗ **Motion Picture Projectionist**

◗ **Operations Assistant (Theater and Gym)**

◗ **Recreation Aide (Bingo, Woodworking, Gear Issue, Youth, Bowling and Sailing)**

◗ **Recreation Assistant (Bowling, Youth and Arts & Crafts)**

◗ **Snack Bar Clerk**

◗ **Ticket Seller**

◗ **Tools and Parts Attendant**

◗ **Waiter/Waitress**

Employment in Armed Forces Recreation

In addition to professional-level positions as MWR recreation specialists and managers, armed forces bases like the Sasebo, Japan, Naval Base offer hundreds of technical or maintenance jobs that are open both to Americans abroad and to local community residents.

PROFESSIONAL IDENTIFICATION IN RECREATION

What does being a *professional* mean? At the simplest level, it indicates that one is paid for one's work—as opposed to an *amateur*, who is not paid for it. Thus, an athlete who receives pay for playing for a team is classified as a professional. (Professional may also imply being very good at one's work; thus, the phrase he—or she—is a real pro!)

But this obviously is not a sufficient definition of the term in that many forms of paid work are *not* considered to be professional. A more complete definition of the term would suggest that a professional is one who has a high degree of status and specialized training and provides a significant form of public or social service. A position paper of the Society of Park and Recreation Educators defined *profession* as follows:

> A profession is a vocation whose practice is founded upon an understanding of the theoretical structure of some department of learning or science and upon the abilities accompanying such understanding. This understanding and these abilities are applied to the vital practical affairs of man. . . . The profession, serving the vital needs of man, considers its first ethical imperative to be altruistic service to the client.[5]

Within a number of specialized leisure-service areas today, such as company-sponsored employee programs, therapeutic recreation, or fitness and health spas, professionalism might be narrowly defined as the possession of a required certification based on a combination of education, experience, and examination. In other situations, membership in a designated professional association or society may be recognized as a hallmark of professionalism. In the public recreation and park field, the following criteria have generally been accepted as key elements of professionalism.

CRITERION 1: SOCIAL VALUE AND PURPOSE

The goals of organized community leisure-service agencies are described in Chapter 7. In general, they deal with such elements as improving the quality of life, contributing to personal development and social cohesion, helping to prevent socially destructive leisure pursuits, and protecting the environment.

In the nonprofit field, the YWCA is dedicated to the empowerment of women and girls and the elimination of racism. The oldest American organization owned and managed by women, its member organizations provide safety; shelter; day care; physical fitness and recreation programs; counseling; and other social, health, educational, and job-related services to millions of women and girls and their communities each year.

Other youth-serving organizations tend to have similar goals. While many of their services may not be specifically concerned with recreation, they *do* provide rich programs in sports, social activities, the arts, outdoor recreation, and other pastimes. In essence, leisure programs are used both as an end in themselves and as a means of achieving other agency goals of personal development and community improvement.

CRITERION 2: PUBLIC RECOGNITION

The rapid expansion of the leisure-service field over the past several decades does not necessarily mean that the public at large understands and respects it fully or that they regard it as a distinct area of professional service. To illustrate, most individuals today know what recreation is, and many regard it as an important part of their lives. Most are prepared to pay substantial portions of their income for recreational goods or services, such as memberships in health clubs, vacations, sports equipment, television sets, and other leisure-related fees and charges. However, they are often less willing to pay taxes in support of public recreation and park facilities and programs than they are to spend privately for their own leisure needs.

However, in a detailed analysis of the public's perception of local public recreation and park agencies, Godbey, Graefe, and James surveyed a broadly representative sample of 1,305 households throughout the United States. A substantial number of those queried had visited parks and playgrounds during the preceding year and had participated in such activities as sports leagues, educational classes, and artistic or cultural events in their communities. The majority of respondents reported significant individual, household, and community benefits provided by their local recreation and park agencies.[6]

Even though the value of organized recreation service may be acknowledged, how aware is the public at large of the leisure-service field *as a profession?* The likelihood is that most individuals recognize the roles of recreation professionals within specific areas of service. For example, they are likely to be familiar with the function of a recreation therapist in a mental hospital or nursing home or the function of a community center director, a park ranger, or a sports specialist in an armed forces recreation program.

What they tend not to understand is that recreation represents a field of practice that requires special expertise and educational preparation in a college or university. At issue is the image of the recreation professional.

Image of the Professional

The public's perception of those working in the recreation field tends to be unclear. Often, the recreation professional is confused with the physical educator because of the strong emphasis on sports in many recreation programs and the close connection between the two fields in early professional preparation.

Recreation professionals themselves have assumed such a wide variety of roles that no single image stands out. Sessoms commented a number of years ago that "we would like to be all things to all people: entertainers, promoters, counselors, psychiatric aides, and social analysts," concluding:

> I am afraid the public sees us either as ex-athletes, or gregarious, fun-and-game leaders wearing short pants, knee socks, and an Alpine hat, calling for all to join in.[7]

He later suggested that one of the problems was that recreation was not perceived as an occupational field that required special preparation and long-term training, and that it was ranked only "average" in remuneration. In part, the question of identity is one that workers in this field must settle for themselves. For example, a study of therapeutic recreation employees in Michigan showed that many respondents did not hold degrees in the field or belong to state or national professional organizations and were not professionally registered. It would seem clear that, if recreation and leisure-service employees are to sharpen their identity and support, they must enrich their own competence through specialized professional study and by joining organizations that strengthen their field.

CRITERION 3: SPECIALIZED PROFESSIONAL PREPARATION

A measure of the professional authority of any given field is the degree of specialized preparation that people must have to function in it. Typically, the most highly regarded professions in modern society, such as medicine or law, have rigorous requirements with respect to professional education. These have evolved through the years and involve higher education curricula on the graduate level, supported in some cases by required internships or periods of professional practice and by comprehensive examinations prepared or administered by professional societies.

Professional Preparation in Recreation and Parks

The early period of the development of higher education in recreation, parks, and leisure services was described earlier in this text. Over the past five decades, college and university curricula in recreation and parks have been developed on three levels: two-year, four-year, and graduate (master's degree and doctorate).

Two-Year Curricula   During the late 1960s and early 1970s, many community colleges began to offer associate degree programs in recreation and parks. Typically, these sought to prepare individuals on para- or sub-professional levels, rather than for supervisory or administrative roles. Most community colleges offered recreation majors a choice of two types of programs: terminal and transfer. *Terminal* programs were intended to equip students immediately for employment and gave heavy emphasis to developing basic, useful recreation leadership skills, often within a specific field of practice. *Transfer* programs were intended for students who hoped to transfer to four-year degree programs.

Four-Year Programs   The most widely found degree program in recreation and parks has been the four-year bachelor's degree curriculum. Initially, most such programs consisted of specialized degree options in college departments of health, physical education, and recreation—although some were located in departments or schools of landscape architecture, agriculture, forestry, or social work. Today, although many departments are still situated administratively in schools or colleges of health, physical education, and recreation, they have achieved a high level of curricular independence—with their own objectives, courses, degree requirements, and faculty.

Four-year programs typically have established degree options in areas such as recreation programming, recreation and park management, resource management, therapeutic recreation, and commercial recreation. The normal pattern has been to require all department majors to take certain *core* courses representing the generic needs of all pre-professionals, including basic courses in recreation history and philosophy, programming, management, and evaluation and/or research—and then to have a separate cluster of specialized courses for each different option.

With the onset of the era of economic austerity, many public recreation and park agencies had either frozen their staffs or cut back on them; as a result, there was little demand for new graduates in governmental leisure-service agencies. However, there was growing academic awareness of the job opportunities in other recreation areas. As a result, a number of college and university programs changed their titles and departmental affiliations to reflect the new interest in commercial recreation, travel and tourism, sports management, hotel and resort management, and similar specializations.

Typically, a considerable number of departments have added the term *tourism* to their titles and established enriched programs in this area—in some cases in collaboration with schools of business in their institutions. In other cases, therapeutic recreation majors were transferred administratively to departments or schools of public health or health-care services. As the most striking example of proliferation in this field, as of the late 1990s there were over 200 independent departments of sports management designed to meet personnel needs in this growing field.

In many cases, curriculum revision was based on the requirements or recommendations of professional societies, such as the Resort and Commercial Recreation Association (RCRA), the North American Society for Sport Management (NASSM), the National Association for Sport and Physical Education (NASPE), and the National Employee Services and Recreation Association (NESRA).

Master's Degree and Doctoral Programs   Although it is generally agreed that the four-year curriculum should provide a broad base of general or liberal arts education along with the core of essential knowledge underlying recreation service, the specific function of graduate education in this field is not as clearly defined. Some authorities have suggested that graduate curricula should accept only those students who have already taken a degree in recreation and should focus on providing advanced professional education within a specialized area of service. However, there tends to be little support for this position, and many graduate programs accept students from other undergraduate disciplines as well as those holding undergraduate degrees in recreation.

In general, authorities agree that master's degree work should involve advanced study in recreation and park administration or in some other specialized area of service, such as therapeutic recreation. The assumption is that individuals on this level are preparing for supervisory or managerial positions or, in some cases, roles as researchers or planners. In a minority of graduate curricula, strong emphasis is placed on the philosophical or sociological analysis of recreation and leisure.

Specialized Body of Knowledge

At the outset, many recreation and park degree programs were established as "minor" specializations in other areas of study, such as physical education. As such, they tended to lack theoretically based courses within the field of study. Over the past four decades, this deficiency has been largely corrected.

However, there continues to be some concern about whether the degree programs in this field are based on a legitimate field of academic study. Typically, critics argue that it is simply an area of practical management or, from a theoretical point of view, a field with a hodgepodge of ideas drawn from other disciplines—but lacking a unique body of knowledge. What *is* a professional body of knowledge? Thomas Yukic writes that it is

> an aggregate of theories, facts, principles, understandings, and skills, formally and systematically organized as academic courses of study. It must be agreed upon by a teaching faculty and approved by field professionals as providing a framework of vocational and educational concepts indispensable to proficiency in a recreation service job at a particular level.[8]

On undergraduate levels, a major element in the process of imparting practical knowledge and skills to students consists of required field work and internship experiences. While these vary from institution to institution, in general they require at least a semester of full-time commitment to work in an agency of high quality within the student's expressed field of professional interest. Such placements should extend far beyond an agency's using field work or internship students in routine or mechanical roles as a source of cheap labor. Instead, they are meant to involve a full range of realistic job assignments and exposures, as well as conscientious counseling and supervision by professional staff members.

The knowledge and skills components of higher education in recreation, parks, and leisure studies—while they may involve content taken from other scholarly disciplines or fields of practice—are formulated in terms that are specifically applicable to the recreation field.

Given the recent impressive growth in both research studies and publication of findings, it seems clear that the field does have a legitimate body of knowledge that must be possessed by professionals. Indeed, within some areas of practice, there has been systematic study of the competencies and knowledge that entry-level practitioners should possess, so as to provide a basis for curriculum development.

Increasingly, undergraduate curricula have been redesigned to include specific areas of knowledge and job performance based on standards of practice or certification examinations that have been developed by professional societies.

Accreditation in Higher Education

The most significant effort that has been made to upgrade curricular standards and practices in recreation, parks, and leisure studies has come in the accreditation process. The first attempt to develop a separate accreditation review process in recreation and parks was undertaken by the Federation of National Professional Organizations for Recreation in 1963, with a threefold purpose: (1) to develop for the National Commission on Accrediting a statement supporting recreation as a significant field of public service and as a profession; (2) to develop standards and evaluative criteria for recreation education at both undergraduate and graduate levels; and (3) to raise funds to carry out the actual process of accreditation.

In order to ensure broader representation in the process, a new Council on Accreditation was formed with representation from both the National Recreation and Park Association and the American Association for Leisure and Recreation. By 1980, approximately 30 college departments had applied for and received accreditation for all or part of their programs. In the course of this process, clearly defined standards and procedural guidelines for departments seeking accreditation had been developed, including guidelines regarding courses, administrative support, student selection and services, faculty resources, and other curriculum components.

In 1982, the Council on Postsecondary Accreditation agreed to consider the NRPA/AALR Council's application, an important first step in the process. In addition, steps were taken to streamline the accreditation operation by limiting its application only to baccalaureate programs and simplifying review procedures. After an arduous series of hearings and a review of the documents supporting the legitimacy of recreation, parks, and leisure studies as an area of significant scholarly concern, the Council on Postsecondary Accreditation finally granted recognition to it as a field of study and to the Council as the accrediting body. This served as a strong stimulus to the accreditation process, with the number of approved curricula increasing steadily from about 50 in the mid-1980s to over 100 in the late 1990s.

Academic accreditation has numerous benefits: (1) internal, in that it requires a focused effort to upgrade curriculum content and program standards and tends to create a higher level of respect for approved departments within overall institutions; and (2) external, in that it improves the level of instruction throughout the field and results in more highly qualified graduates entering the field.

CRITERION 4: EXISTENCE OF A PROFESSIONAL CULTURE

Another important characteristic of professions in modern society is that they have strong organizations, shared values, and traditions. How does the recreation and park field measure up to this criterion?

In both the United States and Canada, professional recreation societies have been in existence for a number of years. Like their counterparts in other professions, recreation and park associations have the following functions: they (1) regulate and set standards for professional development; (2) promote legislation for the advancement of the field; (3) develop programs of public information to improve understanding and support of the field; (4) sponsor conferences, publications, and field services to improve practices; and (5) press for higher standards of training, accreditation, and certification.

National Recreation and Park Association

Because of the varied nature of professional service in recreation and parks and the strong role played by citizens' groups and nonprofessional organizations, many different associations were established through the years to serve the field. Five of these (the National Recreation Association, the American Institute of Park Executives, the National Conference on State Parks, the American Association of Zoological Parks and Aquariums, and the American Recreation Society) merged into a single body in 1965, with Laurance S. Rockefeller as president. Within a year or two, other groups, such as the National Association of Recreation Therapists and the Armed Forces Section of the American Recreation Society, had merged their interests with the newly formed organization.

This national body, the National Recreation and Park Association, is an independent, nonprofit organization intended to promote the development of the recreation and park movement and the conservation of natural and human resources in the United States. It is directed by a board of trustees, which meets several times each year to guide its major policies. Several separate branches carry out the work and serve to coalesce the special interests of members; these include the American Park and Recreation Society, the National Society for Park Resources, the Ethnic Minority Society, the Armed Forces Recreation Society, the National Therapeutic Recreation Society, the Society of Park and Recreation Educators, and the National Student Recreation and Park Society.

Throughout the 1980s and 1990s, NRPA played a vigorous role in helping to bring about a fuller national consciousness of the value of recreation and leisure through varied public information campaigns, publications, research efforts, and legislative presentations. NRPA provides extensive services with respect to general and professionally oriented information through the NRPA/SCHOLE Network with links to Delphi and the Internet, the global database of communication that helps information flow through the government, business, education, research, and computer worlds.

NRPA publishes *Dateline,* a newsletter that focuses primarily on national issues related to recreation and parks. Through its Resource Development Division, it responds to thousands of inquiries and requests for technical assistance from practitioners. NRPA representatives regularly testify before congressional subcommittees in support of legislation and funding proposals dealing with the environment, social needs, and similar national problems. In cooperation with various universities and other professional organizations or through its separate branches or state societies, NRPA sponsors numerous important workshops, management schools, and seminars each year.

Role of NRPA Branches and State Societies

Each of NRPA's branches carries on vigorous programs related to its specialized area of interest. For example, the National Therapeutic Recreation Society is active in developing professional standards and an effective certification process for therapeutic recreation personnel. It also promotes research and publication, sponsors conferences and workshops, helps shape higher education curricula, and carries out legislative and lobbying campaigns to block federal cutbacks in social services and achieve a higher level of support for therapeutic recreation services.

Despite this record of accomplishment, some of NTRS's members were discontented with the support given them by the national organization and complained that it failed to recognize their authority with respect to therapeutic recreation service and programming for special populations. As a result, a number of leading therapeutic recreation specialists formed a new national organization, the American Therapeutic Recreation Association, in the mid-1980s to focus more sharply on the concerns of this specialized field.

The NRPA branch directly concerned with professional education and development is the Society of Park and Recreation Educators (SPRE), which defines its mission as that of an association of scholars who believe that leisure makes a valuable contribution to society:

> The Society facilitates for its members, the park and recreation profession, and society at large the continuing investigation of leisure and the development and dissemination of a body of knowledge that verifies its contributions. . . .
>   Furthermore, the Society supports the development of techniques to improve professional practice and serves as a conduit for demonstrating the impact leisure has on society, including communities, the economy, and the development of individuals.

Canadian Professional Societies.   The major Canadian organization in this field is the Canadian Parks/Recreation Association (CPRA), which has its national office in Ottawa, Ontario. Its major objectives are:

To acquaint Canadians with the significance of leisure in a changing society

To assist in the development, organization, and promotion of the parks and recreation service delivery system in Canada

To involve the membership in the development of national policies of significance to the parks and recreation movement in Canada

To promote effective planning, design, and development of parks and recreation facilities in Canada

The CPRA receives substantial support from the Canadian federal government. It has approximately 3,000 members; publishes a monthly magazine, *Recreation Canada*; and, like NRPA, sponsors an annual conference, provides consultation and technical assistance to both government and nongovernment agencies concerned with recreation, parks, and leisure, and generally promotes this field throughout Canada and internationally. In addition, each of the Canadian provinces has its own recreation and park professional society, and there are specialized organizations related to camping, industrial/employee recreation, and similar functions.

Other Professional Organizations

Many other organizations sponsor programs supporting the recreation and park field or one of its specialized components. For example, the American Alliance for Health, Physical Education, Recreation, and Dance (AAHPERD) has several thousand members who have a specialized interest in education for leisure, school-sponsored recreation, the promotion of school camping and outdoor education, and adapted physical education and recreation programs for the disabled.

The branch of AAHPERD that has been most directly concerned with these functions has been the American Association for Leisure and Recreation (AALR), which has (1) worked closely on the accreditation process with NRPA through the Joint Accreditation Steering Committee and later the National Council on Accreditation; (2) played a key role in promoting community education and leisure education projects; (3) published *Leisure Today*, an outstanding series of special-theme inserts in the

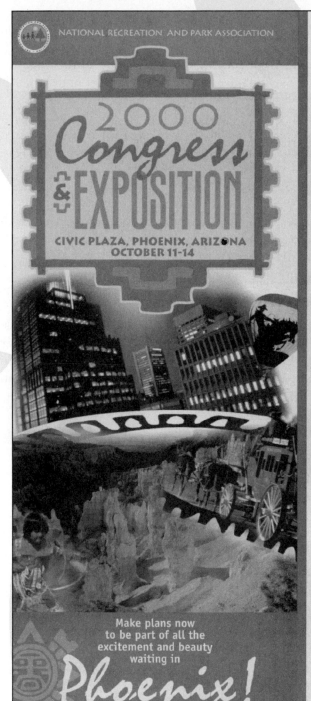

2000
Congress
& EXPOSITION

CIVIC PLAZA, PHOENIX, ARIZONA
OCTOBER 11-14

Make plans now
to be part of all the
excitement and beauty
waiting in

Phoenix!

CONGRESS KEYNOTE SPEAKERS

Tom Whittaker

Opening General Session, Wednesday

On May 27, 1998, an extraordinary event took place on the world's tallest and most treacherous mountain. Tom Whittaker became the first human with a disability to climb to the top of the world.

Nineteen years earlier, his life was drastically altered when a drunk driver hit his vehicle. He sustained multiple fractures to both legs, loss of a kneecap, and amputation of his right foot. His doctors told him he might never walk again.

His recovery, both physical and emotional, is a most inspirational story. Ever aware of the impact of his message on others, he will address the NRPA delegates about his extraordinary experiences. His achievement and the hard work, discipline, confidence, and faith that led to it, form a compelling and universal story. A story that will remind all of us of the infinite power we all possess as individuals.

Bil Keane

Closing General Session, Saturday,

The National Recreation and Park Association is pleased to have Bil Keane as the Keynote Speaker at the Closing General Session. Delegates are aware of Bil's creative ability to portray typical family life in America, through the cartoon "Family Circus."

"Family Circus" regularly rates number one in newspaper surveys and has won several awards. In 1982, Bil was named "Cartoonist of the Year" by the National Cartoonists Society. Millions of Americans regularly follow the lives of Mommy and Daddy, Billy, Dolly, Jeffy, and PJ. Two dogs, a cat, and grandparents round out the cast. These characters—their ups and downs, trials and laughs, and mischief and merrymaking are based on his own family.

This promises to be a most entertaining, illustrative presentation by the creator of a cartoon panel that appears weekly in more than 1,500 newspapers worldwide.

Promoting Professionalism

Each year, thousands of recreation and park professionals, civic officials, board members, educators, and students attend the National Recreation and Park Congress. Varied workshops, general sessions, exhibitor displays and continuing education events provide inspiration and expertise—along with exposure to outstanding programs in different regions of the country.

Journal of Physical Education, Recreation, and Dance; and (4) assisted in job placement of recreation personnel and similar functions.

Other important organizations that have made important contributions to this field include: (1) the American Camping Association, the national professional organization of the organized camping movement; (2) the American College Personnel Association, which includes many people working in student residence halls and campus unions; (3) the American Association of College Unions, which has a similar function; (4) the Amateur Athletic Union, which promotes and sets standards for a wide range of participant sports in the United States; (5) the National Intramural/Recreational Sports Association, which promotes intramural sports competition in colleges and universities; (6) the National Employee Services and Recreation Association (renamed in 2000 the Employee Services Management Association), which serves personnel directors and other professionals providing recreation, fitness, and related personnel services; and (7) the World Leisure and Recreation Association, which deals with the international recreation and leisure movement.

In addition to such organizations, which tend to represent chiefly nonprofit branches of the overall leisure-service movement, there are hundreds of other trade associations that promote individual sports but are also allied with commercial businesses.

It is clear that no one organization can possibly speak for or represent the entire leisure-service field today. As each specialized area of recreation has become more active and successful, it has tended to form its own professional society to deal with its unique needs and interests.

CRITERION 5: CREDENTIALING, STANDARDS FOR SCREENING PERSONNEL

Credentials are qualifications that must be satisfied through a formal review process before an individual is permitted to engage in professional practice in a given field. Obviously, this is a very important criterion of professionalism. If anyone can call himself or herself a qualified practitioner in a given field—without appropriate training or experience—that field has very low standards and is not likely to gain or hold the public's respect.

Because the recreation and park field has been so diversified, no single standard or selection process has been devised for those who seek employment in it. However, within the field of recreation and parks, a number of special screening procedures have been developed, including: (1) registration; (2) certification and licensing; (3) civil service position requirements; and (4) other job specifications or qualification systems, such as those established by national voluntary organizations, which outline personnel qualifications and guidelines for their local branches to follow.

Registration

This procedure represented an early effort to rely on professional societies to screen and identify those who are considered to be qualified in their respective fields. North Carolina in 1954 became the first state to establish a registration plan for recreation administrators in local communities. During the 1950s, a number of recreation and park societies in such other states as California, New York, Wisconsin, Washington, Colorado, and Texas also initiated registration plans that outlined and administered requirements to be met at different levels of professional or paraprofessional practice.

Because of the difficulty of maintaining standards through 50 different state plans, the National Recreation and Park Association developed and implemented a process of national registration. Following guidelines set forth in a model registration plan approved by the NRPA Board of Trustees in 1973, it reviewed and approved the plans of a number of state societies, encouraging a standardized approach to registration and reciprocity agreements among these states.

In 1970, the National Therapeutic Recreation Society developed its own registration plan. However, as the more effective process of certification became accepted, NTRS disbanded its Registration Board and its functions were transferred to the National Council for Therapeutic Recreation Certification, an independently administered body of the National Recreation and Park Association. It was agreed that the existing levels of service would be grouped under a new two-level system: professional (therapeutic recreation specialist) and paraprofessional (therapeutic recreation assistant). It should be noted that at this point the term *registration* was changed to *certification*.

Certification and Licensing

These two terms refer to the process of examining the credentials of persons in given occupational or professional fields and, if they meet stated qualifications, giving them permission to practice. *Licensing* governs the scope of professional practice, defining the specific services that may be provided, the populations to be served, and other conditions. Licensing applies not only to health-related-fields but also to such areas of employment as driving taxis or operating barber shops or beauty parlors. Stumbo cites the U.S. Department of Health, Education, and Welfare's definition of licensing as the process by which an agency of government

> grants permission to persons meeting predetermined qualifications to engage in a given occupation upon finding that the applicant had attained the minimal degree of competency necessary to ensure that the public health [and] safety will be reasonably well protected.[9]

Stumbo goes on to point out that licensing is the most restrictive form of credentialing, since it requires state governments to enact legislation defining the scope of professional practice and makes it illegal for those not licensed to perform services within this scope. Customarily, licensing programs are overseen by state regulatory agencies, which screen applicants, set practice standards and codes of conduct, and investigate charges of incompetence or impropriety against licensees, taking necessary disciplinary action where justified.

In contrast, *certification* refers to the process through which a nongovernmental organization grants recognition—usually in the form of the right to use a professional title—to an individual who has met predetermined qualifications specified by that organization. Certification is usually a voluntary process and is not always required to practice in the profession, although states, voluntary or therapeutic agencies, and other hiring bodies may choose to require a given certification title of candidates for employment.

Certification in Therapeutic Recreation. As indicated earlier, therapeutic recreation was one of the first professional specializations in recreation to initiate a strong national registration plan. Its revised certification standards, instituted in 1981, specified that, to become a qualified therapeutic recreation specialist on the professional level, a person needed to meet one of four optional criteria. These ranged from holding a baccalaureate or higher degree from an accredited curriculum with a major or option in therapeutic recreation to an "equivalency" combination of five years of full-time paid experience in an approved therapeutic recreation setting and a degree in a recreation-related field including upper-division therapeutic recreation credits. On the paraprofessional level, candidates for certification as therapeutic recreation assistants were given five similar but less stringent options.

National Certification in Recreation, Parks, and Leisure Services

In the early 1980s, the NRPA Board of Trustees set in motion a two- to five-year plan that sought to link the three elements of certification, accreditation, and continuing education in a certification procedure that would apply broadly to the overall recreation, parks, and leisure-service field.

The new Model Certification Plan for Recreation, Park Resources, and Leisure Services Personnel was designed to provide a national means of attesting to the educational and experiential qualifications of people receiving compensation in public, quasi-public, and private employment in the recreation field. Its purpose was to

establish standards for certification in recreation, park resources, and leisure-services professions; provide recognition of individuals who have qualified; and afford a guarantee to employers that certified personnel have attained stated education and experience qualifications.

Among the unique elements of the plan was the stipulation that everyone seeking certification after November 1, 1986, would be required to hold a degree from a college or university with a curriculum accredited by NRPA. Other stipulations were that recertification would be mandatory every two years, beginning in 1983, and that individuals would be required to earn a minimum of two Continuing Education Units (CEUs) or equivalent college course work within each 24-month period from the date of certification. Implied in the plan was that many of the professional development programs offered or sponsored by NRPA would be approved for CEU credit.

This ambitious plan, however, was largely unenforced in government or voluntary agencies that chose not to comply with it. A number of professionals were outspoken in their opposition to a strong certification requirement because of its effect on thousands of practitioners and hundreds of institutions not meeting NRPA's criteria.

After a lengthy process of development, a Certified Leisure Professional (CLP) Examination was administered for the first time in October 1990. Testing three ability areas of applicants (knowledge, application to professional concerns, and analysis of program solutions), the examination dealt with four major content areas: (1) leisure-service management, including budget and finance, staff development and supervision, and policy formulation; (2) leisure/recreation program delivery, including assessment, planning, implementation, and evaluation; (3) natural resource facilities management; and (4) therapeutic recreation service.

Under the NRPA plan, three levels of certification are provided: Certified Leisure Professional (CLP), Certified Leisure Provisional Professional (CLPP), and Certified Leisure Technician (CLT).

Continuing Education. A key element in the certification process is the requirement for continuing education participation by professionals. Continuing education represents a noncredit program of study planned and organized around learning experiences designed to meet specific professional objectives. One of the requirements to remain certified is the attainment of two Continuing Education Units (CEUs), requiring 20 contact hours in organized learning activities over a two-year period. Examples of continuing education programs are shown in Figure 11.3, which shows training programs offered by a single organization in Oglebay, West Virginia, throughout the year; and Figure 11.4, an example of many major events sponsored or cosponsored by the National Recreation and Park Association.

Problems with Enforcement. Requirements were established that by 1990 all states have their own professional certification plans based on NRPA's national guidelines—including the stipulation for maintaining certification through continuing education participation—and that the job specifications of all administrative employees in public recreation and park departments include such certification as a requirement. By the late 1980s, it was apparent that such requirements could not be widely enforced in light of the inability of professional societies to impose their standards on legally independent government bodies without formal legislation to support them.

Civil Service in Recreation and Parks

Across a wide range of public, tax-supported departments—including not only local government agencies but also federal, state, provincial, and armed forces recreation programs—the most common means of screening applicants for government employment is through civil service procedures. *Civil service* is a general descriptive term that applies to many different agencies, boards, and personnel systems that attempt to provide a politically neutral method of employment under which individuals are hired because they meet formal qualifications rather than because they have political contacts or influence. Often referred to as the "merit system," civil service involves a complicated job classification system with promotional steps and salary ranges under many job titles. It also includes detailed procedures for eligibility, examinations, appointment, probationary periods, promotion, separation, and personnel rights and benefits.

On the federal level, full-time professional employees in such agencies as the National Park Service or the Veterans Administration are normally part of the federal civil service system. Similarly, most state employees (with the exception of upper-level administrators and part-time or seasonal workers) in hospitals, penal institutions, recreation and park departments, and other agencies fall under civil service.

Management Training Schools & Institutes

at Oglebay

Wheeling, WV

The following nationally recognized training schools will be offered in 2000 for professional staff and management training. Continuing education courses have been presented at Oglebay since 1960.

Supervisors' Management School
In cooperation with North Carolina State University
November 1999

National Institute of Golf Management
In cooperation with the National Golf Foundation
January 2000

Oglebay Entertainment Business Institute
In cooperation with the International Association of Family Entertainment Centers
January 2000

Park & Recreation Maintenance Management School
Presented by National Recreation & Park Association in cooperation with
North Carolina State University
January 2000

Schools for Zoo & Aquarium Personnel
In cooperation with the American Zoological Association
February 2000

School of RV Park & Campground Management
In cooperation with the National Association of RV Parks & Campgrounds
February 2000

School of Sports Management
In cooperation with North Carolina State University
February 2000

Business Institute for Park & Recreation Professionals
Presented by National Recreation & Park Association cooperation with
North Carolina State University
March 2000

Medical Transport Leadership Institute
In cooperation with the Association of Air Medical Services
April 2000

Public Assembly Facility Management School
In cooperation with the International Association of Assembly Managers Foundation
June 2000

Institute for Quality Environmental Management
August 2000

For more information and detailed brochures, call 1-888–OGLEBAY, x4019
www.oglebay-resort.com

Continuing Education Opportunities

For many years, management training programs in a variety of important areas related to recreation and park operations have been offered at Oglebay, West Virginia—in cooperation both with universities and leading national associations.

FIGURE 11.4

National Aquatic Conference

Linking commercial, public, and other special-interest recreation organizations, the National Recreation and Park Association offers a variety of special conferences and management schools each year. Other associations in such areas as theme or water-park management, conference operations, zoo and aquarium maintenance and other specializations, sponsor similar national programs.

Despite such requirements, a number of studies in the 1970s and 1980s indicated that in the United States substantial numbers of superintendents, directors, division heads, and district supervisors of recreation and parks lacked bachelor's degrees in recreation or related fields. Among recreation supervisors and center directors in five major categories, 42 percent had less than a bachelor's degree. Similarly, in Canada, despite efforts to promote certification of personnel, a study in the early 1970s showed a low level of specialized academic training among employees in public recreation and park agencies and in voluntary, nonprofit agencies and institutions.

Clearly, efforts to upgrade civil service standards should continue to be made, in tandem with the efforts being made nationally and on the state level to gain compliance with the NRPA certification plan. The fact that civil service is *in place* and actually governs current hiring and personnel practices means that it has the potential for being strengthened and being used more effectively to improve professional performance. In a number of states, approved standards for therapeutic recreation personnel—not only in state agencies but also in private or voluntary institutions such as nursing homes, which come under the jurisdiction of state health departments—have been modeled on the personnel standards of the National Therapeutic Recreation Society.

Standards in Nonpublic Leisure-Service Agencies

Both the National Recreation and Park Association and the American Association for Leisure and Recreation, which have been the prime movers in the attempt to strengthen professionalism in leisure-service agencies, have had as their main targets either public recreation and park departments or schools and colleges. In general, the employees of voluntary agencies, such as nonprofit, commercial, private, or employer sponsors, have not been identified as key elements in the recreation movement. Hiring in such agencies has therefore not been influenced by the NRPA/AALR accreditation efforts or the certification plan just described.

However, national organizations like the Ys, Scouts, and Boys' and Girls' Clubs are obviously concerned with helping their local councils, branches, or other direct-service units maintain a high level of staff competence. Their national offices therefore typically prepare job descriptions or recommended standards for employment within given categories of professional positions.

The National Council of the YMCA recommends that YMCA staff members have the following qualifications: (1) commitment to YMCA purposes and goals; (2) integrity of character and interest in working with young people for their personal and social growth; (3) sound health; and (4) an undergraduate degree or equivalent, preferably in one of the social or behavioral sciences, such as psychology, economics, sociology, government, or education, or in liberal arts generally. In addition, professional training of YMCA staff directors should cover such areas as leadership of informal groups; counseling and guidance; administration of social and religious agencies; leadership supervision and training; and understanding of the history, objectives, programs, and methods of the YMCA.

Similarly, the Boys and Girls Clubs of America has a recommended personnel hiring policy for professional staff workers. To be certified as a full-time administrator in a Club, one must meet the following criteria: (1) a degree from an accredited four-year college; (2) satisfactory performance in two years of program leadership or administrative work in a Club or as a member of the National Staff; and (3) a total of 10 training credits in conferences and training sessions sponsored by the Regional or National Manpower Development Committees of the Boys and Girls Clubs of America or other authorized training institution.

Beyond such requirements, in such areas as aquatics, fitness services, and varied outdoor recreation skills, leisure-service organizations of all types usually require staff members to hold certification from appropriate professional societies, both to upgrade program quality and to serve as protection against claims of negligence in case of accidents or deaths.

CRITERION 6: CODE OF ETHICAL PRACTICE

A final important measure of any profession is that it typically outlines the public responsibilities of practitioners and sets up a code of ethical behavior. In fields such as medicine or law, where the possibility of malpractice is great and the stakes are high, strict codes of ethics prevail—although they tend to be enforced rather inconsistently.

In the field of leisure services, it might appear that any issues related to ethical practice are not as critical as in these other professions. However, in specialized areas such as therapeutic recreation service, where patients or clients are likely to be physically, emotionally, or economically vulnerable, the opportunities for harmful, negligent, or unprofessional behavior are great. In other areas of leisure service as well, professionals should have a strong sense of obligation to those they serve, to their communities, and to the profession itself.

For these reasons, in the early 1980s, the National Recreation and Park Association prepared a recommended code of ethics, which included general principles that applied to state recreation and park societies and affiliated professional organizations, and a set of special principles that related to such NRPA branches as the Society of Park and Recreation Educators and the American Park and Recreation Society. The general principles presented in this document were broad, including such statements as the need for the professional to be "of high moral character in fulfilling obligations to and protective of the public's trust." Gerald Fain, however, argued that ethical codes should more directly

> reflect the ongoing business of the practitioner, the felt need within the society, and the critical issues identified by the profession. Commitment to the study, promotion, and regulation of ethical practices has a beginning but it has no end. When people actively work to enhance the lives of others, they accept a responsibility that is greater than themselves.[10]

In a 1986 survey of state recreation and park societies, Ira Shapiro found that societies in only 17 states and the District of Columbia reported having a written code of ethics, while even fewer reported having a state code of ethics committee.[11] Nevertheless, NRPA continued to address the ethics issue, forming a new task force in 1991 to formulate a concise code of ethics that would apply to all organization members. It was initially agreed that this code should be short, concise, and backed up by a plan for enforcement. However, in a series of hearings, considerable resistance was expressed to the enforcement concept and to any punitive procedures, and the enforcement element was therefore eliminated from the code.

In a much more extensive statement, the National Therapeutic Recreation Society approved a Code of Ethics in 1990 and a set of Interpretive Guidelines in 1994. This organization's overall code contained an explanatory preamble followed by six detailed sections on the obligations of professionals and the profession itself to individuals served, to other individuals and society, to colleagues, to the profession, and to "professional virtue." One of the specific guidelines in the NTRS Code presents the following statements under the heading of *The Obligation of the Professional to the Individual*:

> A. *Well-Being: Professionals' foremost concern is the well-being of the people they serve. They do everything reasonable in their power and within the scope of professional practice to benefit them. Above all, professionals cause no harm.*
>
> Therapeutic recreation professionals enter into or continue professional relationships based on their ability to meet the needs of clients appropriately. Similarly, they terminate service and professional relationships which are no longer required or which cease to serve the client's best interests. Recognizing that the private and personal nature of the therapeutic relationship may unrealistically intensify clients' feelings toward them, they take special efforts to maintain professional objectivity. They are careful to avoid, and do not initiate, personal relationships or dual roles with clients.
>
> Appropriate settings are chosen for one-on-one interactions, in order to protect both the client and the professional from actual or imputed physical or mental harm.
>
> When the client's condition indicates that there is clear and imminent danger to the client or others, the therapeutic recreation professional must take reasonable personal action or inform responsible authorities. Consultation with other professionals must be used where possible. The assumption of responsibility for the client's behavior must be taken only after careful deliberation.

AGENCY ACCREDITATION PROCESS

A final example of the thrust toward fuller professionalism in the organized recreation, park, and leisure-service field is found in the accreditation process for local, public departments initiated in the mid-1990s. Van Anderson sums up progress in this area:

> Since February of 1994 when the Monmouth County, New Jersey, Park System was accredited by the Commission for the Accreditation of Park and Recreation Agencies (CAPRA), interest in agency accreditation has steadily grown. . . . Those agencies currently accredited range in size from the Metropolitan Dade County, Florida, Park and Recreation Department, serving a population of 2.5 million, to the Newton, Kansas, Recreation Commission, serving 16,000 persons.[12]

At this time, NRPA's executive director commented, "Because the agency accreditation process is voluntary, those who seek or facilitate it represent the best of our profession. For everyone involved, the level of professionalism is increased."[13]

Within the various drives to improve professional practice that have been described in this chapter, periodic monitoring and research projects are carried out to ascertain their progress. For example, M. Deborah Bialeschki has conducted regular surveys of college and university curricula in recreation, parks, and leisure studies, with the most recent report published in February 2000.[14] Similarly, detailed analyses have been conducted of specific curriculum areas such as therapeutic recreation by Stumbo and Carter, among others.[15]

CURRENT LEVEL OF PROFESSIONAL STATUS

When the six accepted criteria of professionalism reviewed here are used as the basis for judgment, it is apparent that the recreation, parks, and leisure-service field has made considerable progress toward becoming a recognized profession.

Some elements are already securely in place, such as the development of a unique body of knowledge and the establishment of a network of college and university programs of professional preparation. As for the professional organization element, the National Recreation and Park Association and other national associations or societies do represent a significant force for upgrading and monitoring performance in the recreation field, but their attempts to serve the interests of a wide variety of leisure-service agencies also illustrate the field's continuing fragmentation. Realistically, many practitioners in such specialized disciplines as therapeutic recreation service, employee services and recreation, and varied aspects of commercial recreation tend to identify more closely with their separate fields than they do with the overall leisure-service field. Even in the more difficult areas of certification and the development of ethical codes, some considerable progress has been made although the concept of enforcement continues to be a problem in both areas.

Not all practitioners and educators are fully in favor of strengthening accreditation and certification requirements. For example, some professors have expressed concern about the impact of accreditation on smaller college leisure-studies curricula that are unable to meet its requirements. Kauffman and Logan write:

> Currently the park and recreation field faces a problem which, if not corrected, may seriously limit the number of students prepared by colleges and universities for careers in the park and recreation field. As accreditation becomes more of a criterion in hiring newly graduated professionals, viable small college programs could be eliminated from the delivery system.[16]

Similarly, in a survey of college and university educators within this field that sought to determine the level of priority that should be given to different needs or professional issues, the goal of strengthening drives toward professionalism was rated relatively low (see page 359).

Nonetheless, professionalism in recreation, parks, and leisure services has increased greatly over the past five decades, along with the growing recognition of the field's value in modern society. Because of the immense scope of the diversified recreation field in terms of employment, it has the potential for becoming even more influential in contributing to community well-being in the years ahead.

SUMMARY

Recreation, parks, and leisure services have grown immensely as a career field, with several million men and women now employed in different areas of organized recreation programming, facilities management, or other leisure-related functions. Of this overall group, it is estimated that several hundred thousand individuals should be regarded as professionals due to their academic training, job functions, and organizational affiliations.

This chapter describes several important criteria of professionalism, including the following:

1. Having a significant degree of social value, in terms of providing benefits to individual participants and/or to community life
2. Being recognized by the public as a meaningful area of social service or as a legitimate occupational field
3. Requiring specialized professional preparation on the college or university level, based on a distinct body of theoretical and practical knowledge
4. Possessing a professional culture that involves national and regional organizations that sponsor conferences, research, publications, and other efforts to upgrade practice, and that promote collegiality and a sense of commitment among the practitioners
5. Having a credentialing system to ensure that only qualified individuals—usually identified through a system of certification or licensing—are permitted to undertake professional-level tasks
6. Having a code of ethics to ensure that responsible and effective service is provided to the public

While the recreation, parks, and leisure-services field has not as yet met all of these criteria of professionalism fully, it has made substantial progress on most of them. As recreation and leisure become increasingly important aspects of life in the years ahead, the challenge to the leisure-service field will be to become even more highly professionalized by building on the foundation that has already been laid.

Chief emphasis is given in the chapter to professionalization in public, tax-supported agencies. However, numerous references are also provided to career development and professionalization in therapeutic recreation, nonprofit agencies, and other types of organizations.

QUESTIONS FOR CLASS DISCUSSION OR ESSAY EXAMINATIONS

1. Before reading this chapter, what was your understanding of the meaning of the term *profession*? Since reading the chapter, has your understanding of this word changed? How important do you believe it is for any occupational field to be regarded as a profession?
2. There are several criteria that are generally accepted as hallmarks of professionalism, such as having a social mandate or set of important social values or having a

body of specialized knowledge. Select any four of these, and discuss the extent to which you believe the recreation, park, and leisure-service field meets these criteria of professionalism.

3. Some educators believe that the field of professional preparation in recreation and parks has two contrasting sets of priorities: (1) the need to provide practical skills in personnel management, budgeting, marketing, programming, and similar functions; and (2) the need to focus on the theoretical (philosophical, historical, etc.) study of recreation and leisure. Do you believe this is a significant concern? Present an argument for either of these two positions.

4. The leisure-service field has developed into 10 different specialized areas, such as public, nonprofit, commercial and therapeutic recreation—with some of these having a number of distinct subspecializations. Do you believe that it is possible for this fragmented field to develop and maintain a single, common identity in order to gain fuller public support and understanding? How could this be done?

ENDNOTES

1 *Occupational Quarterly* (U.S. Department of Labor, 1998–1999): 152–153.

2 C. Edginton, D. Jordan, D. DeGraaf, and S. Edginton, *Leisure and Life Satisfaction: Foundational Perspectives* (Dubuque, Ia.: Brown and Benchmark, 1995): 350.

3 "Professionals in Managed Recreation," *Recreation, Sports, and Leisure* (August 1985): 49.

4 *Statistical Abstract of the United States* (U.S. Department of Labor, 1995): 416, 414, 322.

5 *Education for Leisure*, Position Paper of Society of Park and Recreation Educators (1975).

6 G. Godbey, A. Graefe, and S. James, "Reality and Perception: Where Do We Fit In?" *Parks and Recreation* (January 1993): 76–83.

7 H. Douglas Sessoms, "A Critical Look at the Recreation Movement," *Recreation for the Ill and Handicapped* (Washington, D.C.: National Association of Recreation Therapists, 1965): 11, 14.

8 Thomas Yukic, "Advancing a Professional Body of Knowledge," *California Parks and Recreation* (December 1980/January 1981): 6.

9 Norma Stumbo, "Overview of State Credentialing Concerns: A Focus on Licensure," *Therapeutic Recreation Journal* (2nd Quarter, 1990): 40–59.

10 Gerald Fain, "To Protect the Public: A Matter of Ethics," *Parks and Recreation* (December 1983): 53.

11 Ira Shapiro, "The Existence of Ethical Codes and Ethics Code Committees in State Recreation and Park Societies," *Pennsylvania Recreation and Park Society Magazine* (Summer 1987): 3.

12 V. F. Anderson, "Accreditation: A Standard of Quality for Park and Recreation Agencies," *Parks and Recreation* (July 1997): 40.

13 Ibid.

14 M. D. Bialeschki, "Baccalaureate Programs in Recreation, Park Resources, and Leisure Services," *Parks and Recreation* (February 2000): 82–92.

15 N. Stumbo and M. J. Carter, "National Therapeutic Recreation Curriculum Study, Part A: Accreditation, Curriculum, and Internship Characteristics," *Therapeutic Recreation Journal* (1st Quarter 1999): 46–59.

16 R. Kauffman and A. Logan, "Are We Accrediting Small College Park and Recreation Programs Out of Business?" *Trends* (Vol. 30, No. 3, 1993): 35.

CHAPTER 12

PHILOSOPHY OF RECREATION AND LEISURE:
Future Perspectives

◆ ◆ ◆

Definitions of Philosophy

. . . [T]he science which investigates the most general facts and principles of reality and of human nature and conduct; specifically . . . the science which comprises logic, ethics, aesthetics, metaphysics, and the history of knowledge.

The body of principles or general conceptions underlying a given branch of learning or major discipline, a religious system, a human activity, or the like, and the application of it.

An integrated and consistent personal attitude toward life or reality or toward certain phases of it, especially if this attitude is expressed in beliefs or principles of conduct.[1]

◆ ◆ ◆

INTRODUCTION

The remarkable growth of organized recreation, park, and leisure services throughout the United States and Canada has been documented throughout this text. Despite the impressive recent history of this social movement and field of professional activity, a number of serious questions still exist in regard to the appropriate role of recreation in community and national life as we begin the twenty-first century.

For example, how can recreation contribute more effectively to the battle against such social ills as poverty, racial or ethnic hostility, crime and delinquency, and economic deprivation? What solutions can be found for the overcrowding and vandalism that affect many urban, state, and federal parks and recreation facilities?

How should the major priorities of organized recreation service in the United States and Canada be determined? In what ways can government provide more effective and efficient services in this field? What are the special responsibilities of organized recreation toward the physically and mentally disabled, toward the aging, or toward those who may have had inadequate opportunities in the past because of their gender or other demographic factors?

How have technological developments—especially computers, electronic forms of amusement, and the Internet—affected both leisure patterns and the management of recreation programs? How will leisure-service professionals respond to such changes in the years ahead?

Should recreation sponsors simply seek to meet the expressed wishes of the public for enjoyable play, or do they have a moral responsibility to present only socially constructive and desirable leisure programs? With regard to violence, overemphasis on winning in sport, and policies governing drinking, drugs, gambling, or sexually oriented play, what should the role of recreation professionals be?

How will the changing social and economic conditions in the decades ahead affect the public's leisure values and patterns of participation, and how can recreation, park, and leisure-service professionals and organizations respond effectively to the challenges of the future?

NEED FOR A SOUND PHILOSOPHICAL BASIS

Obviously, such issues should be resolved within the context of a coherent set of values, moral beliefs, and social priorities. What is needed is a sound philosophy of recreation and leisure that can serve the leisure-service field in ongoing policy formulation and program development.

Meaning of Philosophy

The term *philosophy* often conveys an image of ivory tower abstraction, divorced from practical or realistic concerns. Understandably, many practitioners are likely to be suspicious of any approach that appears to be overly theoretical, rather than pragmatic and action-based.

How then is philosophy to be defined? Of the possible examples presented on page 338, the second one, stating that philosophy consists of the body of principles underlying a major discipline or human activity, as expressed in guidelines for conduct, is the most useful for our purpose.

This chapter will *not* present a single philosophy of recreation and leisure and argue that it represents the only acceptable system of goals and values. Instead, it will (1) briefly review a number of approaches taken by philosophers and other scholars to the analysis of recreation and leisure in the past; (2) identify seven prevailing approaches to providing organized recreation services in the present; (3) discuss various changes that are occurring today in terms of work and leisure availability, demographic influences on leisure, and prevailing social values as they affect recreational participation; (4) present a number of forecasts of future trends; and (5) suggest some guiding principles for the organization of community recreation services in the years ahead.

Past Views of Recreation and Leisure

As earlier chapters have shown, recreation, play, and leisure have been examined by numerous philosophers throughout history. Obviously, the views expressed reflected not only the personal beliefs of the individual writers but also the dominant religious and social ideals of each period, ranging from the early Greek and Roman era through the Industrial Revolution.

Greek philosophers like Aristotle and Plato described the significant role of leisure and play in Athenian life and childhood upbringing, and authors during the Renaissance and Reformation periods supported the value of play in early education. During the nineteenth century, fears about the danger of illicit uses of leisure were widely expressed, and a system of "rational" recreation that would support the Protestant work ethic and the expanding capitalist system gained support in the industrialized West.

Early Twentieth-Century Views

In the beginning decades of the twentieth century, as the recreation and park movement gained momentum, pioneer recreation leaders like Joseph Lee, Jane Addams, and Luther Halsey Gulick developed a philosophy of play and recreation that stressed their importance as vital aspects of community life, important forms of education, and essential ways of combatting juvenile delinquency and other problems afflicting urban industrial life. Play was widely viewed as an instrument for spiritual development, and leisure and recreation were praised as a means of achieving the happy life through promoting moral values and engaging in the "best" activities of which one was capable.

Recreation and Leisure as Social Instruments

During the Great Depression of the 1930s, recreation was used to provide an alternative to the civic despair stemming from unemployment and widespread poverty. The federal government spent huge sums on parks and other leisure facilities and employed thousands of recreation leaders, as well as artists, writers, and performers, to enrich popular culture. In the 1960s, recreation was used as a social instrument during the so-called war on poverty. During the late 1960s and early 1970s, as rebellious youth protested against traditional establishment values, leisure came to be perceived as a means of achieving holistic life values. Recreation, with its implied freedom and emphasis on self-discovery and self-actualization, was also perceived as an ideal vehicle for achieving the goals of the "counterculture."

It was at this time that writers like James Murphy, David Gray, and Seymour Greben urged the organized recreation system to respond forcefully to the critical social challenges of disadvantaged urban populations, minority groups, women, the disabled, and environmental population. They sought the fullest possible mobilization of the recreation and park movement to respond in a dynamic way to such needs, to form an effective political force, and to collaborate with other citizen groups and environmental organizations to make recreation and parks a vital force in national life.[2]

Trends in the 1980s and 1990s

The prevailing trend in many public and voluntary recreation and park agencies during the 1980s essentially reflected a cautious philosophy that sought to maintain support by offering programs and services that met important human needs but were non-controversial and did not break new ground. As the fiscal crisis lessened, many recreation and park agencies began to recover, rehabilitating major parks and developing new facilities and programs as part of their cities' efforts to improve their images and popular appeal.

National values changed sharply in the late 1970s and 1980s, resulting in new attitudes toward recreation, leisure, and work. Building successful careers and making impressive incomes became the primary goals of many young people, as evidenced by annual surveys of beginning college students. Social goals and values were no longer in fashion, and a new work ethic seemed to have captured the national consciousness.

However, in the 1990s, many young people evidenced growing concern with social issues and began to devote themselves to community service. At the same time, public and nonprofit leisure-service agencies initiated varied socially purposeful programs, such as those designed to serve at-risk youth (see page 193).

PHILOSOPHICAL ANALYSES OF RECREATION AND LEISURE

Given this historical background, what formal analyses were made of recreation and leisure from a philosophical perspective during the middle decades of the twentieth century? Some textbook authors examined the field making use of widely accepted philosophical systems. Earle Ziegler, for example, examined the field of health, physical education, and recreation in light of several such philosophical systems—including naturalism, realism, idealism, and experimentalism. However, because his primary emphasis was on recreation education rather than recreation and leisure in national culture, his analysis is somewhat remote from the concerns of leisure in modern society.[3] Apart from such generalized analyses, a number of writers examined specific components of leisure behavior in terms of accepted philosophical criteria.

Sport as a Focus of Inquiry

For example, the immense growth of popular interest in sports led a number of writers to examine amateur and professional athletics from a philosophical perspective. Carolyn Thomas studied sports in light of the major branches of philosophical inquiry, including: (1) metaphysics, the branch that explores the nature of being and mankind's relationship to God and nature; (2) epistemology, concerned with the origin and acquisition of knowledge; (3) axiology, which examines human ethics and moral conduct; and (4) aesthetics, which is concerned with the nature, and form of beauty and art.[4]

In *Sport: A Philosophic Inquiry,* Paul Weiss argues that play and games must be defined within the larger context of work and leisure time. Of all forms of experience, he writes, sport constitutes our greatest opportunity for achieving and witnessing human excellence.[5]

Moral Values and Leisure

In another analysis of the philosophy of leisure, Charles Sylvester contrasts the traditional moral view of leisure (as exemplified in the writings of Aristotle and applied in the twentieth century by J. B. Nash) with an existentialist approach based on Sartre, Ortega, and Jaspers. In the older view, Aristotle argued that happiness was the greatest good in human life and that it was the result of having lived one's life virtuously, chiefly through contemplation and exercise of one's intellect in leisure. Following this line of thought, Nash presented a twentieth-century theory of leisure-time morality in which human beings have the freedom to choose between "good," "bad," and "best" uses of leisure. Sylvester points out that Nash's model of leisure ranged from delinquent and destructive acts against oneself and society at the base to creative participation at the pinnacle:

> [I]t also reflected his belief in the moral separation between mind and body. Essentially spiritual, the mind was connected with the highest forms of leisure expression. The body, on the other hand, was linked with appetites, weaknesses, an occasional debauchery. Intellectual and spiritual pursuits were superior to purely physical activities.[6]

In contrast, the existential view of human life rejects any *a priori* laws as to good or bad behavior. Sartre wrote, "Man is nothing else but what he makes of himself," and Ortega argued that man "is the novelist of himself."

That such analyses are not ivory tower abstractions is shown by the continuing conflicts or contradictions in society's approach to controlling varied forms of morally marginal leisure pursuits. For example, while it is widely recognized that gambling, substance abuse, and commercialized or indiscriminate sexual activity have destructive consequences for society, we are ambivalent with respect to public policy and laws regarding them. At the same time that we regulate and prosecute—often inconsistently—private enterprises engaged in providing these forms of play, government condones and promotes the same activities through state liquor stores, through lotteries, legal casinos, and racetracks with parimutuel betting, and through ignoring the open operation of massage parlors and escort services.

Shift in Professional Orientations

As a third example of philosophical analyses in recreation and leisure studies, a number of authors have examined the changing approaches found within the recreation and park profession. To illustrate, Wayne Stormann points out that there has been a pronounced shift from the early decades of the twentieth century—when the field was dominated by progressive reformers who sought to improve community life through organized play—to today, where recreation has become an area of professional service that has been, in his words, "bureaucratized, commercialized, and centralized."[7] The popular idea of the professional as an expert technician who markets leisure "products" or prescribes social services and solutions is in sharp contrast to the idea of leisure as a domain in which participatory democracy can flourish and community residents can gain valuable experience in managing their own lives.

OPERATIONAL PHILOSOPHIES OF RECREATION AND LEISURE

Such analyses may have only limited application for those who are directly concerned with the recreation movement today. For them, it is more helpful to examine the philosophical views of those who *direct* this movement—the boards, administrators, and leaders of recreation and park agencies, voluntary organizations, commercial businesses, and other specialized leisure services. These views are generally expressed in mission statements, membership brochures, or other materials that describe the goals of such organizations.

It is possible to identify several approaches or orientations found in leisure-service agencies today that may be called *operational philosophies*. These include the following: (1) the *quality-of-life* approach; (2) the *marketing* approach; (3) the *human-services* approach; (4) the *prescriptive* approach; (5) the *environmental/aesthetic/preservationist* approach; (6) the *hedonist/individualist* approach; and (7) the *benefits-based* approach.

Quality-of-Life Approach

This approach has been the dominant one in the field of organized recreation service for several decades. It sees recreation as an experience that contributes to human development and to community well-being in various ways: improving physical and mental health, enriching cultural life, reducing antisocial uses of leisure, and strengthening community ties.

The quality-of-life orientation stresses the unique nature of recreation as a vital form of human experience—one that is engaged in for its own sake, rather than for any extrinsic purpose or conscious social goal. Generally, proponents of this view have agreed that recreation satisfies a universal human need that has been made even more pressing by the tensions of modern urban society, the changed nature of work, and other social conditions. In an early text, Meyer, Brightbill, and Sessoms commented that community recreation led to the development of democratic citizenship and sound moral character and to the reduction of social pathology.

Those holding this view argue that the pleasure, freedom, and self-choice inherent in recreation and leisure are their most vital contributions to the lives of participants. Quality-of-life advocates have tended to assume that public recreation should be supported for its own sake as an important area of civic responsibility, and that adequate tax funds should be provided for this purpose.

Marketing Approach

This business-oriented approach to providing organized recreation and park programs and services evolved rapidly during the late 1970s and 1980s as a direct response to the fiscal pressures placed on public and voluntary leisure-service agencies. As noted in earlier chapters, steadily mounting operational costs and a declining tax base during that time forced many recreation and park departments to take drastic measures in order to survive, adopting what has come to be known as the marketing approach to agency management. This approach is based on the idea that public, voluntary, or other leisure-service providers will flourish best if they adopt the methods used by commercial recreation businesses. It argues that they must become more aggressive and efficient in developing and promoting recreation facilities and programs that will reach the broadest possible audience and gain the maximum possible income.

John Crompton, one of the leading exponents of this position, has commented on the growing interest in adapting marketing concepts and techniques (ranging from needs assessments and target marketing to sophisticated pricing methods) to the needs of nonprofit recreation organizations:

> This interest reflects a growing recognition that marketing is the essential core discipline upon which the success or survival of any agency depends. For a park and recreation agency to carry out its mission, it requires resources and support from citizens. It seeks to obtain these ingredients by delivering services which provide benefits sought by client groups. In *exchange* for services delivered, the agency receives resources in the form of tax dollars and/or direct user charges. Thus, marketing may be defined as a set of activities aimed at facilitating and expediting exchanges with target markets.[8]

Proponents of the marketing approach take the position that recreation and park professionals should not have to plead for tax-based support solely on the basis of the social value of their programs, but should seek to become relatively independent as a viable, self-sufficient form of community service.

It should be recognized that the marketing trend has influenced far more than public recreation and park agencies alone. Many large nonprofit youth-serving organizations, such as the YMCA, YWCA, and YM-YWHA, have been forced to increase their reliance on self-generated revenues and to move into more aggressive marketing of a wide range of leisure programs, including their fitness services.

While the marketing approach has been enthusiastically received by many recreation and park managers, it raises a number of issues with respect to the essential purpose of public and voluntary leisure-service agencies. The argument has been made that increased fees and charges—whether imposed by the agencies themselves or by concessionaires or contractors working under privatization plans—tend to exclude the people in greatest need of inexpensive public recreation opportunities, such as children, persons with disabilities, or the economically disadvantaged.

Human-Services Approach

In direct contrast to the marketing approach is the human-services approach to organized recreation service. This approach regards recreation as an important form of social service that must be provided in a way that contributes directly to a wide range of desired social values and goals. The human-services approach received a strong impetus during the 1960s, when recreation programs were generously funded by the federal government as part of the war on poverty, and recreation was used to offer job training and employment opportunities for economically disadvantaged youth and adults in America's ghettos.

The human-services approach is similar to the quality-of-life approach in its recognition of the social value of recreation service. However, it does not subscribe to the latter's idealization of recreation as an inherently ennobling kind of experience, carried on for its own sake. Instead, within the human-services framework, recreation must be designed to achieve significant community change and to use a variety of appropriate modalities.

This does not mean that recreation personnel should seek to *be* health educators, employment counselors, nutritionists, correctional officers, legal advisors, or housing experts. Rather, it implies that they must recognize the holistic nature of the human condition, provide such services when able to do so effectively, and cooperate fully with other practitioners in the various human services fields when appropriate.

Operating under this approach, many public recreation departments have sponsored youth or adult classes in a wide range of educational, vocational, or self-improvement areas and have also provided day-care programs, special services for persons with disabilities, roving leader programs for juvenile gangs, environmental projects, and numerous other functions of this type.

In its forceful emphasis on the need to meet social problems head on and achieve beneficial human goals, the human-services approach to recreation and park programming may at times be at odds with the marketing approach to service. In the marketing approach, efficient management and maximum revenue are often the primary aims. In the human-services orientation, social values and human benefits are emphasized.

Prescriptive Approach

Of the orientations described here, the prescriptive is the most purposeful in the way it defines the goals and functions of the recreational experience. The idea that recreation should bring about constructive change in participants has been stressed in a number of textbooks on programming. For example, Ruth Russell describes "programmed recreation" chiefly as a form of organized and purposeful activity designed in an orderly and deliberate way to achieve desirable individual and group results.[9]

The clearest cases of prescriptive recreation programs are found in therapeutic recreation. For example, Paul Wehman and Stuart Schleien describe the curriculum design sequence in therapeutic recreation as it is used to develop either an individualized education program or an individualized habilitation plan. In order to help patients or clients master important motor skills, improve social behavior, or achieve other goals of treatment, members of the treatment team review the individual's level of illness or disability, past recreation, education, other experiences and skills, and current level of functioning. On the basis of this review, a curriculum is devised to include the following program components: (1) a program goal; (2) an instructional objective (short-term); (3) a task analysis of each skill; (4) the verbal cue required for instruction in the skill; (5) materials that are required for instruction; and (6) teaching procedures and special adaptations for each skill.[10]

While it is similar to the human-services approach in its emphasis on deliberately achieving significant social goals, the prescriptive approach differs in its reliance on the practitioner's expertise and authority. In contrast, a recreation professional working within a human-services framework would be much more likely to value the input of community residents and to involve them in decision making.

Environmental/Aesthetic/Preservationist Approach

This unwieldy title is used as a catch-all model to lump together three elements that are not synonymous but that do exhibit a high degree of similarity. The *environmentalist* obviously is concerned with protecting the outdoor environment and preserving it in as natural and healthy a state as possible. The *aesthetic* position is one that values the appearance of the environment, both natural and artificial, and stresses the inclusion of cultural arts and other creative experiences within a recreation program. The *preservationist* seeks to maintain the physical environment—not simply out of a respect for nature, but to preserve evidence of a historical past and a cultural tradition.

This approach to recreation planning is more likely to be evident in agencies that operate extensive parks, forests, waterfront areas, or other natural or scenic resources. Thus, one might assume that it would chiefly be found in such government agencies as federal, state, or provincial park departments that administer major parks and outdoor recreation facilities.

However, this is not the full picture. Many urban recreation and park planners are responsible for large, older parks. Often they may help to rehabilitate or redesign run-down waterfront areas, industrial sites, or gutted slum areas. In many cases, their purpose is to preserve or rebuild historic areas of cultural interest that will maintain or increase the appeal of cities for tourism and cultural programming.

Environmental Awareness   A key element in this approach is the deep reverence that many individuals have today for nature in its various forms. Daniel Dustin has described the experience of being interconnected with the natural world and the spiritual value that human beings derive from their varied experiences with wilderness.[11] Douglas Knudson points out that love for nature and acceptance of responsibility for it is

> more than watching birds with binoculars or identifying spring wildflowers. It is the perceiving—the understanding—of the ways in which nature operates. The relatedness of all elements of the environment provides the key to perception. The rhythm of natural changes provides the beat. When man perceives the processes, he understands better the Creation and feels the refreshment of recreation in its deepest sense.[12]

However, environmental programming approaches cannot be carried out simply through a poetic evocation of the beauty of nature. Political and economic realities also come into play when environmental decisions must be made. For example, a continuing controversy over opening up redwood forest areas in the West has involved the argument that the lumbering industry provides year-round employment to thousands of workers in states such as California and Oregon—and that this fact outweighs the need to preserve these historic areas.

The last two decades have seen a concerted effort to reverse the progress made in the 1960s and 1970s in protecting and restoring the environment. *New York Times* columnist Anthony Lewis described the efforts of a determined faction of congressional conservatives to cripple the United States Environmental Protection Agency, gut environmental laws, and set up a virtual environmental "exemption bazaar" with bills that would

Open the Arctic National Wildlife Refuge in Alaska, which may be America's greatest unspoiled ecosystem, to oil and gas drilling

Prevent the EPA from keeping possibly toxic fill out of lakes and harbors

Deprive the EPA of funds to keep raw sewage out of rivers and away from beaches

Prohibit for a year the listing of new endangered species for protection and kill most of the funding to carry out the Endangered Species Act

Cut by two-thirds, from 300,000 to 100,000 acres, the wetlands to be bought from farmers by the Agriculture Department for a reserve

Increase logging in the Tongass National Forest, a remarkable rain forest in Alaska[13]

Such legislative assaults, plus other pitched battles over the use of public lands for lumbering, mining, grazing, and oil drilling, represent a continuing threat to the environmental ethic today. In addition, there is a growing realization that recreation itself poses a continuing threat to the wilderness, and that abrasive conflict exists between different groups of outdoor recreation enthusiasts, such as the tensions between snowmobilers and cross-country skiers, canoers and motorboat owners, and hikers and mountain bikers.

These concerns call not only for a carefully defined philosophy to promote the appropriate uses of national and state parks and forests but also for adequate financial support to permit park management of environmental programs to function effectively. This overall issue is not of concern to the United States alone. In Canada, for example, a Task Force on Park Establishment created by the national Minister of Environment issued a report, "Our Parks—Vision for the 21st Century." This report urged that a comprehensive plan be enacted to ensure protection of the nation's natural resources, including proposals for over 500 new parks throughout Canada.

Hedonist/Individualist Approach

This approach to recreational programming is concerned chiefly with providing fun and pleasure. It regards recreation as a highly individualistic activity that should be free of social constraints or moral purposes. The term *hedonist* is used to mean one who seeks personal pleasure—often with the implication that it is of a sensual, bodily nature. The term *individualist* is attached because this philosophical approach stresses the idea that each individual should be free to seek his or her own fulfillment and pleasure untrammeled by group pressures or social expectations.

Obviously, certain forms of leisure activity that have gained increased popularity in American life fit this description. The accelerated use and generally freer acceptance of drugs, alcohol, gambling, sex as a commercialized recreational pursuit, and other forms of sensation-seeking entertainment and play all illustrate the hedonist approach to leisure. These forms of play may best be described as morally marginal, in the sense that they are legal in some contexts or localities and illegal in others, regarded as acceptable leisure experiences by some population groups and condemned by others.

Drug and Alcohol Abuse   The use of mind-altering or mood-changing substances as a form of pleasure-seeking or socializing experience has been found in many cultures and human societies, both past and present. Alcohol may be legally sold and consumed by adults throughout most of the United States and Canada and is generally considered to be a useful social lubricant—consumed at weddings and family parties, business luncheons, neighborhood taverns, and a host of other kinds of recreation settings. In contrast, the use of narcotic drugs is illegal, unless medically prescribed, and provides the basis for an immense underworld industry.

Drugs are generally regarded as a far greater threat to health and safety than alcohol. Yet, each year, while cocaine, crack, and heroin take about 7,000 American lives, alcohol claims about 100,000. Someone is killed by a drunk driver every 24 minutes, and over 500,000 people are injured in alcohol-related traffic accidents each year.

The scope of the problem was indicated at a 1994 United Nations–sponsored conference on organized international crime, where it was reported that drug trafficking worldwide involved annual profits of $500 billion, with the United States representing the major user of illegal narcotics.

One of the newest drug crazes involves the use of "ecstasy"—pills that have become extremely popular at "raves" frequented by teenagers and young adults. While this drug appears to have few negative consequences, federal authorities argue that it has serious short- and long-term dangers.

Organized Gambling   Over the past three decades, organized legal gambling in the form of casinos, lotteries, racetrack betting, and numerous other commercially sponsored games has proliferated at breakneck speed in the United States. *The New York Times* reports that no American industry in the present decade, with the possible exception of computer software and on-line technology, has grown as rapidly and pervaded society as thoroughly as legalized gambling:

> In 1988, casino gambling was legal in only two states—Nevada and New Jersey. Today [November 1995], casinos, including those on Indian reservations, operate or are authorized in 23 states. In 1994, gamblers armed with lottery tickets, chips, and slot machines wagered a whopping $482 billion in this country, which is more than the gross national product of China and represents a 22 percent increase over the previous year.[14]

Throughout the United States, city after city has fallen for the economic lures of legalizing varied forms of gambling, authorizing riverboat casinos that never leave the shore (except when they travel to a more attractive setting financially), and approving offtrack betting parlors and varied slot-machine gaming operations. While the argument is made that tax revenues, gaming-related jobs, and visitor spending help to sustain local economies, there is growing evidence that the social costs of gambling make it an unprofitable enterprise for most localities.

What is most significant about the tremendous growth of the gaming industry is that it illustrates a basic transformation in America's prevailing value system. While some still reject legalized gambling as not only destructive of the lives of millions of compulsive bettors but also as a cynical exploitation of the public trust, the majority of citizens today tend to accept it as an appropriate kind of leisure experience.

Only over the past few years have organized forces, including church, civic, and parents' groups, mobilized to resist the spread of legalized gambling, resulting in the rejection of pro-gambling referenda in a number of states.[15]

Commercialized Sex   A third form of morally marginal play that is a key component of the hedonist approach to recreation and leisure is the use of sex as a form of play or entertainment. Commercialized sex expanded dramatically over the three decades following the counterculture movement of the 1960s. It takes many forms, including legalized houses of prostitution in Nevada, call-girl rings, and the escort services and massage parlors that represent thinly disguised forms of prostitution in many cities; sex films, books, and magazines that may now be legally purchased; the widespread rental

Gambling continues as an immensely profitable industry in the United States in casinos, on riverboats, cruise lines, and airplanes; through the Internet; and on racetrack simulcasts. If it represents a negative and destructive form of play—as many authorities contend—should states, churches, public recreation and park departments, or military MWR programs sponsor it?

of X-rated videocassettes for home viewing; and the increased showing of sexual images and themes on network television programs and of "soft porn" on cable television.

A recent manifestation of commercialized sex as an element in popular culture involves its broader exploitation within the mass media of entertainment and communication. Increasingly, the phenomenon of "cyberporn"—the transmission of varied types of erotica on the Internet—has prompted national concern. Awareness that children have easy access to such materials and that the Internet is being used for recruitment of sexual partners led to an effort in the mid-1990s to curb such abuses.

While public, nonprofit, and other types of community-based leisure-service organizations generally do not sponsor substance abuse, gambling, or sex-oriented types of entertainment, such activities are widely available through commercial sponsorship and, in many cases, have governmental approval or tacit acceptance.

Benefits-Based Management Approach

This final philosophical approach to the design and implementation of recreation, park, and leisure-service programs is relatively new. It was the subject of a number of presentations of NRPA Congresses in the early and mid-1990s and has been discussed in numerous publications. Essentially, this approach holds that it is not enough to verbalize a set of desirable goals or mission statements or to carry out head counts of participation and tally the number of events sponsored by a leisure service agency. Instead, governmental, nonprofit, therapeutic, armed forces, and other types of managed recreation agencies should more clearly define their roles and purposes in terms of community and participant benefits.

In practice, the benefits-based approach is based on a three-step implementation process: (1) *benefits and opportunity identification:* determine a core group of benefits that users seek and agencies can realistically provide, along with the management changes needed for benefits achievement; (2) *program implementation:* make facility or staff modifications needed to achieve desired benefits, and carry out systematic monitoring procedures during programs; and (3) *evaluation and documentation:* analyze data, determine if program benefits were achieved, develop reports, and disseminate findings to appropriate audiences.[16]

Within this process, it is essential that target goals be defined in terms of concrete and measurable benefits. Bill Exham, manager of the Community Services Department in Scottsdale, Arizona, stresses that this should be done in terms of *outcomes* that measure change or effect, rather than *outputs* that simply describe a program.[17]

Lawrence Allen points out that a number of studies are under way to develop a realistic set of significant target benefits for use by public and other community-based leisured-service agencies in implementing a benefits-based management approach. When this has been accomplished and when the recreation, park, and leisure-service profession moves purposefully to accomplish, document, and publicize its important contributions to community life, the field itself should benefit from heightened public awareness and support.[18]

Through the late 1990s, professional publications and conference presentations continued to stress the benefits-based management approach, with recommendations that it be incorporated in the accreditation process of college and university leisure-

Emerging Issues:

Issues relating to military youth have emerged that concern DoD leaders

- Increases in parental deployment absences intensify associated risk factors

- Increases in the reports of youth violence and gang activity around and on military bases

- Lack of positive activities during after-school hours

- Nation-wide increase in youth problems which in turn affect military youth

- Geographical separation of families due to teens in high school

- Problems associated with the transfer of military high school students

Model Communities Program Successes

Results reported by some of the projects include:

- Improved school performance – 85% academically and 77% socially

- A law enforcement mentoring program which resulted in an 84% drop in delinquency and 30% increase in volunteering

- Teen participation at Teen Centers and Outreach Programs tripled

- Local school partnerships which resulted in a 50% decrease in suspensions and 62% decrease in physical violence

- 87% of overseas youth offenders involved with counseling, employment assistance and academic help program remained crime-free after entering

Example of Benefits-Based Planning in Military Recreation

Documentation of positive outcomes of Model Communities Program designed to deal with critical youth issues in armed forces Morale, Welfare, and Recreation operation.

studies curricula. A number of pilot training programs were developed by the National Recreation and Park Association, with the collaboration of Clemson University and Texas A&M's Consortium on Youth at Risk.[19]

Philosophical Approaches: No Pure Models

It should be stressed that, while these seven approaches to the definition and management of organized leisure services are separate and distinct philosophical positions, it is unlikely that any single agency or government department would follow one approach exclusively. Many organizations combine two or more positions in defining their own missions. This blending of emphases was illustrated in the opening statement of the 1987 report of the President's Commission on Americans Outdoors. Entitled *Americans and the Outdoors*, the report begins:

> *It enriches us in many ways . . .*
> The great outdoors is a great health machine, toning up our minds and bodies. The engineer kayaking through a cataract and the assembly-line worker hunting in quiet woods are both recharging themselves for more productive work.
> Our economic health benefits more directly. Recreation products and services are a 300-billion-dollar industry, and the economic web does not stop there. The clothes we wear, the automobile that takes us to recreation areas, and the photographic equipment that records the highlights all derive in part from the outdoor use of leisure time.
> Open space is a silent social worker as well, in its ability to reduce crime and delinquency. A drop in vandalism accompanied the building of small park in Trenton, New Jersey, prompting Mayor Arthur Holland to tell the commission, "You don't throw stones when you've got a basketball to throw around."

This message contains clearly identifiable elements of the quality-of-life, marketing, and human-services approaches, with a strong environmentalist thrust as well.

KEY PRINCIPLES GUIDING LEISURE-SERVICE DELIVERY TODAY

For recreation, parks, and leisure-service practitioners, it is possible to identify a number of key principles that should be used to guide their professional operations today. First, it is assumed that such individuals—no matter what their fields of specialization—regard recreation and leisure as important to human growth and community development. A contemporary philosophy of organized recreation service should therefore deal with such important issues as the place of recreation and leisure in modern life, the role of government, the development of programming based on significant social needs, and the place of leisure education.

Place of Recreation in the Modern Community

In American and Canadian society, our view of recreation as a social phenomenon and area of community involvement is influenced by our governmental systems. In our Constitution and in court decisions that have influenced government policy and practice through the years, we have accepted the view that, on various levels, government has the responsibility for providing certain major services to citizens. These include functions related to safety and protection, education, health, and other services that contribute to maintaining the quality of life of all citizens.

Linked to this system of governmental responsibility is our general acceptance of the Judeo-Christian concepts of the worth and dignity of all human beings and the need to help each person become the most fully realized individual that he or she is capable of being. Through government and through many voluntary community associations, we have accepted the responsibility for providing needed services and opportunities for people at each stage of life and for those who because of disability have been deprived in significant ways.

Needs of Individual Citizens

Recreation and leisure are important aspects of personal experience in modern life for the physical, social, emotional, intellectual, and spiritual benefits they provide. Positive leisure experiences enhance the quality of a person's life and help each person develop to the fullest potential. To make this possible, government and other responsible social agencies should provide recreation resources, programs, and, where appropriate, leisure education to help people to understand the value of free time when constructively and creatively used.

Government's Responsibility

In addition to providing these personal benefits, recreation helps a community to meet health needs, gain economic benefits, and maintain community morale. On each level (local, state or provincial, and federal), appropriate government agencies should therefore be assigned the responsibility for maintaining a network of physical resources for leisure participation—including parks, playgrounds, centers, sports facilities, and other special recreation facilities. Government should be responsible for planning, organizing, and carrying out programs, under proper leadership, for all age levels.

Government cannot and should not seek to meet *all* of the leisure needs of the community. It must recognize that other types of community organizations—including voluntary, private, commercial, therapeutic, industrial, and educational groups—sponsor effective recreation programs, which are often designed to meet specialized needs or more advanced interests. Therefore, its unique role should be to provide a basic floor of recreational opportunity, to fill the gaps that are not covered by other organizations, and to provide coordination and overall direction to community leisure-service programs.

There has been a growing body of opinion that local government recreation and park agencies should take less responsibility for the direct provision of program activities—particularly when limited by fiscal constraints—and should move instead into the role of serving as an advocate for recreation and leisure in community life and providing coordinating or facilitating assistance to other agencies.

A major concern should be to ensure an equitable distribution of recreational opportunities for the public at large. This would not guarantee that all residents will have totally equal programs and services, but would represent a pledge that, within the realities of community needs and economic capabilities, facilities and programs will be distributed so as to bring about a reasonable balance of such opportunities for different neighborhoods and community groups.

Goals of Other Organizations

Each type of organization that makes a contribution to this field should determine its own specialized goals for recreation service, depending on its overall purposes, the nature of its membership, and its available resources.

Armed forces recreation should give its highest priority to helping develop and maintain a high level of physical fitness and positive morale; building an esprit de corps; reducing problems related to alcohol or drug abuse or the taking of unauthorized leave; and providing needed leisure programs for the families of service personnel.

In employee recreation programs, the goal generally is to improve the productivity of workers by enhancing their physical and mental fitness and morale, improving relationships between management and line personnel, assisting in recruitment and retention of skilled employees, and reducing problems related to boredom and monotony on the job.

In therapeutic recreation service, the specific goals of treatment or rehabilitation, as developed by an interdisciplinary team of professionals working in collaboration with clients or patients themselves, serve to direct the course of programming.

A prevailing principle today is that all forms of organized recreation service provided by government or nonprofit community-service organizations should be goal-oriented and purposeful. While recreation may certainly be carried on by individuals without any clear sense of purpose, if leisure-service programs are to justify the support of taxpayers or those who contribute to the funding of community agencies, they *must* be designed to bring results of significant value to the community.

OTHER GUIDELINES

In addition to these general guidelines, there are a number of others that are of particular relevance to the role of leisure-service professionals.

Coordination Among Agencies

American society today has many organizations of various types that provide leisure services, but they often do so with marked duplication and in wasteful competition with each other. At the same time, there are continuing gaps in service that result in unmet needs.

It is therefore essential that public, private, voluntary, commercial, and other types of leisure-service organizations cooperate fully in determining community needs and accepting appropriate functions and roles for themselves in providing recreational opportunities. This will help to prevent unnecessary competition among agencies and help to identify and fill gaps in community leisure services. Similarly, the various types of sponsors could share resources and know-how and even develop joint programming that will be more effective than the work of any single agency could be.

Participant Input

A sound contemporary philosophy of recreation dictates that participants themselves should be as fully involved as possible in the determination of program emphases and needs. This can be accomplished through the use of neighborhood committees or advisory councils, recreation and park boards, task forces, or volunteers. Such participation has a dual benefit: (1) community residents are able to provide leadership, advice, assistance, and other resources to the program; and (2) they are engaged supporters of the program and represent an active constituency for it in political and other strategic terms.

While this principle is most obviously of use in government-sponsored recreation and park programs, it also applies to other types of membership organizations or specialized services. Particularly in such fields as campus, employee, and voluntary-agency recreation, volunteer participation in planning groups and in the actual operation of programs is essential.

Balance of Marketing and Human-Services Approaches

These two approaches to leisure-service management appear to represent sharply opposed philosophical orientations. Can they be reconciled? As earlier chapters have shown, economic and other factors have compelled a much more aggressive and fiscally hardheaded thrust in the marketing of leisure services, among nonprofit as well as profit-oriented agencies. Yet, a number of authors have emphasized that organizations in the public sector—while they may adopt an entrepreneurial approach—must also be concerned with social and economic priorities that benefit the overall community.

For example, Ronald Riggins argues that increasing privatization of public leisure-service agencies, with a strong commercial emphasis, could seriously limit open access to needed recreation facilities and programs.[20] Yet, from a pragmatic point of view, it is necessary to link the marketing and human-services approaches through appropriate objectives, policies, and management techniques. This means that while every effort should be made to plan and market recreation programs and services as efficiently and economically as possible—with the intention of maximizing revenues for support of the department—it is also necessary to establish certain social priorities and to meet these critical needs despite their costs or the inability of recipients of special services to pay their way.

Within this context, the benefits-based management approach described earlier in this chapter provides a potentially useful means of reconciling the marketing and human-services models. Agency targets may incorporate both fiscal and social elements and, when achieved, should result in a higher level of financial support overall for recreation and park budgets.

A useful approach that is followed in armed forces recreation involves classifying varied program elements based on their contribution to the mission of the Morale, Welfare, and Recreation operation. Those with the highest value with respect to MWR's goals receive fuller financial support without fees being imposed for participation. Other program elements must charge fees that support their operational costs and make them self-sustaining.

Need for Effective Leisure Education

Finally, there is a need to promote effective leisure education among the various sectors of the public and among professionals in other areas of community service or in special disciplines. The heritage of our Puritan forebears and our centuries-long dependence on the Protestant work ethic have combined to make many Americans and Canadians suspicious of recreation and to keep them unaware of its potential value in human society and in the day-to-day lives of individuals and families.

The effort to encourage a fuller understanding and appreciation of creative and constructive forms of leisure involvement is particularly critical today, in light of the changes that have occurred over the past two decades. As described in earlier chapters, many of the most popular forms of entertainment in sports, the mass media, tourism, and similar leisure domains are now dominated by a few huge conglomerates—multibillion dollar businesses that determine the kinds of free-time attractions to be presented to the public. Their primary concern is profitability, and often their products and services include negative or self-destructive forms of play that are designed and marketed in highly sophisticated and efficient ways.

In the mid-1990s, it became clear that the nation was greatly concerned about the breakdown of traditional family values and social structures and that the mass media of entertainment were increasingly being seen as a leading cause of major social problems. This development provides an important opportunity for recreation, park, and leisure-service professionals to make their voices heard and to promote a positive and constructive set of leisure values among Americans and Canadians of all ages.

FACING THE CHALLENGE OF THE FUTURE

The principles and guidelines that have been presented here deal essentially with the *present*. However, those who read this book—primarily college and university students in recreation, park, and leisure-studies curricula—are looking ahead to careers in the *future*. What will the rest of the twenty-first century bring us in terms of demographic, social, and economic changes that can radically affect our uses of leisure?

Patricia Farrell and Richard Trudeau argue that we are in the midst of a "social upheaval" that will continue through the next decade and beyond. If professionals in the park and recreation field miss the import of what is occurring today, the danger of their being left behind is all too real. Instead, they must be a part of the nation's development of a new social ethic:

> These times will require an "ethic of commitment" which will demonstrate evidence of growing concern with community and a sensitivity to human relationships. Strategic management of the human climate will be of paramount importance in the decades to come.[21]

Many contemporary authorities in the leisure-service field emphasize that bringing about needed changes will require a new wave of entrepreneurship. Recreation and park professionals in all spheres of service need to think more imaginatively and innovatively, need to be more goal-oriented and flexible, and need to be more willing to take risks in order to achieve outstanding results. They need to cultivate an organizational and professional climate that is interactive, with everyone sharing common purposes and working to achieve them.

EFFORTS TO PREDICT THE FUTURE

A number of major study groups in the United States and Canada have attempted to develop systematic predictions of social changes that will accelerate as we go farther into the twenty-first century. For example, a collaborative study by the Canadian Park and Recreation Association and the Rethink Group, a leading-edge research and planning organization, has identified a number of "macro" trends that are expected to characterize Canadian society in the decades ahead.

These include (1) *"adultism"*—the "altered" family, with many more youth, single adults, and elderly persons, and nontraditional family units; (2) *structural economic change*, with far greater emphasis on computer and telecommunication advances and populations dividing into "technocrats" and "technopeasants"; (3) *greening: the environmental imperative*, with growing concern about waste management, energy management, and the preservation of habitats and at-risk species; and (4) *electronic entertainment cocoons*, with virtual "reality" taking the place of real experiences.[22]

U.S. Views: Agenda for the Twenty-First Century

Many of the same trends described in the Canadian *Leisure Watch* report have been noted by leisure-service professionals and scholars in the United States as well. For example, in the early 1990s, a national conference was held to identify critical needs in the field under the sponsorship of the National Symposium Committee and with the findings published by the National Recreation and Park Association. Somewhat more sharply focused on the direct concerns and priorities of the recreation and park field than was the Canadian report, these conferences led to a substantial number of conclusions, including the following:

> Park and recreation professionals must be able and willing to identify, analyze, promote and respond to change in society.
>
> There is a strong trend toward greater participation in the decision-making process by citizens and employees. New leadership techniques will be required of park and recreation professionals to facilitate consensus building.
>
> Multicultural diversity will continue to grow rapidly. Parks and recreation must find ways to celebrate the variety of cultures within the community.
>
> The wellness movement will continue to grow, and parks, recreation, and leisure services must facilitate and identify directly with the growing wellness movement.
>
> Success will depend on an organization's ability to build cooperative relationships and establish networks and coalitions with other organizations.
>
> It is essential to improve the image of the profession, both externally and internally, so that the relationship between recreation and park programs and values and contemporary issues is clearly apparent.
>
> Tourism has emerged as one of the world's growth industries and an increasingly important part of leisure expression. Parks and recreation must be involved in mutually beneficial partnerships with tourism.

Environment will increasingly become a focus of international concern. The park and recreation profession must take its rightful place as a leader in shaping environmental policy.

The park and recreation profession must develop and articulate clearly defined mission statements, goals, and objectives of the field.[23]

CHALLENGES AND STRATEGIES FOR THE FUTURE

In light of all of the trends for the future that have been outlined in this chapter, numerous professional societies and government agencies have sought to outline appropriate strategies for the decades to come. For example, the Bureau of Land Management in the U.S. Department of the Interior developed a major report, *Recreation 2000*, which identified the specific challenges facing it in the years ahead and suggested strategies to deal with these concerns. Overall, it outlined 14 specific policy statements dealing with such issues as resource monitoring and protection, visitor services, partnership, use limits and allocation of resources, fees for the use of public lands, tourism, and professionalism and career development for BLM resource management specialists.

A number of other government agencies, professional associations, and nonprofit leisure-service organizations also developed planning studies that outlined major policy concerns and strategies needed for success in the years ahead. In September 1998, the author of this text carried out a comprehensive study of recreation, park, and leisure-service educators in the United States and Canada, which asked them to prioritize the importance of major trends and challenges facing the profession in the years ahead. Their findings of the 14 most important challenges for the twenty-first century are shown in Table 12.1. Several of these challenges are discussed in the concluding section of this chapter, grouped under four major headings.

Challenges Linked to Population Diversity

As earlier chapters have shown, both the United States and Canada are undergoing dramatic shifts in their population makeup that affect leisure-service management and programming.

Age Groupings The swelling numbers of school-aged children and the shift of "Baby Boomers" to the already huge number of elderly citizens in each country will require expanded service delivery. Similarly, the dramatic changes in family structure, particularly the increase in the numbers of single adults and single-parent families, will also present challenges to public and nonprofit agencies.

Gender-Related Concerns Chapter 6 describes the progress that has been made by women and girls in terms of leisure opportunities and professional careers that transcend the traditional "glass ceiling," as well as changing expectations of men and boys.

Lifestyle Issues Of growing importance are issues revolving around the leisure roles of gay and lesbian youth and adults. The Supreme Court decision in June 2000 permitting the national Boy Scout organization to ban homosexuals as members or staff

TABLE 12.1

RANKED IMPORTANCE OF CHALLENGES FACING LEISURE-SERVICE FIELD IN TWENTY-FIRST CENTURY

	Weighted Score
1. Serve increasingly diverse society (race, age, gender, etc.).	453
2. Emphasize key social purposes of recreation: working with at-risk youth, serving persons with disabilities, promoting community development, etc.	437
3. Achieve fuller public understanding of value of recreation and parks and of leisure-service profession.	434
4. Upgrade recreation and park programs and facilities, particularly in inner cities and for minority populations.	417
5. Adopt a benefits-based management approach, researching, proving, and publicizing positive outcomes of recreation.	411
6. Promote recreation's identity as health-related field.	392
7. Develop partnerships with environmental organizations to protect and restore wildlands, waterways, etc.	386
8. Employ marketing approach to achieve fiscal self-sufficiency and gain public respect and support.	378
9. Expand and improve family-centered programs and facilities.	373
10. Promote higher values and ethical practices in youth sports competition.	363
11. Strive for fuller mainstreaming of persons with disabilities in community recreation programs.	360
12. Plan for long-term role of recreation and leisure in potentially job-scarce economy.	341
13. Develop higher levels of professionalism, through accreditation, certification, continuing education, or program standards.	340
14. Unify separate branches of leisure-service field (public, nonprofit, commercial, therapeutic, etc.) in common programs and projects.	298

Source: Richard Kraus, *Leisure in a Changing America* (Needham Heights, Mass.: Allyn and Bacon, 2000). *Note:* Each challenge should be preceded by the phrase, "Need to . . . ". They are ranked in order by respondents, with 1 being the highest and 14 the lowest.

leaders led to organized protests based on accusations of civil rights violations, as well as other issues involving the denial of staff tax exemptions and discounts to gay or lesbian couples for pool memberships in Connecticut.[24] Similarly, in California, issues have arisen with respect to county school boards banning student gay and lesbian clubs.

Impact of Racial and Ethnic Diversity   The need to serve a far more diverse population than in the past has become apparent with the rapid growth in numbers of Hispanic-Americans, who have become increasingly active in political life and who—despite their own diversity with respect to their origins—tend to be strongly attached to Latino cultural traditions. As a single example, the fastest-growing television audience in the United States watches Spanish-language programs on two networks, Univision Television and Telemundo Network Group. Other minorities, such as Asian-Americans and Native Americans, symbolize America's role today as a "mosaic," rather than a "melting pot" society.

Religion-Connected Issues   Often race and ethnicity are linked to religious affiliation, as in the case of the rapid growth in the number of Muslims from Mideast and Asian lands who are now part of American society. Often, their beliefs and customs may come into conflict with traditional American values (see page 176) and pose a concern for community organizations that seek to serve them. As a single example, some Boy Scout organizations have rejected Muslims as leaders.[25]

Religion itself has become another major issue facing many leisure-service agencies. The right to say organized prayers at high-school games, to place a Jewish menorah next to a Christmas tree in a public square or park, to offer churchgoing members admission discounts on special days in minor league ballparks, or to hold other religious observances at public events or places have all recently led to lawsuits in American communities. Holding a choir concert in a county park or posting the Ten Commandments on a high-school ballfield fence are similar examples of practices that have led to courtroom conflicts.[26] Clearly, many recreation, park, and leisure-service agencies will continue to face such challenges in the years ahead.

Challenges Linked to Environmental Trends

As the United States and Canada have become increasingly concerned about environmental degradation and the need to preserve the natural environment, a number of areas of conflict have emerged. The most obvious one has to do with the clash of priorities among at least three different groups: those who fight to open up forests and other wilderness areas to logging, grazing, and oil drilling for economic reasons, to support local employment; those who demand the right to use the wilderness or major water areas for recreational pastimes despite possible damage done to the environment, or the infringement on the wishes of other residents or recreational participants; and those who fight vigorously to resist all invasions of the natural environment—to the point of so-called "ecoterrorism."

Beyond such conflicts, which often involve local residents and public officials who resist federal "intrusion" on what they hold should be local rights, a number of other environmental issues pose difficulty. The effort to introduce wild species, such as lynxes, mountain lions, wolves, or grizzly bears, often is resisted by farmers, ranchers, or new residents who have built homes close to wilderness areas.

In some states, the use of jet skis has been banned along populated shorelines, leading to legal confrontations. The building of elaborate ski centers next to wilderness areas has been met by angry sabotage. Off-road vehicles such as snowmobiles have increasingly been barred from forests and major parks.

Urban Conflicts   There have been legal confrontations challenging the right of suburban communities to ban residents from other neighborhoods from using their beaches, tennis courts, or other park areas.[27] Issues of urban sprawl, which increasingly is consuming the urban-wildland interface, pose growing problems for public officials. In the cities themselves, local residents—often members of racial or ethnic minorities in crowded ghettos—have seen their neighborhood gardens that serve as places for community life to flourish destroyed by bulldozers to permit construction of expensive private housing.

All such trends and issues pose challenges for recreation and park professionals, particularly those who administer outdoor recreation and park programs and facilities.

Challenges Linked to Information Technology

One of the most widely heard predictions of the future is that we are increasingly becoming an interactive society—meaning that we have become almost totally dependent on technological tools such as television, cordless telephones, VCRs, answering machines, camcorders, computers, home fax machines, and similar devices, both in the business world and in our personal lives.

Social critics disagree about this trend. Some see it as a marvelous development that enriches our lives, while others argue that it is helping to create an "apartheid" society with growing gaps between the rich and the poor and with the technocrats walling themselves off from those without their expertise—which also has racial and ethnic connotations with respect to computer literacy.[28]

Concerns about the Internet   Over the past decade and a half, the Internet has become a powerful force in education, commerce, and social life. One commentator describes it as "by far the greatest and most significant achievement in the history of mankind."[29] Others refer to this global network as a technology of borderless free markets, which facilitates business and industry on every level, and in which organizational bureaucracies of every kind—corporate, government, and union—suddenly look vulnerable to the Internet's decentralizing powers.

Clearly, telecommuting, job searches, communication, and transactions on all levels are greatly facilitated by the Internet. At the same time, at the turn of the twenty-first century, the popular press began to publicize some of the negative aspects of this new technology.

Impact on Lifestyles   Telecommuting has been seen in both a positive and negative light. Many human resource executives believe that the availability of a sophisticated mobile telecommuting workforce will be the biggest workplace trend in the next millennium.[30] However, other critics suggest that telecommuting may create a nation of isolates, helping to destroy the social nature of work.

The Internet itself has increasingly been shown to provide a medium for a host of "scams" and confidence games, with criminal schemes hooking the unwary. More and more, it is being used to invade personal privacy and to gather intimate information about individuals and families. Pedophiles and other unscrupulous individuals are using the Internet to recruit victims, and there is growing evidence of many individuals becoming addicted to "cyberporn"—online hard-core sexual entertainment.[31] Teenagers and others have been able to buy illegal drugs through the Internet.

Perhaps the most disturbing information comes from a series of research studies conducted through Carnegie Mellon University and Stanford University. These reports indicate that the more time people spend on-line, the less they can spare for real-life relationships with family and friends. Overuse of the Internet is shown to have isolating and alienating effects, with heavy users reporting significant degrees of depression and loneliness.[32]

While such aspects of the interactive society are obviously beyond the ability of leisure-service professionals to control, like addictive gambling, commercialized sex, or substance abuse, they represent powerfully appealing elements within the total spectrum of leisure attractions. As such, they involve negative free-time pursuits in the United States and Canada today that should be counterbalanced by a wealth of healthy, constructive, and readily available recreational attractions to serve all ages and population groups.

Commodification, Privatization, and Future Work/Leisure Trends

Almost every aspect of recreational involvement has been transformed into a product for sale—including many programs offered by public and nonprofit community agencies. Fee-charging and marketing strategies now dominate the recreational landscape, including even programs offered by armed forces, employee-service, and therapeutic recreation sponsors. While a number of analysts have debated the role of marketing in municipal recreation and park agencies or the evolution of "social marketing" in leisure-service management,[33] it is clear that it has become increasingly expensive to engage in any but the most basic leisure activities. Beyond this, it is likely that as fees provide a greater bulk of support for public recreation and park facilities and programs, governmental fiscal support through tax funds may decline—particularly for services that do not yield revenues.

The growing reliance on commercial forms of play in an increasingly affluent society is illustrated vividly in the examples of "luxury fever" cited in earlier chapters (see page 111). The provision of lavish sports and outdoor recreation facilities in private schools or wealthy suburbs may be contrasted with the description of a high-school soccer team's daily travel from a low-income New York neighborhood:

> Changing clothes on the subway because of inadequate locker rooms in the school. . . . Spending 90 minutes taking two trains and a bus to a playing field on Randalls Island. Lugging 40 pounds of nets to practice. Raising money to buy uniforms.
>
> All this when New York City has a budget surplus and is committing generous capital dollars to building two minor-league baseball stadiums for the Yankees in Staten Island and for the Mets in Coney Island.[34]

The separation of the wealthy and poor socioeconomic classes described earlier is accentuated by the increasing privatization of public park and recreation programs also described earlier—and the shift of many middle- and upper-class residents to the use of private or for-profit leisure resources. Former Secretary of Labor Robert Reich writes:

> As public parks and playgrounds deteriorate, there is a proliferation of private health clubs, golf clubs, tennis clubs, skating clubs, and every other type of recreational association in which costs are shared among members. Condominiums and the omnipresent residential communities dun their members to undertake work that financially strapped local governments can no longer afford to do well—maintaining roads, mending sidewalks, pruning trees, repairing street lights, cleaning swimming pools, paying for lifeguards, and, notably, hiring security guards to protect life and property.[35]

Particularly in larger, older cities, there is the risk that as formerly public spaces become disused, they may be taken over for other uses or managed by groups that will discourage their broader social functions. The impact of such privatization represents a retreat, Wayne Stormann writes, from the time-honored "Olmstedian" vision of public space in the city.[36]

Rich and Poor in American Life   In the widespread optimism about the flourishing state of the American economy in the opening years of the twenty-first century—with booming employment, budget surpluses, and rising stock market prices—the continuing plight of the poor tends to be overlooked. The reality is that the "new economy" has had both winners and losers. In many cases, the losers have been those who have been downsized, outsourced, or converted to "temps" employees without job benefits or

Recreation for Rich and Poor

Many American families have private, backyard swimming pools. Others visit lavish resorts, like Mandalay Bay Resort and Casino in Las Vegas, Nevada, with several pools and luxurious accommodations. Many others must rely on the spray from a streetside fire hydrant to keep cool in the ghettos' hot summers. Can the leisure-service profession remedy such contrasts?

security. Globalization of the economy has resulted in whole swathes of the labor force losing their jobs—along with millions of other mid-level and lower-level employees being dismissed because of profit-driven company mergers and downsizing policies in the 1980s and 1990s.

As a consequence of such trends, some analysts question the implications for American society as the rich continue to get richer and the poor get poorer.[37] Based on such trends and on the increasing technology-based transformation of work, many responsible critics have asked the question, "What will we do in a future world without work?" In a discussion of leisure and leisure services in the twenty-first century, Geoffrey Godbey writes that jobs will become the critical issue of the oncoming years.[38]

Too Little Leisure   A paradox is found in the pressure placed on many industrial employees to work long, hard hours of required overtime in the booming economy as a consequence of company executives refusing to hire additional full-time, regular workers. In the mid-1990s, 32,200 members of the United Automobile Workers struck the General Motors Corporation, with the company's refusal to hire additional new workers to reduce overtime and workloads a key issue. Similarly, in August 2000, thousands of employees in health care, communications, and other industries went on strike in protest against mandatory overtime requirements that forced them to choose between jobs and family needs.[39] Increasingly, it has become apparent that for growing numbers of men and women, the search for quality time that can be devoted to family involvement, personal needs, and leisure pursuits has become an important priority in making job choices.

EVER-GROWING LEISURE INVOLVEMENTS: A CAUTION

Linked to concern about future economic developments and their impact on leisure, there is the reality that recreation and leisure, like other elements of national life, cannot continue to expand indefinitely.

Authorities in this field have generally pointed out that expenditures on recreation and leisure have grown steadily, along with statistics of participation, over the past several decades. However, as earlier chapters have shown, there are cycles in public involvement that reflect changing tastes, as well as reactions to such trends as the rising costs in professional sports (see page 292) or the shifts from one type of recreational interest to another. In the last years of the twentieth century, for example, there were striking examples of several elements of public recreational involvements reaching a crest of participation—and then declining.

In both amateur and professional sports and the travel and tourism industry, there were significant declines in attendance and participation at this time. While the wave of construction of new sports stadiums and arenas continued into the early 2000s, a number of analysts warned that many of these costly ventures might risk failure because of oversaturation of the market.

Linked to such trends, such sportswear giants as Nike and the Venator footwear chain suffered major losses in the late 1990s and were forced to close numerous outlets and fire thousands of employees. Two major toy manufacturers or retailers—Hasbro,

Inc., and Toys "R" Us—downsized heavily at this time, eliminating large numbers of workers throughout the nation.

In the late 1990s, Discovery Zone, the nation's largest chain of children's indoor recreation centers, was forced to declare bankruptcy. At the same time, a number of major bookseller chains such as Barnes and Noble experienced sharp declines in sales as a result of lessened consumer demand for mass-market paperbacks. In 2000, a major national chain of movie multiplexes declared bankruptcy.

Even in the flourishing gambling business, exploding competition has meant that many racetracks and casinos have suffered heavy losses and, in some cases, have been forced to close.

PROSPECTS FOR THE FUTURE

These downward trends in the diversified field of commercial leisure ventures must be seen in perspective. They do *not* mean that the public's need for creative, challenging, and accessible forms of play is any less than it was in the past. However, they do illustrate the point that it is possible to provide an oversupply of recreational services and opportunities, and that, within the competitive leisure-service field, different cycles of public interest and involvement will inevitably take place.

The real challenge for the many different kinds of recreation, park, and leisure-service organizations and professionals described in this text will be to develop sound philosophies and programs that fulfill their essential function in society. The potential contribution of recreation and leisure in the decades ahead—in personal, social, environmental, and economic terms—will be greater than ever before.

While it is impossible to define the exact technological or societal changes that will occur throughout the United States and Canada, it is probable that both discretionary time and income will expand for a large sector of the population. For these individuals and for those who continue to be disadvantaged in socioeconomic terms or because of other disabilities, the mission of the organized leisure-service field will be to provide a critical source of enrichment and community involvement.

SUMMARY

Philosophy, seen as a set of carefully evolved principles that express the fundamental values and goals of any field of professional service, is a critical element in professional practice. This chapter presents a brief review of some earlier approaches to defining the meaning of recreation, play, and leisure and their roles in community life, followed by a discussion of recent efforts in this area.

The chapter then identifies seven distinct operational philosophies that influence the provision of organized recreation services today. These range from the quality-of-life and marketing orientations to a more recent model of service, the benefits-based management approach. While the chapter notes that most leisure-service organizations employ a blend of two or more orientations in their policy making and program planning, it suggests that the benefits-based model would appear to be particularly useful in an era of dramatic social change and economic challenge.

The concluding section of the chapter discusses a number of these changes, particularly relating to such areas of concern as population growth, shifts in employment patterns, environmental challenges, the impact of technology and commodification on leisure, privatization of government functions, and the withdrawal of the elite from many areas of community life. Several examples of studies that predict future trends in both Canadian and American society are summarized, with an emphasis on the need to anticipate and deal with change in a proactive way, rather than through passive or reluctant responses. Ultimately, this chapter serves to illustrate the blending of theoretical and practical concerns that must characterize all fields of public service if they are to be successful.

QUESTIONS FOR CLASS DISCUSSION OR ESSAY EXAMINATIONS

1. Define the term *philosophy*. Why is it an important element in recreation, park, and leisure-service planning, policy making, and administrative practice? Give one or more examples of the kinds of issues facing practitioners in this field that involve philosophical issues or require the application of management principles based on a sound set of agency values and goals.

2. What is your personal philosophy with respect to the meaning of recreation and leisure in contemporary society? This may be answered in terms of the functions it fulfills in community life or in terms of the overall mission of a particular type of leisure-service sponsor.

3. Chapter 12 presents seven different approaches to recreation, park, and leisure-service management today (examples: quality-of-life or marketing models of service). Select any three of these orientations and show how their influence is reflected in the practices of recreation agencies with which you are familiar. Which of the seven approaches do you find most compatible with your own views?

4. The Internet has had a tremendous impact on American and Canadian society and on leisure lifestyles in particular. What are some of its major effects—both positive and negative?

5. The chapter presents a number of predictions for the future with respect to demographic, social, economic, and other changes. Which of these do you believe present the most important challenge for the recreation, park, and leisure-service field? In what ways should leisure-service professionals seek to meet them constructively in the twenty-first century?

ENDNOTES

1 Webster's *New International Dictionary*, 1954 edition, s. v. "philosophy."

2 See, for example, D. Gray and S. Greben, "Future Perspectives," *Parks and Recreation* (July 1974): 53.

3 Earle Zeigler, *Philosophical Foundations for Physical, Health, and Recreation Education* (Englewood Cliffs, N.J.: Prentice-Hall, 1964).

4 Carolyn Thomas, *Sport in a Philosophical Context* (Philadelphia: Lea and Febiger, 1983).

5 Paul Weiss, *Sport: A Philosophical Inquiry* (Carbondale, Ill.: Southern Illinois University Press, 1969).

6 Charles Sylvester, "The Freedom to Be What We Want to Be: A Philosophical Comparison of Traditional and Existential Approaches to the Ethics of Leisure" (Presentation at 1986 NRPA Leisure Research Symposium).

7 Wayne Stormann, "The Recreation Profession, Capital, and Democracy," *Leisure Sciences* (Vol. 15, 1993): 49–66.

8 John Crompton, "Selecting Target Markets—A Key to Effective Marketing," *Journal of Park and Recreation Administration* (January 1983): 8.

9 Ruth Russell, *Planning Programs in Recreation* (St. Louis: C. V. Mosby, 1982): Chapter 2.

10 P. Wehman and S. Schleien, *Leisure Programs for Handicapped Persons* (Baltimore, Md.: University Park Press, 1981): 89.

11 Daniel Dustin, "Managing Public Lands for the Human Spirit," *Parks and Recreation* (September 1994): 92–96.

12 Douglas Knudson, *Outdoor Recreation* (New York: Macmillan, 1980): 31.

13 Anthony Lewis, "On Another Planet?" *New York Times* (29 September 1995): A-3.

14 Kevin Sack, "There Are Two Sides to Every Game in Town," *New York Times* (5 November 1995): 4-E.

15 See Margot Hornblower, "No Dice: The Backlash Against Gambling," *Time* (1 April 1996): 29.

16 See Lawrence Allen, "Time to Measure Outcomes" (Presentation at 1994 NRPA Congress).

17 Bill Exham, "Time to Measure Outcomes" (Presentation at 1994 NRPA Congress).

18 Allen, op. cit.

19 Michelle Park, "Where is NRPA Going with Benefits-Based Management?" *Parks and Recreation* (March 1998): 18.

20 Ronald Riggins, "Social Responsibility and the Public Sector Entrepreneur," *Journal of Physical Education, Recreation, and Dance—Leisure Today"* (October 1988): 27–28.

21 "Macro Trends Describe Canada's New National Vision for Recreation and Parks," *Leisure Watch* (Vol. 2, No. 3, 1993): 1–4.

22 P. Farrell and R. Trudeau, "Strategic Management for the Coming Decade," *Journal of Park and Recreation Administration* (July 1984): 1.

23 T. Mobley and R. Toalson, eds., *Parks and Recreation in the 21st Century* (Arlington, Va.: National Symposium Committee and NRPA, 1992).

24 L. Bruch and J. Stoiber, "Ex–Boy Scouts Cut Ties to Organization Over Ban on Gays," *New York Times* (22 August 2000): B-1.

25 "Cub Scouts Reject Muslim as Scout Master [in Kalamazoo, Mich.]" *Associated Press* (23 November 1995).

26 See James Kozlowski, "Religious Symbol a Snake in the Grass," *Parks and Recreation* (September 1999): 50.

27 James Willwerth, "Get Off My Turf," *Time* (24 August 1998): 68.

28 Kirkpatrick Sale, "Information Technology Revolution: Boon or Bane," *The Futurist* (January/February 1997): 10–11.

29 Steve Lohr, "The Economy Transformed, Bit by Bit," *New York Times* (20 December 1999): C-1.

30 "Workplace 2000 Transformed," *Employee Services Management* (January 2000): 30.

31 Jane Brody, "Cybersex Gives Birth to a Psychological Disorder," *New York Times* (16 May 2000): F-7.

32 Joellen Perry, "Only the Cyberlonely," *U.S. News and World Report* (28 February 2000): 62.

33 C. P. Johnson Tew, M. E. Havitz, and R. E. McCarville, "The Role of Marketing in Municipal Recreation Programming Decisions: A Challenge to Conventional Wisdom," *Journal of Park and Recreation Administration* (Spring 1999): 1–20.

34   Joyce Purnick, "No Level Field for Athletes in Schools," *New York Times* (8 January 2000): B-1.

35   Robert Reich, "Secession of the Successful," *New York Times Magazine* (20 January 1991): 44.

36   W. F. Stormann, "The Death of the Olmstedian Vision of Public Space," *Journal of Leisure Research* (Vol. 32, No. 1, 2000): 166–70.

37   James Lardner, "The Rich Get Richer," *U.S. News and World Report* (21 February 2000): 39.

38   Geoffrey Godbey, *Leisure and Leisure Services in the 21st Century* (State College, Pa.: Venture Publishing, 1997): 175.

39   Stephanie Armour, "All Work and No Play Makes Workers Mad," *U.S.A. Today* (18 August 2000): 1-B.

BIBLIOGRAPHY

Austin, David. *Therapeutic Recreation: Processes and Techniques*. Champaign, IL: Sagamore Publishing, 1999.

Bammel, Gene, and Lei Lane Burrus-Bammel. *Leisure and Human Bahavior*. Dubuque, IA: Wm. C. Brown, 1982.

Barnett, Lynn. *Research About Leisure: Past, Present, and Future*. Champaign, IL: Sagamore Publishing, 1995.

Beck, Larry, and Ted Cable, *Interpretation for the 21st Century: Fifteen Guiding Principles*. Champaign, IL: Sagamore Publishing, 1998.

Brymer, Robert. *Hospitality and Tourism: An Introduction to the Industry*. Dubuque, IA: Kendall/Hunt Publishing, 1998.

Bullock, Charles, and Michael Mahon. *An Introduction to Recreation and Therapeutic Recreation Programming for Persons with Disabilities*. Champaign, IL: Sagamore Publishing, 1996.

Caillois, Roger. *Man, Play and Games*. London: Thames and Hudson, 1961.

Cordell, H. Ken. *Outdoor Recreation in American Life: A National Assessment of Demand and Supply Trends*. Champaign, IL: Sagamore Publishing, 1999.

Cross, Gary. *A Social History of Leisure Since 1600*. State College, PA: Venture Publishing 1990.

Crossley, John, and Lynn Jamieson, *Introduction to Commercial and Entrepreneurial Recreation*. Champaign, IL: Sagamore Publishing, 1997.

Dattilo, John. *Leisure Education Program Planning: A Systematic Approach*. State College, PA: Venture Publishing, 1999.

DeGraaf, Donald, Debra Jordan, and Kathy DeGraaf. *Programming for Parks, Recreation, and Leisure Services: A Servant Leadership Approach*. State College, PA: Venture Publishing, 1999.

Driver, B. L., Daniel Dustin, Tony Baltic, Gary Elsner, and George Peterson, eds. *Nature and the Human Spirit: Toward an Expanded Land Management Ethic*. State College, PA: Venture Publishing, 1996.

Driver, B. L., Perry Brown, and George Peterson, eds. *Benefits of Leisure*. State College, PA: Venture Publishing, 1991.

Dulles, Foster. *A History of Recreation: America Learns to Play*. New York; Appleton-Century-Crofts, 1965.

Dumazedier, Joffre. *Sociology of Leisure*. Amsterdam: Elsevier, 1974.

Dustin, Daniel, Leo McAvoy, and John Schultz. *Stewards of Access, Custodians of Choice*. Champaign, IL: Sagamore Publishing, 1995.

Dustin, Daniel. *The Wilderness Within: Reflections on Leisure and Life*. Champaign, IL: Sagamore Publishing, 1999.

Edgell, David. *Tourism Policy: The Next Millennium*. Champaign, IL: Sagamore Publishing, 1999.

Edginton, Christopher, Susan Hudson, and Phyllis Ford. *Leadership for Recreation and Leisure Programs and Settings*. Champaign, IL: Sagamore Publishing, 1999.

Edginton, Christopher, Debra Jordan, Donald DeGraaf, and Susan Edginton. *Leisure and Life Satisfaction: Foundational Perspectives*. Dubuque, IA: Brown and Benchmark, 1995.

Fain, Gerald, Ed. *Leisure and Ethics: Reflections on the Philosophy of Leisure*. Reston, VA: American Alliance for Health, Physical Education, Recreation, and Dance, 1991.

Godbey, Geoffrey. *Leisure in Your Life: An Exploration*. State College, PA: Venture Publishing, 1999.

Godbey, Geoffrey. *Leisure and Leisure Services in the 21st Century*. State College, PA: Venture Publishing, 1997.

Goodale, Thomas, and Geoffrey Godbey. *The Evolution of Leisure: Historical and Philosophical Perspectives*. State College, PA: Venture Publishing, 1988.

Havitz, Mark, ed. *Models of Change in Municipal Parks and Recreation: A Book of Innovative Case Studies*. State College, PA: Venture Publishing, 1995

Henderson, Karla, M. Deborah Bialeschki, Susan Shaw, and Valeria Freysinger. *Both Gains and Gaps: Feminist Perspectives on Women's Leisure*. State College, PA: Venture Publishing, 1996.

Huizinga, Johan. *Homo Ludens: A Study of the Play Element in Culture*. Boston, MA: Beacon Press, 1950.

Hultsman, John, Richard Cottrell, and Wendy Hultsman. *Planning Parks for People*. State College, PA: Venture Publishing, 1998.

Hunnicutt, Benjamin. *Work Without End: Abandoning Shorter Hours for the Right to Work*. Philadelphia, PA: Temple University Press, 1988.

Jackson, Edgar, and Thomas Burton, eds. *Leisure Studies: Prospects for the Twenty-First Century*. State College, PA: Venture Publishing, 1999.

Jordan, Debra. *Leadership in Leisure Services: Making a Difference*. State College, PA: Venture Publishing, 1996.

Kelly, John, and Rodney Warnick. *Recreation Trends and Markets: The Twenty-First Century*. Champaign, IL: Sagamore Publishing, 1999.

Kelly, John, and Valeria Freysinger. *21st Century Leisure: Current Issues*. Needham Heights, MA.: Allyn and Bacon, 2000.

Knapp, Richard, and Charles Hartsoe. *Play for America: The History of the National Recreation and Park Association*. Arlington, VA: National Recreation and Park Association, 1980.

Kraus, Richard. *Leisure in a Changing America: Trends and Issues for the 21st Century*. Needham Heights, MA: Allyn and Bacon, 2000.

Kraus, Richard, Elizabeth Barber, and Ira Shapiro. *Introduction to Leisure Services: Career Perspectives*. Champaign, IL: Sagamore Publishing, 2001.

Kraus, Richard, and Joseph Curtis. *Creative Management in Recreation, Parks and Leisure Services*. St. Louis, MO: McGraw-Hill, 2000.

Larrabee, Eric, and Rolf Meyersohn, eds. *Mass Leisure*. Glencoe, IL: The Free Press, 1958.

Mannell, Roger, and Douglas Kleiber. *A Social Psychology of Leisure*. State College, PA: Venture Publishing, 1997.

McFarland, Elsie. *The Development of Public Recreation in Canada*. Vanier City, Ontario, Canada. Canadian Parks/Recreation Association, 1970.

McGuire, Francis, Rosangela Boyd, and Raymond Tedrick. *Leisure and Aging: Ulyssean Living in Later Life*. Champaign, IL: Sagamore Publishing, 1999.

Mobley, Tony, and Robert Toalson, eds. *Parks and Recreation in the 21st Century*. Arlington, VA: National Recreation and Park Association, 1992, 1993.

Mundy, Jean. *Leisure Education: Theory and Practices*. Champaign, IL: Sagamore Publishing, 1998.

Murphy, James, E. William Niepoth, Lynn Jamieson, and John Williams. *Leisure Systems: Critical Concepts and Applications*. Champaign, IL: Sagamore Publishing, 1991.

O'Sullivan, Ellen, and Kathy Spangler. *Experience Marketing: Strategies for the New Millennium*. State College, PA: Venture Publishing, 1998.

Parkhouse, Bonnie, ed. *The Management of Sport: Its Foundation and Application*. St. Louis, MO: Mosby and National Association for Sport and Physical Education, 1996.

Parks, Janet, Beverly Zanger, and Jerome Quarterman. *Contemporary Sport Management*. Champaign, IL: Human Kinetics, 1998.

Pieper, Josef. *Leisure: The Basis of Culture*. New York: Mentor-Omega, 1963.

Rossman, J. Robert, and Barbara Schlatter. *Recreation Programming: Designing Leisure Experiences*. Champaign, IL: Sagamore Publishing, 2000.

Russell, Ruth. *Pastimes: The Context of Contemporary Leisure*. Dubuque, IA: Brown and Benchmark, 1996.

Samuel, Nicole, ed. *Women, Leisure and the Family in Contemporary Society: A Multinational Perspective*. Wallingford, UK: CAB International, 1996.

Schleien, Stuart, M. Tipton Ray, and Frederick Green. *Community Recreation and People with Disabilities: Strategies for Inclusion*. Baltimore, MD: Paul H. Brookes Publishing, 1997.

Searle, Mark, and Russell Brayley. *Leisure Services in Canada: An Introduction*. State College, PA: Venture Publishing, 2000.

Sessoms, H. Douglas, and Karla Henderson. *Introduction to Leisure Services*. State College, PA: Venture Publishing, 1994.

Stumbo, Norma. *Intervention Activities for At-Risk Youth*. State College, PA: Venture Publishing, 1999.

Walker, John. *Introduction to Hospitality*. Upper Saddle River, NJ: Prentice Hall, 1999.

Weston, Susan. *Commercial Recreation and Tourism: An Introduction to Business-Oriented Recreation*, Dubuque, IA: Brown and Benchmark, 1996.

Witt, Peter, and John Crompton. *Recreation Programs That Work for At-Risk Youth: The Challenge of Shaping the Future*. State College, PA: Venture Publishing, 1996.

Wolfe, Alan. *One Nation, After All*. New York: Viking, 1998.

INDEX

PHOTO CREDITS